# Families
## and
# *Change*

*Dedicated to our maternal grandmothers—*
*Mary Katherine Evans Charles, 1902-1983*
*Delno Phelps Beck, 1883-1971*

# Families and
# *Change*
## Coping With
## Stressful Events

**edited by**

## *Patrick C. McKenry*
## *Sharon J. Price*

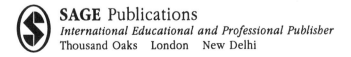

**SAGE** Publications
*International Educational and Professional Publisher*
Thousand Oaks   London   New Delhi

*For information address*:

 SAGE Publications, Inc.
2455 Teller Road
Thousand Oaks, California 91320

SAGE Publications Ltd.
6 Bonhill Street
London EC2A 4PU
United Kingdom

SAGE Publications India Pvt. Ltd.
M-32 Market
Greater Kailash I
New Delhi 110 048 India

Printed in the United States of America

**Library of Congress Cataloging-in-Publication Data**

Main entry under title:

Families and change: coping with stressful events / edited by Patrick
    C. McKenry, Sharon J. Price
        p.  cm.
    Includes bibliographical references and index.
    ISBN 0-8039-4925-1. — ISBN 0-8039-4926-X (pbk.)
    1. Family—United States. 2. Social problems—United States.
3. Social change—United States.   I. McKenry, Patrick C.
II. Price, Sharon J.
HQ534.F35   1994
306.85′0973—dc20                                                93-43064

    95  96  97  10  9  8  7  6  5  4  3

Sage Production Editor: Diane S. Foster

# Contents

# Preface

This book presents a synthesis and analysis of the vast literature that has emerged in recent years detailing families' responses to various problems and change. Scholarly interest in family problems is not new. The social and behavioral sciences evolved during the Progressive Era (1890-1920) out of an interest in the social problems facing families as a result of industrialization and urbanization. The interest at this time was in social reform and the use of research to solve these social problems. During the 1920s and 1930s, scholars began to focus on the internal dynamics of families. Because of disillusionment with the effects of social reform programs and the growing depersonalization of mass society, there was an increasing interest in the well-being and personal adjustment of families and individuals. Researchers became interested in healthy lifestyles, mental health, and child development. Both family sociology and family therapy developed at this time (Cole & Cole, 1993).

Two major societal disruptions, that is, the Great Depression and World War II, prompted further attention to how families coped with unprecedented change. Angell (1936) and Cavan and Ranck (1938) both identified various family characteristics that mediated the impact of the effects of the depression, that is, family organization, integration, and adaptability. These findings remain largely unchallenged today (Boss, 1987). Hill (1949), in his study of wartime family separations, developed a framework for assessing family crisis—the ABC-X model. This framework, with its emphasis on the family resources and definitions that mediate the extent of the stress or crisis response, serves today as the basis for most stress and coping theoretical models. While the 1950s represented a focus on the integrity of the American family as an institution and on traditional family patterns, the social and political revolution of the 1960s and the technological changes accompanying greater industrialization and urbanization of the 1970s and 1980s have resulted in a proliferation of research on families' coping and adaptation to myriad changes and new problems (Cole & Cole, 1993). Prior to undertaking this project, we conducted an extensive review of over 400 randomly selected undergraduate and graduate college and university catalogs. These institutions ranged from small, private, liberal arts colleges to large land-grant/research universities. We found that over 60% of these academic units had courses that dealt with family problems, stress, and/or change. These courses were found in departments of social work, home economics/human ecology, sociology, human services, psychology, human development, family science, family relations, child and family development, health, professional studies, and criminology. We also informally surveyed instructors of such courses at various institutions and discovered that texts representing a compilation of recent research findings in this area were almost nonexistent.

Thus the purpose of this text is to provide a volume appropriate for the study of various family problems, stressors, and changes prevalent in today's society. This text represents an integration of research, theory, and application, drawing on the interdisciplinary scholarship in each topic area. In addition, special attention is given to issues of minority families and gender as these two groups are often disproportionately affected by these problems. This book is intended to serve as a basic or supplementary text for undergraduate and introductory graduate courses on family or social problems. This book will also be useful to professionals, novices, and those with considerable experience, especially in social work, education, and public health, who are increasingly being required to work with family problems.

Each chapter follows a similar outline with the purpose of providing students with an overview of our current understanding of selected family problems and stressors as well as possible mechanisms of intervention and policy development. Each chapter will consist of sections focusing on incidence/epidemiology, etiology, consequences, and programmatic and policy recommendations.

The chapters in the book represent both predictable (normative) and unpredictable (situational) problems or stressors. Predictable family problems would include those stressors that are inherently stressful even though they are foreseen. We take the position that all forms of abrupt or disjunctive changes, although mediated by the family's coping resources, are likely to be stress producing. Such predictable or normative changes include aging, death and dying, adolescent transition, marital problems, em-

ployment changes, illness, and oppressive gender roles. Other problems
are potentially more traumatic because of the very fact that they cannot be
predicted; thus there is insufficient time to gather adequate coping resources. These would include drug and alcohol use, violence, and divorce.
We take the position that many of these problems are interrelated and that
they often combine to produce a stress-related response. For example, gender oppression may lead to marital problems, including violence; this may
then initiate a cycle of divorce, personal and economic disorganization, and
remarriage. Also, we assume that family problems, change, and stress responses are not necessarily "bad" for the family. The disequilibrium that
develops requires new methods for handling problems. Out of this situation
may arise new and creative solutions for organizing activities that are superior to those that were present before the problem occurred. This experience may enable the family to handle future crises in a superior manner,
and it may result in greater individual and group satisfaction with family
life.

Not all family problems could be reviewed due to page constraints. The
topics chosen represent major social issues today and have received considerable social, professional, and research attention. Some family problems that met these criteria were not included as separate chapters (e.g.,
economic problems, AIDS) because they are components of other chapters.

We begin the text with a conceptual overview of the research on family
problems, stressors, change, and coping. The nature and origin of the problems and changes facing families today are delineated, noting that, while
many of today's problems are not new, the extent of change in American
society is unprecedented. The history of systematic inquiry into family
problems and change is traced to individual physiological stress studies in
the late seventeenth century; these studies of individuals have evolved into
today's focus on whole family interaction. A social systems approach is
presented as the integrating framework for studying families under stress.
This paradigm views families as dynamic mechanisms, always in the process of growth and adaptation as they deal with change and stressor events.

Chapter 2 by Katherine Allen and Kristine Baber examines gender as a
source of stress for families in that traditional gender roles serve as a form
of oppression. It is argued that traditional gender-role socialization leaves
women vulnerable to many stressor events. For example, discrimination in
the labor force places women at economic risk. Women in traditional marriages with the male as primary breadwinner may have less influence in
making decisions that affect their lives, may have a disproportionate share
of household tasks, may not feel safe expressing conflict, and may not have

the resources to exit an unsatisfactory relationship. The authors point out that traditional roles also can be problematic for men in terms of creating barriers to intimacy, lower marital quality, and economic strain.

David Wright, Briana Nelson, and Kathleen Georgen review marital problems as stressor events for couples in Chapter 3. Consistent with the social systems model, marital problems are not assumed to have only negative effects on families; often problems indicate the need for couples to make changes in their relationship. In this vein, the authors discuss the dynamics and strengths of long-term stable marriages. Also, consistent with a social systems approach, the impact of marital problems varies by the context in which they occur and the resources the couple has for coping with them. In addition to discussing coping with major marital problems, the authors also review more normative strains and stressors associated with the family life cycle.

Chapter 4 by Sharon Nickols discusses the work system as a contributor to family stress. More specifically, she addresses unemployment and underemployment, the changing nature of the labor force, and women's and men's differential labor force participation and the division of family work as these create difficulties for families. Attention is also given to how employment and family life interface, how families balance these two aspects of their lives, and the impact on marriages and children. Nickols concludes with a discussion of the implications for families, corporate policy, public policy, and education.

The adolescent stage of development is viewed as a source of family stress and crisis by Velma Murry and Patricia Bell-Scott in Chapter 5. The authors point out that changes associated with this developmental stage may lead to an array of stressors and strains for both adolescents and families; these include adolescent individuation and separation from parents, parental control, adolescent sexuality, and adolescent problem behaviors (e.g., acting-act behaviors, drug use, and depression). Attention is given to the role of family relationships as mediators of the stress associated with the adolescent stage of development. The authors note the importance of considering gender, race, and family structure when drawing conclusions about family coping during this stage in the family life cycle.

In Chapter 6, Jay Mancini and Rosemary Blieszner assess the stressors associated with another family life cycle stage, that is, later life. More specifically, they discuss the transitions associated with later life that pose a threat to well-being. Transitions discussed include retirement and relationship loss and changes in health and economic status. Various models are presented to describe these transitions, including a process model, a leisure resources model, and a social provisions and disability model. The authors note that, although these models suggest different approaches to intervention, successful coping has been found to be highly related to social support and individual initiative.

Thomas Campbell discusses the interrelationship between health and families in Chapter 7. The chapter takes a systemic, bidirectional approach (biopsychosocial) in analyzing the role families play in individual physical health; that is, not only does illness affect families, but families very much influence the health status of their members. From health promotion to health intervention, families are seen as the most important context for health and illness. Healthy and unhealthy behaviors are developed and maintained or changed within the family. In addition, families are the most important source of stress and social support, which have a profound effect on the development and course of physical illness. Finally, family members are the primary caregivers for patients with chronic illness, and as a result such families suffer their own stresses and burdens.

Like Campbell, Stephen Gavazzi in Chapter 8 views mental illness as a bidirectional phenomenon. Families play a role in the etiology of mental disorders, and they are severely affected by the mental illness of a family member. The stressors and strains of families with mentally ill family members are often referred to as burdens, consisting of resource contribution (e.g., payment of medical expenses, provision of transportation), stigma, and psychological costs (lower self-esteem, reduced social contacts, job loss, and family relationship difficulties). The author notes that traditionally families have been neglected and even blamed by practitioners who have focused only on the treatment of the individual and the role that family interaction has played in the etiology of the disorder.

Colleen Murray discusses family experiences with death, dying, and bereavement in Chapter 9. She notes that death of a family member is widely considered the most stressful life event that families face. Although a predictable and hence normative event, the death of a family member is not viewed as normal by society, including many researchers and clinicians, and it is often treated as a problem rather than something that can result in growth and strength. Adapting to the loss of a family member is hampered by a lack of cultural support for the bereaved, a minimum of rituals surrounding death, and poorly defined roles for the chronically ill or the bereaved. The author conceptualizes the reaction to the death of a family member as a process, not an event, that does not always follow a linear progression. A social systems perspective is used to describe family reactions, noting that the family responds as a unit to the death of a family member and that a variety of systemic characteristics may influence the outcome for families. Gender, culture, and religion also are identified as important mediating factors in the grief process.

The book's section on unpredictable or situational family problems begins with a discussion of divorce in Chapter 10 by David Demo and Lawrence Ganong. Divorce is viewed as a process, somewhat similar to the reaction of an individual to the death of a family member. Divorce is also seen as a family process that differs significantly for husbands, wives, and children, and thus the perceptions of all three must be considered to understand the divorce process. Although divorce is often viewed as a serious problem, the authors contend that divorce might serve as a potential solution to a series of individual and family problems, and, for most, the crisis period is short-term. The authors, however, suggest that many women and children are at risk for long-term negative consequences of divorce because of a decline in their economic well-being after divorce.

Margaret Crosbie-Burnett discusses remarriage and recoupling as a stressor event in Chapter 11. This chapter presents demographic data on remarriage as well as a model explaining family stress and coping in remarried families. This model has both sociological and psychological components, is based on the ABC-X model, and focuses on the role of hardships and pileups, resources, perception, and adaptation to the recoupling. Crosbie-Burnett emphasizes the need for changes in law, education, and therapy to address the unique needs of remarried families.

In Chapter 12, Robert Lewis and Irwanto assess the family context of alcohol and drug use, focusing on the role of family structure, processes, and history in the etiology of abuse. Consistent with the social systems approach, the authors conceptualize a reciprocal relationship between alcohol and drug use and family dysfunction. They review research that indicates that drugs and alcohol may produce stressful changes within families, changes that are often dysfunctional. In turn, these dysfunctional families may help to continue the transmission of drug and alcohol use from generation to generation. Also consistent with a social systems approach, the authors discuss overlapping system influences, such as schools, peer groups, and the wider society. Cultural explanations of patterns of alcohol and drug use also are identified. Drawing on their theoretical base, it is suggested that preventive programs that reduce demand would be more effective in dealing with the current alcohol and drug problems than the very expensive attempts to control the supply of drugs.

Richard Gelles in Chapter 13 discusses the incidence and etiology of various forms of family violence. Estimates of the extent of family violence would suggest that this event is approaching normative status. The author goes beyond individual explanations to discuss various societal factors that are related to family violence, including gender, race, socioeconomic status, stress, social isolation, and intergenerational patterns. More theoretically, models from psychology, sociology, and biology are used to provide the systems context for family violence. Drawing on the research literature, the most promising preventive measures would focus on reducing stress, providing social support, and facilitating new patterns of interaction.

Elizabeth Lindsey discusses the impact of homelessness on families in Chapter 14. Estimates of the number of families who are homeless suggest this is an increasing problem in our society. The author goes beyond demographic data to a discussion of the reasons families are homeless and the physical and emotional impact on adults and children. Several explanations for homelessness, including both individual and family orientations, are included. The author also discusses various intervention programs that have focused on homeless families and makes suggestions for future work in this area.

Chapter 15 summarizes common themes that emerged from the authors in this volume. These include (a) how families cope as systems, (b) gender and cultural variations in coping, (c) the increasing level of stress facing families, (d) the interrelationship of family problems and other social systems, (e) the ambiguity of chronic stress, and (f) variations in problems and stress across the family life cycle.

The support, advice, and encouragement of several colleagues and friends were instrumental in the conceptualization and production of this book. We would like to express our appreciation to Kathryn Beckham and Albert Davis. We also would like to thank the many students who through the years have asked for a book of this type and contributed to our ideas for this text.

We are very grateful to the authors of this book for their impressive, thoughtful, and well-written contributions. Their enthusiasm for this project and their timely revisions certainly helped to make the project less onerous.

We also are indebted to Judie Strain for her valuable assistance. Finally, a very special note of appreciation must go to Debi Combs, secretary, and Mary McKelvey, graduate research associate, who managed the project, including many hours editing our work.

# References

Angell, R. C. (1936). *The family encounters the depression.* New York: Scribner.

Boss, P. (1987). Family stress. In M. B. Sussman & S. K. Steinmetz (Eds.), *Handbook of marriage and the family.* New York: Plenum.

Cavan, R. S., & Ranck, K. H. (1938). *The family and the depression.* Chicago: University of Chicago Press.

Cole, C. L., & Cole, A. L. (1993). Family therapy theory implications for marriage and family enrichment. In P. G. Boss, W. J. Doherty, R. LaRossa, W. R. Schumm, & S. K. Steinmetz (Eds.), *Sourcebook of family theories and methods: A contextual approach.* New York: Plenum.

Hill, R. (1949). *Families under stress.* New York: Harper & Row.

# 1

❀

# Families Coping
# With Problems and Change

## A Conceptual Overview

PATRICK C. MCKENRY
SHARON J. PRICE

American families today are experiencing unprecedented change and are coping with a variety of problems, both old and new (Toffler, 1990). It is impossible to read extensively in either scholarly or lay publications without encountering a discussion of stress in American society.

Technology accompanying industrialization and urbanization frequently is identified as making daily life more complex and impersonal. Variations in gender roles have blurred, traditional values are being questioned, and even traditional conceptualizations of family have changed in response to the increasing options of a postmodern society. Feminists and others have challenged prevailing assumptions about the family by raising questions about family boundaries, equity in family relationships, and the viability of a monolithic family form.

The "Ideal of Progress" that emerged with industrialization proclaimed that scientific advances would always make life progressively better (Naisbitt & Aburdene, 1990). However, as American families have strived for a continuing improvement in their quality of life, they have actually experienced a decrease in economic and socioemotional well-being in recent years. A changing economy has introduced uncertainty into the lives of many family members; job security and advancement are less certain even to those who have formal preparation for a career. Both parents usually must work outside the home, while women and minorities are still facing economic discrimination. Day care as well as adequate health care have become luxuries beyond the reach of many families. The rate of families in poverty has actually increased in recent years. Overpopulation accompanying industrialization has resulted in transportation problems, pollution, and a shortage of resources. Societal alienation has resulted in a steady increase in major mental disorders and related self-destructive behaviors, including drug and alcohol abuse, suicide, and violence.

The family, which was once a haven for individuals who were stressed by external problems, increasingly is challenged to meet individual affective and other emotional needs. There is decreasing time for leisure as both parents are working longer hours outside the home; youth also are working additional hours outside the home or are otherwise heavily involved in extrafamilial activities.

Families are faced with many unique problems as a result of societal change. Technology, which has facilitated an increasing life span, has also brought about a growing aged population with whom overextended and mobile families must cope. Young family members must contend with the realization that there are fewer opportunities and resources available for them as compared with their parents. And the fluidity of family structures requires most families to deal with several family structural transitions during the life course (Spanier, 1989).

Change results in a stress response whether or not that change is "good" or "bad." The effect of the change is dependent on the family's coping ability. Boss (1988) defines *family stress* as pressure or tension in the family system. It is a disturbance of the family's steady state. It is normal and even desirable at times. Life transitions and events often provide an essential condition for psychological development. Family stress is perceived as inevitable because people and hence families develop and change over time. With change comes disturbance and pressure—what is termed *stress*. Changes affecting families also occur externally (e.g., unemployment, natural disasters), and these also create stress within the family system. Change becomes problematic only when the degree of stress in the family system reaches a level at which family members and/or the family system become dissatisfied or show symptoms of disturbance.

## The Study of Family Stress and Coping

In comparison with the long history of research in the general area of stress and coping, theoretical and clinical interest in family stress, problems, and coping styles is a rather recent phenomenon (McCubbin, Cauble, & Patterson, 1982). Research on family stress and coping has gradually evolved from various disciplines that have examined stress and coping from more of an individualistic perspective.

According to the *Oxford English Dictionary,* the term *stress* can be traced back to the early fourteenth century when *stress* had several distinct meanings, including hardship, adversity, and affliction (Rutter, 1983). Even among stress researchers today, *stress* is variably defined as a stimulus, an inferred inner state, and an observable response to a stimulus or situation; also there is debate concerning the extent to which stress is chemical, environmental, or psychological in nature (Lazarus & Folkman, 1984; McCubbin et al., 1980).

In the late seventeenth century, Hooke used *stress* in the context of physical science, although the usage was not made systematic until the early nineteenth century. Stress and strain were first conceived as a basis of ill health in the nineteenth century (Lazarus & Folkman, 1984). In the twentieth century, Cannon (1932) laid the foundation for systematic research on the effects of stress in detailed observations of bodily changes. He showed that stimuli associated with emotional arousal (e.g., pain, hunger, cold) caused changes in basic physiological functioning (Dohrenwend & Dohrenwend, 1974). Selye (1978) was the first researcher to define and measure stress adaptations in the human body. He defined *stress* as an orchestrated set of bodily defenses against any form of noxious stimuli (General Adaptation Syndrome). In the 1950s social scientists became interested in his conceptualization of stress, and even today Selye's seminal work accounts for much of the scholarly interest in stress and coping (Lazarus & Folkman, 1984).

Meyer in the 1930s taught that life events may be an important part of the etiology of a disorder and that the most normal and necessary life events may be potential contributors to pathology (Dohrenwend & Dohrenwend, 1974). More recently Holmes and Rahe (1967) have used the Myerian perspective to study life events and their connection to the onset and progression of illness. Through their Schedule of Recent Events, which includes many family events, Holmes and Rahe have related the accumulation of life changes and those of greater magnitude to a higher chance of associated illness or disease.

In the social sciences, both sociology and psychology have long histories of study related to stress and coping. Sociologists Marx, Weber, and Durkheim wrote extensively about "alienation." Alienation was conceptualized as synonymous with powerlessness, meaninglessness, and self-estrangement, clearly under the general rubric of stress (Lazarus & Folkman, 1984).

In psychology, stress was implicit as an organizing framework for thinking about psychopathology, especially in the theorizing of Freud and later psychodynamically oriented writers. Freudian psychology also highlighted the process of coping and established the basis for a developmental approach that considered the effect of life events on later development and gradual acquisition of resources over the life cycle. Early psychologists used anxiety to denote stress, and it was seen as a central component in psychopathology through the 1950s. The reinforcement-learning theorists (e.g., Spence, 1956) viewed anxiety as a classically conditioned response that led to unserviceable (pathological) habits of anxiety reduction. Existentialists (e.g., May, 1950) also focused on anxiety as a major barrier to self-actualization (Lazarus & Folkman, 1984). Developmentalists (e.g., Erikson, 1963) have put forth various stage models that demand that a particular crisis be negotiated before the individual can cope with subsequent developmental stages. Personal coping resources accrued during the adolescent-young adult years are thought to be integrated into the self-concept and shape the process of coping throughout adulthood (Moos, 1986). Crisis theorists (e.g., Caplan, 1964) conceptualized these life changes as crises, with the assumption that disequilibrium may provoke stress in the short run but can promote the development of new skills in the long run.

Since the 1960s, there has been growing interest in coping responses in adaptational outcomes. Researchers have attempted to delineate the coping strategies that individuals and families employ in successfully managing stress (Coelho, Hamburg, & Adams, 1974; McCubbin, 1979; Moos, 1976). Coping in the study of families involves the integration of both sociological and psychological perspectives. Lazarus's (1966) psychological taxonomy emphasized two major categories of coping responses: (a) direct actions and (b) palliative modes (use of thought or actions to relieve the emotional impact of stress). The sociological perspective of coping underscores the importance of individual and family resources, such as cohesion and adaptability, in the management of stress (e.g., Burr, 1973; Hill, 1949).

Many researchers from a variety of disciplines have presented data that support the relationship between social support and the ability to adjust to and cope with crises and change. Caplan (1964, 1974) notes that social support allows the individual to adapt more easily to change and appears to protect him or her from the typical physiological and psychological health consequences of life stress (McCubbin et al., 1982). From this line of research, others have attempted to explore the contribution of other variables and processes as mediators of the stressor-stress response relationship. In the study of family stress and coping per se, much of the work has used some variation of Hill's (1949) social system model of family stress.

## Family Stress Theory

### Social Systems Perspective

Family theorists typically have used a social systems approach in their conceptualization of families under stress. Thus families are viewed as living organisms with both symbolic and real structures. They have boundaries to maintain, and they have a variety of instrumental and expressive functions to perform to ensure growth and survival (Boss, 1988). As any social system, families strive to maintain a steady state. Families are the products of both subsystems (e.g., individual members, dyads) and suprasystems (e.g., community, culture, nation).

While most general stress theories have focused only on the individual, the primary interest of family stress theory is the family unit as a whole. Systems theory states that the system is more than the sum of its parts (Hall & Fagan, 1968). In terms of families, this means that the collection of family members is not only a specific number of people but also an aggregate of particular relationships and shared memories, successes, failures, and aspirations (Boss, 1988). However, systems theory is also interested in studying the individual to more completely understand a family's response to stress.

A social systems approach allows the researcher to focus beyond the family and the individual to the wider social system (suprasystem). Families do not live in isolation; they are part of the larger social context. This external environment in which the family is embedded is referred to as the "ecosystem," according to social systems theory. This ecosystem consists of historical, cultural, economic, genetic, and developmental influences (Boss, 1988). Thus the family's response to a stressor event is influenced by living in a particular historical period, its cultural identification, the economic conditions of society, its genetic stamina and resistance, and its stage in the family life cycle.

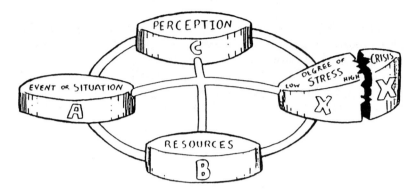

**Figure 1.1.** ABC-X Model of Family Crisis

SOURCE: Hill, R. (February, 1958). Social stresses on the family: Generic features of families under stress, *Social Casework*, pp. 139-150. Copyright © Families International Incorporated. Reprinted by permission.

### ABC-X Model

The foundation for a social systems model of family stress lies in Hill's (1949) classic research on war-induced separation and reunion. His ABC-X formulation has withstood careful assessment and has remained virtually unchanged (McCubbin & Patterson, 1985). This family stress framework may be stated as follows:

> A (the provoking or stressor event)—interacting with B (the family's resources or strengths)—interacting with C (the definition or meaning attached to the event by the family)—produces X (stress or crisis).

The main idea is that the X factor is influenced by several other mediating phenomena. Stress or crisis is not seen as inherent in the event itself but conceptually as a function of the response of the disturbed family to the stressor (Burr, 1973; Hill, 1949). (See Figure 1.1.)

### Stressor Events

A stressor event is an occurrence that provokes a variable amount of change in the family system. Anything that changes some aspect of the system such as the boundaries, structures, goals, processes, roles, or values can produce stress. This variable denotes something different than the routine changes within a system that are expected as part of its regular, routine operation. This variable is a dichotomy, that is, an event not changing the system and one changing the system (Burr, 1982). The stressor event by definition has the potential to raise the family's level of stress. However, the degree of stress is dependent on the magnitude of the event as well as other mediating factors to be discussed. Also, both positive and negative events can be stressors. Life events research has clearly indicated that normal and/or positive changes can increase an individual's risk for illness. Also, stressor events do not necessarily increase stress levels to the point of crisis; the family's stress level can be managed and the family can return to a new equilibrium.

Researchers have attempted to describe various types of stressor events (e.g., Boss, 1988; Hansen & Hill, 1968; Rees & Smyer, 1983). Lipman-Blumen (1975) has described family stressor events in terms of eight dimensions: internal versus external, intense versus mild, pervasive versus bounded, transitory versus chronic, precipitate onset versus gradual, random versus expectable, natural generation versus artificial, and perceived insolvable versus solvable. The type of event may be highly correlated with the family's ability to manage stress. (These dimensions are defined in Table 1.1.) Other researchers (e.g., McCubbin, Patterson, & Wilson, 1981; Pearlin & Schooler, 1978) have classified stressor events in terms of their intensity or hardship on the family.

One dichotomous classification that is often used by family stress researchers and clinicians is normal or predictable events versus nonnormative or unpredictable or situational events. Normal events are part of everyday life and represent transitions inherent in the family life cycle, such as birth or death of a family member, child's school entry, and retirement. Normative stressor events by definition are of short duration. Although predictable and normal, such life-cycle events have the potential of changing a family's level of stress because they disturb system equilibrium. These events lead to crisis only if the family does not adapt to the changes brought about by these events (Carter & McGoldrick, 1989).

Nonnormative events are the product of some unique situation that could not be predicted and is not likely to be repeated. Examples of nonnormative events would include natural disasters, loss of a job, or an automobile accident. Unexpected events that are not disastrous may also be stressful for families, such as promotion or winning the lottery. Although these events are positive, they do change or disturb the family's routine and thus have the potential of raising the family's level of stress (Boss, 1988).

There has been much recent interest in the study of isolated versus accumulated stressors. Various life events inventories (e.g., Holmes & Rahe,

**Table 1.1.** Ten Dimensions of Family Stressor Events

(1) Internality versus Externality: refers to whether the source of the crisis was internal or external to the social system affected.

(2) Pervasiveness versus Boundedness: refers to the degree to which the crisis affects the entire system or only a limited part.

(3) Precipitate onset versus Gradual onset: marks the degree of suddenness with which the crisis occurred, i.e., without or with warning.

(4) Intensity versus Mildness: involves the degree of severity of the crisis.

(5) Transitoriness versus Chronicity: refers to the degree to which the crisis represents a short- or long-term problem.

(6) Randomness versus Expectability: marks the degree to which the crisis could be expected or predicted.

(7) Natural generation versus Artificial generation: connotes the distinction between crises that arise from natural conditions and those that come about through technological or other human-made effects.

(8) Scarcity versus Surplus: refers to the degree to which the crisis represents a shortage or overabundance of vital commodities—human, material and nonmaterial.

(9) Perceived solvability versus Perceived insolvability: suggests the degree to which those individuals involved in the crisis believe the crisis is open to reversal or some level of resolution.

(10) Substantive content: (This dimension differs from the previous nine in that it subsumes a set of subject areas, each of which may be regarded as a separate continuum graded from low to high.) Using this dimension, the analyst can determine whether the substantive nature of the crisis is primarily in the political, economic, moral, social, religious, health, or sexual domains or any combination thereof.

1967; McCubbin et al., 1981; Sarason, Johnson, & Siegel, 1978) have been used to indicate that it is the accumulation of several stressor events rather than the nature of one isolated event that determines a family's level of stress. The clustering of stressor events (normative and/or nonnormative) is termed *stress pileup*. An event rarely happens to a family in total isolation. Normal developmental changes are always taking place and nonnormative events tend to result in other stressors; for example, loss of job may result in moving, marital disruption.

### Resources

The family's resources mediate the impact of the stressor event on the family's level of stress. Hansen (1965) uses the term *vulnerability* to denote this phenomenon. This mediator denotes variation in a family's ability to prevent a stressor event or change from creating disruptiveness in the system (Burr, 1973). When members have sufficient appropriate resources, they are less likely to view a stressful situation as problematic. McCubbin and Patterson (1985) define *resources* as traits, characteristics, or abilities of (a) individual family members, (b) the family system, and (c) the community that can be used to meet the demands of a stressor event. Individual or personal resources include finances (economic well-being), education (problem solving), health (physical and emotional well-being), and psychological resources (self-esteem).

The term *family system resources* refers to internal attributes of the family unit that protect the family from the impact of stressors and facilitate family adaptation during family stress and/or crisis. Family cohesion (bonds of unity) and adaptability (ability to change) (Olson, Russell, & Sprenkle, 1979, 1983) have received the most research attention. These two dimensions are the major axes of the Circumplex Model (Olson et al., 1979). This model suggests that families who function moderately along the dimensions of cohesion and adaptability are likely to make a more successful adjustment to stress (Olson, Russell, & Sprenkle, 1980). However, it should be noted that the family literature contains studies and writings that qualify or refute the curvilinear interpretation of the relationship between adaptability and cohesion and effective functioning; instead, these studies support a linear relationship between these two dimensions and effective outcomes (Anderson & Gavazzi, 1990).

*Community resources* refers to those capabilities of people or institutions outside the family upon which the family can draw for dealing with stress. Social support is one of the most important community resources. Social support may be viewed as information disseminated to facilitate problem solving and as development of new social contacts who provide help and assistance. Social support offers information at an interpersonal level that provides (a) emotional support, (b) esteem support, and (c) network support (Cobb, 1976). In general, social support serves as a protector against the effects of stressors and promotes recovery from stress or crisis.

### Definition of the Event/Perceptions

The impact of the stressor event on the family's level of stress is also mediated by the definition or meaning the family gives to the event. This variable is also synonymous with family appraisal, perception, and assessment of the event. Thus subjective definitions can vary from viewing circumstances as a challenge and an opportunity for growth, to the negative view that things are hopeless, too difficult, or unmanageable (McCubbin & Patterson, 1985). Empirical findings suggest that an individual's cognitive appraisal of life events strongly influences the response (Lazarus & Launier, 1978).

This idea has a long tradition in social psychology in terms of the self-fulfilling prophecy that, if something is perceived as real, it is real in its consequences (Burr, 1982). Families who are able to redefine a stressor event more positively (i.e., reframe it) appear to be better able to cope and adapt. By redefining, families are able to (a) clarify the issues, hardships, and tasks to render them more manageable and responsive to problem-solving efforts; (b) decrease the intensity of the emotional burdens associated with stressors; and (c) encourage the family unit to carry on with its fundamental tasks of promoting individual member social and emotional development (McCubbin & Patterson, 1985).

Lazarus and Launier (1978) have discussed the impact of an individual's learned cognitive attributional style on the stress response; this work has been applied to the study of families as well (e.g., Boss, 1988). For example, a family may respond to an event in terms of "learned helplessness," thereby increasing their vulnerability due to low self-esteem and feelings of hopelessness. Such a family would react to the unemployment of a spouse by failing to look for another job or supporting that family member in the search for another job.

*Stress and Crisis*

According to social systems theory, stress represents a change in the family's steady state. Stress is the response of the family to the demands experienced as a result of a stressor event. Stress is not inherently bad; it becomes problematic when the degree of stress in the family system reaches a level at which the family becomes disrupted or individual members become dissatisfied or display physical or emotional symptoms. The degree of stress ultimately depends on the family's definition of the stressor event as well as the adequacy of the family's resources to meet the demands of the change associated with the stressor event.

The terms *stress* and *crisis* have been used inconsistently in the literature. In fact, many researchers have failed to make a distinction between the two. Boss (1988) makes a useful distinction as she defines crisis as (a) a disturbance in the equilibrium that is so overwhelming, (b) pressure that is so severe, or (c) change that is so acute that the family system is blocked, immobilized, and incapacitated. When a family is in a crisis state, at least for a time it does not function adequately. Family boundaries are no longer maintained, customary roles and tasks are no longer performed, and family members are no longer functioning at optimal physical or psychological levels. The family has thus reached a state of acute disequilibrium and is immobilized.

Family stress, on the other hand, is merely a state of changed or disturbed equilibrium. Family stress therefore is a continuous variable (degree of stress), whereas family crisis is a dichotomous variable (either in crisis or not). A crisis does not have to permanently break up the family system. It may only temporarily immobilize the family system and then lead to a different level of functioning than that experienced before the stress level escalated to the point of crisis. Many family systems, in fact, become stronger after they have experienced and recovered from crisis (Boss, 1988).

## Coping

Family stress researchers have increasingly shifted their attention from crisis and family dysfunction to the process of coping. Researchers have become more interested in explaining why some families are better able to manage and endure stressor events rather than documenting the frequency and severity of such events. In terms of intervention, this represents a change from crisis intervention to prevention (Boss, 1988; McCubbin et al., 1980).

The study of family coping has drawn heavily from cognitive psychology (e.g., Lazarus, 1976; Lazarus & Folkman, 1984) as well as sociology (e.g., Pearlin & Schooler, 1978). *Cognitive coping strategies* refers to the ways in which individual family members alter their subjective perceptions of stressful events. Sociological theories of coping emphasize a wide variety of actions directed at either changing the stressful situation or alleviating distress by manipulating the social environment (McCubbin et al., 1980). Thus family coping has been conceptualized in terms of three types of responses: (a) direct action (e.g., acquiring resources, learning new skills); (b) intrapsychic (e.g., reframing the problem); or (c) controlling the emotions generated by the stressor (e.g., social support, use of alcohol) (Boss, 1988; Lazarus & Folkman, 1984; Pearlin & Schooler, 1978). These responses can be used individually, consecutively, or, more commonly, in various combinations. Specific coping strategies are not inherently adaptive or maladaptive; they are very much situation specific. Flexible access to a range of responses appears to be more effective than any one response (Moos, 1986).

Coping interacts with both family resources and perceptions as defined by the "B" and "C" factors of the ABC-X Model. However, coping actions are different than resources and perceptions. Coping represents what people do—their concrete efforts to deal with a stressor (Pearlin & Schooler, 1978). Having a resource or a perception of an event does not imply whether or how a family will react (Boss, 1988; Lazarus & Folkman, 1984).

Although coping is sometimes equated with adaptational success (i.e., a product), from a family systems perspective, coping is a process, not an outcome per se. *Coping* refers to all efforts expended to manage a stressor regardless of the effect (Lazarus & Folkman, 1984). Thus the family strategy of coping is not instantly created but is progressively modified over time. Because the family is a system, coping behavior involves the management of various dimensions of family life simultaneously: (a) maintaining satisfactory internal conditions for communication and family organization, (b) promoting member independence and self-esteem, (c) maintenance of family bonds of coherence and unity, (d) maintenance and development of social supports in transactions with the community, and (e) maintenance of some efforts to control the impact of the stressor and the amount of change in the family unit (McCubbin et al., 1980). Coping is thus a process of achieving balance in the family system that facilitates organization and unity and promotes individual growth and development. This is consistent with systems theory, which suggests that the families that cope the best with stress are strong as a unit as well as in individual members (Buckley, 1967).

Boss (1988) cautions that coping should not be perceived as maintaining the status quo; rather, the active managing of stress should lead to progressively new levels of organization as systems are naturally inclined toward greater complexity. In fact, sometimes it is better for a family to "fail to cope" even if that precipitates a crisis. After the crisis, the family can reorganize into a better functioning system. For example, a marital separation may be very painful for a family, but it may be necessary to allow the family to grow in a different, more productive direction.

In addition to serving as a barrier to change and growth, coping also can serve as a source of stress. There are three ways that coping itself may be a source of additional hardship (Roskies & Lazarus, 1980). One way is by indirect damage to the family system. This occurs when a family member inadvertently behaves in such a way as to put the family in a disadvantaged position. For example, a father may become ill from overwork to ease his family's economic stress. The second way that coping can serve as a source of stress is through direct damage to the family system. For example, family members may use an addictive behavior or violence to personally cope, but this will be disruptive to the family system. The third way that coping may increase family stress is by interfering with additional adaptive behaviors that could help preserve the family. For example, denial of a problem may preclude getting necessary help and otherwise addressing the stressor event (McCubbin et al., 1980).

## Adaptation

Another major interest of family stress researchers in recent years has been the assessment of how families are able to "recover" from stress or crisis. Drawing from Hansen's (1965) work, Burr (1973) described this process in terms of a family's "regenerative power," denoting a family's ability to recover from stress or crisis. According to McCubbin and Patterson (1982), the purpose of postcrisis or poststress adjustment is to reduce or eliminate the disruptiveness in the family system and restore homeostasis. However, these authors also note that family disruption has the potential of maintaining family relations and stimulating desirable change. Because system theorists (e.g., Buckley, 1967; Hill, 1972) hold that all systems naturally evolve toward greater complexity, it may be inferred that family systems initiate and capitalize on externally produced change in order to grow. Therefore reduction of stress or crisis alone is an incomplete index of a family's adjustment to crisis or stress.

McCubbin and Patterson (1982) use the term *adaptation* to describe a desirable outcome of a crisis or stressful state. *Family adaptation* is defined as the degree to which the family system alters its internal functions (behaviors, rules, roles, perceptions) and/or external reality to achieve a system (individual or family)-environment fit. Adaptation is achieved through reciprocal relationships in which (a) system demands (or needs) are met by resources from the environment and (b) environmental demands are satisfied through system resources (Hansen & Hill, 1964).

According to McCubbin and Patterson (1982), demands include normative and nonnormative stressor events as well as the needs of individuals (e.g., intimacy), families (e.g., launching of children), and social institutions and communities (e.g., governmental authority). Resources include individual (e.g., education, psychological stability), family (e.g., cohesion, adaptability), and environmental (social support, medical services) attributes.

Adaptation is different than adjustment. Adjustment is a short-term response by a family that changes the situation only momentarily. Adaptation

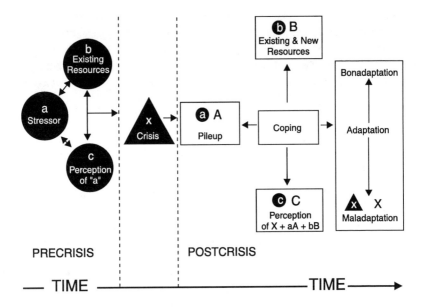

**Figure 1.2.** Double ABC-X Model

SOURCE: From McCubbin, H. I., & Patterson, J. M. (1982). *Family Stress, Coping, and Social Support.*
Reprinted by courtesy of Charles C Thomas, Publisher, Springfield, Illinois.

implies a change in the family system that evolves over a longer period of
time or is intended to have long-term consequences involving changes in
family roles, rules, patterns of interaction, and perceptions (McCubbin &
Patterson, 1980).

McCubbin and Patterson (1982) have expanded Hill's (1949) ABC-X
Model by adding postcrisis/poststress factors to explain how families achieve
a satisfactory adaptation to stress or crisis. Their model consists of the
ABC-X Model followed by their "Double ABC-X" configuration. (See
Figure 1.2.)

McCubbin and Patterson's (1982) "Double A" factor refers to the stressor pileup in the family system, and this includes three types of stressors.
The family must deal with unresolved aspects of the initial stressor event,
the changes and events that occur regardless of the initial stressor (e.g.,
changes in family membership), and the consequences of the family's
efforts to cope with the hardships of the situation (e.g., intrafamily role
changes).

The family's resources, the "Double B" factor, are of two types. The first are those resources already available to the family and that minimize the impact of the initial stressor. The second are those coping resources (personal, family, and social) that are strengthened or developed in response to the stress or crisis situation.

The "Double C" factor refers to (a) the perception of the initial stressor event and (b) the perception of the stress or crisis. The perception of the stress or crisis situation includes the family's view of the stressor and related hardships and the pileup of events as well as the meaning families attach to the total family situation. The family's postcrisis/poststress perceptions involve religious beliefs, redefining (reframing) the situation, and endowing the situation with meaning.

The "Double X" factor includes the original family crisis/stress response and subsequent adaptation. Family crisis/stress is at one end of the continuum of family adjustment over time, and family adaptation is the outcome at the other end of the continuum.

Boss (1988) cautions against use of the term *adaptation* to refer to the optimal outcome of a stressful or crisis state. She contends that the family literature appears to assume that calm, serenity, orderliness, and stability are the desired ends for family life. Like Hoffman (1981), Boss maintains that systems naturally experience discontinuous change through the life cycle in the process of growth. If adaptation is valued over conflict and change, then families are limited to a perspective that promotes adjustment to the stressor event at the expense of individual or family change. Boss contends that sometimes dramatic change must occur for individual and family well-being, including breaking family rules, changing boundaries, and revolution within the system. For example, an abused wife may need to leave or at least dramatically change her family system to achieve a sense of well-being for herself and perhaps for other family members. Boss prefers use of the term *managing* to refer to the coping process that results from the family's reaction to stress or crisis.

## Conclusions

Families today are being challenged with numerous changes and problems that have the capacity to produce stress and crisis. After many years of focusing on individual stress responses, researchers have begun systematic assessments of whole family responses. The major theoretical paradigm that has been used to study family responses to stressor events has been the social systems model. Developing from Hill's (1949) work on the effect of wartime separation, various characteristics of stressor events as well as the mediating effects of perceptions and resources have been studied, suggesting that there is nothing inherent in the event per se that is stressful or crisis producing.

More recently, family stress research has moved beyond the linear relationship of stressor, mediator, and response to look at the process of coping and adaptation over time, that is, how families actually manage stress and/or crisis. Coping is conceptualized as an ongoing process that facilitates family organization but also promotes individual growth. Increasingly, the outcome of interest is adaptation, that is, the ability of a family to recover from stress and crisis; however, this concept, like coping, is perceived by some researchers as not a definitive end product because families are always growing and changing and the serenity and stability synonymous with adaptation are not always functional for family members.

## References

Anderson, S. A., & Gavazzi, S. M. (1990). A test of the Olson Circumplex Model: Examining its curvilinear assumption and the presence of extreme types. *Family Process, 29,* 309-324.

Boss, P. G. (1988). *Family stress management.* Newbury Park, CA: Sage.

Buckley, W. (1967). *Sociology and modern systems theory.* Englewood Cliffs, NJ: Prentice Hall.

Burr, W. R. (1973). *Theory construction and the sociology of the family.* New York: John Wiley.

Burr, W. R. (1982). Families under stress. In H. I. McCubbin, A. E. Cauble, & J. M. Patterson (Eds.), *Family stress, coping, and social support* (pp. 5-25). Springfield, IL: Charles C Thomas.

Cannon, W. B. (1932). *The wisdom of the body.* New York: Norton.

Caplan, G. (1964). *Principles of preventive psychiatry.* New York: Basic Books.

Caplan, G. (1974). *Support systems and community mental health.* New York: Behavioral Publications.

Carter, B., & McGoldrick, M. (1989). Overview: The changing family life cycle—A framework for family therapy. In B. Carter & M. McGoldrick (Eds.), *The changing family life cycle: A framework for family therapy* (2nd ed., pp. 3-28). Boston: Allyn & Bacon.

Cobb, S. (1976). Social support as a moderator of life stress. *Psychosomatic Medicine, 38,* 300-314.

Coelho, G., Hamburg, D., & Adams, J. (1974). *Coping and adaptation.* New York: Basic Books.

Dohrenwend, B. S., & Dohrenwend, B. P. (1974). *Stressful life events: Their nature and effects.* New York: John Wiley.

Erikson, E. H. (1963). *Childhood and society.* New York: Norton.

Hall, A. D., & Fagan, R. E. (1968). Definition of system. In W. Buckley (Ed.), *Modern systems research for the behavioral scientist* (pp. 81-92). Chicago: Aldine.

Hansen, D. A. (1965). Personal and positional influence in formal groups: Propositions and theory for research on family vulnerability to stress. *Social Forces, 44*, 202-210.

Hansen, D. A., & Hill, R. (1964). Families under stress. In H. Christensen (Ed.), *Handbook of marriage and the family* (pp. 215-295). Chicago: Rand McNally.

Hill, R. (1949). *Families under stress*. Westport, CT: Greenwood.

Hill, R. (1972). *The strengths of black families*. New York: Emerson Hall.

Hoffman, L. (1981). *Foundation of family therapy: A conceptual framework for systems change*. New York: Basic Books.

Holmes, T. H., & Rahe, R. H. (1967). The social readjustment rating scale. *Journal of Psychosomatic Research, 11*, 213-218.

Lazarus, R. (1966). *Psychological stress and the coping process*. New York: McGraw-Hill.

Lazarus, R. (1976). *Patterns of adjustment*. New York: McGraw-Hill.

Lazarus, R. S., & Folkman, S. (1984). *Stress, appraisal, and coping*. New York: Springer.

Lazarus, R. S., & Launier, R. (1978). Stress-related transactions between person and environment. In L. A. Pervin & M. Lewis (Eds.), *Perspectives in interactional psychology* (pp. 360-392). New York: Plenum.

Lipman-Blumen, J. (1975). A crisis framework applied to macrosociological family changes: Marriage, divorce, and occupational trends associated with World War II. *Journal of Marriage and the Family, 27*, 889-902.

May, R. (1950). *The meaning of anxiety*. New York: Ronald.

McCubbin, H. I. (1979). Integrating coping behavior in family stress theory. *Journal of Marriage and the Family, 41*, 237-244.

McCubbin, H. I., Cauble, A. E., & Patterson, J. M. (1982). *Family stress, coping, and social support*. Springfield, IL: Charles C Thomas.

McCubbin, H. I., Joy, C. B., Cauble, A. E., Comeau, J. K., Patterson, J. M., & Needle, R. H. (1980). Family stress and coping: A decade review. *Journal of Marriage and the Family, 42*, 125-141.

McCubbin, H. I., & Patterson, J. M. (1982). Family adaptation to crisis. In H. I. McCubbin, A. E. Cauble, & J. M. Patterson (Eds.), *Family stress, coping, and social support*. Springfield, IL: Charles C Thomas.

McCubbin, H. I., & Patterson, J. M. (1985). Adolescent stress, coping, and adaptation: A normative family perspective. In G. K. Leigh & G. W. Peterson (Eds.), *Adolescents in families* (pp. 256-276). Cincinnati, OH: Southwestern.

McCubbin, H. I., Patterson, J. M., & Wilson, L. (1981). *Family inventory of life events and changes (FILE): Research instrument*. St. Paul: University of Minnesota, Family Social Science.

Moos, R. H. (1976). *Human adaptation: Coping with life crisis*. Lexington, MA: D. C. Heath.

Moos, R. H. (1986). *Coping with life crises: An integrated approach*. New York: Plenum.

Naisbitt, J., & Aburdene, P. (1990). *Megatrends 2000: Ten new directions for the 1990s*. New York: Morrow.

Olson, D. H., Russell, C. S., & Sprenkle, D. H. (1979). Circumplex Model of Marital and Family Systems: Cohesion and adaptability dimensions, family types, and clinical applications. *Family Process, 18*, 3-28.

Olson, D. H., Russell, C. S., & Sprenkle, D. H. (1980). Marital and family therapy: A decade review. *Journal of Marriage and the Family, 42*, 239-260.

Olson, D. H., Russell, C. S., & Sprenkle, D. H. (1983). Circumplex Model of Marital and Family Systems: VI. Theoretical update. *Family Process, 22*, 69-83.

Pearlin, L., & Schooler, C. (1978). The structure of coping. *Journal of Health and Social Behavior, 19,* 2-21.

Rees, H., & Smyer, M. (1983). The dimensionalization of life events. In E. Callahan & K. McCluskey (Eds.), *Life span developmental psychology: Non-normative life events* (pp. 328-359). New York: Academic Press.

Roskies, E., & Lazarus, R. (1980). Coping theory and the teaching of coping skills. In D. Davidson & S. Davidson (Eds.), *Behavioral medicine: Changing health lifestyles* (pp. 38-69). New York: Brunner/Mazel.

Rutter, M. (1983). Stress, coping, and development: Some issues and questions. In N. Garmezy & M. Rutter (Eds.), *Stress, coping, and development* (pp. 1-41). New York: McGraw-Hill.

Sarason, I., Johnson, J., & Siegel, J. (1978). Assessing the impact of life changes: Development of the life experiences survey. *Journal of Consulting and Clinical Psychology, 64,* 932-946.

Selye, H. (1978). *The stress of life.* New York: McGraw-Hill.

Spanier, G. B. (1989). Bequeathing family continuity. *Journal of Marriage and the Family, 51,* 3-13.

Spence, K. W. (1956). *Behavior therapy and conditioning.* New Haven, CT: Yale University Press.

Toffler, A. (1990). *Power shift: Knowledge, wealth, and violence at the edge of the 21st century.* New York: Bantam.

# PART I

# Stress and Change
# Over the Family Life Cycle

# 2

❀

# Issues of Gender

## *A Feminist Perspective*

KATHERINE R. ALLEN
KRISTINE M. BABER

Gender is a central organizing principle of contemporary social life. Gender issues permeate physiological functioning, identity, personality, relationships, social roles, and institutional structures. Children become aware of who they are as gendered beings by age 3, but individuals continue to be socialized as males and females throughout their lives. Gender plays a critical role in people's experiences and opportunities from birth to death. Sometimes the effects of gender are clear and explicit, while at other times they are subtle and elusive.

Gender is a pervasive force in family life. We are assigned a gender as either a male or a female based on biological sex at birth. However, the meanings and implications of gender are developed through intimate interactions with others, primarily in association with parents, siblings, and other close connections (Ferree, 1990). These interactions occur in a societal context that provides different opportunities for and has different expectations of males and females (Thompson & Walker, 1989).

We see gender, then, as a process rather than a category. What it means to be a male or female in our society is socially constructed, not something that is innately given. Although there are biosocial theories that place greater emphasis on human physiology and evolution (Troost & Filsinger, 1993), we take the position that gender must be understood primarily within its social context. The idea that gender and gender roles are socially constructed carries with it the possibility, and indeed the likelihood, of change over time.

Gender is a particularly charged issue in contemporary family life. Although women have moved in significant numbers into the paid workforce, and there are growing expectations for men to be involved in household work and child care, traditional stereotypes of men as providers and women as primary caregivers are deeply rooted in the social consciousness. The belief that breadwinning is central to male identity and purpose in the family historically has provided a justification for discrimination against women in the labor force and reinforced women's dependence on a male partner (Potuchek, 1992). Men continue to have more opportunities and accrue greater rewards through their paid work, making it more likely that a husband's job will be given priority in a family. Because their jobs are often lower status and lower paying, wives who work outside the home often plan their occupational lives around family support and caregiving activities, which are less valued and unpaid. The inequities in the labor force and the resulting differential access to resources that women and men experience translate into differential power in the family. Women in traditional marriages in which husbands are seen as the primary breadwinners will have less influence regarding family and marital decision making, may not feel safe raising controversial issues, and may not have the resources to leave a problematic or dangerous relationship if it becomes necessary or desirable (Okin, 1989).

Increased fertility control through effective contraception and legal abortions has allowed women to break out of confining gender expectations that define women primarily as nurturers—wives and mothers. By being able to make active decisions about whether to have children, as well as when to have them and how many to have, women have freed themselves to access educational and occupational opportunities. As a result, women, individually and collectively, are amassing greater resources, which are providing a basis for greater influence in relationships with male or female partners and in society in general (Aptheker, 1989; Blumstein & Schwartz, 1983; Faderman, 1991).

Women's greater involvement in work outside the home has significant consequences for what goes on inside the family—particularly in regard to expectations of men and their participation in family work. These expectations sometimes challenge traditional beliefs about responsibility for family work and can contribute to conflict between partners. Men are struggling with uncertainty about what it means to be a man today, and some feel they are asked to take on responsibilities and show care in ways that are unmasculine or require skills they do not have (Levant, 1992). Some men are becoming more involved in family work, particularly in interactions with their children. To a certain extent, men's increased involvement in child care may be traced to divorce, to women's decreased availability for child care because of their own employment, and/or pressure from female partners for more equitable sharing. However, other men are becoming more involved in parenting because they want to be the kind of father that they themselves never had, or they desire to share parenting because of a sense of equity and fairness to their partners (Ehrensaft, 1987; Hochschild, 1989).

However, the perception that men have drastically increased their involvement in parenting is deceptive (Pleck, 1987). Research indicates that, although we are developing a culture of fatherhood and male nurturance, the conduct of fathers—the actual time spent caring for children—has not changed significantly (LaRossa, 1988). Men can still see themselves and be seen by others as "good fathers" without being deeply involved in child care or spending a lot of time with their children; they are able to justify their lack of direct involvement on the grounds that they are working hard to provide for the family (Phoenix & Woollett, 1991). In fact, many men define being a good father as providing for their families and being there to solve problems when they arise; they feel devalued by contemporary critiques of fathering (Levant, 1992).

## Current Research on Gender and Families

### A Feminist Perspective on Gender

A feminist perspective illuminates the gendered nature of family life, allowing us to examine the contradictions contained in the previously mentioned examples. Feminism points to the pervasive ways in which women and men are not equal. The inequities are relative, complex, and multidimensional: "Relationships between women and men vary from equality or near equality to marked inequality" (Morgan, 1990, p. 74). Feminism points to the interplay of power in private relations among family members and in public access to control over resources.

In any society in which a social hierarchy exists, gender is a key way in which rewards and opportunities are handed out according to systematic structures and expectations and is designed to benefit those who hold power and who maintain the status quo. A hierarchical system based on gender is referred to as *patriarchy,* which literally means "male domination." Some feminists prefer the term *social stratification* to *patriarchy,* in which gender is seen as affecting all aspects of life, in variable, not universal, ways (Acker, 1989). Feminism provides a language to critique the status quo on the basis of inequity and to identify which groups or individuals are being more or less oppressed by existing social structures, just as a perspective on racism allows an analysis of differential access to rewards and opportunities based on race (Andersen & Collins, 1992).

Traditional marriage as an institution contributes to the vulnerability of women in our society (Okin, 1989). Females are socialized to shape their lives around caring for husbands and children and make career choices that do not conflict with their ability to meet these caregiving responsibilities. Because women's wages and status in the workplace are usually less than their male partners', it appears beneficial to give priority to the husbands' work. Women in traditional marriages therefore tend to be economically dependent on their husbands.

The fact that the male's paid work takes priority increases his status and earnings, giving him more power both within and outside the family. Okin (1989) points out that the "asymmetric dependency of wives on husbands affects their potential for a satisfactory exit, and thereby influences the effectiveness of their voice within the marriage" (p. 167). Women who devote themselves to furthering their husbands' careers while sacrificing their own may lack the social and economic resources to maintain a base of power in the relationship or to leave the relationship if necessary.

### Gender and Caregiving

Children's experience of being cared for primarily by a female in American society reinforces the expectation that nurturance and love are provided by women (Chodorow, 1978). Parenthood has come to be synonymous with women, and women are expected to structure their lives around the role and identity of being a mother. In this way, motherhood becomes perceived as "natural" for women, and women become associated with the acts of care that they are supposed to perform.

A growing understanding and body of evidence suggests, however, that motherhood, in particular, and caregiving, in general, are not synonymous with the female gender. About 20% of women do not become mothers, and half of these women avoid motherhood voluntarily (Baber & Allen, 1992). In addition, many women who become mothers have had unplanned, and sometimes unwanted, children. Some mothers, particularly those who are in professional positions, pay other women to act in their place by employing family home day-care providers (Nelson, 1990). When men provide nurturing behavior toward children, as in the example of single fathers, children experience such mothering-like behavior not as a biological property but as a practice that is defined by the situation of caregiving, regardless of gender (Risman, 1986).

If men can mother and not all women want to be caregivers, why, then, are women disproportionately the individuals who provide nearly all of the care in families? Why is it that following the birth of a baby, even egalitarian couples succumb to a traditionalization process, with the mother providing nearly all of the primary care for the infant and the father providing only occasional care (LaRossa & LaRossa, 1989)? Why is it that wives, daughters, and daughters-in-law are the primary caregivers to the frail elderly, even if the care recipient is the parent of an adult son (Stone, Cafferata, & Sangl, 1987)? Why is it that women who work for wages outside the home have a "second shift," which is a double burden of work that involves coming home to housework and child care after leaving their paid jobs (Hochschild, 1989)?

Why is it, then, that both men *and* women are capable of acting as caregivers, but women still do the vast majority of family care? Part of the problem is that women continue to accept society's justifications for their husband's small contributions to family work (Thompson, 1991). Some women may be reluctant to give up control over traditional female responsibilities that provide them with some power and place women in the center of the family by virtue of care, attention, and connection (Kranichfeld, 1988). Women also may have concerns about husbands performing tasks up to their own standards, feel guilty about shirking what they perceive to be their own responsibilities, or sense pressure from friends and family (Baber & Allen, 1992).

Men's resistance to relinquishing the benefits they derive from gendered arrangements in intimate and social life is a more serious obstacle to change. In a classic statement explaining men's resistance to changing gender roles, Goode (1982) speculates that men receive too many benefits from current gendered arrangements to be motivated to change and take on additional duties simply because of fairness or altruism, even if requested by their female partners. The structural justifications for male dominance, however, are changing, and men's rights to (a) greater freedom from domestic work and (b) privilege in the workforce are being challenged on many fronts. Male privilege used to be based on an ideology of men's superior strength, but "because of the increased use of various mechanical gadgets and devices, fewer tasks require much strength. As to those that still require strength, most men cannot do them either" (Goode, 1982, p. 144). Furthermore, the kinds of qualities required by political and business leaders no longer benefit the stereotypical aggressive male. Rather, top positions in government and business are best filled "by people, male or female, who are sensitive to others' needs, adept at obtaining cooperation, and skilled in social relations" (Goode, 1982, p. 145). Goode (1982) concludes that the old structural supports that allowed men greater protection from an additional burden of work at home are gradually giving way through forces outside the home. Still, only a small minority of men take seriously the feminist challenge to traditional masculinity by dealing with gender issues in male-focused groups (Bubolz & McKenry, 1993).

### Gender and Breadwinning

*Breadwinning,* defined as the activities and the ideology involved in the economic support of families, is central to reconstructions of gender roles that are more equitable and less constraining for both men and women. The ideology of the breadwinner role particularly affects men's lives (Morgan, 1990) but has far-reaching consequences for women and children. Men's experience and value in families are defined and evaluated by their success in providing for their families. Yet, because of changes in the economy and the nature of work, there has been a weakening of men's abilities to provide the sole income for their families (Wilkie, 1991). Traditional gender ideology equates men with their capacity to earn a substantial wage. At the same time, we live in a postindustrial society, where structural supports such as secure jobs and steady promotions are no longer guaranteed, even for men in elite positions (Stacey, 1990). As a result of these structural changes in society, men are becoming less able to fulfill their traditional gender roles, but there has been little change in the expectation that they should do so. A complete reorganization of men's family experiences must be undertaken to understand the diversity of men's lives; it is no longer acceptable to assign men to the outdated solo identity of breadwinner (Morgan, 1990), and it may be costly to everyone involved.

Dual-earner, and particularly dual-career, families tend to have more egalitarian gender beliefs. As women amass personal and financial resources through paid work, they are more likely to expect equal relationships (Gerson, 1985; Gerstel & Gross, 1987). However, several studies have found that, even when they are working full time, wives may not expect their husbands to participate equally in family work (Ferree, 1990; Hochschild, 1989; Thompson, 1991; Yogev, 1981). Ferree (1990) proposed that women's labor force participation is necessary but not sufficient in renegotiating more equitable responsibilities. She argued that women who participate in supporting their families and whose work is seen as an important contribution to family well-being are better able to renegotiate the distribution of household work.

Breadwinning and labor force participation are not synonymous. Breadwinning is not just the behavior but, more important, the meaning attached to that behavior in the family (Potuchek, 1992). Potuchek's study of 153 dual-earner couples found that the wives varied considerably in their orientation to breadwinning. She identified seven different categories of orientation from co-breadwinners to employed homemakers. Co-breadwinners, who constituted 15% of the sample, reported that their jobs were critical to the support of the family and were at least as important as their husbands'. Employed homemakers, who were 21% of the total, did not define their employment as a source of financial support for their families, and 97% saw their husbands' jobs as more important than their own. The rest of the women were in "mixed" categories depending on the centrality of work to their sense of self and the contribution they saw themselves making to the support of their families. However, most of these women reported that their husbands' jobs were more important than their own and that the breadwinner role should be allocated primarily to males.

Couples in which both partners are involved in breadwinning and in which there is a commitment to equality are most likely to negotiate a satisfactory distribution of family work (Baruch, Barnett, & Rivers, 1983; Hochschild, 1989; Lein, 1984). Women are more empowered when they can support themselves and their children. Women with incomes similar to their partners' are most likely to be seen as breadwinners. In Potuchek's (1992) study, the cobreadwinners were concentrated in relatively high-paying professional and managerial positions and earned about the same amount as their husbands.

### Economic and Human Costs of Gender Inequities

Caregiving labor in families is unpaid, unrecognized, unrewarded, and highly gendered. The market value of a homemaker's activities is estimated to be more than $50,000 a year (Strong & DeVault, 1992), but in most families, this work is taken for granted unless it is not done. Women are the primary caregivers and homemakers in society, yet the work that women do at home is often experienced as invisible to those who benefit from it.

Although the majority of women are now in the workforce, men are not assuming equal responsibility for housework and child care. One major study that examined men's and women's contributions to housework found that women did over 80% of the cooking, cleaning, and laundry (Robinson, 1988). Even men in marriages where partners are committed to sharing report that men devote less time to family work than do their wives; the time they do spend is more likely to be spent in parenting rather than housework (Gilbert, 1985). Women's typical response to the situation has been to cut back the total number of hours of housework that they do (Robinson, 1988).

Hochschild (1989) interviewed 50 dual-worker couples and found that in only 20% of the couples did men share housework equally with their wives; 70% of the men did less than half but more than one third of the work, and 10% did less than one third. Many of the men resisted sharing household work and used resistant strategies such as doing tasks in a distracted way, waiting to be asked to help out, or working on projects other than those that needed to be done most. The men who were most likely to share were those whose wives had advanced degrees, careers, and incomes similar to their husbands'—indicators of what Hochschild referred to as "cultural capital." The 20% of men who shared equally in family work also seemed to have deep feelings and beliefs about equality.

For most women, the dilemmas associated with paid labor aggravate and reinforce inequities that characterize family life. In 1989, 57% of all women aged 16 and over were in the paid labor force (U.S. Bureau of the Census, 1991), and 51% of all mothers of newborns were in the workforce in 1988 (U.S. Bureau of the Census, 1989). Yet, women are still concentrated in traditionally female jobs characterized by lower status and lower salaries. In 1991, 86% of elementary school teachers, 95% of nurses, and 99% of all secretaries were women (U.S. Bureau of the Census, 1992). Although women are gaining entry into traditionally male-dominated occupations, the transition has been slow. Even in 1991, only 20% of physicians, 19% of lawyers, and 8% of engineers were women (U.S. Bureau of the Census, 1992). Women and minorities who seek advanced positions run into attitudinal or organizational biases that act as a "glass ceiling" by blocking their advancement in ways that are not easily detected (U.S. Department of Labor, 1991).

Wage discrimination by gender continues to pervade the workplace. In 1990 the median income for males was $20,293, and the median income for females was $10,070 (U.S. Bureau of the Census, 1992). Contributing to the gender gap in wages is the fact that men predominate in higher-status professions that tend to pay more than the professions that women tend to occupy, such as teaching, nursing, and human service. Considering incomes among college-educated men and women, a study conducted by the Census Bureau in 1989 and 1990 reported that college-educated white men earned on average $41,090, and college-educated white women earned on average $27,440. The gender gap still prevailed when race was added to the analysis: College-educated black men earned on average $31,380, and college-educated black women earned on average $26,730 (Bovee, 1991).

Recent studies suggest that women are not complacent about the unequal burden of work that they carry in families. As gender ideologies and expectations are changing, many women may no longer accept that it is women's "lot in life" to do more work for little or no reward. Dressel and Clark (1990) found that women are highly ambivalent about their double burden. In a study investigating the kinds of care men and women provide in families and how they define and interpret acts of family care, Dressel and Clark found that three quarters of the women expressed "emotional dissonance" about their caregiving activities.

The researchers asked the respondents to keep diaries of their activities. Women reported negative feelings associated with the routine acts they integrated into their daily lives—grocery shopping, baby-sitting, sewing, ironing, vacuuming, and cooking. These women seemed to be providing care to others in the form of "personal service," including routinely doing things for others that others could have done themselves. Men, on the other hand, did not report such ambivalent feelings. Dressel and Clark (1990) speculated that perhaps men were more rewarded by participating in family care "precisely because it was not expected from them" (p. 779). Another explanation of men's lesser participation is the fact that they are not expected to plan or coordinate any of the family activities but only to participate in them; they were saved from feeling the ambivalent emotions that women felt. Dressel and Clark's (1990) analysis reveals how complicated women's and men's relationship to family work is. Gender alone is not enough to account for women's disproportionate acts of care; women's feelings of oppression in participating in these activities and in providing these services to others must also be examined.

### Gender and Violence

Domestic violence is a pervasive and disturbing aspect of American family life. There is a great deal of controversy about who perpetrates most of the violence in families, but it is clear that it is usually women and children who get hurt. Women report being the victim of violence three times as frequently as men, and this violence is suffered generally at the hands of their husbands, ex-husbands, or boyfriends (Harlow, 1991). Harlow found that 28% of female murders in 1989 were believed to have been committed by husbands or boyfriends. Although it occurs among all social classes, marital violence is more likely to happen in low-income families and to be associated with different expectations about the division of household work, husbands' frequent drinking, and wives' attaining more education than their husbands (Hotaling & Sugarman, 1990).

Men are traditionally socialized to repress their emotions rather than to identify or express them. However, anger and rage are among the few emotions that men have legitimately expressed, so many other feelings such as hurt, disappointment, and fear get funneled into them (Levant, 1992). As a result, the potential for violent anger and rage may lie close to the surface, particularly for men who are unable to communicate their emotions in other ways. In addition, our social constructions of masculinity include the notions of power and dominance. Violence may be seen as legitimate for a man who feels inadequate or believes his control threatened by a partner (Gelles & Strauss, 1988). Violence is more likely to occur in relationships in which one partner has most of the power rather than in relationships characterized by shared decision making (Gelles & Strauss, 1988).

### Reconstructing Marriage

Continuing gender inequity in marriage no doubt contributes in numerous, yet often subtle, ways to the deterioration of relationships. The high rate of divorce in the United States attests to the difficulties that men and women encounter in their intimate relationships. Some have predicted that as many as two out of three marriages may end in divorce in the future (Martin & Bumpass, 1989).

It is not enough simply to look at marriage survival, however. The happiness and satisfaction of those individuals with enduring marriages deserve consideration. Glenn (1991) estimated that only one third of those couples who married in the early 1970s were still married *and* satisfied to be in their marriages. There appears to be a continuing downward trend in the percentage of people who report that they are very happy in their marriages—from 60% in the mid-1970s to 54% in the late-1970s and early 1980s to 49% in the mid-1980s. Glenn's findings led him to propose that the probability of marital success is so low that "to make a strong, unqualified commitment to a marriage—and to make the investments of time, energy, and foregone opportunities that entails—is so hazardous that no totally rational person would do it" (Glenn, 1991, p. 269).

Marriages that are successful and rewarding to the individuals provide information that may be useful in reconstructing gender expectations in intimate relationships. Baruch, Barnett, and Rivers (1983) studied 300 women aged 35 to 50 and focused on aspects of their lives and relationships that brought them pleasure and satisfaction. Married women in this study expressed more satisfaction, happiness, and optimism than single women; the researchers attributed this difference to higher family income and having a regular sexual partner. Women who had successful marriages indicated the importance of communication with and support from their partners. Poor communication between partners, emotionally distant husbands, and lack of companionship caused the most problems in relationships. The most rewarding marriages were similar to relationships among loving friends and were characterized by mutual care and cooperation.

Research by Vannoy-Hiller and Philliber (1989, 1992) also emphasizes the importance of husbands' sensitivity and supportiveness to the success of the marriage, particularly among dual-worker couples. Gender-role identities and expectations were found to be much more important in determining the quality of marriage than were socioeconomic, life cycle, educational, or occupational status variables (Vannoy-Hiller & Philliber, 1992). Husbands' role expectations, gender-role identity, and support were more related to marital quality than were the attitudes of the wives. Husbands with sensitive, supporting personalities not only contribute to higher quality marriages for their wives but also indicate more satisfying marriages themselves. Women who perceived their husbands to have more egalitarian expectations also reported higher marital satisfaction.

### Interventions

We begin our suggestions for intervention with the assumption that gender equality in families and intimate relationships is desirable and possible through the restructuring of traditional gender roles. Changes are needed at all levels of society to reverse the pattern of gender discrimination and to create a more equitable society for women, men, and children. Intervention at one societal level is not sufficient; we should simultaneously work for change at the individual, family, and societal levels.

*Individuals*

Personal empowerment is necessary to create and promote societal change. Empowerment is a consequence of individuals joining together to act against intolerance and inequity. People who are empowered have a voice in which to speak their own opinions and to advocate for changes that improve their lives and well-being (Baber & Allen, 1992).

Economic autonomy is critical for women to become and remain empowered in their families. A woman who has the psychological and economic means to be independent is less vulnerable to abuse within a relationship. She is more likely to have the power to raise and negotiate difficult issues and the potential to leave an abusive relationship (Okin, 1989). Because of the high divorce rate in our society and the likelihood that women will need to support themselves and their children at some point in their lives, it is no longer reasonable to expect that women will be able to depend on a partner for support. Traditional female gender expectations are a potentially costly luxury that today's women cannot afford.

Likewise, neither males nor females should be absolved of the responsibility for nurturance and caregiving (Thompson, 1992). Levant (1992) has argued that one of the major reasons men do not get more involved in child care is because of skill deficits. This could be remedied through a wide range of fatherhood education programs. A proactive approach would be to implement a "curriculum of caring" in the schools (Bronfenbrenner & Weiss, 1983) that would give both male and female children an opportunity to learn the skills and integrate caregiving into their gender scripts.

The experience of caregiving can be beneficial for men. It can provide men with an opportunity to develop a closer relationship with their children and allow them to directly influence the growth and development of their daughters and sons. Contrary to traditional beliefs, research indicates that the quality of men's parental and marital roles contributes as much to their mental health as does their work role (Barnett, Marshall, & Pleck, 1992).

Comprehensive sexuality education is also needed to prepare people for the realities of a sexually active life—to control and limit fertility and to guard against sexually transmitted diseases. Young people need knowledge about the kinds of relationship options that might be best suited to them, rather than imposing the assumption that marriage is the best or only way to live. They need valid information about the reality of adult relationships and to anticipate the consequences of relationship impermanence.

Consciousness-raising groups have always been an important feature of women's collective empowerment. Now, men are finding that they, too, need to work with members of their own gender to discover previously unexamined aspects of their lives and experiences and to help each other toward restructuring their roles and identities (Kimmel & Messner, 1992). There are various men's movements with diverse purposes and styles that are nevertheless united in their recognition of the costs to men of "the economic, legal, social, and political rewards that patriarchy has conferred upon them in the 20th Century" (Bubolz & McKenry, 1993).

Men express anxiety and concern about changing roles. In his book, *How Men Feel,* Astrachan (1986) found that men are anxious about new roles because they blur the boundaries by which men orient themselves, raise the possibility of women no longer needing men, and provoke fear of losing advantage in the relationship. However, there are benefits that accrue to men as the result of role changes. Men feel relief when they learn that women can bring in money that is needed by the family and gain a new sense of intimacy through equitable roles.

*Families*

Family relationships need to be predicated upon explicit expectations of reciprocal caring, support, and equity. One of the greatest challenges of parenting in the 1990s is preparing children for the social and technological changes they will face. Continually evolving gender roles demand that parents are sensitive to and aware of subtle differences in the ways in which they interact with their male and female children and the opportunities that they provide for them. From an early age, girls and boys should have the opportunity to develop the skills and gain the information they will need to be sensitive caregivers and adequate breadwinners. Males and females need to be reared with the expectation that they will participate in both paid and family work.

An important gift that parents can give their children is the model of a loving, supportive, and egalitarian adult intimate relationship. The safest and most fulfilling kind of intimate relationship is egalitarian (Hochschild, 1989; Thompson & Walker, 1989). Thompson (1992) draws upon Cancian's image of interdependent marriages to suggest a model for a relationship in which both partners are expected to nurture the other, attend and respond to the other's needs, and encourage the other's projects. Such a relationship rejects traditional gender expectations about responsibility for care and reduces the likelihood for exploitation within the relationship. Such a model is consistent with Okin's (1989) notion of a just family—a family in which the quality of one's life would not depend upon whether one had been born a male or a female.

Clear and open communication is essential to the development and maintenance of healthy intimate relationships. Communication between women and men is often hampered by the different ways they use and understand language. Tannen (1990) claims that men and women speak different "genderlects" so that talk between them is almost like communicating cross-culturally. Women and men learn to use language differently—men to maintain status and independence and women to encourage connection and intimacy—but then try to interpret each other's ways of talking in terms of their own style. The result is misunderstanding and the feeling of not being heard. Understanding interactional differences between men and women is an important intervention that should be included in communication courses in school curricula and family life education.

*Public Policy*

The stark reality of the power of public policy to affect family life was demonstrated clearly in the transition from the Bush administration to the Clinton administration. In a matter of weeks, the threat to women's reproductive rights was greatly diminished, a family leave bill was passed, and women were appointed to new positions of power in the government. It is imperative that women and men committed to gender equality advance to positions of social influence where they can facilitate changes that will result in the dismantling of social structures perpetuating inequities.

Individuals who are concerned about gender equality need to contribute to the process of defining the family agenda that is put before elected officials. The governmental neglect of family policies leaves couples struggling to work out equitable distributions of labor, women struggling with the conflicting demands of work and parenting, employers struggling to meet the new demands of a changing workforce, and domestic partners who are not legally married struggling to secure personnel benefits for their families (Baber & Allen, 1992). Programs that need to be addressed are pay equity, high-quality subsidized child and elder care, flexible work schedules, adequate health care, and comprehensive employee benefits that are not discriminatory.

## Future Directions

Analyses that are sensitive to the interlocking ways in which gender, race, class, age, sexual orientation, and physical capacity structure individual and family lives are becoming central to our understanding of families. It is no longer possible to design research in which it is assumed that there is one standard family form (Cheal, 1991). Diversity and plurality in family structures and processes are more normative than the old notion of the "benchmark family" of the 1950s (Scanzoni, Polonko, Teachman, & Thompson, 1989). This means that we need to consider and include all the variations in and orientations to mothering and fathering as well as the variety of configurations that characterize contemporary families.

In considering the effects of diversity, it is important that our research and theorizing about gender do not continue to be biased toward white, middle-class families. The dynamics of gender in African-American families, for example, challenge much of our traditional theorizing. Staples and Johnson (1993) note that many of the conditions that white feminists have found oppressive, such as not working outside the home, are seen as luxuries not historically available to African-American women. Although black women have been family breadwinners for generations, severe competition for the small pool of educated, employed black men may mean that these women will still have to take relationships on men's terms (Staples & Johnson, 1993).

New research questions must be asked that allow us to examine the effects of postmodern society on families as well as how diverse family forms are altering society (Cheal, 1991). There is a developing body of knowledge regarding how families can be described from the previously unexamined perspectives of women (Baber & Allen, 1992). To complement this information, we need research that examines men's roles and contributions (Morgan, 1990). These new analyses allow us to ask questions about conceptualizations of family life that were once considered sacrosanct. For example, when is marriage harmful to women (Okin, 1989)? Under what conditions can divorce lead to kinship extension rather than kinship disruption (Stacey, 1990)? What are the unexamined emotional costs of divorce for men (Morgan, 1990)? How important is legal marriage to the stability of an intimate relationship, regardless of the sexual orientation of the partners (Baber & Allen, 1992)? Women, men, and children are already living out the responses to these questions in their daily lives. Family scholars need to examine these experiences in more realistic ways. Research methods that are sensitive to diversity, particularly many qualitative approaches, allow families to define their own experiences (Gilgun, Daly, & Handel, 1992) and thereby provide a richer and more valid picture of family life.

## Conclusion

In this chapter, we have examined how gender is a compelling and pervasive feature of individual and family life. As a socially constructed phenomenon, gender is created through daily interaction with self and others. The family is a leading way in which gender is learned, experienced, and transformed over the life course. But gender is also more than a social construction. Like race, class, age, and sexual orientation, gender is a system of opportunity and oppression in which individual lives are constrained and channeled according to whether one is male or female. Perhaps this reality may explain the contradiction as to why gender roles seem to be changing at an unprecedented rate yet are so resistant to change.

As the twentieth century comes to a close, one thing is certain. Successful adulthood depends on the ability of women and men to provide for themselves and their families. It means that both women and men should share in the distribution of household work and child care, something that has been slower to change than participation in breadwinning. Family life education needs to provide ways of helping children and adults participate in the life-sustaining activities that traditionally have been the province of women. Sharing the burdens and rewards of family nurturance and breadwinning is an important message to give the next generation.

## References

Acker, J. (1989). The problem with patriarchy. *Sociology, 23,* 235-240.

Andersen, M. L., & Collins, P. H. (Eds.). (1992). *Race, class, and gender: An anthology.* Belmont, CA: Wadsworth.

Aptheker, B. (1989). *Tapestries of life: Women's work, women's consciousness, and the meaning of daily experience.* Amherst: University of Massachusetts Press.

Astrachan, A. (1986). *How men feel: Their response to women's demands for equality and power.* Garden City, NY: Doubleday.

Baber, K. M., & Allen, K. R. (1992). *Women and families: Feminist reconstructions.* New York: Guilford.

Barnett, R. C., Marshall, N. L., & Pleck, J. H. (1992). Men's multiple roles and their relationship to men's psychological distress. *Journal of Marriage and the Family, 54,* 358-367.

Baruch, G., Barnett, R., & Rivers, C. (1983). *Life prints.* New York: McGraw-Hill.

Blumstein, P., & Schwartz, P. (1983). *American couples: Money, work, sex.* New York: William Morrow.

Bovee, T. (1991, September 20). Wide gap found in earnings by white, black college graduates. *The Boston Globe,* pp. 1, 7.

Bronfenbrenner, U., & Weiss, H. B. (1983). Beyond policies without people: An ecological perspective on child and family policy. In E. F. Zigler, S. L. Kagan, & E. Klugman (Eds.), *Children, families and government: Perspectives on American social policy* (pp. 393-414). London: Cambridge University Press.

Bubolz, M. M., & McKenry, P. C. (1993). Gender issues in family life education: A feminist perspective. In M. Arcus, J. Schvaneveldt, & J. Moss (Eds.), *Handbook of family life education* (Vol. 1, pp. 131-161). Newbury Park, CA: Sage.

Cheal, D. (1991). *Family and the state of theory.* Toronto: University of Toronto Press.

Chodorow, N. (1978). *The reproduction of mothering.* Berkeley: University of California Press.

Dressel, P., & Clark, A. (1990). A critical look at family care. *Journal of Marriage and the Family, 52,* 769-782.

Ehrensaft, D. (1987). *Parenting together: Men and women sharing the care of their children.* New York: Macmillan.

Faderman, L. (1991). *Odd girls and twilight lovers: A history of lesbian life in twentieth-century America.* New York: Penguin.

Ferree, M. M. (1990). Beyond separate spheres: Feminism and family research. *Journal of Marriage and the Family, 52,* 866-884.

Gelles, R. J., & Strauss, M. A. (1988). *Intimate violence.* New York: Simon & Schuster.

Gerson, K. (1985). *Hard choices: How women decide about work, career, and motherhood.* Berkeley: University of California Press.

Gerstel, N., & Gross, H. E. (1987). Commuter marriage: A microcosm of career and family conflict. In N. Gerstel & H. E. Gross (Eds.), *Families and work* (pp. 422-433). Philadelphia: Temple University Press.

Gilbert, L. A. (1985). *Men in dual-career families.* Hillsdale, NJ: Lawrence Erlbaum.

Gilgun, J. F., Daly, K., & Handel, G. (Eds.). (1992). *Qualitative methods in family research.* Newbury Park, CA: Sage.

Glenn, N. D. (1991). The recent trend in marital success in the United States. *Journal of Marriage and the Family, 53,* 261-270.

Goode, W. J. (1982). Why men resist. In B. Thorne with M. Yalom (Eds.), *Rethinking the family: Some feminist questions* (pp. 131-150). New York: Longman.

Harlow, C. W. (1991). *Female victims of violent crimes.* Washington, DC: U.S. Department of Justice.

Hochschild, A. (1989). *The second shift: Working parents and the revolution at home.* New York: Viking.

Hotaling, G. T., & Sugarman, D. B. (1990). A risk marker analysis of assaulted wives. *Journal of Family Violence, 5,* 1-14.

Kimmel, M. S., & Messner, M. A. (Eds.). (1992). *Men's lives* (2nd ed.). New York: Macmillan.

Kranichfeld, M. L. (1988). Rethinking family power. In N. D. Glenn & M. T. Coleman (Eds.), *Family relations: A reader* (pp. 230-241). Chicago: Dorsey.

LaRossa, R. (1988). Fatherhood and social change. *Family Relations, 37,* 451-457.

LaRossa, R., & LaRossa, M. M. (1989). Baby care: Fathers vs. mothers. In B. J. Risman & P. Schwartz (Eds.), *Gender in intimate relationships* (pp. 138-154). Belmont, CA: Wadsworth.

Lein, L. (1984). *Families without victims*. Lexington, MA: D. C. Heath.

Levant, R. F. (1992). Toward the reconstruction of masculinity. *Journal of Family Psychology, 5*, 379-402.

Martin, C. S., & Bumpass, L. (1989). Trends in marital disruption. *Demography, 26*, 37-52.

Morgan, D. H. J. (1990). Issues of critical sociological theory: Men in families. In J. Sprey (Ed.), *Fashioning family theory: New approaches* (pp. 67-106). Newbury Park, CA: Sage.

Nelson, M. K. (1990). Mothering others' children: The experiences of family day care providers. *Signs, 15*, 586-605.

Okin, S. M. (1989). *Justice, gender, and the family*. New York: Basic Books.

Phoenix, A., & Woollett, A. (1991). Introduction. In A. Phoenix, A. Woollett, & E. Lloyd (Eds.), *Motherhood: Meanings, practices, and ideologies* (pp. 1-12). Newbury Park, CA: Sage.

Pleck, J. H. (1987). American fathering in historical perspective. In M. S. Kimmel (Ed.), *Changing men* (pp. 83-97). Newbury Park, CA: Sage.

Potuchek, J. L. (1992). Employed wives' orientations to breadwinning: A gender theory analysis. *Journal of Marriage and the Family, 53*, 548-558.

Risman, B. J. (1986). Can men "mother"? Life as a single father. *Family Relations, 35*, 95-102.

Robinson, J. P. (1988). Who's doing the housework? *American Demographics, 10*, 24-27.

Scanzoni, J., Polonko, K., Teachman, J., & Thompson, L. (1989). *The sexual bond: Rethinking families and close relationships*. Newbury Park, CA: Sage.

Stacey, J. (1990). *Brave new families: Stories of domestic upheaval in late twentieth century America*. New York: Basic Books.

Staples, R., & Johnson, L. B. (1993). *Black families at the crossroads: Challenges and prospects*. San Francisco: Jossey-Bass.

Stone, R., Cafferata, G. L., & Sangl, J. (1987). Caregivers of the frail elderly: A national profile. *Gerontologist, 27*, 616-626.

Strong, B., & DeVault, C. (1992). *The marriage and family experience* (5th ed.). New York: West.

Tannen, D. (1990). *You just don't understand: Women and men in conversation*. New York: William Morrow.

Thompson, L. (1991). Family work: Women's sense of fairness. *Journal of Family Issues, 12*, 181-196.

Thompson, L. (1992, November). *Conceptualizing gender: The example of nurturance in marriage*. Paper presented at the annual meeting of the National Conference on Family Relations, Orlando, FL.

Thompson, L., & Walker, A. J. (1989). Gender in families: Women and men in marriage, work, and parenthood. *Journal of Marriage and the Family, 51*, 845-871.

Troost, K. M., & Filsinger, E. (1993). Emerging biosocial perspectives on the family. In P. G. Boss, W. J. Doherty, R. LaRossa, W. R. Schumm, & S. K. Steinmetz (Eds.), *Sourcebook of family theories and methods: A contextual approach* (pp. 677-710). New York: Plenum.

U.S. Bureau of the Census. (1989). Fertility of American women: June 1988. *Current population reports* (Series P-20, No. 436). Washington, DC: Government Printing Office.

U.S. Bureau of the Census. (1991). *Statistical abstract of the United States*. Washington, DC: Government Printing Office.

U.S. Bureau of the Census. (1992). *Statistical abstract of the United States*. Washington, DC: Government Printing Office.

U.S. Department of Labor. (1991). *A report on the glass ceiling initiative*. Washington, DC: Government Printing Office.

Vannoy-Hiller, D., & Philliber, W. W. (1989). *Equal partners: Successful women in marriage.* Newbury Park, CA: Sage.

Vannoy-Hiller, D., & Philliber, W. W. (1992). Wife's employment and quality of marriage. *Journal of Marriage and the Family, 54,* 387-398.

Wilkie, J. R. (1991). The decline in men's labor force participation and income and the changing structure of family economic support. *Journal of Marriage and the Family, 53,* 111-122.

Yogev, S. (1981). Do professional women have egalitarian marital relationships? *Journal of Marriage and the Family, 43,* 865-871.

# 3

❀

# Marital Problems

DAVID W. WRIGHT
BRIANA S. NELSON
KATHLEEN E. GEORGEN

The current divorce rate is but one indicator that marriages experience problems. Because life is inherently stressful and challenging and because it is difficult to have a relationship without conflict, it is not difficult to imagine that nearly all spouses encounter marital problems. Some of these problems are relatively minor irritations, whereas others are severe and challenge the stability of marriages. The variety of possible marital problems, along with the vast variation in the ways couples view them, makes them difficult to understand. In fact, few studies have directly examined marital problems. Instead, researchers have examined marital difficulties through the study of marital satisfaction, marital adjustment, marital stability, and marital quality. *Marital satisfaction* is the marital partners' subjective satisfaction with their marriage; *marital adjustment* is the degree to which partners have mastered the various tasks and obstacles inherent in marriage; *marital stability* is an indicator of the persistence of the marital relationship; and *marital quality* is the objective assessment of a marriage by a researcher or clinician. These concepts overlap, but it is important to recognize they are also distinct. For instance, a marriage may be deemed low in quality but persist over time, possibly because spouses see no alternatives or they perceive that barriers are insurmountable, thereby preventing them from divorcing. In contrast, a couple may view their marriage as not meeting their expectations even though it might be viewed by professionals as being of high quality.

It should not be assumed that the existence of problems necessarily has a negative effect on the marital relationship or that problems are always negative events. The occurrence of a positive or negative event often signals to a couple that some change in their relationship is required. In this sense, problems may reflect the existence of a developmental transition, the resolution of which may increase spouses' life skills (Caplan, 1964). Furthermore, the effect of problems on a marriage will depend on the context in which they occur and the resources that spouses implement in addressing problems (McCubbin & Patterson, 1985). For instance, spouses' perception and definition of a problem is a function of, among other things, values, past marital history, individual histories within their families of origin, current state of mind, and prevailing mores within society. Success in resolving the problem is a function of the spouses' perception of the problem, their personal characteristics, the support available to them from family and community, their commitment to one another, and available resources such as education, money, health, and psychological well-being. Thus, in reading this chapter, one should keep in mind that there is far more variation across couples than findings of studies may suggest. Rather, a marriage is a complex and changing mix of individual and relationship characteristics, history, and hopes and expectations.

## Review of Current Research

The following overview of marital problems focuses on empirical studies published since 1980 that have examined issues related to marital problems, marital adjustment, marital quality, marital satisfaction, and marital stability. (A large body of clinical literature is excluded because of space constraints.) Findings are grouped into four categories: (a) factors that predispose a couple to problems, (b) topics that are related to a couple's life together, (c) aspects of relating to one another, and (d) major marital problems.

### Factors Predisposing to Marital Problems

The existence of several circumstances prior to marriage increases the likelihood that a couple will experience problems in their marriage. Some are demographic in nature, whereas others are related to the characteristics of the partners.

There is considerable evidence that marrying at a young age is a strong predictor of later marital problems (Thornton & Rodgers, 1987; Witt, Davidson, Sollie, Lowe, & Peek, 1987). However, it is not simply chronological age that makes the difference. Rather, marrying early may lower spouses' attainment of education and thus increase their employment instability, which increases the negative effect of age on marital dissolution, especially during the early years (Bahr & Galligan, 1984). Greater levels of partners' warmth and outgoingness may offset the effects of early marriage (Levine & Hennessy, 1989). Waite, Haggstrom, and Kanouse (1985) reported that the birth of the first child had a strong stabilizing effect on early marriages, although Moore and Waite (1981) found the effect of young marriage on long-term stability to be independent of early childbearing. However, the evidence is quite clear that premarital pregnancy and/or childbearing contributes to higher levels of marital stress, especially for white couples (Billy, Landale, & McLaughlin, 1986; Martin & Bumpass, 1989).

Several authors have found stronger religious beliefs to be positively associated with marital satisfaction and stability (Heaton & Pratt, 1990; Wilson & Filsinger, 1986), and there is evidence that religious beliefs and participation may compensate for a lack of marital satisfaction, especially for women (Hansen, 1987a). Several studies have reported that those who have religious homogamy have less marital discord than those who have religious heterogamy (Chi & Houseknecht, 1985; Heaton & Pratt, 1990; Ortega, Whitt, & William, 1988), possibly because similar religious beliefs, joint church attendance, and a common network of friends result in less conflict over values and lifestyles. However, this relationship appears to be clearer for Protestants than for Catholics (Chi & Houseknecht, 1985; Ortega et al., 1988). Also, it has been suggested that the apparent general effect of religious homogamy on marital satisfaction actually is a reflection of higher religiosity among homogamous partners.

Three additional factors that are often considered from a standpoint of heterogamy and homogamy are cultural background, age, and education. Two studies, one examining couples in Israel (Weller & Rofe, 1988) and another examining Puerto Rican couples in New York City (Rogler & Procidano, 1989), failed to find negative effects of cultural heterogamy on marital quality. Weller and Rofe (1988) found that differences in marital quality disappeared after controlling for socioeconomic status. Tynes (1990) reported that, when husbands had more education than their wives, both partners reported less happy marriages with more disagreement and less positive feedback compared with marriages where the wives had a level of education comparable to their husbands'. A possible explanation given for this is that rigid adherence to traditional sex roles, which sometimes creates problems for couples, is more likely to occur in couples when the husband has more education than the wife.

Several studies have linked premarital cohabitation with lower marital satisfaction and higher rates of marital dissolution. Bennett, Blanc, and Bloom (1988) found that women who engaged in premarital cohabitation had almost 80% higher marital dissolution rates than those who did not cohabit. Similarly, Booth and Johnson (1988) concluded that premarital cohabitation was correlated with lower marital satisfaction and divorce. According to DeMaris and Leslie (1984), cohabitation was associated with lower perceived quality of communication for wives and low marital satisfaction for both spouses. The negative effect of cohabitation on marriages may be accounted for by personality characteristics, drug use, problems with the law, and unemployment factors that sometimes coexist with cohabitation (Booth & Johnson, 1988). Thus factors that predispose individuals to cohabit may contribute to marital problems.

### Problems Associated With Major Aspects of Marriage

Marriage generally implies the intense involvement of two people through some period of their lives. During their time together, they experience various life-cycle transitions, health changes, the influence of children and other family members, the negotiation of various roles and work to support themselves, and the synthesis of personality and interpersonal styles.

*Across the life cycle.* Marriage is not static and constant; it undergoes numerous changes over the course of the family life cycle. The early family life-cycle stages are particularly difficult for many couples (Kotler, 1985a; Swensen, Eskew, & Kohlhepp, 1981), whereas later life stages are frequently easier (Swensen et al., 1981). Marital quality across the life cycle perhaps can best be described by a U-shaped curve, with lowest quality during the child-rearing stage (Anderson, Russell, & Schumm, 1983), and the highest levels early in the marriage (before the birth of children) and after the children are grown and leave the home. This curvilinear pattern may be explained by the life transitions that marital partners must make throughout their marriage (Reinke, 1985). There is also evidence that the success of life-cycle transitions may be most dependent on the quality of the marriage prior to the transition (Vinick & Ekerdt, 1989).

Several studies have examined long-term marriages and factors that are related to their longevity and quality. Lauer and Lauer (1986) considered factors present in long-term (15 or more years) marriages for happy marriages versus those marriages that survived but were described as unhappy, and found that unhappily married couples stayed together primarily because of their children and their view that marriage is a long-term commitment.

Several studies have focused on the effects of variables outside the marital relationship. Retirement appears to be a particularly significant transition in later life. Although it has been found that retirement community couples spend less time with friends (Ade-Ridder, 1985; Brubaker & Ade-Ridder, 1987), other research has shown that interaction with friends is an important predictor of marital satisfaction in later life (Lee, 1988). Family support continues to be important for later life because of the many transitions faced by older couples (e.g., retirement, declining health, disability, economic instability, and moving to new locations) (Walsh, 1989). Finally, although Vinick and Ekerdt (1989) found little negative change in marital satisfaction after husbands' retirement, retired couples faced difficult adjustments. For instance, women complained of a lack of privacy because of their husbands' increased time at home, and husbands voiced concerns about their wives' mundane daily routine.

*Health.* Across the course of their lives, spouses will experience different states of health. Studies have focused on rheumatoid arthritis, myocardial infarction, chronic pain, and Alzheimer's disease, among others. It appears that health problems influence marriage but the effect may be dependent on the type and severity and on whether or not the health problems occur later in life (Johnson, 1985). The extent to which physical health is a problem also seems to depend on spouses' support networks (Revenson & Majerovitz, 1991) and the amount of control they feel over the circumstances surrounding the illness (Coyne & Smith, 1991; Elliott, Trief, & Stein, 1986).

One problem with studies of depression and marriage is that they primarily focus on wives' depression, because women are more likely to report and be diagnosed with depression (Avison & Mcalpine, 1992; Boggiano & Barrett, 1991; Fabrega, Mezzica, Ulrich, & Benjamin, 1990; Potts, Burnam, & Wells, 1991). However, Gotlib and Whiffen (1989), who conducted a study of depressed men and women, nondepressed female and male medical patients, and nonpatient control couples, found depressed couples showed more negative perceptions of their spouses than did the other groups. Similarly, most examinations of the influence of psychological health on marriage have focused on depression. Schafer (1985) studied married couples in four life-cycle stages and found a direct relationship between the wives' perception of their husbands' evaluation of them and their level of depression. It appears there is a reciprocal relationship between health and marital satisfaction. Schmoldt, Pope, and Hibbard (1989) found that spouses experience better health when the marital relationship is cohesive, companionable, and cooperative. (See Chapter 7 for additional discussion of the reciprocal relationship between health and family functioning.) A similar reciprocal relationship has been found between psychological health and marital quality (Kotler & Omodei, 1988; Whisman & Jacobson, 1989).

*Children.* Several studies have provided evidence that the presence of children has a negative effect on marriage (Glenn & McLanahan, 1982; LaRossa & LaRossa, 1981; Miller, 1976; Rollins & Galligan, 1978). However, it may not be the mere presence of children that affects marital disruption (Johnson & Johnson, 1980) but variables related to the presence of children. For example, the presence of children requires more of parents; they must take on new roles, and it becomes difficult to perform role behaviors as effectively given the increase in demands generated by children. Some research shows that families with young children and those with a large number of children may have greater problems (Abbott & Brody, 1985; Menaghan, 1983). Other studies have found that marital dissolution is lowest when couples have very young children and adult children (Heaton, 1990). Finally, research on the effects of the gender of the child show mixed results. Some point to more marital problems with female children (Morgan, Lye, & Condran, 1988), and others indicate more negative effects if there are male children (Abbott & Brody, 1985).

Because the birth of a child represents one of the most significant events in marriage, several studies have examined how this major transition affects marital quality. Some have failed to find a relationship between pregnancy and marital satisfaction across the course of the pregnancy (MacDermid, Huston, & McHale, 1990; Schuchts & Witkin, 1989; Snowden, Schott, Awalt, & Gillis-Knox, 1988). However, Waldron and Routh (1981), Belsky, Lang, and Rovine (1985), and Wallace and Gotlib (1990) all report declines in various aspects of the marital relationship during the first several months of the transition to parenthood.

Among families with young and school-age children, it appears there is a strong reciprocal relationship between marital problems and child problems, especially those related to children's conduct disorders (Frick, Lahey, Hartdagen, & Hynd, 1989; Jouriles, Pfiffner, & O'Leary, 1988; Kolko & Kazdin, 1990; Smith & Jenkins, 1991). It is difficult to determine causality between child problems and marital problems, but Shaw and Emery (1988) found that an accumulation of stressors predicted higher levels of child behavior problems. The influence of these variables on childrens' behavior may actually be the result of their effect on parents' parenting skills (Stoneman, Brody, & Burke, 1989).

There have also been studies on the effects of childlessness on couples, although much of the research does not distinguish between voluntary and involuntary childlessness. Sabatelli, Meth, and Gavazzi (1988), in their study of involuntarily childless couples, found a decrease in the frequency of intercourse and satisfaction with sex and, for women, a decrease in comfort with sexuality after an infertility problem had been detected. Pepe and Byrne's (1991) study focused particularly on the effects of infertility treatments on the marital and sexual relationship and found marital satisfaction to be significantly lower during treatment than before treatment.

Studies of voluntarily childless couples' marriages are limited and findings are mixed, although Houseknecht (1987) concludes these marriages do not appear to suffer. Indeed, she notes that a common motivation given for voluntary childlessness is the desire for a more satisfactory marital relationship. Similarly, one study (Maschoff, Fanshier, & Hansen, 1976) found that having a vasectomy was associated with improved marital stability; wives became more assertive in initiating sexual intercourse, and there was an increase in the mutual initiation of sex. These authors noted, however, that couples in the sample who sought permanent birth control also seemed to have stable marital histories.

*Division of labor and roles.* The findings of several studies suggest that the division of labor in marriages fluctuates depending on life-cycle circumstances. For parents, the division of labor appears to be somewhat more nontraditional during pregnancy and early childhood, changing to more traditional patterns as time passes after the birth of a child (Cowan & Cowan, 1988; MacDermid et al., 1990; Schuchts & Witkin, 1989). This change from nontraditional to traditional may be the cause of considerable conflict and negative feelings after the birth of a child (Belsky & Pensky, 1988), especially for mothers who find themselves performing more housework and child-care tasks than they expected (Ruble, Fleming, Hackel, & Stangor, 1988).

It continues to be documented that women continue to do the major portion of housework and child care in marriages, and this traditional division of labor may not always lower marital satisfaction (Perry-Jenkins & Crouter, 1990; Smith & Reid, 1986). Yogev (1981), studying the division of labor in dual-career families, found that women spend about 23 hours more a week on child care than their husbands and 16 hours more on housework. Yet only 13% of the women thought the husband did less than his share of child care, and only 24% felt the husband was not doing enough housework.

It may be that the traditional division of labor persists at least partially because women do not want, or do not expect, their husbands to share these responsibilities equally. Obtaining greater participation from husbands may not be worth the effort for some women. Baruch and Barnett (1986) found that, although men's participation in child care increased their family involvement, it was also associated with effects that could be negative for the marital relationship such as dissatisfaction with the amount of time the wife spends with children, the husband reporting that family responsibilities interfered with his work, and the wife reporting that work interferes with her family responsibilities.

Marriages are happier if the spouses possess personality traits associated with both female and male traits, that is, androgyny (Kurdek & Schmitt, 1986; Peterson, Baucom, & Elliott, 1989; Zammichielli, Gilroy, & Sherman, 1988). Androgynous couples report fewer destructive disagreements, higher accomplishment of necessary tasks, and higher expressiveness (Kurdek & Schmitt, 1986). Perhaps the flexibility these couples possess in their sex-role definitions translates into an ability to engage in a variety of situations more effectively than those whose adherence to more traditional sex role norms makes them more rigid.

*Work and careers.* Most of the research that has focused on work and families has examined the effect of dual careers on marriages. When both spouses work outside of the home, it appears that mutual support by spouses is pivotal to the success of the marriage. Thus dual-career couples appear to live in greater harmony when the husband supports the wife's employment, does not feel competitive with her, the wife feels supported, and the husband views housework and child care as joint spousal responsibilities and participates accordingly (Fendrich, 1984; Gilbert, 1985; Thomas, Albrecht, & White, 1984). Furthermore, contrary to the expectations that dual-career couples have little time to spend together, resulting in lower marital quality, they appear to spend as much time together as single-earner couples in marriage-enhancing activities such as recreation, homemaking, and activities related to children (Kingston & Nock, 1987).

Dual-career families with preschool children experience lower marital quality (Cooper, Chassin, & Braver, 1986; Cooper, Chassin, & Zeiss, 1985; Thomas, Albrecht, & White, 1984), but, when compared with single-earner families with at least one preschool child, both groups report lower marital quality than when they had no children. This is consistent with the findings that families in the preschool years of the family life cycle experience lower marital satisfaction because of the demands of this transition and the amount of care required for preschool children (Benin & Nienstedt, 1985). Thus, although dual-career couples report decreased marital satisfaction in the transition to parenthood and the elementary school years, the effect may be the result of stress normally associated with this life-cycle stage.

*Income and money.* In general, socioeconomic well-being is highly related to favorable marital outcomes. Thoresen and Goldsmith (1987) found a positive relation between financial well-being and marital satisfaction and general well-being. Similarly, Jorgensen (1979) found socioeconomic rewards to be moderately related to wives' perceptions of their husbands as competent providers and their satisfaction with husbands' income; however, husbands' perceptions of marital satisfaction were not associated with the level of socioeconomic rewards. On the other hand, there is evidence that economic strain increases the hostility and decreases the warmth and supportiveness of husbands toward their wives, resulting in lower marital satisfaction for both men and women (Conger et al., 1990). When financial strain does exist, it appears that agreement about expenditures can mediate the effect of the strain on marital satisfaction (Berry & Williams, 1987).

*Sexuality.* A variety of sexual dysfunction occurs in marriages, including premature ejaculation, unresponsiveness or low levels of desire, lack of orgasm, and difficulties with erections. Sexual dysfunction is found in both troubled and untroubled marriages (Frank, Anderson, & Rubinstein, 1978), and it is important to remember that not all couples who experience sexual dysfunction label it as a problem for their marriage (Heiman, Gladue, Roberts, & LoPiccolo, 1986). However, couples who report sexual dysfunction have been found to demonstrate poor communication, low self-esteem, depression, and rigid sex roles (Arentewicz & Schmidt, 1983; LoPiccolo, 1977). It is important to note that the direction of causality is not clear here. Rather, it is likely there is a bidirectional relationship between some of these variables and sexual dysfunction.

*Remarriage.* Contrary to common assumptions, remarried couples are not more prone to having marital problems than those in first marriages (Vemer, Coleman, Ganong, & Cooper, 1989). Instead, it is a combination of variables that contributes to the quality of a remarriage relationship (Guisinger, Cowan, & Schuldberg, 1989) and, as with first marriages, satisfaction changes over the course of the remarriage. It appears that satisfaction may be especially low for remarrieds during the first 3 years of their marriage (Guisinger et al., 1989). Especially predictive of marital problems are competitiveness and dissimilar perceptions (James & Johnson, 1988; Pasley, Ihinger-Tallman, & Coleman, 1984).

According to Whitsett and Land (1992), the most common problems facing remarried couples with children are factors related to discipline, the other biological parent, and the relationship with the stepchild. Participation in decision making may enhance adjustment in remarriage, especially for stepfathers (Orleans, Palisi, & Caddell, 1989). Two common problem areas for stepmothers are confusion about their position in the family hierarchy (Pasley & Ihinger-Tallman, 1989) and lack of role clarity (Guisinger et al., 1989; Whitsett & Land, 1992).

A major problem for remarrieds is the fact that many aspects of their lives fall outside of the institutional role prescriptions and guidelines for family members, that is, the "incomplete institutionalization" of remarriage in our society (Cherlin, 1978). Many areas of society, for example, schools and churches, still have not changed their practices to accommodate the demands of remarriage and "step-relationships."

*Continuing Relationships in Marriage*

A number of authors have examined why spouses continue in their marital relationships and the ways they relate to one another. Two theories of dyadic interaction, attachment and social exchange, have been especially useful in understanding the persistence of relationships and the ways spouses interact. Attachment between partners constitutes a bond that can help buffer the negative effects of problems while the exchange model provides a way of understanding how partners' assessments of the outcomes of their ongoing marital interactions contribute to variations in their attraction to their relationship.

*Attachment.* Marriages usually are relationships that can be characterized as having some degree of attachment or deep enduring affection between the partners. This mutual provision of security by partners serves as a stabilizing function in marriage (Kotler, 1985b). Kobak and Hazan (1991) found that marital partners who felt able to rely on their partners and who viewed their partners as psychologically available were better able to control their emotions and reported higher marital adjustment. Although Kotler (1985b, 1989) described the influence of childhood experiences on attachment, she noted that marital attachment also evolves in an ongoing reciprocal process between spouses. Part of this process is the sharing of pleasure and leisure time and not allowing the presence of children to interrupt the development and maintenance of the relationship (Hill, 1988). It should be noted that, although the security inherent in attachment is important, relationships that nurture change and development are those best able to maintain intimacy (Kotler, 1989).

*Exchange.* There is evidence that spouses who feel emotionally and financially rewarded in their marriages experience greater marital adjustment (Hansen, 1987b). It is not just self-centered individuals who hold exchange orientations in marriages; individuals with high levels of moral reasoning appear to be just as likely (for men) or more likely (for women) to be exchange oriented in their marriages (Hansen, 1991). Spouses who perceive themselves as equal partners experiencing equality in exchanges also report greater marital satisfaction with their marriages (Aida & Falbo, 1991; Buunk & Van Yperen, 1991; Houlihan, Jackson, & Rogers, 1990), although cultural and ethnic variations may exist (Gray-Little, 1982). Unfortunately, because there is evidence that women are not as satisfied with marriage as men (Buunk & Van Yperen, 1991; Houlihan et al., 1990), this perception of equity may not exist in many marriages.

*Interaction.* Effective marital interaction is commonly considered to be one of the most critical factors contributing to marital quality. High levels of positive messages, low levels of negative messages, agreement, feeling understood, self-disclosure, patience, and humor are of particular importance for intimacy and marital satisfaction (Allen & Thompson, 1984; Barling, Bluen, & Moss, 1990; Rust & Goldstein, 1989; Schafer & Keith, 1984). There appears to be a reciprocal relationship between the character of interactions and spouses' satisfaction with their relationship. For example, having and demonstrating positive and caring feelings about a spouse has a positive effect on marital satisfaction (Broderick & O'Leary, 1986; Martin, Blair, & Nevels, 1990; Tolstedt & Stokes, 1983), whereas dissatisfied couples report more hostility, withdrawal, and displeasure (Roberts & Krokoff, 1990).

When couples must resolve problems, active discussion rather than avoidance, along with low levels of negative affect and hostile behavior, contributes to effectiveness and satisfaction with solutions (Miller, Lefcourt, & Holmes, 1986). Open conflict and self-interest in coping appear to be characteristics of unhappy marriages (Bowman, 1990). However, two studies show that existing levels of marital problems appear to be strongly predictive of the types of strategies couples use. Sabourin, Laporte, and Wright (1990) found less problem-solving confidence, greater avoidance of difficult problem-solving activity, and less control over behavior in distressed couples. Distressed couples also used less negotiation and optimistic comparisons to solve problems. Menaghan (1982) suggests there probably exists a worsening spiral for distressed couples when encountering problems; as problems mount, they experience greater stress and decreased coping abilities, thereby leading to more problems.

It is likely that the relationship between communication and marital satisfaction is reciprocal. Good communication increases marital satisfaction, and marital satisfaction positively influences communication. However, time is also an important variable in the relationship between communication and marital satisfaction. Two longitudinal studies found that some patterns of interaction considered harmful at one point in time do not necessarily predict an expected decline in marital satisfaction over time. Gottman and Krokoff (1989) reported that, although defensiveness, whining, stubbornness, and withdrawal from interactions were associated with longitudinal deterioration of marital satisfaction, disagreement and expression of anger were not. Huston and Vangelisti (1991) found negativity of either husbands or wives to be associated over time with lower marital satisfaction for wives, but not for husbands.

Blaming one's spouse for marital difficulties has also been found to influence the quality of marital satisfaction. There is evidence that perceiving one's spouse as a source of marital conflict is associated with less marital satisfaction (Fincham, 1985; Sabourin, Lussier, & Wright, 1991), whereas perceived personal control over conflicts is associated with higher marital satisfaction (Madden & Janoff-Bulman, 1981). Similarly, several studies have reported partners' internal locus of control, that is, making decisions based on one's own desires as opposed to those of others, to be positively associated with the quality of a marriage (Clayson & Frost, 1984; Madden, 1987; Miller et al., 1986). Possibly because persons with an internal locus of control more actively engage in problem solving and are more effective in communicating and achieving their desired goals (Miller et al., 1986), they have been found to have higher self-concepts than those who are more externally oriented, especially when not under stress (Clayson & Frost, 1984). Contrary to their expectations, Sabatelli, Dreyer, and Buck

(1983) found that husbands married to externally oriented wives had more complaints about their marital relationships. It appears that partners who have autonomy are better able to develop and maintain quality relationships than those who are controlling, compliance gaining, or nonmotivated (Blais, Sabourin, & Boucher, 1990; Dillard & Fitzpatrick, 1985).

Congruence of spouses' perceptions is also associated with greater marital satisfaction (Plechaty, 1987) as is the ability to take the spouse's perspective—an ability that wives excelled at compared with husbands in Long and Andrews's (1990) study. Madden and Janoff-Bulman (1981) found that wives perceived their husbands as determining the negativity of marital problems and themselves as influencing the more positive aspects of resolving or avoiding conflicts. However, attributions such as these appear less likely when spouses believe their relationships are influenced by external factors (McRae & Kohen, 1988). There is also evidence that a spouse's perceptions may be more important than the actual attitudes of the other spouse (Broderick & O'Leary, 1986; Merves-Okin, Amidon, & Bernt, 1991).

### Major Problems

Three problem areas—extramarital sex, alcohol, and violence—generally are considered especially distressing for marriages. Although there is research examining these problems, the inherent complexity of these problems makes them difficult to understand.

*Extramarital sex.* Although surveys in the early 1940s and 1950s revealed much higher rates of extramarital coitus for men compared with women, it appears that currently about 50% of both men and women engage in extramarital sex (Macklin, 1987). Numerous reasons are given by persons for their participation in extramarital coitus: frustration, boredom, desire for broader sexual experiences, and lack of self-control (Lawson, 1988). Extramarital affairs are more likely to occur during the personal disruption associated with major life transitions (Reinke, 1985) or when men and women perceive themselves to be in inequitable and underbenefited relationships (Walster, Traupmann, & Walster, 1978).

The suspected impact of extramarital coitus on marriages may not be as strong as many would think. In a study of individuals who had been separated less than 26 months, Spanier and Margolis (1983) found that extramarital coitus was more often an effect rather than a cause of marital problems, and there was no relation between presence or absence of extramarital coitus and marital quality at the time of separation. They also found levels of religiosity did not predict extramarital coitus, but for those who had engaged in extramarital sex, religiosity was associated with a longer time between marriage and its first occurrence. Similarly, in a follow-up of subjects from a 1978 study comparing open marriages with sexually exclusive marriages, Rubin and Adams (1986) found 68% of the spouses in sexually open marriages were still together compared with 82% of those who were sexually exclusive. They noted that in 1978 there were no differences between the groups on levels of dyadic adjustment, and they found few differences in the effect of sexual openness on marital satisfaction. However, any conclusions about the effect of extramarital sex on marriages must be regarded as tentative because of the meager body of empirical research on the topic and the fact that little recent research exists on the topic.

*Alcohol.* It is estimated that nearly 9 million Americans are alcoholics, a figure representing about 4% of the population, although the figure may be as high as 10% in some high-risk groups (Royce, 1981). Several studies report negative effects of alcohol on couples' interactions (e.g., Jacob & Krahn, 1988; O'Farrell & Birchler, 1987; Zweben, 1986) although there is some evidence that couples with an alcoholic spouse are very similar to other conflicted couples on measures of marital stability, desired change, struggles for control, and levels of positive communication (O'Farrell & Birchler, 1987). Zweben (1986) found that marital disruption was more common in heavy drinking households than in non-heavy drinking households. However, the differences between these households decreased after controlling for a number of consequences resulting from the use of alcohol. Thus, when drinking results in negative consequences, it does not have to be heavy drinking to constitute a problem. Similarly, Jacob and Leonard (1988) described different patterns of interactions for couples that included episodic alcoholics compared with steady-drinking alcoholics. Episodic-drinking couples, compared with steady-drinking couples, showed less problem solving, husbands were more negative than wives, and their interaction suggested a coercive control pattern. Among steady-drinking couples, wives were more negative than the alcoholic husband, and there were patterns of interaction that suggest these couples have a lot of experience solving problems. There is evidence that alcohol consumption may serve a function in some marriages by allowing each partner to fulfill role behaviors developed in their families of origin or reinforced by society (e.g., Bepko & Krestan, 1985; Dunn, Jacob,

Hummon, & Seilhamer, 1987; Steinglass, Tislenko, Reiss, & Kaufman, 1985).

*Violence.* In her thorough review of the family violence literature, Steinmetz (1987) notes that between 50% and 60% of couples who were subjects in studies of violence during the 1970s reported that physical violence had occurred in their relationships. In a follow-up to their 1975 survey (Straus & Gelles, 1985; Straus, Gelles, & Steinmetz, 1980), Straus et al. reported a reduction in marital violence over the decade, but rates remained alarmingly high. (See Chapter 13 for discussion of marital violence.)

Despite the recognition of marital violence as a major marital problem by most scholars and clinicians and a corresponding large body of literature addressing family violence, there is a scarcity of empirical work that actually clarifies its causes and effects. Most studies focus on violence toward wives rather than toward husbands (Gelles & Conte, 1990), although the latter should not be considered insignificant (Steinmetz, 1987). Research on causes has examined characteristics of individuals (e.g., biological and psychological factors) and relationship perspectives, such as the cyclical models that view violence from intergenerational or relationship process models (Giles-Sims, 1983; Walker, 1979). Although there is some evidence that marital violence occurs more in blue-collar marriages and that its occurrence decreases with social class, education, and financial resources, it is clear that it occurs in all segments of society. From clinical literature, it appears that violence often is associated with a buildup of other problems (e.g., alcohol) and stressors but that it also occurs in marriages where these are not present. Furthermore, although it is difficult to know exactly which couples will be involved in violence and how that violence will occur, there are consistent findings in support of an intergenerational transmission of abuse (Corenblum, 1983; Hershorn & Rosenbaum, 1985; Kalmuss, 1984; Malone, Tyree, & O'Leary, 1989).

### Interventions

Although some marital problems may be resolved with time or by efforts of the couple, others require professional assistance. Some problems are best handled by specific interventions, whereas others call for broader policy or legislative actions.

*Clinical and therapeutic.* The approach of marriage and family therapy to treating marital problems has changed over the past few years. Common approaches to intervention have become more brief and solution focused (Piercy & Sprenkle, 1991), although the teaching of problem-solving and communication skills continues to receive support (Jacobson, 1977; Rabin, Blechman, Kahn, & Carel, 1985; Reid & Strother, 1988). Clinicians have also found it necessary to broaden their perceptions of presenting problems beyond the family system and consider the impact of various societal systems (e.g., schools, churches, and community) and cultural beliefs (e.g., those related to ethnicity and gender-role socialization). It has become increasingly more apparent that marital problems seen in clinical settings are the result of a complex network of marital and extramarital systems; it is only through untangling and understanding these systems that solutions can be found.

Instead of attempting to "solve" the problems after the damage has been done, enrichment programs may be more effective answers to marital problems (Guerney & Maxson, 1990). A focus on programs that strengthen areas of the marital relationship and help couples cope with life problems should buffer marital problems. Programs that prepare couples for marriage also may help, although premarital programs may be hampered because, during engagement, partners frequently do not believe they have, or will have, problems.

*Policy.* Most of the policy discussion related to marriage focuses on legislation that might relieve stresses associated with the work-family interface. There are three broad areas of concern. First, many would like to see the government mandate job-protected dependent care leave for a period of 24 weeks—a period many experts believe to be minimally adequate for a parent to bond with a newborn (Hewlett, 1991). This leave would be offered to all working parents for the purpose of looking after a newborn baby, a newly adopted child, or a seriously ill child or elderly parent and would help reduce the stress on marriages that occurs during those transitions. Second, many marital relationships are stressed by consistent concerns about day care for their children. Therefore there is a need for policies that both increase parents' buying power (e.g., through earned-income tax credits and vouchers) and improve the standard of day care through regulation and subsidies to day-care providers (Hewlett, 1991). Third, there is a need for a more fluid, less rigid workplace that enables married workers a choice over how best to manage their own work-family interfaces. Although corporate America is developing elaborate family support policies, government can help shape and complement these private sector efforts by providing incentives for employers. These policies have been shown to be win-win policies. For businesses, they result in greater worker productivity, less turnover, and less money lost. For families, they result in more flexible schedules, part-time employment, and job security (Hewlett, 1986, 1991; Wright-Edelman, 1992). Other topics that deserve greater attention include better preparation of young people for marriage through family life education for marriage, recognition of the need for health insurance coverage for mental health treatment, and employee assistance programs, especially for marriages where there are problems with drugs or alcohol.


## Summary and Conclusions

There is a broad body of literature examining various aspects of marital problems. Several generalizations can be made about these studies. First, samples for the majority of studies are small and gathered by means of convenience. Although there are a number of studies with large probability samples, the nature of the methods used reduces the depth and richness of the data.

Second, although many studies in the area of marital problems are theoretically based, most examine pragmatic issues, simple propositions, or questions related to clearly observable variables (Glenn, 1990). Of those studies that are strongly based in theory, most use variations of exchange theory, which has as its basic premise the notion that individuals make choices based on rational comparisons of the costs and rewards in their relationships. Equity theory, which proposes that individuals will be most satisfied when they are in equitable relationships, also is common. Several other social psychological theories or perspectives, including attribution theory and cognitive consistency theory, have also been used. Recently, feminist thinking has emerged as an important perspective in understanding marriages, especially in clinical writings, but few empirical studies have used it. One consequence of this eclectic approach to the subject of marital problems is a lack of standardization in how topics are viewed and studied. This has led to much inconsistency in findings and hence difficulty in drawing clear conclusions.

Third, there are few answers as to why marital problems affect couples differentially. Clearly, there is considerable variation in how couples encounter problems and the degree of success they achieve in resolving them. Most research focuses on what problems exist and how often they occur rather than on the processes couples engage in concerning them. Researchers have largely failed to examine factors that help couples develop resilience to the stresses of life and relationships. One area of focus here might be examining how encountering and overcoming problems constitutes a resource that contributes to growth of the individuals and strengthening of their relationship.

In conclusion, marital relationships are certain to undergo many internal and external changes, whether those relationships last 5 years or 50. Although we are unable to differentiate precisely couples who have problems that will strain their relationships from those with problems that will result in divorce, it is important to recognize that there are many variables that affect marriages and that it often is the accumulation or combination of problems, not specific problems, that reduces the stability of marriages.

## References

Abbott, D. A., & Brody, G. H. (1985). The relation of child age, gender, and number of children to the marital adjustment of wives. *Journal of Marriage and the Family, 47,* 77-84.

Ade-Ridder, L. (1985). Quality of marriage: A comparison between golden wedding couples and couples married less than fifty years. *Lifestyles: A Journal of Changing Patterns, 7,* 224-237.

Aida, Y., & Falbo, T. (1991). Relationships between marital satisfaction, resources, and power strategies. *Sex Roles, 24,* 43-56.

Allen, A., & Thompson, T. (1984). Agreement, understanding, realization, and feeling understood as predictors of communicative satisfaction in marital dyads. *Journal of Marriage and the Family, 46,* 915-921.

Anderson, S. A., Russell, C. S., & Schumm, W. R. (1983). Perceived marital quality and family life-cycle categories: A further analysis. *Journal of Marriage and the Family, 45,* 127-139.

Arentewicz, G., & Schmidt, G. (1983). *The treatment of sexual disorders.* New York: Basic Books.

Avison, W. R., & Mcalpine, D. D. (1992). Gender differences in symptoms of depression among adolescents. *Journal of Health and Social Behavior, 33,* 77-96.

Bahr, S. J., & Galligan, R. J. (1984). Teenage marriage and marital stability. *Youth and Society, 15,* 387-400.

Barling, J., Bluen, S., & Moss, V. (1990). Type A behavior and marital dissatisfaction: Disentangling the effects of achievement striving and impatience-irritability. *The Journal of Psychology, 124,* 311-319.

Baruch, G., & Barnett, R. (1986). Consequences of fathers' participation in family work: Parents' role-strain and well-being. *Journal of Personality and Social Psychology, 51,* 983-992.

Belsky, J., Lang, M. E., & Rovine, M. (1985). Stability and change in marriage across the transition to parenthood: A second study. *Journal of Marriage and the Family, 47,* 855-865.

Belsky, J., & Pensky, E. (1988). Marital change across the transition to parenthood. *Marriage and Family Review, 12,* 133-156.

Benin, M. H., & Nienstedt, B. C. (1985). Happiness in single and dual-career families: The effects of marital happiness, job satisfaction, and life-cycle. *Journal of Marriage and the Family, 47,* 975-984.

Bennett, N., Blanc, A., & Bloom, D. (1988). Commitment and the modern union: Assessing the link between premarital cohabitation and subsequent marital stability. *American Sociological Review, 53,* 127-138.

Bepko, C., & Krestan, J. A. (1985). *The responsibility trap: A blueprint for treating the alcoholic family.* New York: Free Press.

Berry, R., & Williams, F. (1987). Assessing the relationship between quality of life and marital and income satisfaction: A path analytic approach. *Journal of Marriage and the Family, 49,* 107-116.

Billy, J., Landale, N., & McLaughlin, S. (1986). The effect of marital status at first birth on marital dissolution among adolescent mothers. *Demography, 23,* 329-349.

Blais, M. R., Sabourin, S., & Boucher, C. (1990). Toward a motivational model of couple happiness. *Journal of Personality and Social Psychology, 59,* 1021-1031.

Boggiano, A. K., & Barrett, M. (1991). Gender differences in depression in college students. *Sex Roles, 25,* 595-605.

Booth, A., & Johnson, D. (1988). Premarital cohabitation and marital success. *Journal of Family Issues, 9,* 255-272.

Bowman, M. L. (1990). Coping efforts and marital satisfaction: Measuring marital coping and its correlates. *Journal of Marriage and the Family, 52,* 463-474.

Broderick, J. E., & O'Leary, K. D. (1986). Contributions of affect, attitudes, and behavior to marital satisfaction. *Journal of Consulting and Clinical Psychology, 54,* 514-517.

Brubaker, E., & Ade-Ridder, L. (1987). Relationships between marital quality, social, and familial interactions by residential location: Implications for human service professionals. *Lifestyles: A Journal of Changing Patterns, 8,* (137)7-(145)15.

Buunk, B. P., & Van Yperen, N. W. (1991). Referential comparisons, relational comparisons, and exchange orientation: Their relation to marital satisfaction. *Personality and Social Psychology Bulletin, 17,* 709-717.

Caplan, G. (1964). *Principles of preventative psychiatry.* New York: Basic Books.

Cherlin, A. J. (1978). Remarriage as an incomplete institution. *American Journal of Sociology, 84,* 634-650.

Chi, S. K., & Houseknecht, S. K. (1985). Protestant fundamentalism and marital success: A comparative approach. *Sociology and Social Research, 69,* 351-375.

Clayson, D. E., & Frost, T. F. (1984). Impact of stress and locus of control on the concept of self. *Psychological Reports, 55,* 919-926.

Conger, R. D., Elder, G. H., Lorenz, F. O., Conger, K. J., Simons, R. L., Whitbeck, L. B., Huck, S., & Melby, J. N. (1990). Linking economic hardship to marital quality and instability. *Journal of Marriage and the Family, 52,* 643-656.

Cooper, K., Chassin, L., & Braver, S. (1986). Correlates of mood and marital satisfaction among dual-worker couples and single-worker couples. *Social Psychology Quarterly, 49,* 322-329.

Cooper, K., Chassin, L., & Zeiss, A. (1985). The relation of sex-role self-concept and sex-role attitudes to the marital satisfaction and personal adjustment of dual-worker couples with preschool children. *Sex Roles, 12,* 227-241.

Corenblum, B. (1983). Reactions to alcohol-related marital violence. *Journal of Studies on Alcohol, 44,* 665-674.

Cowan, C. P., & Cowan, P. A. (1988). Who does what when partners become parents: Implications for men, women, and marriage. *Marriage and Family Review, 12,* 105-131.

Coyne, J. C., & Smith, D. A. (1991). Couples coping with a myocardial infarction: A contextual perspective on wives' distress. *Journal of Personality and Social Psychology, 61,* 404-412.

DeMaris, A., & Leslie, G. R. (1984). Cohabitation with the future spouse: Its influence upon marital satisfaction and communication. *Journal of Marriage and the Family, 46,* 77-84.

Dillard, J. P., & Fitzpatrick, M. A. (1985). Compliance-gaining in marital interaction. *Personality and Social Psychology Bulletin, 11,* 29-33.

Dunn, N. J., Jacob, T., Hummon, N., & Seilhamer, R. A. (1987). Marital stability in alcoholic-spouse relationships as a function of drinking pattern and location. *Journal of Abnormal Psychology, 96,* 99-107.

Elliott, D. J., Trief, P. M., & Stein, N. (1986). Mastery, stress, and coping in marriage among chronic pain patients. *Journal of Behavioral Medicine, 9,* 549-558.

Fabrega, H., Mezzica, J., Ulrich, R., & Benjamin, L. (1990). Females and males in an intake psychiatric setting. *Psychiatry, 53,* 1-16.

Fendrich, M. (1984). Wives' employment and husbands' distress: A meta-analysis and a replication. *Journal of Marriage and the Family, 46,* 871-879.

Fincham, F. D. (1985). Attribution processes in distressed and nondistressed couples: Responsibility for marital problems. *Journal of Abnormal Psychology, 94,* 183-190.

Frank, E., Anderson, A., & Rubinstein, D. (1978). Frequency of sexual dysfunction in "normal" couples. *The New England Journal of Medicine, 299,* 111-115.

Frick, P. J., Lahey, B. B., Hartdagen, S., & Hynd, G. W. (1989). Conduct problems in boys: Relations to maternal personality, marital satisfaction, and socioeconomic status. *Journal of Clinical Child Psychology, 18,* 114-120.

Gelles, R. J., & Conte, J. R. (1990). Domestic violence and sexual abuse of children. *Journal of Marriage and the Family, 52,* 1045-1058.

Gilbert, L. (1985). *Men in dual-career families: Current realities and future prospects.* Hillsdale, NJ: Lawrence Erlbaum.

Giles-Sims, J. (1983). *Wife battering: A systems theory approach.* New York: Guilford.

Glenn, N. D. (1990). Quantitative research on marital quality in the 1980s: A critical review. *Journal of Marriage and the Family, 52,* 818-831.

Glenn, N. D., & McLanahan, S. (1982). Children and marital happiness: A further specification of the relationship. *Journal of Marriage and the Family, 44,* 63-72.

Gotlib, I. H., & Whiffen, V. E. (1989). Depression and marital functioning: An examination of specificity and gender differences. *Journal of Abnormal Psychology, 98,* 23-30.

Gottman, J. M., & Krokoff, L. J. (1989). Marital interaction and satisfaction: A longitudinal view. *Journal of Consulting and Clinical Psychology, 57,* 47-52.

Gray-Little, B. (1982). Marital quality and power processes among black couples. *Journal of Marriage and the Family, 44,* 633-646.

Guerney, B., & Maxson, P. (1990). Marital and family enrichment research: A decade review and look ahead. *Journal of Marriage and the Family, 52,* 1127-1135.

Guisinger, S., Cowan, P. A., & Schuldberg, D. (1989). Changing parent and spouse relations in the first years of remarriage of divorced fathers. *Journal of Marriage and the Family, 51,* 445-456.

Hansen, G. L. (1987a). The effect of religiosity on factors predicting marital adjustment. *Social Psychology Quarterly, 50,* 264-269.

Hansen, G. L. (1987b). Reward level and marital adjustment: The effect of weighting rewards. *Journal of Social Psychology, 127,* 549-551.

Hansen, G. L. (1991). Moral reasoning and the marital exchange relationship. *The Journal of Social Psychology, 131,* 71-81.

Heaton, T. B. (1984). Religious homogamy and marital satisfaction reconsidered. *Journal of Marriage and the Family, 46,* 729-733.

Heaton, T. B. (1990). Marital stability throughout the child-rearing years. *Demography, 27,* 55-63.

Heaton, T. B., & Pratt, E. L. (1990). The effects of religious homogamy on marital satisfaction. *Journal of Family Issues, 11,* 191-207.

Heiman, J. R., Gladue, B. A., Roberts, C. W., & LoPiccolo, J. (1986). Historical and current factors discriminating sexually functional from sexually dysfunctional married couples. *Journal of Marital and Family Therapy, 12,* 163-174.

Hershorn, M., & Rosenbaum, A. (1985). Children of marital violence: A closer look at the unintended victims. *American Journal of Orthopsychiatry, 55,* 260-266.

Hewlett, S. A. (1986). *A lesser life: The myth of women's liberation in America.* New York: Warner.

Hewlett, S. A. (1991). *When the bough breaks: The cost of neglecting our children.* New York: Harper Perennial.

Hill, M. S. (1988). Marital stability and spouses' shared time: A multidisciplinary hypothesis. *Journal of Family Issues, 9,* 427-451.

Houlihan, M. M., Jackson, J. L., & Rogers, T. R. (1990). Decision making of satisfied and dissatisfied married couples. *The Journal of Social Psychology, 130,* 89-102.

Houseknecht, S. K. (1987). Voluntary childlessness. In M. B. Sussman & S. K. Steinmetz (Eds.), *Handbook of marriage and the family* (pp. 369-395). New York: Plenum.

Huston, T. L., & Vangelisti, A. L. (1991). Socioemotional behavior and satisfaction in marital relationships: A longitudinal study. *Journal of Personality and Social Psychology, 61,* 721-733.

Jacob, T., & Krahn, G. L. (1988). Marital interactions of alcoholic couples: Comparison with depressed and nondistressed couples. *Journal of Consulting and Clinical Psychology, 56,* 73-79.

Jacob, T., & Leonard, K. E. (1988). Alcoholic-spouse interaction as a function of alcoholism subtype and alcohol consumption interaction. *Journal of Abnormal Psychology, 97,* 231-237.

Jacobson, N. S. (1977). Training couples to solve their marital problems: A behavioral approach to relationship discord, Part 1: Problem-solving skills. *International Journal of Family Counseling, 5,* 22-31.

James, S. D., & Johnson, D. W. (1988). Social interdependence, psychological adjustment, and marital satisfaction in second marriages. *The Journal of Social Psychology, 128,* 287-303.

Johnson, C. L. (1985). The impact of illness on late-life marriages. *Journal of Marriage and the Family, 47,* 165-172.

Johnson, F. C., & Johnson, M. R. (1980). Family planning: Implications for marital stability. *Journal of Divorce, 3,* 273-281.

Jorgensen, S. (1979). Socioeconomic rewards and perceived marital quality: A re-examination. *Journal of Marriage and the Family, 41,* 825-835.

Jouriles, E. N., Pfiffner, L. J., & O'Leary, S. G. (1988). Marital conflict, parenting, and toddler conduct problems. *Journal of Abnormal Child Psychology, 16,* 197-206.

Kalmuss, D. (1984). The intergenerational transmission of marital aggression. *Journal of Marriage and the Family, 46,* 11-19.

Kingston, P., & Nock, S. (1987). Time together among dual-earner couples. *American Sociological Review, 52,* 391-400.

Kobak, R. R., & Hazan, C. (1991). Attachment in marriage: Effects of security and accuracy of working models. *Journal of Personality and Social Psychology, 60,* 861-869.

Kolko, D. J., & Kazdin, A. E. (1990). Matchplay and firesetting in children: Relationship to parent, marital, and family dysfunction. *Journal of Clinical Child Psychology, 19,* 229-238.

Kotler, T. (1985a). A balanced distance: Aspects of marital quality. *Human Relations, 38,* 391-407.

Kotler, T. (1985b). Security and autonomy within marriage. *Human Relations, 38,* 229-321.

Kotler, T. (1989). Patterns of change in marital partners. *Human Relations, 42,* 829-856.

Kotler, T., & Omodei, M. (1988). Attachment and emotional health: A life span approach. *Human Relations, 41,* 619-640.

Kurdek, L., & Schmitt, J. (1986). Interaction of sex-role self-concept with relationship quality and relationship beliefs in married, heterosexual cohabitating, gay and lesbian couples. *Journal of Personality and Social Psychology, 51,* 365-370.

LaRossa, R., & LaRossa, M. M. (1981). *Transition to parenthood: How infants change families.* Beverly Hills, CA: Sage.

Lauer, R. H., & Lauer, J. C. (1986). Factors in long-term marriages. *Journal of Family Issues, 7,* 382-390.

Lawson, A. (1988). *Adultery: An analysis of love and betrayal.* New York: Basic Books.

Lee, G. R. (1988). Marital satisfaction in later life: The effects of nonmarital roles. *Journal of Marriage and the Family, 50,* 775-783.

Levine, K. S., & Hennessy, J. J. (1989). *Personality influences in teenage marital stability.* Paper presented at the annual meeting of the American Psychological Association, New Orleans, LA.

Long, E. C., & Andrews, D. W. (1990). Perspective taking as a predictor of marital adjustment. *Journal of Personality and Social Psychology, 59,* 126-131.

LoPiccolo, J. (1977). Direct treatment of sexual dysfunction in the couple. In J. Money & H. Musaph (Eds.), *Handbook of sexology* (1227-1244). New York: Elsevier North Holland.

MacDermid, S. M., Huston, T. L., & McHale, S. M. (1990). Changes in marriage associated with the transition to parenthood: Individual differences as a function of sex-role attitudes and changes in the division of household labor. *Journal of Marriage and the Family, 52,* 475-486.

Macklin, E. D. (1987). Nontraditional family forms. In M. B. Sussman & S. K. Steinmetz (Eds.), *Handbook of marriage and the family* (pp. 317-353). New York: Plenum.

Madden, M. E. (1987). Perceived control and power in marriage: A study of marital decision making and task performance. *Personality and Social Psychology Bulletin, 13,* 73-82.

Madden, M. E., & Janoff-Bulman, R. (1981). Blame, control, and marital satisfaction: Wives' attributions for conflict in marriage. *Journal of Marriage and the Family, 43,* 663-674.

Malone, J., Tyree, A., & O'Leary, K. D. (1989). Generalization and containment: Different effects of past aggression for wives and husbands. *Journal of Marriage and the Family, 51,* 95-99.

Martin, J. D., Blair, G. E., & Nevels, R. (1990). A study of the relationship of styles of loving and marital happiness. *Psychological Reports, 66,* 123-128.

Martin, T. C., & Bumpass, L. L. (1989). Recent trends in marital disruption. *Demography, 26,* 37-51.

Maschoff, T. A., Fanshier, W. E., & Hansen, D. J. (1976). Vasectomy: Its effect upon marital stability. *Journal of Sex Research, 12,* 259-314.

McCubbin, H. I., & Patterson, J. M. (1985). Adolescent stress, coping, and adaptation: A normative family perspective. In G. K. Leigh & G. W. Peterson (Eds.), *Adolescents in families* (pp. 256-276). Cincinnati, OH: Southwestern.

McRae, J. A., & Kohen, J. A. (1988). Changes in attributions of marital problems. *Social Psychology Quarterly, 51,* 74-80.

Menaghan, E. (1982). Measuring coping effectiveness: A panel analysis of marital problems and coping efforts. *Journal of Health and Social Behavior, 23,* 220-234.

Menaghan, E. (1983). Coping with parental problems: Panel assessments of effectiveness. *Journal of Family Issues, 4,* 483-506.

Merves-Okin, L., Amidon, E., & Bernt, F. (1991). Perception of intimacy in marriage: A study of married couples. *The American Journal of Family Therapy, 19,* 110-118.

Miller, B. C. (1976). A multivariate developmental model of marital satisfaction. *Journal of Marriage and the Family, 38,* 643-658.

Miller, P. C., Lefcourt, H. M., & Holmes, J. G. (1986). Marital locus of control and marital problem solving. *Journal of Personality and Social Psychology, 51,* 161-169.

Moore, K., & Waite, L. (1981). Marital dissolution, early motherhood, and early marriage. *Social Forces, 60,* 20-40.

Morgan, S. P., Lye, D. N., & Condran, G. A. (1988). Sons, daughters, and the risk of marital disruption. *American Journal of Sociology, 94,* 110-129.

O'Farrell, T. J., & Birchler, G. R. (1987). Marital relationships of alcoholic, conflicted, and nonconflicted couples. *Journal of Marital and Family Therapy, 13,* 259-274.

Orleans, M., Palisi, B., & Caddell, D. (1989). Marriage adjustment and satisfaction of stepfathers: Their feelings and perceptions of decision making and stepchildren relations. *Family Relations, 38,* 371-377.

Ortega, S. T., Whitt, H. P., & William, A. J. (1988). Religious homogamy and marital happiness. *Journal of Family Issues, 9,* 224-239.

Pasley, K., & Ihinger-Tallman, M. (1989). Boundary ambiguity in remarriage: Does ambiguity differentiate degree of marital adjustment and integration? *Family Relations, 38,* 46-52.

Pasley, K., Ihinger-Tallman, M., & Coleman, C. (1984). Consensus styles among happy and unhappy remarried couples. *Family Relations, 33,* 451-457.

Pepe, M. V., & Byrne, T. J. (1991). Women's perceptions of immediate and long-term effects of failed infertility treatment on marital and sexual satisfaction. *Family Relations, 40,* 303-309.

Perry-Jenkins, M., & Crouter, A. (1990). Men's provider-role attitudes: Implications for household work and marital satisfaction. *Journal of Family Issues, 11,* 136-156.

Peterson, C., Baucom, D., & Elliott, M. (1989). The relationship between sex role identity and marital adjustment. *Sex Roles, 21,* 775-787.

Piercy, F. P., & Sprenkle, D. H. (1991). Marriage and family therapy: A decade review. In A. Booth (Ed.), *Contemporary families: Looking forward, looking back* (1116-1126). Minneapolis, MN: National Council on Family Relations.

Plechaty, M. (1987). Perceptual congruence of five attitudes among satisfied and unsatisfied couples. *Psychological Reports, 61,* 527-537.

Potts, M. K., Burnam, M. A., & Wells, K. B. (1991). Gender differences in depression detection: A comparison of clinician diagnosis and standardized assessment. *Psychological Assessment, 3,* 609-615.

Rabin, C., Blechman, E. A., Kahn, D., & Carel, C. A. (1985). Refocusing from child to marital problems using the marriage contract game. *Journal of Marriage and the Family, 11,* 75-85.

Reid, W. J., & Strother, P. (1988). Super problem solvers: A systematic case study. *Social Service Review, 62,* 430-445.

Reinke, B. J. (1985). Psychosocial changes as a function of chronological age. *Human Development, 28,* 266-269.

Revenson, T. A., & Majerovitz, S. D. (1991). The effects of chronic illness on the spouse: Social resources as stress buffers. *Arthritis Care and Research, 4,* 63-72.

Roberts, L. J., & Krokoff, L. J. (1990). A time-series analysis of withdrawal, hostility, and displeasure in satisfied and dissatisfied marriages. *Journal of Marriage and the Family, 52,* 95-105.

Rogler, L. H., & Procidano, M. E. (1989). Marital heterogamy and marital quality in Puerto Rican families. *Journal of Marriage and the Family, 51,* 363-371.

Rollins, B. C., & Galligan, R. (1978). The developing child and marital satisfaction of parents. In R. M. Lerner & G. P. Spanier (Eds.), *Child influences on marital and family interaction: A life-span perspective* (pp. 71-105). New York: Academic Press.

Royce, J. E. (1981). *Alcohol problems and alcoholism.* New York: Free Press.

Rubin, A. M., & Adams, J. R. (1986). Outcomes of sexually open marriages. *Journal of Sex Research, 22,* 311-319.

Ruble, D. N., Fleming, A. S., Hackel, L. S., & Stangor, C. (1988). Changes in the marital relationship during the transition to first time motherhood: Effects of violated expectations concerning division of household labor. *Journal of Personality and Social Psychology, 55,* 78-87.

Rust, J., & Goldstein, J. (1989). Humor in marital adjustment. *Humor, 2-3,* 217-223.

Sabatelli, R. M., Dreyer, A., & Buck, R. (1983). Cognitive style and relationship quality in married dyads. *Journal of Personality, 51,* 192-201.

Sabatelli, R. M., Meth, R. L., & Gavazzi, S. M. (1988). Factors mediating the adjustment to involuntary childlessness. *Family Relations, 37,* 338-343.

Sabourin, S., Laporte, L., & Wright, J. (1990). Problem solving self-appraisal and coping efforts in distressed and nondistressed couples. *Journal of Marital and Family Therapy, 16,* 89-97.

Sabourin, S., Lussier, Y., & Wright, J. (1991). The effects of measurement strategy on attributions for marital problems and behaviors. *Journal of Applied Social Psychology, 21,* 734-746.

Schafer, R. B. (1985). Effects of marital role problems and the self-concept on wives' depressed mood. *Journal of Consulting and Clinical Psychology, 53,* 541-543.

Schafer, R. B., & Keith, P. M. (1984). A causal analysis of the relationship between the self-concept and marital quality. *Journal of Marriage and the Family, 46,* 909-914.

Schmoldt, R. A., Pope, C. R., & Hibbard, J. H. (1989). Marital interaction and the health and well-being of spouses. *Women and Health, 15,* 35-56.

Schuchts, R. A., & Witkin, S. L. (1989). Assessing marital change during the transition to parenthood. *Social Casework, 70,* 67-75.

Shaw, D. S., & Emery, R. E. (1988). Chronic family adversity and school-age children's adjustment. *Psychiatry, 27,* 200-206.

Smith, A., & Reid, W. (1986). Role expectations and attitudes in dual-earner families. *Social Casework, 67,* 394-402.

Smith, M. A., & Jenkins, J. M. (1991). The effects of marital disharmony on prepubertal children. *Journal of Abnormal Child Psychology, 19,* 625-644.

Snowden, L. R., Schott, T. L., Awalt, S. J., & Gillis-Knox, J. (1988). Marital satisfaction in pregnancy: Stability and change. *Journal of Marriage and the Family, 50,* 325-333.

Spanier, G. B., & Margolis, R. L. (1983). Marital separation and extramarital sexual behavior. *Journal of Sex Research, 19,* 23-48.

Steinglass, P., Tislenko, L., Reiss, D., & Kaufman, E. (1985). Stability/instability in the alcoholic marriage: The interrelationships between course of alcoholism, family process, and marital outcome. *Family Process, 24,* 365-376.

Steinmetz, S. K. (1987). Family violence: Past, present, and future. In M. B. Sussman & S. K. Steinmetz (Eds.), *Handbook of marriage and the family* (pp. 725-765). New York: Plenum.

Stoneman, Z., Brody, G. H., & Burke, M. (1989). Marital quality, depression, and inconsistent parenting: Relationship with observed mother-child conflict. *American Journal of Orthopsychiatry, 59,* 105-117.

Straus, M. A., & Gelles, R. J. (1985, November). *Is family violence increasing? A comparison of 1975 and 1985 national survey rates.* Paper presented at the annual meeting of the American Society of Criminology, San Diego, CA.

Straus, M. A., Gelles, R. J., & Steinmetz, S. K. (1980). *Behind closed doors: Violence in the American family.* Garden City, NY: Anchor.

Swensen, C. H., Eskew, R. W., & Kohlhepp, K. A. (1981). Stage of family life cycle, ego development, and the marriage relationship. *Journal of Marriage and the Family, 43,* 841-853.

Thomas, S., Albrecht, K., & White, P. (1984). Determinants of marital quality in dual-career couples. *Family Relations, 33,* 513-521.

Thoresen, R. J., & Goldsmith, E. B. (1987). The relationship between army families' financial well-being and depression, general well-being, and marital satisfaction. *The Journal of Social Psychology, 127,* 545-547.

Thornton, A., & Rodgers, W. (1987). The influence of individual and historical time on marital dissolution. *Demography, 24,* 1-22.

Tolstedt, B. E., & Stokes, J. P. (1983). Relation of verbal, affective, and physical intimacy to marital satisfaction. *Journal of Counseling Psychology, 30,* 573-580.

Tynes, S. R. (1990). Educational heterogamy and marital satisfaction between spouses. *Social Science Research, 19,* 153-174.

Vemer, E., Coleman, M., Ganong, L. H., & Cooper, H. (1989). Marital satisfaction in remarriage: A meta-analysis. *Journal of Marriage and the Family, 51,* 713-725.

Vinick, B. H., & Ekerdt, D. J. (1989). Retirement and the family. *Generations, 13,* 53-56.

Waite, L., Haggstrom, G., & Kanouse, D. (1985). The consequences of parenthood for the marital stability of young adults. *American Sociological Review, 50,* 207-216.

Waldron, H., & Routh, D. K. (1981). The effect of the first child on the marital relationship. *Journal of Marriage and the Family, 43,* 785-788.

Walker, L. E. (1979). *The battered woman.* New York: Harper & Row.

Wallace, P. M., & Gotlib, I. H. (1990). Marital adjustment during the transition to parenthood: Stability and predictors of change. *Journal of Marriage and the Family, 52,* 21-29.

Walsh, F. (1989). The family in later life. In B. Carter & M. McGoldrick (Eds.), *The changing family life cycle: A framework for family therapy* (2nd ed., pp. 312-334). Needham Heights, MA: Allyn & Bacon.

Walster, E., Traupmann, J., & Walster, G. W. (1978). Equity and extramarital sexuality. *Archives of Sexual Behavior, 7,* 127-142.

Weller, L., & Rofe, Y. (1988). Marital happiness among mixed and homogeneous marriages in Israel. *Journal of Marriage and the Family, 50,* 245-254.

Whisman, M. A., & Jacobson, N. S. (1989). Depression, marital satisfaction, and marital personality measures of sex roles. *Journal of Marital and Family Therapy, 15,* 177-186.

Whitsett, D., & Land, H. (1992). Role strain, coping, and marital satisfaction of stepparents. *Families in Society, 73,* 79-92.

Wilson, M. R., & Filsinger, E. E. (1986). Religiosity and marital adjustment: Multidimensional interrelationships. *Journal of Marriage and the Family, 48,* 147-151.

Witt, D. D., Davidson, B., Sollie, D. L., Lowe, G. D., & Peek, C. W. (1987). The consequences of early marriage on marital dissolution. *Sociological Spectrum, 7,* 191-207.

Wright-Edelman, M. (1992). *The measure of our success: A letter to my children and yours.* Boston: Beacon.

Yogev, S. (1981). Do professional women have egalitarian marital relationships? *Journal of Marriage and the Family, 43,* 865-871.

Zammichielli, M., Gilroy, F., & Sherman, M. (1988). Relation between sex-role orientation and marital satisfaction. *Personality and Social Psychology Bulletin, 14,* 747-754.

Zweben, A. (1986). Problem drinking and marital adjustment. *Journal of Studies on Alcohol, 47,* 167-172.

# 4

# Work/Family Stresses

SHARON Y. NICKOLS

The entry of large numbers of women into the paid labor force during the 1970s has been called a "subtle revolution" (R. E. Smith, 1979). This revolution occurred in both families and employment settings and is manifested in a variety of family/work issues including child care, family stress, and the division of household tasks.

In the "traditional" family, husbands were the "breadwinners" and wives the "breadbakers." This family, which emerged with the advent of industrialization, was considered the norm in the 1950s, even though other types of families coexisted. However, in recent decades the "dual-worker family," in which both spouses are gainfully employed, has emerged to the extent that it is increasingly considered the norm. Another significant trend has been the increase in the number of unmarried women and men who support families and are in the labor force; Hayghe (1990) has thus concluded there is no longer a "typical family" when it comes to employment and families. The revolution is not over, however, as the reciprocal adjustments between families and employment settings continue.

## Labor Force Participation
## and the Changing Economy

*Men's and Women's*
*Attachment to the Labor Force*

There is an abundance of demographic and historical data available on employment of women and men but less documentation of employment patterns related to families (see Chafe, 1976; Hayghe, 1990). In 1992 58.4% of women and 77.3% of men 20 years and older were in the labor force (either employed or looking for employment) (U.S. Bureau of Labor Statistics, 1993c). Women make up 45% of the total workforce in the United States (Ferber & O'Farrell, 1991) and vary by age, marital status, and presence of children. These variations, however, have decreased during the last few years, and increasingly men's and women's labor force behavior is similar. Unemployment rates, which have been historically lower for men, were lower for women, 7% and 6.3%, respectively, in 1992 (U.S. Bureau of Labor Statistics, 1993c).

In the past, it was predominately young, single, and childless women who were in the labor force. Today, having children is not an inhibitor to women's labor force participation. In 1990 63% of mothers were in the labor force (Moen, 1992) and 59.4% of mothers of preschoolers were employed. It is increasingly evident that "the economic well-being of most families is increasingly dependent on having two wage earners" (Ferber & O'Farrell, 1991, p. 41). For example, in families in which wives were employed full-time and year-round, wives' earnings constituted nearly 40% of total family income in 1977 and 1986 (Moen, 1992).

Bernard (1975) used the concept of "tipping point" to note this change in women's employment. The tipping point is a statistical assessment of social norms. According to this measure, half of the population of women are assuming roles and behaviors that were formerly not accepted, whereas the remainder continue in traditional roles and behaviors accepted in the past. Socially, the tipping point is a period of normlessness when old social norms are declining in importance but new social norms have yet to emerge. Thus it has become the norm for women to be employed, especially if their children are school age, but revised norms relative to family values and expectations have not emerged that create new patterns of family and work life. Nor have support systems or work schedules emerged to facilitate the institutionalization and integration of employment and family roles. As previously noted, women's labor force participation increasingly resembles that of men. There are two explanations given for this trend: (a) The labor force participation of women is steadily increasing and is less affected by age (Shank, 1988), and (b) men at all stages past age 24 are reducing their participation in the labor force (Gendell & Siegel, 1992). For example, married men's labor force participation fell from 91% in 1955 to 79% in the 1985-1987 period (Hayghe & Haugen, 1987).

Several demographic variables are related to men's participation in the labor force. For example, married men are more likely to be in the labor force than never-married, divorced, or widowed men. The labor force participation rates of Hispanic husbands are higher than those of whites and African Americans; however, Hispanic husbands experience higher rates of unemployment than African Americans or whites (Hayghe & Haugen, 1987).

In contrast, the proportion of women who work for pay varies little by race and ethnicity (Ferber & O'Farrell, 1991). African American women are only marginally more likely to be employed than white women (58.7% and 57.2%, respectively), whereas the labor force participation rate of Hispanic women was 53.5% in 1989 (Ferber & O'Farrell, 1991).

### The Impact of a Dynamic Economy on Families

The U.S. economy has changed dramatically in recent years. Structural changes (i.e., decline in the manufacturing sector, increases in the service sector) coupled with the pattern of higher weekly earnings in the declining sectors and lower weekly earnings in the expanding sectors have squeezed family incomes. The restructuring of many businesses (i.e., moving low-skill jobs to other countries, robotics and other technology that replace operatives and other skilled laborers, mergers and acquisitions) has resulted in the elimination not only of industrial jobs but also of management positions. Other employment-related problems in the 1980s that affect earnings and family income include wage concessions in several unionized industries, differential wage systems in which new employees are hired for lower pay that increases at a slower rate than that of employees hired previously, and increases in part-time and part-year employment (Harrison & Bluestone, 1988, cited in Voydanoff, 1990).

During the economic shifts of the 1980s, men were more likely to be displaced than women (Herz, 1991). Because, on the average, men's earnings are higher than women's, men's job losses more severely affect family incomes. Bowman (1988) observes that the "deindustrialization" of the U.S. economy threatens to erase the industrial job categories (e.g., operatives and semiskilled laborers) that brought stable employment for African American men and economic security for African American families during the twentieth century. The loss of jobs in the manufacturing sector is creating ripple effects for the African American family: Fathers are experiencing "provider role strain" and becoming marginalized from their families, whereas mothers are experiencing multiple-role strain and ever-larger numbers are rearing their children alone (Bowman, 1988).

Because women typically have dominated as employees in jobs in the service sector, expansion in this sector increases the demand for women in the workforce. This demand is compounded by the demographic factors of a shrinking cohort of young workers and the continuation of the trend of early retirement (Gendell & Siegel, 1992). In their report *Workforce 2000,* Johnston and Packer (1987) predict that two thirds of the new entrants into the labor force between the late 1980s and 2000 will be women. These new women entrants are likely to be heads of single-parent households and wives and mothers, not single women, because nearly all of the women in this group are already in the workforce. Thus business and industry will need to be cognizant of the dual family and work roles of these new employees. The characteristics of jobs in the service sector also have implications for families. Service sector jobs are more likely than industrial sector jobs to be short term and/or to have flexible or part-time schedules. About two thirds of part-time and temporary employees are women who take such jobs to accommodate both work and family roles, but as Moen (1992) points out, the trade-off for such flexibility has a negative side for women and their families because (a) wages are lower, (b) there are few if any benefits, and (c) there is little opportunity for advancement.

Unemployment seriously affects the economic security of families. Although the number of families with at least one jobholder grew during 1992 (U.S. Bureau of Labor Statistics, 1993b), about 10% of all U.S. families (6.7 million) had one or more unemployed members as of the first quarter in 1993 (U.S. Bureau of Labor Statistics, 1993a). The official unemployment rate includes only those individuals who have been laid off and are waiting to be recalled and others who are actively seeking employment; these figures do not show the number of workers who have become discouraged and have abandoned their search for employment.

The economy and the labor force are dynamic systems, thus the total number of persons who experience unemployment sometime during a year, or the past several years, is substantially greater than the number who experience unemployment at any one time (Hefferan, 1983). Consequently, unemployment data for a given time underestimate the number of individuals and families affected by unemployment and the nature of the impact. Data from the Panel Study of Income Dynamics indicate that about 10% of prime-age male household heads experienced some unemployment in a given year, but nearly 40% were unemployed at least once in the decade between 1967 and 1976 (Duncan et al., 1984).

Most unemployment data are reported for individuals, which conceals patterns of unemployment according to family types and within families (Voydanoff, 1990). The unemployment rate for married men (spouse present) and for married women (spouse present) was identical (5%) in 1992; however, in 1992, as in 1986, unemployment was twice as high among women maintaining families as among married women with spouse present (U.S. Bureau of Labor Statistics, 1993d; Voydanoff, 1990). Young workers experience unemployment rates two to three times greater than the overall rate, but when older persons are unemployed, they tend to remain jobless longer than younger workers (Hefferan, 1983). In reviewing the impact of job loss during the 1975 recession, Moen (1983) reports that families with preschoolers (young families), as well as single-parent and African American families, were most vulnerable to financial loss.

A growing concern in the United States is the "working poor"—those who have employment but whose earnings are insufficient for them to live above the poverty level. During the decade of the 1980s, the probability that a year-round, full-time worker would have low annual earnings increased (Levitan & Shapiro, 1987; "Workers with Low Earnings," 1992). Being of Hispanic origin, having less than 12 years of education, and being in the 18- to 24-year-old age group enhance the likelihood of being a worker with low annual earnings. Women heading families with children are most affected by low wages, and three fourths of these women who worked full time in 1987 were living below the poverty level (Klein & Rones, 1989). Another difference between poor and nonpoor families is that a higher proportion of poor families (76% versus 39% of nonpoor families) had only one member in the labor force at least 27 weeks during 1987 (Klein & Rones, 1989).

Poverty rates for the population in general have hovered around 13% in the late 1980s ("Changes in Income," 1992; "Money Income and Poverty Status," 1990). Since the mid-1970s, the poverty rate for children has been higher than for any other age group ("Money Income and Poverty Status," 1990), yet nearly two thirds of all poor children in the United States lived in households where the members were working (Chilman, 1991). The higher incidence of single-parent households among African Americans combined with their lower levels of education, and consequently lower earnings, makes African American families more vulnerable to poverty despite labor force participation (Gardner & Herz, 1992). Although the incidence of married-couple families is higher among Hispanic workers, the low labor force participation by Hispanic wives and the low earnings of Hispanic workers in general make these families vulnerable to poverty. Poverty rates in married-couple white, African American, and Hispanic families were 3%, 6%, and 11%, respectively, in 1990 (Gardner & Herz, 1992). Among families maintained by women, the rates were 11% for white families, 21% for African American families, and 20% among Hispanic-origin families.

There is relatively little research on how families cope with unemployment and other economic hardships (see Voydanoff, 1990; Voydanoff & Majka, 1988), and what there is focuses on the unemployment of husbands, not wives. In general, informal supports—in particular, family members and relatives—are used more frequently and are considered more acceptable than the services of agencies and professionals. Women report using a relatively wide spectrum of supports, including family, friends, and coworkers, whereas men depend more exclusively on their spouses for support. Among the coping behaviors used by families to deal with economic setbacks are realigning family work efforts, participating in the informal economy, use of relatives for social support, and reducing expenditures (Hefferan, 1983; Perrucci & Targ, 1988; Retherford, Hildreth, & Goldsmith, 1988; Voydanoff, 1990).

Studies of unemployed men in particular jobs or locations indicate that there are complex psychological effects and adjustments for both wives and husbands following husband's job loss (Conger et al., 1990; Larson, 1984; Liem & Liem, 1988). Perrucci and Targ's (1988) study of blue-collar workers displaced in a midwest plant closing indicates the importance of advance notice and the positive support of spouses in effectively coping with job loss. Aspects of the marital relationship have an important influence on how individuals adapt to underemployment (Zvonkovic, Guss, & Ladd, 1988), and approaches to financial management in the face of reduced economic resources affect how spouses experience the stress of a husband's unemployment (Wilhelm & Ridley, 1988).

In summary, the recent rapid changes in the U.S. economy have introduced new role opportunities for women and reduced the opportunity for employment of men in jobs they have traditionally held. Many of the structural changes in the economy, coupled with the changing composition of U.S. households, have contributed to economic stress among a sizable number of households. Although the majority of married women and women heading families alone are now in the labor force, the norms pertaining to employment and household roles are still in flux.

## Division of Household Work

Women's participation in paid employment is often stressful because they continue to have primary responsibility for unpaid household work. Men have begun increasing the time they spend in unpaid household work; however, this increase has not been revolutionary. Several studies have reported contrasting data. Comparing the time spent in all household activities and in specific activities by husbands, wives, and children in 1967 and 1977, Sanik (1981) reported that, even though there were slight decreases in dish washing and clothing care, and a slight increase in shopping activities (primarily because of the increased time children spent shopping), there were no significant differences in the amount of time spouses spent in household work. Similarly, Coverman and Sheley (1986) found no change in men's housework or child-care time between 1965 and 1975.

In contrast, a study of the same married couples in 1975-1976 and 1981 and 1982, by Juster (1985), reported that work for pay declined for men and remained basically unchanged for women. However, men's time involved in housework increased "noticeably," whereas women's time remained about the same. A trend in increased father participation in child care has been documented (Darling-Fisher & Tiedje, 1990; Pleck, 1985). However, fathers tend to be more involved in play activities with their children than in providing direct care for them (Berk & Berk, 1979; Darling-Fisher & Tiedje, 1990; Pleck, 1985). Pleck (1985) reports that husbands of full-time employed women in occupations classified as professions are the most involved in child-care activities.

The most influential factor determining the amount of time wives spend in housework is whether or not they are employed and how many hours they work per week (Abdel-Ghany & Nickols, 1983; Fox & Nickols, 1983; Nickols & Fox, 1983; Timmer, Eccles, & O'Brien, 1985). Studies consistently show that the more time wives spend at paid work, the less time they spend at housework. It might be expected that wives with more demanding occupations could command more housework time from their husbands;

however, dual-career couples are not any more egalitarian than other couples (dual earner and single earner) in the time husbands and wives allocate to doing household tasks (Berardo, Shehan, & Leslie, 1987).

Nickols and Metzen (1978) found that wives' wages are negatively related to the number of hours they spend doing housework, whereas Abdel-Ghany and Nickols (1983) found no significant relationship between wage rate and household work time of wives. Education has been found to be related negatively to the amount of time wives spend in housework (Abdel-Ghany & Nickols, 1983; Berardo et al., 1987; Ericksen, Yancey, & Ericksen, 1979; Rexroat & Shehan, 1987).

Influences on husband's housework time are less clear. Robinson's (1977) data indicate that higher income husbands spend more time in household work than lower income husbands, but Ericksen, Yancey, and Ericksen (1979) and Nickols and Metzen (1978) found that husbands with higher wage rates spend less time doing housework than husbands with lower wage rates. Most studies show that more highly educated husbands spend more time in housework (Berardo et al., 1987; Hardesty & Bokemeier, 1989; Nickols & Metzen, 1978; Ross, 1987). In addition, the more time husbands spend at paid work, the less time they spend at housework (Abdel-Ghany & Nickols, 1983; Nickols & Fox, 1983; Nickols & Metzen, 1978; Rexroat & Shehan, 1987; Sanik, 1981). When husbands are employed fewer hours, they have a larger relative share of housework (Coltrane & Ishii-Kuntz, 1992).

Having an employed wife does not appear to be related to husbands' participation in housework. However, several studies have shown that the smaller the gap between husband's earnings and the wife's, the more likely the husband is to take some responsibility for household tasks (Bird, Bird, & Scruggs, 1984; Maret & Finlay, 1984; Model, 1981) and the greater is his relative contribution to household work (Ross, 1987).

Nickols and Metzen (1978) reported husbands in larger families spend less time in housework. This is probably because wives in these families are less likely to be in the labor force and thus spend more time in child care. Fathers whose wives are employed differ from other fathers in only two ways according to Timmer, Eccles, and O'Brien (1985). They were found to be less likely to spend time caring for a baby and to do less grocery shopping and other household errands.

Several theories have been proposed to explain why and how housework is divided between spouses. Coltrane and Ishii-Kuntz (1992) have identified three theories: (a) relative resources, (b) ideology, and (c) time availability, and Hardesty and Bokemeier (1989) base their explanations on a fourth theory—Marxist-feminism. As the studies reviewed in this chapter indicate, there is some support for each of these theories, but empirical evidence suggests that they do not offer a sufficient explanation.

Relative resources theory typically measures the gap between spouses' incomes, wage rates, educational levels, or occupational prestige. The conclusion—that the smaller the difference between wife's and husband's resources, the less disparity there is in the division of household labor between spouses—is justified by some studies and refuted by others.

Gender ideology studies attempt to determine the relationship between beliefs and attitudes about gender roles and how family work is divided between spouses. Again, the evidence is contradictory. Small shifts in husbands' housework time have been associated with changes in men's sex role attitudes such that men with less traditional beliefs are more involved in family work (Coltrane & Ishii-Kuntz, 1992; Hiller & Philliber, 1986; Kamo, 1988; Model, 1981). In contrast, other researchers found no such relationship between attitudes supporting gender equity and men's level of household work (Coverman, 1985; Crouter, Perry-Jenkins, Huston, & McHale, 1987; Geerken & Gove, 1983). Furthermore, it is not clear whether the husband's or wife's attitudes exert the most influence on the division of household work. Ross (1987) argues that change in the division of labor at home is set in motion by women taking jobs outside the home but must be completed by men's adoption of less traditional sex role beliefs.

Time availability theory uses measures of employment status or hours of employment to explore the division of household work. Theoretically, husbands of wives who are employed or wives who spend more hours at a paid job than unemployed or part-time employed wives would be expected to spend more time in household tasks. Although wife's employment hours and her housework time are highly negatively correlated, most studies find no relationship between wife's employment and the husband's housework time (see Spitze's, 1988, review article). Researchers have observed that increases in husbands' proportionate share of household labor are probably the result of wives doing less rather than husbands doing significantly more (Berardo et al., 1987; Pleck, 1985; Rexroat & Shehan, 1987; Thompson & Walker, 1989).

Marxist-feminist theory suggests that structural sources of gender inequality place women in a subordinate position within the paid labor force and that these patriarchal social norms justify an inequitable distribution of labor in the household (Hardesty & Bokemeier, 1989; Hartmann, 1981). Marxist-feminist theory builds on the relative resources theory by introducing the idea of relative power between the spouses and recognizing the contextual influence of cultural norms. Whatever the theoretical explanation, accomplishing the work of the home can be a source of stress for families. Women are especially susceptible to role overload as they continue to be responsible for and to perform the majority of household work as well as taking on employment roles. The negotiation of the division of household work can create stress for families as they move through the ever-changing demands of the family life cycle and changing employment situations.

## Balancing Employment and Family Life

The complex interactions between the employment sector and the family system create challenges for contemporary families in terms of managing multiple roles, and they affect families in terms of the marital adjustment of spouses and the well-being of children. Both theoretical explanations and empirical findings contribute to the understanding of these complex relationships.

### Understanding the Family/Work Interface

Pleck (1977) offers an explanation of the relationship between work and family in his conceptual framework of the work-family role system. The work-family role system comprises four interconnected roles—the male work role, the female work role, the female family role, and the male family role. Pleck suggests that the boundaries between the various roles are asymmetrically permeable, resulting in the demands of family roles being allowed to intrude into the work role of wives, whereas the demands of the work role are not allowed to intrude into the family role of husbands. Pleck further suggests that the sex-segregated occupational structure relegates women into different and inferior jobs. Because wives' jobs generally carry less occupational status and lower earnings compared with husbands' jobs, wives have less bargaining power with which to pressure their husbands into accepting more responsibility for family roles.

In seeking the overall economic and social well-being of the family, spouses seem to realize that increasing men's family roles probably means reducing their paid work time, which can potentially result in economic loss for the family (Pleck, 1985). During times of employment uncertainty, including slow growth in workers' wages and stagnated productivity levels, families may not be willing to take these risks, even if the result is role overload for wives.

Gender roles and the extent of control one has over one's work situation, as well as the cumulative effect of role demands, influence the degree of role conflict (Staines & Pleck, 1983; Voydanoff, 1988). Several researchers have observed a direct relationship between the number of hours on the job and work/family conflict (Keith & Schafer, 1980; Staines & Pleck, 1983; Voydanoff & Kelly, 1984). Working overtime and "moonlighting" (i.e., holding two jobs) create perceived time shortages for employed parents (Kelly & Voydanoff, 1985; Voydanoff & Kelly, 1984), and an irregular pattern of workdays is related to work/family conflict (Staines & Pleck, 1983). With surprising findings, Staines and Pleck (1983) and Weiss and Liss (1989) report that parents, especially mothers, working the night shift spend more time with their children and indicate they are able to participate in children's extracurricular activities. Recent articles in the popular press identify both the positive and the negative aspects of shift work ("Living on Dracula Time," 1993). Pleck (1985) found that time in family and job roles has a relatively positive influence on family adjustment of husbands, but he also found that this is likely to have a negative influence on wives' family adjustment.

There are both similarities and differences in the factors that create work/ family role strain for men and women. Work hours, spouse's work hours, and number of children in the home have been shown to create role strain for women, whereas work hours, age, and number of children in the home create role strain for men (Keith & Schafer, 1980). In addition, work role characteristics have a slightly greater impact on work/family conflict for men, whereas family structure demands have marginally more impact for women. Studies of role strain among African American women have identified having more children as contributing to (a) greater role strain among employed, middle-class mothers (Katz & Piotrkowski, 1983; McAdoo, 1982) and (b) using relatives rather than day care (McAdoo, 1982). Job autonomy (Katz & Piotrkowski, 1983) and having mothers who had provided role models of an employed mother (McAdoo, 1982) significantly reduced role strain among African American women.

Despite these findings, it appears that both husbands and wives experience work stress intruding into their family roles. Analyses of diaries indicate that people who have had a hectic day at work decrease their involvement at home, but their spouses (more frequently the wives) increase their involvement at home in order to compensate for the other. Thus wives often act as "buffers for their husbands, protecting them from excessive accumulation of role demands" (Bolger, DeLongis, Kessler, & Wethington, 1989, p. 181).

Being a single-parent, female employee is related to high levels of job tension (Kelly & Voydanoff, 1985); however, Googins and Burden (1987) report that married female parents exhibited the highest levels of role strain in their study, followed by single female parents. Women in all marital and parental statuses reported higher role strain than men. Among men, those whose wives were employed exhibited the highest role strain (Googins & Burden, 1987). Moen and Dempster-McClain (1987) contend that men and women experience role strain because in nearly half the dual-earner families in their study one or both parents, usually the father, worked at their jobs more than 40 hours per week, and approximately 60% of the sample were employed in nonprofessional occupations with little flexibility or autonomy.

### Marital Adjustment: The Importance of Attitudes

Two researchers (Fendrich, 1984; D. S. Smith, 1985) reviewed numerous studies and concluded there is no direct relationship between the wife's employment and the husband's well-being or various aspects of marital adjustment. There are, however, many employment circumstances (e.g., work hours, schedule flexibility, travel demands, weekend work, job security, autonomy) and personal and family characteristics that make the relationship between spousal employment and marital satisfaction highly complex (see Hughes & Galinsky, 1988; Hughes, Galinsky, & Morris, 1992; Menaghan & Parcel, 1990). Based on her review of studies, Spitze (1988) concludes that any effect of wife's employment on marital satisfaction seems to have changed from negative to null, or perhaps positive and negative effects appear to be a result of specific aspects of her employment (e.g., dissatisfaction with her job, scheduling), but there is a large body of research emphasizing the importance of spouses' attitudes toward employment on the quality of the marital relationship.

A husband's attitudes toward his wife's employment are a major determinant of marital quality. Thomas, Albrecht, and White (1984) found a strong positive relationship between the husband's approval and satisfaction with the wife's employment and his marital quality, and Vannoy and Philliber (1992) found the most important factor influencing the wife's marital quality was her *perception* of her husband's role expectations for her. The congruence of beliefs about provider and homemaker roles and

the enactment of roles within the home foster higher levels of marital satisfaction among men (Perry-Jenkins & Crouter, 1990). For example, McHale
and Crouter (1992) found wives with nontraditional sex role attitudes but
a traditional division of family roles, and husbands with traditional attitudes but an egalitarian division of family roles, were less satisfied with
their marriages.

### Children's Adjustment

Many have posed questions regarding the relationship between mother's
employment and children's adjustment, but questions rarely are asked about
father's employment and children's adjustment except to explore the impact of father's unemployment on children's health and adjustment (see
Voydanoff, 1990).

The Panel on Work, Family, and Community of the National Research
Council produced two reports, *Families That Work* (Kamerman & Hayes,
1982) and *Children of Working Parents* (Hayes & Kamerman, 1983) in
which they explored the research on the relationship between parents' employment, especially mother's employment, and children's socialization
and education. They concluded:

> There is no conclusive research evidence to suggest that mother's employ-
> ment per se (by single mothers or mothers in two-parent families) has con-
> sistent, direct effects, either positive or negative, on children's development
> and educational outcomes. (Hayes & Kamerman, 1983, p. 221)

Furthermore, a longitudinal study of effects of mother's employment on
cognitive, academic, or social and behavior developmental domains shows
no long-term or "sleeper" effects from infancy throughout the early school
years (Gottfried, Gottfried, & Bathurst, 1988). Another longitudinal study
(D'Amico, Haurin, & Mott, 1983) of adolescents and young adults concludes that mother's employment has "neither the pervasive beneficial
role-modeling influences that some suggest nor the consistent detrimental
effects due to maternal deprivation that others decry" (p. 150). The relationships are complex and are related to the age of the child at the time of
mother's employment, gender of the child, and outcome variables under
consideration (i.e., educational achievement, gender-role attitudes, propen-
sity to be employed while in high school, career preferences).

Moen (1992) summarizes the tentative conclusions about specific relationships and outcomes as follows:

1. Daughters appear to benefit from having an employed mother more than do sons (because they are likely to develop independence, to plan for future employment, and to have higher academic achievement; see Spitze, 1988).
2. The effects of maternal employment on sons are ambiguous, with possible negative effects in middle-class families. However, studies reviewed by Spitze (1988) report that both sons and daughters of employed mothers hold more egalitarian gender-role attitudes and view women as more competent. Also, the longitudinal analyses of Gottfried, Gottfried, and Bathurst (1988) do not support the conclusion of negative outcomes for boys.
3. Maternal employment affects not only the mother-child relationship but also the father-child relationship (also see Gottfried et al., 1988).
4. The mother's attitude toward her employment or nonemployment (i.e., satisfaction with the job, working outside the home by choice) may be more important than the employment itself.
5. Characteristics of the mother's job (whether part time or full time) greatly influence child outcomes.
6. Young children when exposed to group situations are more often sick compared with those cared for in individual homes.

Hoffman (1987) cautions analysts to remember the historical/social context when studying the effects of maternal employment on children. She notes that, compared with previous generations, present-day decisions about employment are made in a different climate where there is a different demand for women's labor, the housewife/mother role is different and the satisfactions from that role are altered, technology has changed, and economic insecurity has increased for many families. To analyze the effects of maternal employment as though it were occurring in yesterday's "traditional" family would be a fallacy.

The quality of child care arrangements is an important issue for families. The quality components of child care have to do with social structural features of care (e.g., group size, caregiver training, child-caregiver ratios) that influence the quantity and quality of time caregivers spend interacting with children (Belsky, 1990). Studies show positive benefits for children's cognitive and social development when group size and child-staff ratios are appropriate, caregivers are well trained, classroom space is adequate and interesting, and there is stability of care (Belsky, 1990; Hayes, Palmer, & Zaslow, 1990; Phillips, 1987). Because families under stress and with more limited economic and personal resources secure lower quality care for their toddlers and preschoolers, these children thus are more vulnerable (Belsky, 1989; Gamble & Zigler, 1988).

## Implications for
## Corporate Policy, Public Policy, and Education

Just as families are adjusting to the changes in the work-family system, so too are corporations and the government. The implicit assumption that the "traditional family" (an employed husband/father, a homemaker wife/ mother, and their children) would organize its life to accommodate the schedules and policies of business and industry is giving way to an explicit examination of reducing the tensions between families and work, achieving mutual benefits for families and employing institutions, and implementing programs at the workplace to support families. Exemplary "family-friendly" programs in the corporate sector recently have achieved cover story status ("Work & Family," 1993). Although there is still no comprehensive public policy pertaining to families in the United States, passage of the Family and Medical Leave Act in 1993 and federal support of child care in the 1990s indicate that public policymakers are more cognizant of family issues.

Historically, family life has been viewed as a very private matter in U.S. society. The government took a "hands-off" approach that was reflected in ambivalence toward family-related policies. Two examples of this are the Child Care Act of 1971, which was passed by Congress but vetoed by President Nixon, and the Family and Medical Leave Act, which was passed by Congress in 1990 but vetoed by President Bush. The rationales for these vetoes were that child-care subsidies would undermine family-centered child rearing (Moen, 1992), and the unpaid leaves provided in the Family and Medical Leave Act would be too costly for business. With the exception of national emergencies such as the Civil War and World War II, the prevailing ideology has expected individuals to accommodate to the demands of the workplace. Friedman and Galinsky (1992) point out: "The pressures of work and home life are accelerating, and families, which already bear the greater burden of conflicts experienced between home and work, can do little more to sustain the balance" (p. 175). They predict that the 1990s will bring about institutional change that will address the tensions between the two systems. Kamerman (1983) identified four reasons that employers are becoming more responsive to family needs: The labor force is changing, becoming more diverse and comprising people who hold different values than previous cohorts; family composition, gender roles, and events during the life course are different; there is growing pressure on the private sector to take up the slack caused by reductions in the 1980s in social programs previously supported by the government; and concern about productivity in an increasingly competitive world economy compels employers to respond.

The more family-friendly environment of the workplace includes such provisions as information and counseling to help reduce stress associated with balancing work and family roles; dependent-care (child and elder care) centers, referral services, and financial assistance to defray the cost of dependent care; family and medical leave; alternative work schedules, including flextime and job sharing; and work at home (see Peters, Peters, & Caropreso, 1990, and "Work & Family," 1993, for examples of programs; and Friedman & Galinsky, 1992, and Kamerman, 1983, for studies of these programs). These programs and policies are in addition to the standard benefits (e.g., health and life insurance, pensions) that firms have provided to employees for many years. The value of benefit packages in 1987 was over $10,000 per employee, or 39% of payroll (Friedman, 1991).

Managers must contend with absenteeism, employee turnover, and distracted workers when the stresses of family life intrude upon the workplace. Friedman (1991) reports, "The research indicates that the stress produced by work-family conflict is due to daily hassles, and not necessarily catastrophes" (p. 7). There are, however, significant life events that place particular demands on families, including pregnancy, childbirth, and adoption; relocation, especially when spouses have careers and children are at critical stages of development; and care of elderly members. Although the problems of securing quality child care have received the most attention and employers have been the most responsive to this aspect of family life, Friedman (1991) points out that the complexity and duration of caregiving to elder family members often increases stress levels, absenteeism, and resignation rates beyond those caused by child care. Thus, as older persons make up a bigger proportion of the population, more employees will face this aspect of dependent care.

Friedman and Galinsky (1992), Co-directors of the Work and Families Institute, and Moen (1992) advocate taking a "life-cycle approach" to family issues in the workplace. A more sensitive and less stressful work environment could be created if it was acknowledged that all employees at some point in their lives will experience a tension between work and family life, but these tensions will be different for different people depending on their stage of the life cycle and their family situation. As Moen (1992) points out, due to smaller family size and increases in longevity, the period of child rearing is not long lasting. Contemporary parents typically will have preschoolers in the home for 2 or 3 years, probably twice in their lives. Facilitating the integration of employment and parental roles for a short-term period with greater flexibility for parents would be expected to benefit both employers and employees. Policies and programs that recognize the differing family demands at various life-cycle stages do not serve all employees at any given time; however, they potentially reach most employees at some time when they are in the workforce (Friedman & Galinsky, 1992).

The growing literature on balancing the demands of work and family indicates that what employees most need and desire is greater flexibility, as one employee put it, "to get more control over my life" (Peters et al., 1990, p. 13). The implications for employers and public policymakers are clear. For the sake of productivity and competitiveness, the U.S. workplace must become more flexible in responding to the family component of workers' lives. The growing diversity among workers and families and innovations in technology and management approaches provide both the stimulus and response structures for flexible and family-friendly policies and programs.

## Summary

The difficulties of balancing the competing demands of work and family roles continue to challenge family members, educators, and policymakers. Among the most stressful experiences for families are adaptation to a changing economy that offers different opportunities for women's and men's employment; periods of unemployment and economic hardship; dividing the workload in the home; and arranging quality care for children, especially infants, during the time parents are on the job. The changing demographic characteristics of the United States, which indicate rapidly increasing growth in the number of elderly, soon will make elder care as stressful a challenge as child care. The importance of spousal attitudes regarding wife's employment on the quality of the marital relationship and the apparent lack of negative outcomes for children of mother's employment per se reinforce the importance of the qualitative aspects of balancing the relationship between work and families. Families will continue to depend on employment for income and a multitude of benefits, and employers will continue to depend on families for reliable, productive workers. This reciprocal relationship between work and families requires that ways be found to minimize the stress points between the two systems so that people can function optimally in both settings and a satisfying quality of life and a thriving economy can be attained.

# References

Abdel-Ghany, M., & Nickols, S. Y. (1983). Husband/wife differentials in household work time: The case of dual-earner families. *Home Economics Research Journal, 12*(2), 159-167.

Belsky, J. (1989). Infant-parent attachment and day care: In defense of the strange situation. In J. S. Lande, S. Scarr, & N. Gunzenbhauser (Eds.), *Caring for children: Challenge to America* (pp. 23-47). Hillsdale, NJ: Lawrence Erlbaum.

Belsky, J. (1990). Parental and nonparental child care and children's socioemotional development: A decade review. *Journal of Marriage and the Family, 52,* 885-903.

Berardo, D. H., Shehan, C. L., & Leslie, G. R. (1987). A residue of tradition: Jobs, careers, and spouses' time in housework. *Journal of Marriage and the Family, 49,* 381-390.

Berk, R. A., & Berk, S. F. (1979). *Labor and leisure at home: Content and organization of the household day.* Beverly Hills, CA: Sage.

Bernard, J. (1975). *Women, wives, and mothers: Values and options.* New York: Aldine.

Bird, G. W., Bird, G. A., & Scruggs, M. (1984). Determinants of family task sharing: A study of husbands and wives. *Journal of Marriage and the Family, 46,* 345-355.

Bolger, N., DeLongis, A., Kessler, R. C., & Wethington, E. (1989). The contagion of stress across multiple roles. *Journal of Marriage and the Family, 51,* 175-183.

Bowman, P. J. (1988). Postindustrial displacement and family role strain: Challenges for the black family. In P. Voydanoff & L. C. Majka (Eds.), *Families and economics distress: Coping strategies and social policy* (pp. 75-96). Newbury Park, CA: Sage.

Chafe, W. H. (1976). Looking backward in order to look forward: Women, work, and social values in America. In J. M. Kreps (Ed.), *Women and the American economy: A look to the 1980s* (pp. 6-30). Englewood Cliffs, NJ: Prentice Hall.

Changes in income, 1984-89. (1992). *Family Economics Review, 5*(3), 25-26.

Chilman, C. S. (1991). Working poor families: Trends, causes, effects, and suggested policies. *Family Relations, 40,* 191-198.

Coltrane, S., & Ishii-Kuntz, M. (1992). Men's housework: A life course perspective. *Journal of Marriage and the Family, 54,* 43-57.

Conger, R. D., Elder, G. H., Jr., Lorenz, F. O., Conger, K. J., Simons, R. L., Whitbeck, L. B., Huck, S., & Melby, J. N. (1990). Linking economic hardship to marital quality and instability. *Journal of Marriage and the Family, 52,* 643-656.

Coverman, S. (1985). Explaining husband's participation in domestic labor. *The Sociological Quarterly, 26,* 81-97.

Coverman, S., & Sheley, J. F. (1986). Change in men's housework and child-care time, 1965-1975. *Journal of Marriage and the Family, 48,* 413-422.

Crouter, A., Perry-Jenkins, M., Huston, T., & McHale, S. (1987). Processes underlying father involvement in dual-earner and single-earner families. *Developmental Psychology, 23,* 431-440.

D'Amico, R. J., Haurin, R. J., & Mott, F. L. (1983). The effects of mothers' employment on adolescent and early adult outcomes of young men and women. In C. D. Hayes & S. B. Kamerman (Eds.), *Children of working parents: Experiences and outcomes* (pp. 130-219). Washington, DC: National Academy Press.

Darling-Fisher, C. S., & Tiedje, L. B. (1990). The impact of maternal employment characteristics on fathers' participation in child care. *Family Relations, 39,* 20-26.

84 Stress and Change Over the Life Cycle

22Duncan, G. J. with Coe, R. D., Corcoran, M. E., Hill, M. S., Hoffman, S. D., & Morgan, J. N. (1984). *Years of poverty, years of plenty.* Ann Arbor: University of Michigan, Survey Research Center, Institute for Social Research.

Ericksen, J. A., Yancey, W. L., & Ericksen, E. P. (1979). The division of family roles. *Journal of Marriage and the Family, 41,* 301-313.

Fendrich, M. (1984). Wives' employment and husbands' distress: A meta-analysis and a replication. *Journal of Marriage and the Family, 46,* 871-879.

Ferber, M. A., & O'Farrell, B. (1991). *Work and family: Policies for a changing work force.* Washington, DC: National Academy Press.

Fox, K. D., & Nickols, S. Y. (1983). The time crunch: Wife's employment and family work. *Journal of Family Issues, 4*(1), 61-82.

Friedman, D. E. (1991). *Linking work-family issues to the bottom line.* New York: Conference Board.

Friedman, D. E., & Galinsky, E. (1992). Work and family issues: A legitimate business concern. In S. Zedeck (Ed.), *Work, families, and organizations* (pp. 168-207). San Francisco: Jossey-Bass.

Gamble, T. J., & Zigler, E. (1988). Effects of infant day care: Another look at the evidence. In E. F. Zigler & M. Frank (Eds.), *The parental leave crisis: Toward a national policy* (pp. 77-99). New Haven, CT: Yale University Press.

Gardner, J. M., & Herz, D. E. (1992). Working and poor in 1990. *Monthly Labor Review, 115*(12), 20-28.

Geerken, M., & Gove, W. R. (1983). *At home and at work: The family's allocation of labor.* Beverly Hills, CA: Sage.

Gendell, M., & Siegel, J. S. (1992). Trends in retirement age by sex, 1950-2005. *Monthly Labor Review, 115*(7), 22-29.

Googins, B., & Burden, D. (1987). Vulnerability of working parents: Balancing work and home roles. *Social Work, 32,* 295-300.

Gottfried, A. E., Gottfried, A. W., & Bathurst, K. (1988). Maternal employment, family environment, and children's development: Infancy through the school years. In A. E. Gottfried & A. W. Gottfried (Eds.), *Maternal employment and children's development: Longitudinal research* (pp. 11-58). New York: Plenum.

Hardesty, C., & Bokemeier, J. (1989). Finding time and making do: Distribution of household labor in nonmetropolitan marriages. *Journal of Marriage and the Family, 51,* 253-267.

Hartmann, H. I. (1981). The family as the locus of gender, class and political struggle: The example of housework. *Signs: Journal of Women in Culture and Society, 6*(3), 366-394.

Hayes, C. D., & Kamerman, S. B. (1983). *Children of working parents: Experiences and outcomes.* Washington, DC: National Academy Press.

Hayes, C. D., Palmer, J., & Zaslow, M. (Eds.). (1990). *Who cares for America's children? Child care policy for the 1990s* (Report of the Panel on Child Care Policy, Commission on Behavioral and Social Sciences and Education, National Research Council). Washington, DC: National Academy Press.

Hayghe, H. V. (1990). Family members in the work force. *Monthly Labor Review, 113*(3), 14-19.

Hayghe, H. V., & Haugen, S. E. (1987). A profile of husbands in today's labor market. *Monthly Labor Review, 110*(10), 12-17.

Hefferan, C. (1983). Unemployment: The effects on family income and expenditures. *Family Economics Review, 1,* 2-9.

Herz, D. E. (1991). Worker displacement still common in the late 1980's. *Monthly Labor Review, 114*(5), 3-9.

Hiller, D. V., & Philliber, W. W. (1986). The division of labor in contemporary marriage: Expectations, perceptions, and performance. *Social Problems, 33,* 191-201.

Hoffman, L. (1987). The effects on children of maternal and paternal employment. In N. Gerstel & H. E. Gross (Eds.), *Families and work* (pp. 362-395). Philadelphia: Temple University Press.

Hughes, D., & Galinsky, E. (1988). Balancing work and family lives: Research and corporate applications. In A. E. Gottfried & A. W. Gottfried (Eds.), *Maternal employment and children's development: Longitudinal research* (pp. 233-268). New York: Plenum.

Hughes, D., Galinsky, E., & Morris, A. (1992). The effects of job characteristics on marital quality: Specifying linking mechanisms. *Journal of Marriage and the Family, 54,* 31-42.

Johnston, W. B., & Packer, A. (1987). *Workforce 2000: Work and workers for the 21st century.* Indianapolis, IN: Hudson Institute.

Juster, F. T. (1985). A note on recent changes in time use. In F. T. Juster & F. P. Stafford (Eds.), *Time, goods, and well-being* (pp. 313-332). Ann Arbor: University of Michigan, Survey Research Center, Institute for Social Research.

Kamerman, S. B. (1983). *Meeting family needs: The corporate response.* New York: Pergamon.

Kamerman, S. B., & Hayes, C. D. (1982). *Families that work: Children in a changing world.* Washington, DC: National Academy Press.

Kamo, Y. (1988). Determinants of household labor: Resources, power, and ideology. *Journal of Family Issues, 9,* 177-200.

Katz, M. H., & Piotrkowski, C. S. (1983). Correlates of family role strain among employed black women. *Family Relations, 32,* 331-339.

Keith, P. M., & Schafer, R. B. (1980). Role strain and depression in two-job families. *Family Relations, 29,* 483-488.

Kelly, R. F., & Voydanoff, P. (1985). Work/family role strain among employed parents. *Family Relations, 34,* 367-374.

Klein, B. W., & Rones, P. L. (1989). A profile of the working poor. *Monthly Labor Review, 112*(10), 3-13.

Larson, J. H. (1984). The effect of husband's unemployment on marital and family relations in blue-collar families. *Family Relations, 33,* 503-511.

Levitan, S. A., & Shapiro, I. (1987). *Working but poor: America's contradiction.* Baltimore, MD: Johns Hopkins University Press.

Liem, R., & Liem, J. H. (1988). Psychological effects of unemployment on workers and their families. *Journal of Social Issues, 44,* 87-105.

Living on Dracula time. (1993, July 12). *Newsweek,* pp. 68-69.

Maret, E., & Finlay, B. (1984). The distribution of household labor among women in dual-earner families. *Journal of Marriage and the Family, 46,* 357-364.

McAdoo, H. P. (1982). Stress absorbing systems in black families. *Family Relations, 31,* 479-488.

McHale, S. M., & Crouter, A. C. (1992). You can't always get what you want: Incongruence between sex-role attitudes and family work roles and its implications for marriage. *Journal of Marriage and the Family, 54,* 537-547.

Menaghan, E. G., & Parcel, T. L. (1990). Parental employment and family life: Research in the 1980s. *Journal of Marriage and the Family, 52,* 1079-1098.

Model, S. (1981). Housework by husbands: Determinants and implications. *Journal of Family Issues, 2*(2), 225-237.

Moen, P. (1983). Unemployment, public policy, and families: Forecasts for the 1980s. *Journal of Marriage and the Family, 45,* 751-760.

Moen, P. (1992). *Women's two roles: A contemporary dilemma.* New York: Auburn House.

Moen, P., & Dempster-McClain, D. I. (1987). Employed parents: Role strain, work time, and preferences for working less. *Journal of Marriage and the Family, 49,* 579-590.

Money income and poverty status of households and families. (1990). *Family Economics Review, 3*(2) 13-14.

Nickols, S. Y., & Fox, K. D. (1983). Buying time and saving time: Strategies for managing household production. *Journal of Consumer Research, 10,* 197-208.

Nickols, S. Y., & Metzen, E. J. (1978). Housework time of husband and wife. *Home Economics Research Journal, 7*(2), 85-97.

Perrucci, C. C., & Targ, D. B. (1988). Effects of a plant closing on marriage and family life. In P. Voydanoff & L. C. Majka (Eds.), *Families and economics distress: Coping strategies and social policy* (pp. 55-71). Newbury Park, CA: Sage.

Perry-Jenkins, M., & Crouter, A. C. (1990). Men's provider-role attitudes: Implications for household work and marital satisfaction. *Journal of Family Issues, 11,* 136-156.

Peters, J. L., Peters, B. H., & Caropreso, F. (Eds.). (1990). *Work and family policies: The new strategic plan.* New York: Conference Board.

Phillips, D. (Ed.). (1987). *Quality in child care: What does research tell us?* Washington, DC: National Association for the Education of Young Children.

Pleck, J. H. (1977). The work-family role system. *Social Problems, 24,* 417-427.

Pleck, J. H. (Ed.). (1985). *Working wives, working husbands.* Beverly Hills, CA: Sage.

Retherford, P. S., Hildreth, G. J., & Goldsmith, E. B. (1988). Social support and resource management of unemployed women. In E. B. Godsmith (Ed.), *Work and family: Theory, research, and applications* (pp. 191-204). Newbury Park, CA: Sage.

Rexroat, C., & Shehan, C. (1987). The family life cycle and spouses' time in housework. *Journal of Marriage and the Family, 49,* 737-750.

Robinson, J. P. (1977). *How Americans use time.* New York: Praeger.

Ross, C. E. (1987). The division of labor at home. *Social Forces, 65*(3), 816-833.

Sanik, M. M. (1981). Division of household work: A decade comparison—1967-1977. *Home Economics Research Journal, 10*(2), 175-180.

Shank, S. E. (1988). Women and the labor market: The link grows stronger. *Monthly Labor Review, 111*(3), 3-8.

Smith, D. S. (1985). Wife employment and marital adjustment, a cumulation of results. *Family Relations, 34,* 483-490.

Smith, R. E. (1979). The movement of women into the labor force. In R. E. Smith (Ed.), *The subtle revolution: Women at work* (pp. 1-29). Washington, DC: Urban Institute.

Spitze, G. (1988). Women's employment and family relations: A review. *Journal of Marriage and the Family, 50,* 595-618.

Staines, G. L., & Pleck, J. H. (1983). *The impact of work schedules on the family.* Ann Arbor: University of Michigan, Survey Research Center, Institute for Social Research.

Thomas, S., Albrecht, K., & White, P. (1984). Determinants of marital quality in dual-career couples. *Family Relations, 33,* 513-521.

Thompson, L., & Walker, A. J. (1989). Gender in families: Women and men in marriage, work, and parenthood. *Journal of Marriage and the Family, 51,* 845-871.

Timmer, S. G., Eccles, J., & O'Brien, K. (1985). How children use time. In F. T. Juster & F. P. Stafford (Eds.), *Time, goods, and well-being* (pp. 353-382). Ann Arbor: University of Michigan, Survey Research Center, Institute for Social Research.

U.S. Bureau of Labor Statistics. (1993a, April). *Employment and earnings characteristics of families: First quarter 1993.* Washington, DC: U.S. Department of Labor.

U.S. Bureau of Labor Statistics. (1993b, February). *Employment and earnings characteristics of families: Fourth quarter 1992.* Washington, DC: U.S. Department of Labor.

U.S. Bureau of Labor Statistics. (1993c, May). Table 4: Employment status of the population by sex, age, race, and Hispanic origin, monthly data seasonally adjusted. *Monthly Labor Review, 116*(5), 85.

U.S. Bureau of Labor Statistics. (1993d, May). Table 6: Selected unemployment indicators, monthly data seasonally adjusted. *Monthly Labor Review, 116*(5), 87.

Vannoy, D., & Philliber, W. W. (1992). Wife's employment and quality of marriage. *Journal of Marriage and the Family, 54,* 387-398.

Voydanoff, P. (1988). Work role characteristics, family structure demands, and work/family conflict. *Journal of Marriage and the Family, 50,* 749-761.

Voydanoff, P. (1990). Economic distress and family relations: A review of the eighties. *Journal of Marriage and the Family, 52,* 1099-1115.

Voydanoff, P., & Kelly, R. F. (1984). Determinants of work-related family problems among employed parents. *Journal of Marriage and the Family, 46,* 881-892.

Voydanoff, P., & Majka, L. C. (1988). *Families and economic distress: Coping strategies and social policy.* Newbury Park, CA: Sage.

Weiss, M. G., & Liss, M. B. (1989). Night shift work: Job and family concerns. In E. B. Goldsmith (Ed.), *Work and family: Theory, research, and applications* (pp. 279-286). Newbury Park, CA: Sage.

Wilhelm, M. S., & Ridley, C. A. (1988). Stress and unemployment in rural nonfarm couples: A study of hardships and coping resources. *Family Relations, 37,* 50-54.

Work & family. (1993, June 28). *Business Week,* pp. 80-88.

Workers with low earnings: 1964 to 1990. (1992). *Family Economics Review, 5*(4), 32-33.

Zvonkovic, A. M., Guss, T., & Ladd, L. (1988). Making the most of job loss: Individual and marital features of underemployment. *Family Relations, 37,* 56-61.

# 5

❈

# Dealing With Adolescent Children

VELMA MCBRIDE MURRY
PATRICIA BELL-SCOTT

Most research investigations on adolescent development within the context of the family use the perspectives of psychoanalytic theory, family systems theory, cognitive developmental theory, social learning theory, and social exchange theory. Perhaps such wide variability exists because of the history of disciplinary isolation in adolescent and family research. For example, clinicians often focus on improving approaches to therapy or comparing clinical and nonclinical samples in post hoc designs, whereas developmental researchers typically examine the role of family structure, process, and function with regard to various measures of children's competence and social emotional development. Accompanying this variability in approaches are differences in methodological assumptions, such as what data are relevant to the questions under investigation, the principles of sample selection, and even what constitutes acceptable evidence.

Over the past 10 years, researchers, mental health providers, policymakers, and educators have begun to recognize the importance of studying adolescent development within a family context. Unfortunately, most of these studies have not included African American, Hispanic American, Asian American, or Native American family-adolescent relationships (Bell-Scott & McKenry, 1985), or if they are included, they are usually viewed from a social problem perspective. Lack of representation of all families with adolescents should be considered as students explore the areas discussed in this chapter.

Developmental changes associated with adolescence pose an array of stressors and strains on adolescents and their families. This chapter focuses on issues of life change events, stress, coping, and adaptation in families with adolescents. The first section includes a brief discussion of the significance of adolescent development from the individual as well as the family perspective. The second section identifies and discusses theoretical and empirical issues relevant to antecedents that minimize and maximize stress in families with adolescents. Next, a discussion of familial factors that predict high-risk behaviors, such as pregnancy and childbearing, suicide, and substance and drug abuse among adolescents, is provided. Also presented in this section is a brief overview of coping strategies used by adolescents and families. The chapter concludes with a brief discussion of the usefulness of this information for educators, clinicians, and researchers.


## Adolescence:
## A Crucial Developmental Period

Adolescence is a crucial period for the individual and family for several reasons. First, it is a milestone in an individual's life marked by a dramatic change in one's physical, intellectual, and social development. Physically, there are noticeable changes in outward appearances; the intellectual changes reflect modifications in the way experiences are viewed; and social changes occur as a result of the individual's position in the larger society (Hill, 1980). Second, changes associated with adolescent development require family systems to adjust and modify customary interaction processes so that relationships are more consistent with the needs of the developing family member. Third, developmental changes associated with adolescence challenge the family at the very core of its operating assumptions about childhood, adulthood, and the role of the family and parents in the transition from one role to the other. In addition, demands placed on families during this stage of the life cycle may be more stressful because parents are also experiencing developmental changes related to their midlife transition. Finally, the adolescent period is crucial because the intensity of demands imposed by the imminent change within the family, as well as the way in which families respond to the demands, can precipitate family stress and crises (McCubbin & Patterson, 1986).

## Antecedents of
## Family Stress During Adolescence

Despite various developmental changes associated with adolescence, issues of rebellion, family storm and stress, and conflict between adolescents and parents do not characterize all family systems during this stage of development. What antecedent factors might be useful to understand how families minimize or maximize the likelihood of experiencing high levels of family stress during the adolescent stage of the family life cycle?

### Theoretical Explanations

Major work investigating the association between adolescent development and changing familial patterns tends to use the psychosocial and biosocial perspectives. The psychosocial perspective examines the interface between the psychological process of adolescent individuation and the social process of family interactions (Hauser et al., 1984). Biosocial research examines the interface between the biological process of physical maturation and the social process of family relations (Petersen & Taylor, 1980). Illustrations of the use of these approaches in the study of adolescents and families are presented below.

Puberty is assumed to be the life change event that begins the process of family transformation. The onset of puberty disrupts family functioning, requiring the family to readjust to achieve a new level of homeostasis. However, the extent to which the experience is conflictual, stressful, and stormy for families depends on intergenerational issues (Lerner, Karson, Meisels, & Knapp, 1975), on whether the family accepts the viewpoint that conflictual parent-adolescent relationships are inevitable (Adelson & Doehrman, 1980; Blos, 1970), on the degree of noticeable physical changes in the adolescent (Crockett & Petersen, 1987), and on adolescent and parents' response as well as family characteristics.

## Effects of Pubertal Status
## and Pubertal Timing on Families

### Parents' Response

Physical changes in adolescents reflect an emerging adult with reproductive potential. This new status affects family behaviors and processes.

The stage termination hypothesis has been useful in explaining parents' response to pubertal development. Based on this hypothesis, it is assumed that puberty marks the end of childhood and the beginning of adolescence. Differential responses of parents to pubertal development are influenced by whether the adolescent is in the early, middle, or late stage of development. For example, Hauser and associates (1984) reported increased stress and strain in mother-daughter relations shortly after menarche, especially among early maturers. In addition, immediately postmenarcheal daughters perceive their mothers as less accepting than do premenarcheal daughters, and the family is seen as being more controlling. Early maturing daughters were subjected to more constraining behaviors than "on-time" or late maturers. It has been suggested that change in family interactional patterns during pubertal development can be attributed to parental fear of daughters' reproductive maturity, which results in more restrictive monitoring by parents (Newman & Newman, 1986).

Results from a longitudinal study revealed a significant link between the pubertal status of boys and parent-child interaction patterns. Steinberg (1981) observed that change in parent-child interactions was most noticeable during the early period of pubertal development. During early adolescence, both mothers and sons explained themselves less and interrupted each other more. As sons matured, conflict and negativity between mothers and sons increased. Also, mothers deferred more to their sons, becoming less effective monitors of their behavior and activities during the later stage of pubertal development. Steinberg (1987) refers to this change in family process during puberty as the "distancing hypothesis."

Although altercations and decreased control are most characteristic of mother-son relationships, fathers appear to become more influential with sons as physical maturation increases (Hill, Holmbeck, Marlow, Green, & Lynch, 1986). This process occurs even though fathers demonstrate less affection and involvement with their sons across puberty (Papini & Datan, 1983). In general, fewer behavioral changes are observed by the fathers in response to maturation of their children. One study, however, noted that fathers increased flirtatious expressions of warmth toward pubescent daughters. This interactional pattern may explain increased tension between husbands and wives when their daughters are going through puberty (Hill et al., 1986).

One reason offered for the increase in mother-son altercations during puberty is that as adolescent males mature they tolerate less maternal control (Steinberg, 1987). Another explanation is related to the new styles that families use to communicate with each other during various segments of the pubertal phase (Danon-Boileau, 1982; Wendt, 1983). In fact, Papini and Datan (1983) have argued that changing behavior patterns of families during puberty are not related to physical maturation but to fewer instances of positive supportive statements during family interactions than the adolescent experienced during the prepubertal stage of development. According to Steinberg (1981), physical changes associated with puberty may function as cues to the adolescent and his parents to modify their interactional patterns.

### Adolescents' Response

Adolescents' response to developmental transitions may influence their parents' response to them. Differential response of adolescents to puberty depends on (a) the timing of the event, (b) the characteristics of the change, (c) the characteristics of the individual, and (d) the outcome area at issue (Simmons & Blyth, 1987). For instance, research studies have indicated that, compared with "on-time" maturing girls, early maturing females experience undue self-consciousness about breast development (Rutter, 1980), stress and introversion (Peskin, 1973), embarrassment and sexual frustration (Tanner, 1972), as well as increased confrontation and more structured patterns of interaction with parents (Hauser et al., 1984). In contrast, boys who mature early tend to be more assertive, popular, and accepted more readily by adults than later developing males. Increased acting-out and noncompliant behavior were evident as boys matured through puberty. Late maturing girls and boys were more likely to feel less secure and more vulnerable to problems (Rutter, 1980).

Being "off-time" is thought to have a significant impact on the adolescent and parents because families share societal values about when major life events should occur (Neugarten, 1979). These beliefs are internalized by adolescents, affecting their sense of self, social prestige, social adaptation, as well as expectations of others and themselves (Neugarten & Datan, 1973). Being an early or late maturer places adolescents in a position of being "socially deviant," with social advantages and disadvantages. However, difficulties associated with being off-time are more pronounced among early maturing girls and late maturing boys. Such difficulties occur because of their status relative to their peers; for example, girls who mature early are much earlier than the majority of their peers, and boys who mature late are much later than their peers (Tanner, 1972).

## *Family Structure and Composition*

Reactions of parents and adolescents to pubertal development also appear to vary depending on family structure and whether families consist of only girls, only boys, or a combination of girls and boys. Fewer associations have been found between puberty, family relations, and child adjustment in nondivorced families with daughters only. Data that are available show a decline in mothers' abilities to monitor the behavior of their maturing daughters. The same pattern was exhibited by fathers in daughter-only families. That is, fathers had less control and were less effective monitors of daughters' behavior as the girls matured through puberty (Anderson, Hetherington, & Clingempeel, 1989). Despite the noted change in parents' abilities to monitor the behavior of maturing daughters, Anderson and colleagues (1989) found little support for decreased parental warmth and increased conflict between parents and children as daughters matured. In contrast, results from a study conducted by Hill and associates (1986) reported increased conflict in families with sexually maturing daughters. However, fathers appear to be less affected by daughters' pubertal status than mothers (Anderson et al., 1989).

Fewer changes have been observed in the parent-child relationship in divorced families during pubertal development of the adolescent. One developmental transition associated with puberty has been that divorced single mothers become less effective monitors of their daughters' behaviors as the girls' mature. In contrast to shifts in mother-son relationships in nondivorced families, conflict between divorced single mothers and sons was lower (Anderson et al., 1989). One explanation offered for this finding is that the necessary transformation of the relationship during this developmental phase occurs earlier in divorced families. Therefore, as sons mature, there is little need for mothers and sons to undergo the process a second time (Hetherington, 1988).

The response of remarried families to the pubertal status of adolescents is similar to that observed in nondivorced families, particularly with mother-son interactional patterns. According to Hollier (1988), however, high levels of conflict among stepfamily members during adolescence may be attributed to high levels of disengagement from the family by children after the remarriage (Hetherington, 1972) rather than the pubertal or maturational level of the adolescent. Or changes in the mother-son relationship during puberty in stepfamilies may reflect reorganization that occurs in remarried families. Thus increased tension between a mother and an early adolescent son may be more pronounced because of the concomitant adjustments of the family to the child entering puberty. Moreover, adolescents in the later stages of puberty may be more socially competent and have the resources to disengage successfully from a chaotic family environment (Hetherington, 1988).

### Adolescent Stressor and Strain Pileup

Developmental transitions and day-to-day hassles have been identified as the most important types of stress experienced by adolescents. McCubbin, Patterson, Bauman, and Harris (1981) reported that over half of the stressors that adolescents experienced could be attributed to conflict with parents. Although many of them had experienced a family member's hospitalization, seriously ill grandparent, death of a close family member, or problems in school, these life events seemed to have less impact than hassles and conflicts with parents. Tolan (1986) has suggested that the timing and relative "pileup" or accumulation of developmental changes and daily hassles that occur during adolescence may be important in understanding youth at risk of delinquency and patterns of high-risk behavior.

In fact, Jessor and Jessor (1977) have pointed out that, to deal with an accumulation of transitions, adolescents often initiate behaviors that are defined as "problem" behavior (i.e., cigarette smoking, alcohol use, sexual behavior). Moreover, Petersen (1982) argues that most of these behaviors would not be considered alarming or inappropriate in adults but are perceived as evidence of delinquency for youngsters. In reality, excessive engagement in many behaviors can have negative consequences with lasting developmental effects at any age. For adolescents, short-term engagement in these so-called problem behaviors may be purposeful and self-regulating and aimed at coping with the numerous changes associated with this developmental stage (Kaplan, 1980; Petersen, Ebata, & Graber, 1987; Silberison & Noack, 1988).

### Families With High-Risk Adolescents

Over the past few decades, researchers have begun to recognize that the root of high-risk behavior lies within the family. Early aggressive behaviors, such as temper tantrums and grade school misbehavior, have been identified as significant predictors of later delinquent behavior. This relationship is more pronounced in males than in females (Loeber & Dishion, 1983). To successfully intervene, however, it is not enough to know when such behavior begins; one must also look at the causes. In this section, a brief overview of family characteristics thought to impede or foster high-risk behaviors among adolescents will be provided. Then, attention will be given to specific aspects of parental control, quality of parent-child relationship, and family dynamics that increase adolescents' vulnerability to high-risk behavior, such as pregnancy and childbearing, suicide, and substance abuse.

### Family Characteristics

In the literature, families of high-risk adolescents are characterized by a triadic pattern of relationship with one overly involved parent and one punitive or distant parent. In addition, parents of high-risk adolescents tend to be more rigid in their roles and exhibit less emotional closeness than do parents of non-high-risk adolescents. According to Olson and McCubbin (1983), families with adolescents function most favorably with balanced levels of cohesion and adaptability, whereas problem families are more likely to be either disengaged or enmeshed, and rigid or chaotic.

### Parental Control

Parental control is basically the degree of intensity to which parents influence their adolescents to comply with parental wishes (Olson & Cromwell, 1975; Rollins & Thomas, 1979). Parental control has been differentiated primarily in two areas: (a) the extent to which parents allow children to participate in decision making and (b) techniques of parenting styles. These two areas are often described in terms of two orthogonal dimensions: warmth/hostility and control/authority (Maccoby & Martin, 1983; Schaefer, 1965). In recent years, Baumrind (1989) labeled parenting control in terms of degrees of demandingness and responsiveness, which are manifested in parent-child relationships as firm control/restrictiveness and warmth/noncoerciveness. These various dimensions of parental control (behaviors) were categorized in Elder's (1962) classic study of structural variations in child-rearing relationships. Seven child-rearing (parenting) styles were identified in this study: autocratic (authoritative), authoritarian, democratic, egalitarian, permissive, laissez-faire, and ignoring. These typologies have been repeatedly used as researchers have attempted to relate parental behaviors to meaningful aspects of adolescent development. The role of parental control in promoting high-risk behaviors among adolescents is unclear. One proposed explanation is that exposing a child to inept parenting practices increases adolescents' vulnerability to high-risk behaviors (Simons, Whitbeck, Conger, & Conger, 1991). According to this hypothesis, parents of troubled adolescents tend to make use of authoritarian or laissez-faire disciplining styles, whereas parents of non-high-risk adolescents are more likely to use authoritative or democratic styles. Adolescents who characterize their parents as authoritarian are described as being obedient and conforming to standards of adults. They also do well in school and are less likely than their peers to engage in deviant activities. On the other hand, adolescents' perception of self-reliance, in terms of social and academic abilities, is lacking compared with those whose parents use authoritative styles (Jurich, Polson, Jurich, & Bates, 1985). It is thought that authoritarian parenting during adolescence may produce social and instrumental incompetence and problematic behavior (Baumrind, 1968). Moreover, problems occur for children of laissez-faire parents because these parents remove all controls so as not to impose their values on their adolescents; yet, these children exhibit hostile and indifferent feelings toward their parents. Lack of structure and monitoring, as well as low responsiveness, are thought to result in impulsiveness, delinquent behavior, and precocious experimentation with sex, drugs, and alcohol among adolescents (Lamborn, Mounts, Steinberg, & Dornbusch, 1991). In contrast, adolescents who characterize their parents as authoritative are better adjusted, more competent and confident about their abilities, and less likely than their peers to get into trouble (Lamborn et al., 1991).

Attention also has been given to understanding the impact of parental neglect and indulgence on adolescent adjustment. Results from one investigation revealed that adolescents who characterize their parents as neglectful are consistently compromised in areas of competence, self-perception, and misbehavior and tend to be psychologically distressed. Adolescents who are indulged are similar to those from neglectful homes in that they are relatively disengaged from school, have higher involvement in drug and alcohol use, and frequently engage in school misconduct (Fletcher, 1992; Maccoby & Martin, 1983; Schaefer, 1965; Steinberg, Mounts, & Dornbusch, 1991). Overall, research seems to suggest that too much or too little positive parental involvement promotes negative outcomes for adolescents.

Inflexible families may, unintentionally, create irresponsible, high-risk behavior in their adolescents (Steinberg et al., 1991). According to Peterson, Rollins, and Thomas (1985), adolescents whose parents exercise very strict discipline and a high degree of control are at high risk for pregnancy and childbearing. However, moderate to slight strictness from parents results in delayed onset of first coitus and decreased likelihood of adolescent pregnancy among their daughters. Results from Miller, McCoy, Olson, and Wallace (1986) are in agreement with these findings. An examination of parental control and sexual activity among white Mormon adolescents revealed that those whose parents were very lenient and imposed few rules and minimum restrictions had a high incidence of pregnancy. However, excessive strictness and many rules increased risk of pregnancy and childbearing. Similar findings were reported in African American adolescent females (Hogan & Kitagawa, 1985; Murry, 1992). Taken together, these findings seem to suggest that very strict discipline and a high degree of control may result in short-term effectiveness in deterring the development of behavioral problems. In the long run, adolescents may rebel against these coercive strategies.

*Family Dynamics*

In addition to parental control, empirical research indicates that the quality of the relationship between adolescents and parents also appears to influence the extent to which adolescents engage in high-risk behaviors (Roebuck & McGee, 1977; Zelnik, Kantner, & Ford, 1981). For example, some researchers suggest that adolescents are more vulnerable to pregnancy when their families do not foster emotional connectedness because the adolescent feels socially and emotionally isolated. That is, adolescent pregnancy and childbearing may be a mechanism for compensating for these feelings (Grotevant & Cooper, 1985). In fact, lack of happiness in the parental home and feelings of social and emotional isolation have been found to be associated with greater incidence of multiple sex partners among adolescents (Lewis, 1973). Another hypothesis is that pregnancy and childbearing may be hostile acts of defiance toward parents as adolescents attempt to establish identity in an enmeshed family (Nadelson, Notman, & Gillon, 1978).

After thoroughly reviewing the literature, Phipps-Yonas (1980) found that adolescents who had become pregnant during the 1960s and early 1970s were more likely to come from homes marked by poor family relationships and were somewhat more socially isolated and untrusting. Inadequate bonding between parent and child appears to be a strong predictor of high-risk behaviors among adolescents (Gove & Crutchfield, 1982). Moreover, family stress, strain, and conflict have been identified as the most important predictors of adolescent pregnancy and childbearing (Knowles & Tripple, 1986; Robbins, Kaplan, & Martin, 1985). Research results revealed that pregnant adolescents were more likely than nonpregnant adolescents to see their families as exhibiting less pride and strength, perceiving their parents as being more problematic and closed (Barnett, Papini, & Gbur, 1991) and as exhibiting inconsistent, noncohesive, and maladaptive behaviors (Romig & Bakken, 1980).

*Suicide*

Transitions associated with adolescence and individual and family responses to these changes can precipitate crises in the developing adolescent's life. It is not uncommon for adolescents to respond to these changes by developing feelings of alienation, emotionally distancing themselves from others, and even fantasizing about death. While the number of adolescents who attempt and commit suicide is less than in many adult cohorts, the rates of suicide among all youth aged 15 to 24 years have tripled in the last 20 years (Macdonald, 1987; Schuckit & Schuckit, 1989). As alarming as these figures are, they often do not include deaths that may have been victim precipitated but are recorded as accidents (e.g., drownings, single-person car crashes, drug overdoses, homicides). An examination of racial differences in suicide rates reveals that Native Americans have the highest rates (19.4 per 100,000), followed by whites (13.4 per 100,000), with 7 per 100,000 for African Americans. Although African American adolescents have the lowest suicide rate, the greatest change in suicide among adolescents from 1960 to 1980 was attributed to increased rates among these youths. In fact, suicide is now the third leading cause of death among African American youth (Myers, 1989; U.S. Bureau of the Census, 1986).

Several explanations have been offered for the increased adolescent suicide rate among African Americans. One thought is that stress associated with being poor, discriminated against, dealing with everyday life in urban areas (i.e., excessive overcrowding of neighborhoods, high levels of crime and violence, and social isolation from mainstream society) may be manifested by feelings of depression, powerlessness, despair, and suicide (Myers, 1989). Others suggest a link between suicide and homicide (Gibbs, 1988; Hendin, 1987; Weddle & McKenry, in press). Recent data indicate that African American males are five times more likely than white males to be murdered, and African American females are four times more likely than white females to be murdered (Hacker, 1983). Thus homicide among African American youth, particularly males, may be "victim-precipitated" murders in many cases, provoked by the adolescent as a way out (Seiden, 1972). The interconnectedness of suicide, homicide, and accidents among adolescents has been referred to as the "new morbidity" and may more adequately reflect the increasing self-destructive behaviors among African American males (Gibbs, 1988).

Given that adolescent behavior appears to be associated with various aspects of family dynamics and family functioning, a discussion of adolescent suicidal behavior would be incomplete without giving some consideration to these contributions and influences. The types of families at risk of having a suicidal adolescent have not been clearly identified. Nevertheless, research demonstrates a positive correlation between family stress and limited ability to respond appropriately to a suicidal crisis (Palozny, Davenport, & Kim, 1991).

Several salient characteristics continue to manifest themselves in families of suicidal adolescents (Cosand, Bourque, & Kraus, 1982; Tishler, McKenry, & Morgan, 1981). These families frequently have a closed system and rules of communication that do not permit the suicidal adolescent to openly state his or her needs (Pfeffer, 1981, 1986). In addition, suicidal adolescents tend to describe their family environments as negative, less cohesive, higher in conflict, less supportive, stressful, and less controlled than nonsuicidal adolescents (Pfeffer, Zuckerman, Plutchik, & Mezruchi, 1984). It is also not uncommon for adolescents at risk of suicide to describe their parents' marital interactions in terms of ambivalence and anger (Pfeffer, 1981) or as one parent being frequently angry or depressed much of the time (Wright, 1985). This family atmosphere creates a feeling of gloom throughout the family (Sands & Dixon, 1986). Moreover, an adolescent may internalize the family conflict and feel guilty, unloved, and rejected as well as experiencing self-hate. Under these circumstances, an adolescent may view suicide as a means of escaping the pain of living in a dysfunctional family.

Cohen-Sandler, Berman, and King (1982) postulated that children in a context of intensely stressful, chaotic, and unpredictable family events use suicide as a means of interpersonal coercion or retaliation (p. 184). Others suggest that the suicidal act itself communicates that there are long-standing family problems that have interfered with adolescents' struggle to get their needs met in dysfunctional family systems (Pfeffer, 1981). Thus a closed family system, intense ambivalence, marital conflict, and lack of emotional closeness in the family appear to be important antecedents to adolescent suicide.

Substance and drug abuse, either by adolescents or someone in their families, has been associated with increase risk of suicide. Recent national data revealed that 30% to 40% of adolescents who attempt suicide have parents who abuse alcohol (Report of the Secretary's Task Force on Youth Suicide, 1989). Many suicidal adolescents have a history of drug use and/or use drugs in their attempts.

### Drug Abuse

Separate and apart from being associated with suicide, substance and drug use and abuse among adolescents continue to be serious problems and national concerns. Results from a study of a nationally representative sample of high school seniors revealed that alcohol and cigarettes are by far the most commonly used "legal" drugs (Johnston, O'Malley, & Bachman, 1989). Almost all high school seniors had tried alcohol; about half had tried marijuana (one fourth within the month of the survey); and more than two thirds had tried cigarettes. Of those who used alcohol, 64% indicated that they drink on a regular basis. Over one third of the seniors reported having abused alcohol (had more than five drinks in a row) on frequent occasions. Research studies also revealed that males drink more than females; Hispanic adolescents, particularly Dominican adolescents, are at greatest risk of alcohol abuse, followed by white adolescents, with the lowest frequency of alcohol use found among African American high school seniors (Benson & Donahue, 1989; Johnston et al., 1989).

An examination of patterns of substance and drug use among adolescents over time revealed that the proportion of seniors reporting daily use of marijuana and alcohol peaked in the late 1970s, declined steadily during the early 1980s, and plateaued during the mid-1980s. Further, Johnston and associates (1989) reported that use of other drugs among adolescents followed a similar pattern, with one exception. Cocaine use was greater among high school seniors during the mid-1980s than in previous decades (Johnston et al., 1989). Further, although alcohol, cigarette, and marijuana use among adolescents declined during the early-1980s, the overall pattern of use has remained unchanged since the mid-1980s. This pattern suggests that a large proportion of adolescents remain at risk of abuse.

Many factors appear to influence whether adolescents will use harder drugs. Some suggest that use of alcohol by parents and siblings, family stress, and level of parents' depression are the most influential factors

(Onestak, Forman, & Linney, 1989). Others have found that, compared with families of non-substance abusing adolescents, those who were substance abusers had families characterized as rigidly enmeshed, with unclear generational boundaries, overly involved mother-child relationships, and strained father-child relationships (Levine, 1985; Volk, Edwards, Lewis, & Sprenkle, 1989). Moreover, Kaufman (1985), as well as Stanton (1985), indicated that certain qualities of substance abusers' family systems differ from those of other dysfunctional families and "normal" families. These qualities include (a) the prevalence of multigenerational chemical dependency, (b) explicit alliances with primitive and direct expressions of conflict, (c) artificial independence of substance abusers through affiliation with a drug-oriented peer group, (d) symbiotic ties between the mother and substance abusers lasting into the child's adult life, (e) a preponderance of death themes and premature, unexpected or untimely deaths, and (f) pseudoindividuation of the substance abuser that maintains family equilibrium through a facade of defiance.

Results from one study revealed that families of substance abusing adolescents had experienced a higher incidence of loss and critical changes, such as death of a spouse or close friend, divorce, relocation, and launching children (Harkins, Linney, & Forman, 1989). Within the same context, others have focused on the extent to which lack of opportunities, because of inadequate educational opportunities and economic resources, leads to frustration and results in adolescents searching for alternative pathways to rewards and fulfillment (Cloward & Oblin, 1960). However, this theory has weak empirical support (Bachman et al., 1981; Kandel, 1980). During the 1980s the life opportunity theory was expanded to include a broader view of adolescents' social and economic situation. This approach is called the "social stress" model and focuses on the long-term outcome individuals experience with significant others and social systems from birth through adolescence (Rhodes & Jason, 1990). According to this perspective, adolescents initiate substance use as a means of coping with a variety of stressors and influences that may arise within the family, school, peer group, or community. Individuals in a less than optimal social environment will be more resilient or invulnerable to substance and drug abuse if they are members of prosocial, supportive social networks.

The social stress model may be useful in understanding substance and drug use and abuse among urban youth. Rhodes and Jason (1990) cited the following reasons for testing this model on this subpopulation. First, because of the prevalence of alcohol, drugs, and gang activity, urban families are continually faced with the challenge of preventing substance use and abuse among their children. Second, living in impoverished neighborhoods, many urban youth find themselves confronted by life options that are not viewed as acceptable pathways to adulthood but are more feasible in their culture of disempowerment. For example, gang activity and drug dealing create extremely powerful positions in urban settings. Third, greater incidence and frequency of drug taking occurs, in general, in this subgroup, compared with declines elsewhere. Fourth, given the social environment of urban life, many norms and behaviors once thought to be pathogenic are often quite functional. A fifth reason for studying urban youth is that examining variations in these adolescents' behavior will provide useful information about the pathways to delinquency and substance abuse.

Investigations of urban African American youth reveal that the primary influences on the severity of drug use are poor family environment and low assertiveness (Ensminger, 1990; Volk et al., 1989). More specifically, weak sibling and parental relationships, a lack of perceived support and encouragement, and a high degree of family problems are related to a higher level of usage. Other empirical studies on nonurban youth also indicate that family functioning and support appear to serve as a buffer in creating stress-resilient adolescents with regard to substance abuse. Further, youth who are able to set limits with their peers and feel comfortable asserting their own opinions and needs are more resilient to drug use (Barrett, Simpson, & Lehman, 1988; Huba, Wingard, & Bentler, 1980).

It has been suggested that paternal absence is equated with substance abuse because disrupted families negatively influence the emotional development (Wallerstein & Kelly, 1980), social development (Hetherington, 1972), and interpersonal relationships (Hetherington, 1988) of adolescents. This perspective has been supported by the work of Brook, Whiteman, and Gordon (1985). After examining the interrelationships among parental absence, family characteristics, and adolescent's drug use, these authors found that youth in homes where the father was absent reported higher use of drugs than did those from father-present homes. Further, the absence or presence of the father appeared to be associated with two aspects of parent-adolescent relationships: (a) Adolescents in father-absent homes significantly exceeded adolescents in father-present homes in reporting less parental warmth and identification, lower parental expectations, and more paternal models of drug use (drinking, smoking cigarettes, and marijuana use); (b) adolescents from father-absent homes in comparison to those from father-present homes reported less maternal warmth and permissiveness, more maternal negative, rejecting behavior, and higher levels of maternal drug use (smoking and marijuana use); and (c) adolescents from father-

absent homes reported greater parental conflict and sibling drug use than
did those from father-present homes. Adolescents in father-absent homes
may be more susceptible to substance abuse because they have to cope not
only with the absence of a parent but also with family conditions that are
less than optimal (Volk et al., 1989). For example, virtually all data on the
income status of families indicate that father-absent/female-headed families are among the poorest of U.S. families.

Gender differences in substance use have been observed among adolescents from divorced families. Higher levels of substance use were found
among males. However, the rate of substance involvement decreased for
boys when their parent remarried. At the same time, adolescent females'
substance use tended to increase when their parent remarried (Manners &
Smart, 1992; Needle, Su, & Doherty, 1990). It is possible that adolescent
males in stepfather families are more independent than their counterparts
in other family types. Or the presence of a stepfather may mitigate the
adverse effects of the biological father's absence, as the adolescent male
becomes attached to his stepfather (White, Brinkerhoff, & Booth, 1985).
Finally, a parent's remarriage may generate a less favorable family environment for adolescent females.

## Coping and Adaptation Strategies

Coping is an important component of the stress process. Families with
adolescents may use several approaches to meet the demands associated
with this stage of development. To understand this phenomenon, it seems
central to ask: What type of families and adolescents, under what conditions, use certain coping strategies in response to the timing and relative
"pileup" or accumulation of changes associated with this developmental
stage? Researchers have identified differential coping patterns of families
with high- versus low-risk adolescents. More specifically, families with
non-high-risk adolescents are more likely to seek information and advice
from relatives, friends, and professionals as well as use prayer to cope with
stressful situations, whereas families with high-risk adolescents tend to use
avoidance or denial, keep feelings inside, or use drugs and alcohol to ease
tension (Manners & Smart, 1992).

Adolescent coping strategies appear to differ depending on gender, with
girls having a broader range of coping patterns than males. For example,
female coping patterns are geared toward reducing demands (i.e., problem
solving, ventilating feelings), increasing personal resources (e.g., develop-

ing self-reliance and investing in close relationships), and increasing community resources (e.g., developing social support and seeking professional support). Adolescent males, on the other hand, engage in activities that divert their attention from the tension, such as engaging in social activities (movies, watching television, working on a hobby), avoiding the problem, and being humorous (Hauser et al., 1984; Patterson & McCubbin, 1987).

In sum, families can minimize stress and decrease the potential for high-risk behavior among adolescents if they are accepting and understanding (Hauser et al., 1984), when there is a balance of family connectedness and adaptability (Grotevant & Cooper, 1985; McCubbin & Patterson, 1986), and when social support systems are available for families confronted with economic and interpersonal crises. Effective coping among adolescents is evidenced by their ability to "manage individual and family-related demands with capabilities and achieve a fit both within the family and within the community" (Patterson & McCubbin, 1987, p. 164).

## Conclusions and Implications

Adolescence has been described as a time of intense demands for the individual and the family. This chapter has incorporated, for the most part, empirical and theoretical writings reflecting the nature, antecedents, and consequences of the families' and individuals' responses to adolescent development. The information presented may have implications for understanding and identifying stressors, strains, stress, and potential crises associated with rearing an adolescent. The extent to which this developmental stage precipitates family stress and crisis, however, depends on various individual, familial, and social factors.

For instance, overall, girls fare better with their families than boys (Csikszentmihalyi & Larson, 1984). Evidence presented in this chapter shows that females may be more prepared than males to manage and endure the piling-up effects of daily hassles and developmental transitions of adolescence. More specifically, adolescent females use coping strategies that are aimed at reducing demands and increasing personal resources. They are also more likely to seek assistance from community resources. On the contrary, adolescent males tend to use coping strategies characterized by avoidance—attempting to escape from the emotional stress and demands created by stressors. Unfortunately, this style of coping prolongs, rather than resolves or manages, the situation.

The literature reviewed in this chapter has several implications for family life educators, counselors, and practitioners as well as researchers. For family life educators, efforts should be devoted to assisting families in providing a basis for adolescent identity exploration, which promotes individuality as well as family connectedness. Educational programs designed for these families must include goals aimed at improving stress management skills, building family strengths, and enhancing family communication skills. Counselors and practitioners working with parents of adolescents should explore ways of helping families effectively balance cohesion and adaptability to mesh with the needs of the developing family member. Clinicians, as well as parents and educators, need to develop ways of broadening and enhancing the coping repertoire of adolescent males.

In future research, consideration should be given to examining various family-adolescent relationships of African American, Asian, Hispanic, and Native American families from a normative perspective rather than from a social problem perspective. Information obtained from such studies should be useful in developing family intervention and prevention programs for families of color. There is also a need to know more about stress, coping, and adaptation of low-income, urban families with adolescents. For example, how do these families effectively meet the pileup of stressors resulting from both "normal" and extraordinary tasks associated with living in a severely oppressed social and economic environment? There is a need to know more about the extent to which gender-role socialization influences the coping repertoire of adolescent males and females. In addition, future inquiry should focus on furthering our understanding of why males fare less well than females in families that successfully "weather" this developmental stage.

## References

Adelson, J., & Doehrman, M. J. (1980). The psychodynamic approach to adolescence. In J. Adelson (Ed.), *Handbook of the psychology of adolescence* (pp. 99-116). New York: John Wiley.

Anderson, E. R., Hetherington, E. M., & Clingempeel, W. G. (1989). Transformations in family relations on puberty: Effects of family context. *Journal of Early Adolescence, 9*, 310-334.

Bachman, J. G., Johnston, L. D., & O'Malley, P. M. (1981). Smoking, drinking, and drug use among high school students: Correlates and trends. *American Journal of Public Health, 71*, 59-68.

Barnett, J. K., Papini, D. R., & Gbur, E. (1991). Familial correlates of sexually active pregnant and nonpregnant adolescents. *Adolescence, 26*, 458-472.

Barrett, M. E., Simpson, D., & Lehman, W. (1988). Behavioral changes of adolescents in drug abuse intervention programs. *Journal of Clinical Psychology, 44*, 462-463.

Baumrind, D. (1968). Authoritarian vs authoritative control. *Adolescence, 3*, 154-162.

Baumrind, D. (1989). Parenting styles and adolescent development. In J. Brooks-Gunn, R. Lerner, & A. C. Peterson (Eds.), *The encyclopedia on adolescence* (pp. 746-758). New York: Garland.

Bell-Scott, P., & McKenry, P. C. (1985). Black adolescents and their families. In G. K. Leigh & G. W. Peterson (Eds.), *Adolescents in families* (pp. 410-432). Cincinnati, OH: South-Western Publishing.

Benson, P. L., & Donahue, M. J. (1989). Ten-year trends in at-risk behaviors: A national study of African-American adolescents. *Journal of Adolescent Research, 4*, 125-139.

Blos, P. (1970). *The adolescent passage*. New York: International Universities Press.

Brook, J. S., Whiteman, M., & Gordon, A. S. (1985). Father absence, perceived family characteristics and stage of drug use in adolescence. *British Journal of Developmental Psychology, 2*, 87-94.

Cloward, R. A., & Oblin, L. E. (1960). *Delinquency and opportunity*. New York: Free Press.

Cohen-Sandler, R., Berman, A. L., & King, R. A. (1982). Life stress and symptomatology determinants of suicidal behavior in children. *Journal of the American Academy of Child Psychiatry, 21*, 178-186.

Cosand, B. J., Bourque, L. B., & Kraus, J. F. (1982). Suicide among adolescents in Sacramento County, California 1950-1979. *Adolescence, 17*, 917-930.

Crockett, L. J., & Petersen, A. C. (1987). Pubertal status and psychosocial development: Finding from the early adolescence study. In R. Lerner & T. T. Foch (Eds.), *Biological-psychological interactions in early adolescence: A life-span perspective* (pp. 173-188). Hillsdale, NJ: Lawrence Erlbaum.

Csikszentmihalyi, M., & Larson, R. (1984). *Being adolescent: Conflict and growth in the teenage years*. New York: Basic Books.

Danon-Boileau, H. (1982). Parental crisis facing their child. *L'Evaluation Psychiatrique, 47*, 157-157.

Elder, G. H. (1962). Structural variations in the childrearing relationships. *Sociometry, 25*, 141-162.

Ensminger, M. E. (1990). Sexual activity and problem behaviors among African American, urban adolescents. *Child Development, 61*, 2032-2046.

Fletcher, A. C. (1992, March). *Parenting style and aggressive versus nonaggressive misconduct in preadolescence*. Paper presented at the Biennial Society for Research on Adolescence Conference, Washington, DC.

Gibbs, J. T. (1988). The new morbidity: Homicide, suicide, accidents, and life-threatening behaviors. In J. T. Gibbs (Ed.), *Young, black, and male in America: An endangered species* (pp. 258-293). Dover, MA: Auburn House.

Gove, W. R., & Crutchfield, R. D. (1982). The family and juvenile delinquency. *Sociological Quarterly, 23*, 301-319.

Grotevant, H. D., & Cooper, C. R. (1985). Patterns of interaction in family relationships and the development of identity explanation in adolescence. *Child Development, 56*, 415-428.

Hacker, A. (1983). *U.S.: A statistical portrait of American people*. New York: Penguin.

Harkins, C., Linney, J. A., & Forman, S. G. (1989, August). *The ecology of substance use: Family characteristics of high-risk teens.* Paper presented at the annual meeting of the American Psychological Association.

Hauser, S. T., Liebman, W., Houlihan, D., Powers, S. I., Jacobson, A. M., Noam, G. G., Weiss, B., & Follansbee, D. C. (1984). Family contexts of pubertal timing. *Journal of Youth and Adolescence, 14*, 317-337.

Hendin, H. (1987). Youth suicide: A psychological perspective. *Suicide and Life-Threatening Behavior, 17*, 151-165.

Hetherington, E. M. (1972). Effects of father absence on personality development in adolescent daughters. *Developmental Psychology, 26*, 97-136.

Hetherington, E. M. (1988). Parents, children, and sibs 6 years after divorce. In R. Hinde & J. Stevenson-Hinde (Eds.), *Relationships within families: Mutual influence* (pp. 311-331). Oxford: Clarendon.

Hill, J. (1980). The family. In M. Johnson (Ed.), *Toward adolescence: The middle school years* (pp. 32-55). Chicago: University of Chicago Press.

Hill, J. P., Holmbeck, G. N., Marlow, L., Green, T. M., & Lynch, M. E. (1986). Menarcheal status and parent-child relations in families of seventh-grade girls. *Journal of Youth and Adolescence, 14*, 301-316.

Hogan, D. P., & Kitagawa, E. N. (1985). The impact of social status, family structure, and neighborhood on the fertility of African-American adolescents. *American Journal of Sociology, 90*, 825-855.

Hollier, E. A. (1988). *Parent-child relationships during remarriage.* Unpublished doctoral dissertation, University of Virginia, Charlottesville.

Huba, G. J., Wingard, J. A., & Bentler, P. M. (1980). Applications of a theory of drug use to prevention programs. *Journal of Drug Education, 10*, 25-38.

Jessor, R., & Jessor, S. L. (1977). *Problem behavior and psychosocial development: A longitudinal study of youth.* New York: Academic Press.

Johnston, L. D., O'Malley, P. M., & Bachman, J. G. (1989). *Drug use, drinking and smoking: National survey results from high school, college, and young adult populations, 1975-1988* (DHHS Publication No. ADM89-1638). Washington, DC: Government Printing Office.

Jurich, A. P., Polson, C. J., Jurich, J. A., & Bates, R. A. (1985). Family factors in the lives of drug users and abusers. *Adolescence, 20*, 143-159.

Kandel, D. B. (1980). Drug and drinking behavior among youth. *Annual Review of Sociology, 6*, 235-285.

Kaplan, H. B. (1980). *Deviant behavior in defense of self.* New York: Academic Press.

Kaufman, E. (1985). Family systems and family therapy of substance abuse: An overview of two decades of research and clinical experience. *The International Journal of the Addictions, 20*, 897-916.

Knowles, G. A., & Tripple, P. A. (1986). Teen pregnancy: Effect on family well-being. *Journal of Home Economics, 78*, 25-29.

Lamborn, S. D., Mounts, N. S., Steinberg, L., & Dornbusch, S. M. (1991). Patterns of competence and adjustment among adolescents from authoritarian, authoritative, indulgent, and neglectful families. *Child Development, 62*, 1049-1065.

Lerner, R., Karson, M., Meisels, M., & Knapp, J. R. (1975). Actual and perceived attitudes of late adolescents: The phenomenon of the generation gaps. *Journal of Genetics Psychology, 126*, 197-207.

Levine, B. L. (1985). Adolescent substance abuse: Toward an integration of family system and individual adaptation theories. *The American Journal of Family Therapy, 13*, 3-16.

Lewis, R. A. (1973). Parents and peers: Socialization agents in the coital behavior of young adults. *Journal of Sex Research, 9,* 156-170.

Loeber, R., & Dishion, T. (1983). Early predictors of male delinquency: A review. *Psychological Bulletin, 94,* 68-94.

Maccoby, E., & Martin, J. (1983). Socialization in the context of the family: Parent-child interaction. In E. M. Hetherington (Ed.), *Handbook of child psychology: Vol. 4. Socialization, personality, and social development* (pp. 1-101). New York: John Wiley.

Macdonald, D. I. (1987). *Suicide among youth: ADMHA Update.* Washington, DC: Government, Alcohol, Drug Abuse and Mental Health Administration.

Manners, P., & Smart, D. (1992, April). *Family type as a predictor of sexual intercourse and alcohol use in young adolescents.* Paper presented at the annual meeting of the American Educational Research Association, San Francisco.

McCubbin, H. I., & Patterson, J. M. (1986). Adolescent stress, coping, and adaptation: A normative family perspective. In G. Leigh & G. Peterson (Eds.), *Adolescence in families* (pp. 256-276). Cincinnati, OH: South-Western Publishing.

McCubbin, H. I., Patterson, J. N., Bauman, E., & Harris, L. (1981). *A-FILE: Adolescent-Family Inventory of Life Events and Changes.* St. Paul: University of Minnesota, Family Social Science.

Miller, B. C., McCoy, J. K., Olson, T. D., & Wallace, C. N. (1986). Parental discipline and control attempts in relation to adolescent sexual attitudes and behavior. *Journal of Marriage and the Family, 48,* 503-512.

Murry, V. M. (1992, November). *Family and individual predictors of first coitus among middle-class African American adolescent females.* Paper presented at the National Council on Family Relations Annual Conference, Orlando, FL.

Myers, H. F. (1989). Urban stress and the mental health of Afro-American youth. In R. Jones (Ed.), *Black adolescents* (pp. 123-152). Berkeley, CA: Cobb & Henry.

Nadelson, C. C., Notman, M. T., & Gillon, J. (1978). *The woman patient: Medical and psychological interfaces.* New York: Plenum.

Needle, R. H., Su, S. S., & Doherty, W. G. (1990). Divorce, remarriage, and adolescent substance use: A prospective longitudinal study. *Journal of Marriage and the Family, 52,* 157-169.

Neugarten, B. L. (1979). Time, age, and life-cycle. *The American Journal of Psychology, 136,* 887-894.

Neugarten, B. L., & Datan, N. C. (1973). Sociological perspectives on the life-cycle. In P. Bates & K. W. Schaie (Eds.), *Life-span developmental psychology: Personality and socialization* (pp. 53-69). New York: Academic Press.

Newman, B. M., & Newman, P. R. (1986). *Adolescent development.* Columbus, OH: Charles E. Merrill.

Olson, D. H., & Cromwell, R. E. (1975). Power in families. In R. E. Cromwell & D. H. Olson (Eds.), *Power in families* (pp. 114-132). New York: John Wiley.

Olson, D. H., & McCubbin, H. I. (1983). *Families: What makes them work.* Beverly Hills, CA: Sage.

Onestak, D. M., Forman, S. G., & Linney, J. A. (1989, August). *Family variables and alcohol use in high risk adolescents.* Paper presented at the annual meeting of the American Psychological Association.

Palozny, M., Davenport, C., & Kim, W. J. (1991). Suicidal attempts and ideation: Adolescents evaluated on a pediatric ward. *Adolescence, 26,* 210-215.

Papini, D. R., & Datan, N. (1983). *The transitions into adolescence: An interactional perspec-tive.* Paper presented at the biennial meeting of the Society for Research in Child Develop-ment, Detroit, MI.

Patterson, J. M., & McCubbin, H. I. (1987). Adolescent coping style and behaviors: Concep-tualization and measurement. *Journal of Adolescence, 10,* 163-186.

Peskin, H. (1973). Influence of the developmental schedule of puberty on learning and ego functioning. *Journal of Youth and Adolescence, 4,* 273-290.

Petersen, A. C. (1982). Developmental issues in adolescent health. In T. J. Coates, A. C. Petersen, & C. Perry (Eds.), *Promoting adolescent health: A dialog on research and prac-tice* (pp. 61-72). New York: Academic Press.

Petersen, A. C., Ebata, A. T., & Graber, J. A. (1987). *Coping with adolescence: The functions and dysfunction of poor achievement.* Presented at the biennial meeting of the Society of Research on Child Development, Baltimore, MD.

Petersen, A. C., & Taylor, B. (1980). The biological approach to adolescence. In J. Adelson (Ed.), *Handbook of adolescent psychology* (pp. 117-155). New York: John Wiley.

Peterson, G. W., Rollins, B. C., & Thomas, D. L. (1985). Parental influence and adolescent conformity: Compliance and internalization. *Youth and Society, 16,* 397-420.

Pfeffer, C. R. (1981). The family system of suicidal children. *American Journal of Psycho-therapy, 35,* 207-219.

Pfeffer, C. R. (1986). *The suicidal child.* New York: Guilford.

Pfeffer, C. R., Zuckerman, S., Plutchik, R., & Mezruchi, M. S. (1984). Suicidal behavior in normal school children: A comparison with child psychiatric inpatients. *Journal of the American Academy of Child Psychiatry, 23,* 416-423.

Phipps-Yonas, S. (1980). Teenage pregnancy and motherhood: A review of the literature. *American Journal of Orthopsychiatry, 50,* 210-225.

Report of the Secretary's Task Force on Youth Suicide. (1989). *Overview and recommendations* (Vol. 1, DHHS Publication No. ADM 89-1621). Washington, DC: Government Printing Office.

Rhodes, J. E., & Jason, L. A. (1990). A social-stress model of substance abuse. *Journal of Consulting and Clinical Psychology, 58,* 395-401.

Robbins, C., Kaplan, H. B., & Martin, S. S. (1985). Antecedents of pregnancy among unmar-ried adolescents. *Journal of Marriage and the Family, 47,* 567-583.

Roebuck, J., & McGee, N. G. (1977). Attitudes toward pre-marital sex and sexual behavior among African-American high school girls. *Journal of Sex Research, 13,* 104-114.

Rollins, B. C., & Thomas, D. L. (1979). Parental support, power, and control techniques in the socialization of children. In W. R. Burr, F. I. Nye, R. Hill, & I. L. Reiss (Eds.), *Contempo-rary theories about the family* (Vol. 1, pp. 317-364). New York: Free Press.

Romig, C. A., & Bakken, L. (1980). Teens at risk for pregnancy: The role of ego development and family processes. *Journal of Adolescence, 13,* 195-199.

Rutter, N. (1980). *Changing youth in a changing society: Patterns of adolescent development and disorder.* Cambridge, MA: Harvard University Press.

Sands, R. G., & Dixon, S. L. (1986). Adolescent crises and suicidal behavior: Dynamics and treatment. *Child and Adolescent Social Work, 3,* 109-122.

Schaefer, E. S. (1965). Children's reports of parental behavior: An inventory. *Child Develop-ment, 36,* 413-424.

Schuckit, M. A., & Schuckit, J. J. (1989). Substance use and abuse: A risk factor in youth suicide. In J. Kagan (Ed.), *The emergence of moral concepts in young children* (pp. 155-172). Chicago: University of Chicago Press.

Seiden, R. H. (1972). Why are suicides of young African Americans increasing? (H.S.M.H.A.) *Health Report, 87,* 3-8.

Silberison, R. K., & Noack, P. (1988). On the constructive role of problem behavior in adolescence. In N. Bolger, A. Caspi, G. Downey, & M. Moorhouse (Eds.), *Persons and context, developmental processes* (pp. 152-180). Cambridge: Cambridge University Press.

Simmons, R. G., & Blyth, D. A. (1987). *Moving into adolescence: The impact of pubertal change and school context.* New York: Aldine.

Simons, R. L., Whitbeck, L. B., Conger, R. D., & Conger, K. J. (1991). Parenting factors, social skills, and value commitments as precursors to school failure, involvement with deviant peers, and delinquent behavior. *Journal of Youth and Adolescence, 20,* 645-663.

Stanton, M. D. (1985). The family and drug abuse. In T. E. Bratter & G. G. Forrest (Eds.), *Alcoholism and substance abuse: Strategies for clinical intervention* (pp. 398-430). New York: Free Press.

Steinberg, L. D. (1981). Transformations in family relations at puberty. *Developmental Psychology, 17,* 833-840.

Steinberg, L. D. (1987). Family processes at adolescence: A developmental perspective. *Family Therapy, 14,* 77-86.

Steinberg, L., Mounts, N. S., & Dornbusch, S. (1991). Authoritative parenting and adolescent adjustment across various ecological niches. *Journal of Research on Adolescence, 1,* 19-36.

Tanner, J. M. (1972). Sequence, tempo, and individual variation in growth and development of boys and girls aged 12 and 16. In J. Kagan & R. Coles (Eds.), *12 to 16: Early adolescence* (pp. 1-24). New York: Norton.

Tishler, C. L., McKenry, P. C., & Morgan, K. C. (1981). Adolescent suicide attempts: Some significant factors. *Suicide and Life-Threatening Behavior, 11,* 86-92.

Tolan, P. (1986, August). *Social stress dimensions and antisocial and delinquent behaviors in adolescents.* Paper presented at the annual convention of the American Psychological Association, Washington, DC.

U.S. Bureau of the Census. (1986). *Statistical abstract of the United States.* Washington, DC: U.S. Department of Commerce.

Volk, R. J., Edwards, D. W., Lewis, R. A., & Sprenkle, D. H. (1989). Family system of adolescent substance abusers. *Family Relations, 38,* 266-272.

Wallerstein, J. S., & Kelly, J. B. (1980). *Surviving the break-up: How children and parents cope with divorce.* New York: Basic Books.

Weddle, K. D., & McKenry, P. C. (in press). Self-destructive behaviors among black youth: Suicide and homicide. In R. Taylor (Ed.), *Black youth: Perspectives on their status in the United States.* Newbury Park, CA: Sage.

Wendt, H. (1983). Crisis in our life: The crisis of puberty and the crisis of midlife. *Partnerberatung, 20,* 96-106.

White, L. K., Brinkerhoff, D. B., & Booth, A. (1985). The effect of marital disruption on child's attachment to parents. *Journal of Family Issues, 6,* 5-22.

Wright, L. S. (1985). Suicidal thoughts and their relationship to family stress and personal problems among high school seniors and college under-graduates. *Adolescence, 20,* 575-580.

Zelnik, M., Kantner, J. F., & Ford, K. (1981). *Sex and pregnancy in adolescence.* Beverly Hills, CA: Sage.

# 6

# Coping With Aging

JAY A. MANCINI
ROSEMARY BLIESZNER

Transition and developmental change characterize the later years of the life cycle. The often-called "golden years" have great potential for equanimity and satisfaction while at the same time may be tarnished by changes in family structure, health, economic security, and close relationships. Many of these changes result in added stress for family members across generations.

If we live long enough, we can expect that certain events will intersect our lives, among them physical aging. These events reflect role transitions because a person's place in society and what is expected of a person shift, and are greatly affected by demographic factors, health, retirement, economics, intergenerational relationships, and loss of relationships.

## The Aging Society and Family Demographic Factors

Brubaker (1990) has summarized a number of salient dimensions of societal and individual aging. Since 1900 the number of Americans at least 65 years of age increased from about 3 million to about 30 million; their percentage of the U.S. population increased from about 4% to about 11%.

AUTHORS' NOTE: We appreciate the participation of Dan M. Sandifer in the preparation of this chapter.

According to the U.S. Senate Special Committee on Aging (1991), black and Hispanic populations have fewer elderly; in 1989 13% of whites, 8% of blacks, and 5% of Hispanics in the United States were 65 years old and older. Eight of ten men who are between 65 and 74 years old are married, as are about 54% of women (about four of ten women in this cohort are widows); for people 75 years of age and older, 70% of men are married and about 24% of women are married (for this cohort, 70% of women are widowed). Divorce rates for older people have risen dramatically over the past 20 years: 5% of men and women 65-74 are divorced, and the percentage divorced in the 75 years old and above group is about 2.5%. About 5% of older people have never married. Approximately 6% of older men and 11% of older women live with their children. Living alone in old age is more common among women, mainly because of widowhood (Arber & Ginn, 1991). Widowhood rates also differ by race. For example, for women 65 to 74 years old, 36% of whites, 34% of Hispanics, and 47% of blacks have lost a spouse through death. For men, 8% of whites are widowed whereas 9% of Hispanics and 18% of black men are widowed (U.S. Senate Special Committee on Aging, 1991). Beyond the mere demographic characteristics of aging lie a set of transitions that older individuals and families experience in varying degrees and with differential success.

### Changing Health

There is no more critical issue to older people and their families than health. One of the more observable aspects of aging involves changes in health and physical abilities. The Medicare program (Social Security Act health insurance for the aged) provides coverage for almost all older Americans. However, whites are twice as likely as blacks to also have private health insurance (U.S. Senate Special Committee on Aging, 1991).

Numerous studies of well-being in the later years have indicated the importance of health and substantiate that it is a crucial variable in successful aging. The literature on health and aging categorizes disease as acute (specific onset and limited duration) and chronic (conditions that persist over time). On average, acute disease can be cured, whereas chronic disease cannot. Although age itself is not a disease, the chances of having a chronic disease dramatically increase with advancing age. Approximately eight out of ten older people have at least one chronic disease (Soldo & Agree, 1988). Arthritis, hypertension, heart disease, and hearing difficulties account for about 60% of chronic diseases among older people (U.S. Senate Special Committee on Aging, 1991). Organic mental disorders, including Alzheimer's disease, afflict between 4% and 6% of older people (Soldo & Agree, 1988). Functional health problems, that is, problems in accomplishing activities of daily living, substantially increase for people 65 years of age and older, and this is especially so for those over 80 years old. For groups of people who are 80 years old and above, about half experience some self-care disability. However, the majority of older people who are not institutionalized exhibit relatively few functional difficulties (Soldo & Agree, 1988).

*Retirement*

Labor force participation is a major organizing theme for both men and women. In the late 1980s almost 70% of men and about 42% of women between the ages of 55 and 64 were employed; for men 65 years old and beyond, the figure was 16%, and the figure for women was about 7% (Matras, 1990). Compared with earlier periods in the twentieth century, far fewer older men now remain in the labor force. For example, in 1920 almost 60% of older men were working. Today, it is common for aged men to have many more postretirement years.

Therefore another pivotal transition in later life occurs when a person retires from paid work. The retiree is most directly touched by the event, but the lives of the retiree's spouse and children are changed as well. The retiree loses a major mechanism whereby time is arranged and structured and in which self-worth has been experienced. A retiree's spouse (in most cases, the wife) may have her routine dramatically changed by the husband's increased presence in the home. In some instances, children may also be affected by the parent's or parents' increased leisure.

*Economic Conditions*

The economic condition of older adults has been a subject of much debate. The economic status of older people is varied, perhaps more than any other age group. A report on the economic condition of older Americans for the 1980s found that, compared with younger adult groups, older adults have less cash income, are more likely to be poor, and are more likely to be near-poor. However, since 1960 the standard of living of older adults has risen, especially through 1974. For a 20-year period beginning in 1964, the median income of families with older adults as head has risen while that of families with heads younger than 65 has declined; Social Security has become more important and earnings have become less important to the economic status of older people; older people spend more of their income on necessities; and their expenses for health care are twice that of younger people (U.S. Senate Special Committee on Aging, 1985-1986). Soldo and Agree (1988) reported that 15% of older people's income comes from earnings, 40% from Social Security, and 26% from assets. These authors also provided some startling data on poverty rates of older people. Among the elderly, poverty rates increase with age. In 1986 one in ten people between 65 and 74 lived in poverty compared with 20% of those who were 85 years old and above. There were proportionally more older women and older African Americans who were impoverished. Fully 60% of black women 65 years old and above who were not living in families were living below the poverty line.

*Intergenerational Relationships*

The lengthening of the life cycle has several important outcomes for relationships. Aging individuals have the opportunity to amass social and psychological experience, to make a greater number of changes in their lives, and in general to "exercise new and expanded options" (Riley & Riley, 1986, p. 55).

One dimension of change in the later years involves one's adult children. An important family developmental task as both children and parents age centers on their "new" relationship. Families spend a lot of time together throughout the life cycle; this does not change as families age. Studies of older people and their offspring suggest that contact is ongoing, whether it is face-to-face or over the phone (Mancini & Blieszner, 1989). One of the myths about aging families is that older members are neglected and abandoned. In fact, the exchange of goods and services, and of emotional and social support, rarely ceases (Mancini & Blieszner, 1989). For example, older people may need assistance with transportation, and younger generations may need assistance with child care.

*Relationship Loss*

The loss of a spouse through death is a common experience during old age, especially for women. Over half of women 65 years of age and older are widowed, compared with 15% of men (Cavanaugh, 1993). The life expectancies of women are longer, and on average women marry men who are older than they are. Heinemann and Evans (1990) suggest that role involvement, flexibility, better health, and higher income are related to better adaptation to the loss of a spouse. Successful coping with spousal loss is also associated with planning for widowhood; there are those situations where the process of dying is prolonged, thereby providing an opportunity for mental rehearsal for the eventuality of death.

Separation and divorce in the later years have not received much attention in the literature. A U.S. Bureau of the Census study in the later 1980s reported that about 5% of men and almost 6% of women 65-74 years of age were divorced; for those 75 years of age and older, the figures were about 3% for both men and women. The proportion of older people who divorce is expected to continue to rise; although the numbers are small, the divorce rate among older people has doubled over the past 20 years.

## Stress/Coping Models: Examples From Family Gerontology

Our discussion of change and transition in old age has focused on experiences that are common, even though the timing of the experience is often unknown. Although these changes are normative, the way individuals and families cope widely varies. For some, these events are stressful but manageable, whereas for others the result is catastrophe and less control. There are many models of stress and coping that are pertinent to our discussion. In many respects, these approaches are malleable enough to have merit for a number of family situations.

### Process Model of Loss: Heinemann and Evans

Heinemann and Evans (1990) have presented a process model of loss and change that is organized around three stages of loss: preparation, grief and mourning, and adaptation. The example to which the authors apply their approach is widowhood. Among the assumptions in this model are that change can be internal or external to the self; a loss and change situation can include gains, additional losses, or both; changes that a person experiences may be short-lived (for example, feelings of insecurity) or long term (for example, new goals in life); adaptation occurs over a long period of time; and considerable individual variation in adaptation exists. The preparation period precedes the loss event and includes three adaptive processes (learning adaptive behavior, developing skills and abilities, and anticipatory behavior). There are situations where one can generally know when loss will occur, especially in the case of known terminal illness. The grief and mourning period roughly begins as a loss occurs. Within this phase, the person passes through shock, intense emotional pain, working through feelings of grief, and coming to terms with new realities of life. At the end of the second phase, the person is at a point of accepting the loss and is poised to rebuild her or his life. At this juncture, phase three, the actual adaptation begins. Within phase three, the following occurs: development and use of resources, reorganization of roles and reference groups, reintegration, and the development of new images, attitudes, and values. The result of successful passage through the adaptation period is a new identity and lifestyle.

Heinemann and Evans (1990) suggest that many healthy adult life skills support preparation for widowhood. People who are lonely prior to widowhood and those who are characteristically withdrawn adapt less well, as do those with a narrow gender-role socialization. Individual resources accumulated over a lifetime are also helpful, especially skills (goal setting and substantial personal achievements). Rehearsing for widowhood is a way to ease into the reality of loss of a spouse. Some research shows that grief resolution is enhanced by rehearsing and planning, especially in situations where death is prolonged. On the other hand, the effectiveness of anticipatory grieving is not unilaterally supported by research. Heinemann and Evans suggest that a curvilinear pattern best describes anticipatory grieving. That is, a very sudden or a very prolonged death can result in coping difficulties.

Coping during the second phase of grief and mourning includes responses to the spouse's death, specific coping strategies, and the role of social supports. Physical and emotional responses range from sadness and crying to memory loss and sleep disorders. Among older widows, there is a decline in how positively they perceive their own health. Research indicates that over the course of the grieving process a range of coping skills are brought into play. Some coping skills that are effective early in the process may not be as effective later. Heinemann and Evans (1990) give denial as an example. Denying a spouse's death in the short run may give the person time to accept the loss but in the long term may prevent necessary grieving. Among the coping strategies reported by widows are staying busy, participating in social groups, keeping a journal or diary, owning a pet, and attending support groups. Social support is pivotal for successful adaptation and is typically provided by family, friends, and other widows rather than professionals.

The final phase in this model is adaptation—that place where the person discovers new meaning and new social roles. Widows reorganize their social lives—a major difference being in regard to couple-oriented activities and relationships. During this reorganization phase, an older person relies considerably on adult offspring. How an older person defines her- or himself also changes. Research has shown that widows become more independent and widowers become more involved with others. Not surprisingly, widowers are more likely to remarry, whereas many widows do not consider remarriage as an option.

The model that Heinemann and Evans (1990) developed is based on numerous research studies, although they have noted that more research on these processes should be conducted. A strength of this model is its focus on development and personal reorganization and on the emergence of a new identity and lifestyle. This model also accounts for personal and interpersonal resources in adaptation.

*Leisure Resources Model: Kelly*

A second model of coping with change was developed by Kelly (1987) and emerged from a study of time use in old age. This model is not closely tied to a particular event or circumstance in old age but represents a panoramic view of coping focusing on a range of coping styles and resources. Kelly identified three types of life courses and nine coping styles. The life course types are "straight arrow," "turning point," and "zigzag." Those persons classified as "straight arrow" types experienced no major disruption in their lives; they experienced normative, predictable changes involving launching children and retirement. Those classified as "turning point" types were required to respond to an event that forever changed their life course, such as premature death, debilitating illness of a spouse, severe economic downturn, their own severe illness, divorce, or alcoholism. "Zigzag" older people experienced two or more events that mandated substantial change and included a series of stops and starts, especially in those cases where economic constraints were compounded by health difficulties.

Kelly (1987) identified nine coping styles that are descriptive of ways that older people attempt to reorganize their lives. These are based on in-depth personal interviews with adults:

1. *Balanced investors*: These persons decide to invest their energies in two or more central domains, such as family and economic roles and work, leisure, and community roles.

2. *Family focused*: These people's lives are deeply embedded in their family relationships. All decisions, major or minor, are made within the context of how the family will be affected. Family is viewed as the principal provider of emotional support in times of trauma, and leisure has the purpose of family integration.

3. *Work-centered*: These adults invest themselves in the world of work as their primary means of identity.

4. *Leisure-invested*: These persons achieve their identity and life's meaning through leisure pursuits.

5. *Faithful members*: There are persons for whom the church and accompanying activities are the organizing theme in life.

6. *Self-sufficient*: These persons cope with change by consistently relying on themselves. They do not turn to others for advice or emotional support and are not deeply involved in work or leisure roles. Furthermore, they have relationships in which communication is minimal.

7. *Accepting adaptors*: These are passive persons who expect little help from others and redirect their lives only as necessary.

8. *Resistant rebels*: These persons live in relative isolation and believe they have been exploited by society and angrily respond.

9. *Diffuse dabblers*: These persons appear to have few inner resources for coping and appear to have no consistent investment in life. Rather, they wander between unsatisfying personal relationships and social roles.

Balanced investors were the most common type (40% of the sample), followed by the family-focused (19%), self-sufficients (12%), and accepting adaptors (12%); fewer than 5% of the sample were in any of the other coping types. Life satisfaction scores were higher among the balanced investors, family-focused, and faithful members.

Kelly (1987) asked, "What does it take to make it?" He noted two common elements: courage and community. Those persons who had reconstructed their lives and had exhibited courage had taken risks, reached out to others, and tried new activities. Underlying courage was a sense of self-worth and competence. Most people had others who believed in them and encouraged them to take risks. Kelly (1987) stated: "Without question, some access to reliable and responsive relationships is crucial. The reality of sharing in a time of coping with traumatic change is an irreplaceable dimension of coping" (p. 153).

Although Kelly's (1987) focus was on sources of social support, he also found that personal resources are used in the process of coping. One resource involves experiencing previous life events that convince the individual that she or he is "able." That is, past success leads people to believe they can create order out of chaos when experiencing a new crisis. A second personal resource is described as a "myth" or meaningful story that gives coherence and meaning to life. The third personal resource is motivational orientation. This research can take several forms, including primary relationships, a sense of challenge and accomplishment, and a variety of experiences. This sense of direction keeps people moving and able to adapt to change.

### Social Provisions and Disability Model: Felton

In recent years family gerontologists have been adapting the work of Robert Weiss (1969) to issues of aging (Mancini & Blieszner, 1992). Felton (1990) uses Weiss's model and suggests a framework that accounts for influences of disability/chronic illness and social networks on social relationships and psychological well-being. Social support takes different forms and consequently results in a range of outcomes. Felton suggests it is important to focus on the content of support, that is, what relationships provide.

Weiss (1969) identified six social provisions: reassurance of worth (competence and esteem that come from interacting with others), opportunity for nurturance (responsible for the care of others), attachment (feelings of intimacy and security), social integration (belonging to a group with whom one shares common interests and activities), obtaining guidance (having relationships with people who can provide advice and expertise), and a sense of reliable alliance (knowing that one can count on receiving assistance in times of need). A key component in Felton's (1990) model is hierarchy—a component that was not part of Weiss's original model. Felton suggests that a hierarchical approach is needed to reflect a range of difficulties in maintaining various social provisions. Felton placed the six social provisions into three levels: Higher-order provisions include components beyond the person or the pair and move them into a world other than their own (e.g., reassurance of worth and opportunity for nurturance); middle-level provisions focus on the pair and their relationship (e.g., attachment and social integration); and lower-level social provisions focus on the individual recipient of support (e.g., obtaining guidance and reliable alliance). In a relationship, exchanges occur at all three levels, vary over time, and are subject to changing relationship needs. The importance of social provisions varies and those that are more important in the hierarchy are more difficult to maintain.

The examples given are for the social provisions of nurturance and attachment. Much is required in providing nurturance because it requires empathy and skills in caregiving; attachment persists without quite so much intent. Being on the receiving end of aid requires even less maintenance by a person. The hierarchical approach also recognizes the extent to which a person's social relationships interface with issues outside the self or the dyad.

Felton (1990) discussed her model within the context of serious illness and disability. She noted that such illness encompasses one's energies and attention and depletes one's ability to interact productively with others. Therefore certain social provisions may be very difficult to maintain. According to Felton, higher-order provisions are retained by people who still have relatively robust emotional, physical, and psychic capacities. Those with lesser abilities do not have the "luxury" of retaining them but must center their attention on everyday life concerns.

Felton (1990) speculated about the interplay between the nature of the disability, characteristics of the social network, the social provisions hierarchy, and resultant well-being. Disability alters the provisions that are received and prevents a person from fully participating in social relationships because interpersonal exchanges become more focused on the self. Relationships with friends tend to operate at higher hierarchy levels (outerworld-directed provisions), whereas family relationships tend to operate at lower levels. People who have more specialized social networks are more involved in higher-level social provisions. More specialized functions will lead to a broader array of social interactions. If a severely disabled person has relationships that sustain more than one social provision (e.g., the same people in one's network may provide attachment, reliable alliance, and reassurance of worth), then higher levels of social provisions will be maintained. Social networks in which most people know each other will tend to reflect middle-level social provisions because shared knowledge may support focusing on commonly held relationships. Positive affect is associated with higher-level provisions. Under high disability conditions, middle-level provisions will also promote positive affect. As self-esteem is lowered by increasing disability, the importance of middle-level social provisions increases (these are provisions that are more easily maintained). Persons with severe disabilities will experience less negative affect by having lower-level social provisions. Provisions that are enacted by others rather than those that require more intense interaction will counter severe stress for those severely disabled.

Felton's (1990) approach receives some support from research but is open to additional work on the hierarchical nature of social provisions. For example, if certain provisions are more important or more helpful in particular situations, strategies for enhancing the development of those provisions should be encouraged. However, this framework is particularly useful in giving greater meaning to the nature of interpersonal relationships as they are affected by severe chronic illness or disability.

## Family Intervention Issues

There are several interventions that have been developed to facilitate later life transitions and family well-being. The following interventions are from the models of stress and coping.

### Adding Life to Years: Theoretical Lenses

*Coping and recovery is a process and therefore is developmental.* The process perspective was a major component of Heinemann and Evans (1990) in their discussion of preparation, grief and mourning, and adaptation. Successful achievement of tasks in the earlier stages of the process enables more enduring recovery responses.

*Social support is an important component of successful responses to stress and change.* Felton's (1990) focus on the range of social provisions indicates that a variety of social relationship characteristics (e.g., attachment, guidance) interact to support well-being. Kelly's (1987) research on styles of coping suggests that "balanced investors" (people who placed considerable energy in several interpersonal-oriented life roles) were among those highest in psychological well-being. Kelly concludes that "reliable and responsive relationships" are pivotal to successful coping. Heinemann and Evans (1990) concurred by suggesting that people who are lonely prior to widowhood and who tend to be withdrawn from others adapt less well.

*Individual initiative and abilities are significant resources for coping and recovery.* In discussing older people with severe disabilities, Felton (1990) suggests that those with more severe disabilities are less likely to maintain higher-order social provisions. Kelly (1987) found that an important element of coping was personal "courage," and Heinemann and Evans (1990) indicated that adaptation is made up primarily of proactive behaviors; that is, people who develop resources adapt with greater success.

*A renewed definition of "self" is part of successful recovery.* According to Heinemann and Evans (1990), successful adaptation requires a new identity and lifestyle. Kelly (1987) suggests that older people who define themselves as able and competent because of past experience are better able to meet the challenge of a potential crisis. In Felton's (1990) discussion of social provisions, reassurance of worth (sense of competence and esteem) is an important function of interpersonal relationships. Felton's model also suggests that particular relationship provisions will become more important as self-esteem declines due to increasing disability.

*Individuals vary in patterns of coping and adaptation.* Kelly's (1987) styles of coping describe the variety of ways that people reorganize their lives in the face of change and adversity. About 60% of the older adults in Kelly's sample were spread across eight coping styles and 40% were classified as "balanced investors." Within these styles there were individuals who organized their lives around the church, who passively approached stress, who felt exploited and were angry, and who focused their lives around the welfare of their family. The hierarchical component of Felton's (1990) model suggests that the process of coping is variant and requires differential amounts of energy.

Although the approaches to stress and coping share some common characteristics, they also have unique qualities. Heinemann and Evans's (1990) process model is developmental, Kelly's (1987) leisure resources model is typological and broader in its focus, and Felton's (1990) social provisions and disability model is focused on personal relationships. Each model provides insight for an understanding of the stress and coping associated with aging. Using retirement as an example, the approach of Heinemann and Evans suggests that interventionists inquire into feelings of loss related to exiting the workforce. In contrast, Kelly's perspective indicates that intervention should be focused on the balancing of major roles and a person's sense of direction. Felton's social provisions orientation suggests that practitioners uncover the specific content of relationship support that facilitates coping with changes in the work role.

### Intervention Typology: Gottlieb

Gottlieb's (1988) typology includes five major levels of support interventions: individual, dyadic, group, social system, and community. Support comes from a variety of sources ranging from professionals to church groups to radio call-in shows. The *individual* level of intervention includes providing as well as receiving support. Providers of support promote network orientation and methods that invite the support of others. At this level, recipients support intervention by managing their distress while interacting and receiving support from others. There are two dimensions of *dyadic* intervention—support from a key person and the introduction of an outsider (e.g., buddy, coach, mentor, companion). *Group* interventions include support from a collection from one's existing network and what Gottlieb calls the "grafting of new ties," which is essentially the development of support groups. *Social system* intervention pertains to the larger context, including physical and sociocultural aspects. At this level the focus is on a reframing process that permits new approaches and new views on issues and problems. Also, emphasis is placed on structural change, which places people in a different contiguity to one another and to the institution. The final intervention is at the *community* level and pertains to widespread initiatives to promote social support through public campaigns.

### Approaches to Intervention

It has long been recognized that effective intervention takes multiple forms. As society ages, there will be a greater need to develop and maintain a range of individual and family supports that are broad and inclusive.

The friendship network is a powerful force in giving people meaning in their lives. The role that close friends can play in coping cannot be ignored. Many older adults place high value on relationships with their friends, and they become substantial support sources (Blieszner & Adams, 1992).

Increasingly, therapists are dealing with older clients and are developing a variety of approaches to be used with this population (Storandt, 1983). These include individual approaches such as behavioral, psychodynamic, and cognitive orientations as well as relationship-oriented approaches such as family and group therapy. Greene (1989) suggests that an important goal of family therapy with older clients is the promotion of positive interdependence. This goal is consonant with the research literature on how middle and older generations interact (Mancini & Blieszner, 1989). Keller and Bromley (1989) identify seven process-oriented components of successful therapy: (a) having the whole family involved, (b) assisting the family to identify their goals for therapy, (c) identifying family strengths, (d) encouraging independence so family members can do things for themselves during therapy, (e) identifying needs and expectations of all family members,

(f) identifying underlying beliefs that people have about one another, and (g) developing adaptation options. Whether intervention is in the form of a friend or a therapist, it is likely to move the older person toward new ways of coping and recognizing a wider range of resources.

There are many organizational approaches to supporting families and their older members. Kirschling (1987) discusses hospice programs and their important role in helping families with terminally ill members. She notes that professionals working with these families in this situation of family stress must address their needs to be reassured that their loved one is being kept as comfortable as possible, must keep them informed of the person's condition, must provide them the opportunities to express their emotions, and must link them to professional help with legal and financial issues. An important feature of the hospice approach is its use of an intervention team, focusing on both the older adult and the family.

Montgomery and Hatch (1987) have discussed volunteer respite services for older people and their families. Although the use of volunteers is common in institutional settings, it has been used less extensively in family caregiving. Research on the effectiveness of such support shows there are many implementation difficulties; however, it also shows that volunteers can benefit caregivers by relieving some of the daily burdens of care. This level of intervention provides direct support to both the frail family member and her or his family caregivers.


## Conclusions

A broad approach toward understanding aging and family well-being has been presented. There are predictable and unpredictable events that families will experience that involve older members. Resources that individuals and families may use in coping with these events have been identified through the presentation of various stress models. While there are many additional approaches to meeting the needs of families and their older members, those interventions discussed are consistent with many of the identified and relevant issues. Consistent with various stress models, they contain elements of process, development, and resources and involve friends, helping professionals, and formal and informal programs. The problems of aging individuals and their families are diverse and thus respond to a wide range of interventions. Those families that access their own personal resources, as well as those provided by people and groups outside of the family, are better equipped to master change and transition.

# References

Arber, S., & Ginn, J. (1991). *Gender and later life*. Newbury Park, CA: Sage.

Blieszner, R., & Adams, R. G. (1992). *Adult friendship*. Newbury Park, CA: Sage.

Brubaker, T. H. (1990). An overview of family relationships in later life. In T. H. Brubaker (Ed.), *Family relationships in later life* (pp. 13-26). Newbury Park, CA: Sage.

Cavanaugh, J. C. (1993). *Adult development and aging*. Pacific Grove, CA: Brooks/Cole.

Felton, B. J. (1990). Coping and social support in older people's experiences of chronic illness. In M. A. P. Stephens, J. H. Crowther, S. E. Hobfoll, & D. L. Tennenbaum (Eds.), *Stress and coping in later-life families* (pp. 153-171). New York: Hemisphere.

Gottlieb, B. H. (1988). Support interventions: A typology and agenda for research. In S. Duck (Ed.), *Handbook of personal relationships* (pp. 519-541). Chichester, England: Wiley.

Greene, R. (1989). A life systems approach to understanding parent-child relationships in aging families. In G. A. Hughston, V. A. Christopherson, & M. J. Bonjean (Eds.), *Aging and family therapy* (pp. 57-69). New York: Haworth.

Heinemann, G. D., & Evans, P. L. (1990). Widowhood: Loss, change, and adaptation. In T. H. Brubaker (Ed.), *Family relationships in later life* (pp. 142-168). Newbury Park, CA: Sage.

Keller, J. F., & Bromley, M. C. (1989). Psychotherapy with the elderly: A systemic model. In G. A. Hughston, V. A. Christopherson, & M. J. Bonjean (Eds.), *Aging and family therapy* (pp. 29-55). New York: Haworth.

Kelly, J. R. (1987). *Peoria winter: Styles and resources in later life*. Lexington, MA: Lexington Books/D. C. Heath.

Kirschling, J. M. (1987). The interface among terminally ill elderly, their families, and hospice. In T. H. Brubaker (Ed.), *Aging, health, and family: Long-term care* (pp. 216-231). Newbury Park, CA: Sage.

Mancini, J. A., & Blieszner, R. (1989). Aging parents and adult children: Research themes in intergenerational relationships. *Journal of Marriage and the Family, 51,* 275-290.

Mancini, J. A., & Blieszner, R. (1992). Social provisions in adulthood: Concept and measurement in close relationships. *Journal of Gerontology: Psychological Sciences, 47,* P14-P20.

Matras, J. (1990). *Dependency, obligations, and entitlements: A new sociology of aging, the life course, and the elderly*. Englewood Cliffs, NJ: Prentice Hall.

Montgomery, R. J. V., & Hatch, L. R. (1987). The feasibility of volunteers and families forming a partnership for caregiving. In T. H. Brubaker (Ed.), *Aging, health, and family: Long-term care* (pp. 143-161). Newbury Park, CA: Sage.

Riley, M. W., & Riley, J. W. (1986). Longevity and social structure: The potential of the added years. In A. Pifer & L. Bronte (Eds.), *Our aging society: Paradox and promise* (pp. 53-77). New York: Norton.

Soldo, B. J., & Agree, E. M. (1988). America's elderly. *Population Bulletin, 43,* 1-51.

Storandt, M. (1983). *Counseling and therapy with older adults*. Boston: Little, Brown.

U.S. Senate Special Committee on Aging. (1985-1986). *Aging America: Trends and projections*. Washington, DC: Government Printing Office.

U.S. Senate Special Committee on Aging. (1991). *Aging America: Trends and projections*. Washington, DC: Government Printing Office.

Weiss, R. S. (1969). The fund of sociability. *Trans-action/Society, 6,* 36-43.

# 7

❀

# Physical Illness

### THOMAS L. CAMPBELL

Until recently, family scientists have shown little interest in biological or health issues. Although there is a long history of research on families and mental illness, most of the studies on families and physical health have been conducted over the last two decades. As Doherty and Campbell (1988) have commented, it is as if scholars have ignored the fact that families are composed of individuals who have bodies.

At the same time, medicine and other health sciences have largely ignored families and the role they play in the health care system. Physicians, nurses, and other health practitioners have focused almost exclusively on the individual, devoid of social and interpersonal context. Only recently has the medical profession begun to recognize that families are the primary caregivers for most patients with chronic illness and that many chronic illnesses impose enormous burdens on family members. Furthermore, recent research has shown that social relationships, particularly within the family, have an enormous impact on health—as important as any biological factors (House, Landis, & Umberson, 1988).

This chapter will review the recent research on the family and physical health including studies that look at the impact of family factors on physical health and the effects of physical illness on families. The implications of this research and challenges for family professionals will be discussed.

The neglect of biological issues by family scientists, and family issues by health professionals, results from a deep-rooted split in our society between mind and body that goes back to the seventeenth century. Descartes's belief that the human body is like a machine and should be studied separately from the mind or human spirit continues to have a profound effect upon Western thinking. Despite enormous evidence that there are no clear distinctions between physical and mental processes, medicine continues to divide diseases into mental and physical disorders. For example, there is little justification to distinguish Alzheimer's disease as a neurological disorder and schizophrenia as a psychiatric illness. Both disorders are associated with well-defined neurophysiological and neuroanatomical changes in the brain and result in disturbed thinking and feelings, including delusions and hallucinations. Ironically, schizophrenia is much more responsive to drug therapy than Alzheimer's. Both disorders also can be highly influenced by psychosocial factors including the family environment. Research on family expressed emotion has shown how certain types of family environments and family psychoeducation can influence the course of schizophrenia (Goldstein, 1987). Family expressed emotion has also been shown to affect the caregivers of Alzheimer's patients (Vitaliano, Becker, Russo, Magna-Amato, & Mariuvo, 1988); for example, how well the Alzheimer patient functions and whether the patient needs to be placed in a nursing home are strongly influenced by how well the family caregivers are able to cope with the burdens and problems associated with this disease (Houlihan, 1987).

In 1977 Engel first proposed the biopsychosocial model—an approach for medicine that integrates psychosocial and biomedical domains and avoids the mind-body split (Engel, 1977). Using a general systems framework, Engel recognized there are many levels of relevant data that influence health and illness, ranging from the molecular (e.g., certain genetic diseases) to macroenvironmental issues (e.g., thinning of the ozone layer). (See Figure 7.1.) He described how changes in any one level in the system affect every other level. The biopsychosocial model emphasizes that illness occurs within the social context and that the family can influence the individual's physical health and vice versa.

Since Engel's classic article written in the journal *Science* 15 years ago, the biopsychosocial model has gradually gained momentum within medicine. Most of the primary care specialties of family practice, pediatrics, and general internal medicine have adopted many of the principles of the biopsychosocial approach. More research is being funded and conducted on links between psychological and physical processes. For example, research in the new field of psychoimmunology has demonstrated how psychosocial stress can impair the immune process and make individuals more suscep-

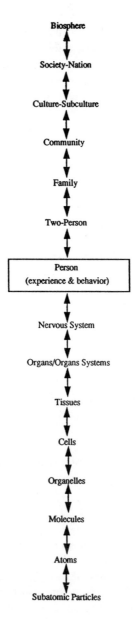

**Figure 7.1.** Systems Hierarchy

SOURCE: Engel, G. L., The clinical applications of the biopsychosocial model. *American Journal of Psychiatry*. Copyright May 1980. The American Psychiatric Association. Reprinted by permission.

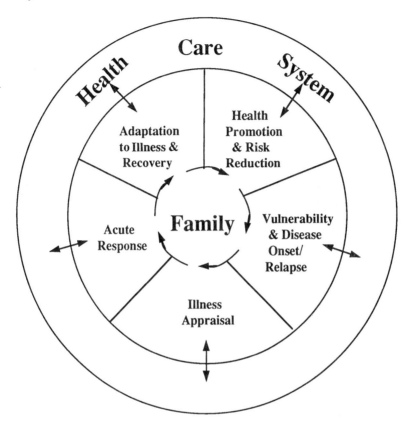

**Figure 7.2.** Family Health and Illness Cycle
SOURCE: Doherty and Campbell (1988, p. 23); reprinted by permission of authors.

tible to many different illnesses (Ader, 1981). The biopsychosocial model
provides a framework for understanding the reciprocal influences of families and physical health.

## The Family Health and Illness Cycle

The family health and illness cycle (see Figure 7.2), developed by
Doherty, is a useful method for organizing disparate areas of research on
families and health, providing an orderly sequence of family experiences

with health and illness (Doherty & Campbell, 1988). The two-way arrows between the family and health care systems emphasize the importance of families' ongoing interactions with physicians and other health care professionals. Beginning at the top of the cycle with health promotion and risk reduction, research in each of the six categories will be reviewed.

### Family Health Promotion and Risk Reduction

During this century, most life-threatening, acute, and infectious diseases (except AIDS) have been either eliminated or largely controlled through vaccination, improved sanitation, and antibiotics. Most of the current suffering and mortality from physical illness now results from chronic, degenerative diseases. A major challenge in the 1990s and into the next century is the prevention of chronic diseases. Ironically, most of these diseases result from unhealthy behaviors. For example, cardiovascular disease and cancer, which currently account for 75% of all deaths in the United States, are largely the result of unhealthy lifestyles (Califano, 1979). As a result, the federal government has initiated a major program titled *Healthy People 2000* to help promote health and reduce health risks (Public Health Service, 1990).

The family is the primary social context in which health promotion and disease prevention take place. The World Health Organization (1976) has characterized the family as the "primary social agent in the promotion of health and well being." Research on families and health demonstrates that the family strongly influences health behaviors and that a family-oriented approach is the most effective and efficient way to meet the health objectives for the year 2000 (McDaniel, Campbell, & Seaburn, 1990). A healthy lifestyle is usually developed, maintained, or changed within the family setting. Behavioral health risk factors cluster within families, as family members tend to share similar diets, physical activities, and use of substances (e.g., tobacco, alcohol, and illicit drugs) (Doherty & Campbell, 1988). Parents' health-related behaviors strongly influence whether a child or adolescent will adopt healthy behaviors, and family support is an important determinant of an individual's ability to change an unhealthy lifestyle. In a 1985 Gallup survey of health-related behaviors, over 1,000 adults reported that their spouse or significant other was more likely to influence their health habits than anyone else, including the family doctor (Gallup Poll, 1985).

Almost every important health behavior is a family activity or is strongly influenced by the family. An emphasis on physical activity and fitness is usually a shared family value, and parents' exercise habits and attitudes have a strong influence on their children's level of physical activity (Sallis & Nader, 1988). Men at high risk for cardiac disease are more likely to participate in an exercise program if their spouses are supportive (Heinzelman & Bagley, 1970).

Nutrition is an obvious family activity. Despite changes in traditional family roles, women still do most of the meal planning and preparation for the entire family. Counseling men with elevated cholesterol levels about nutrition is unlikely to be successful if wives are not involved. It is well documented that family members have similar diets and ingest similar amounts of salt, calories, cholesterol, and saturated fats (Campbell & Treat, 1990). Studies have shown that eating behaviors and obesity can play important homeostatic functions within families (Barbarin & Tirado, 1984). Of mothers surveyed, 25% report that they use food as a reward for their children, and 10% use it as punishment (Bryan & Lowenberg, 1958). Parents' encouragement of children to eat has been shown to correlate with childhood obesity (Klesges, Coates, & Brown, 1983). It is no surprise that the family plays an important role in the development and treatment of the major eating disorders—anorexia nervosa and bulimia. In terms of the treatment of obesity, several randomized controlled trials have shown how the involvement of the spouse in weight reduction programs significantly improves long-term results (Campbell, 1986).

Smoking remains the number one health problem in the United States today with 350,000 deaths per year directly attributed to smoking. Smoking contributes to just about every serious chronic illness and form of cancer. It has been estimated that approximately 5 minutes of life is lost for every cigarette smoked—about half the time it takes to smoke one cigarette (Greene, Goldberg, & Ockene, 1988).

Like other health behaviors, the initiation, maintenance, and cessation of smoking are strongly influenced by the family. Adolescents are much more likely to smoke if either parent or a sibling smokes. A teenager who has a parent and older sibling who smoke is five times more likely to smoke than a teenager from a nonsmoking family (Bewley & Bland, 1977).

There is a very high concordance in smoking behavior within married smokers. Smokers are much more likely to marry smokers, to smoke the same number of cigarettes as their spouses, and to quit at the same time (Venters, Jacobs, Luepker, Maiman, & Gillum, 1984). While some of this is explained by assortative mating (smokers marry smokers), studies also show smoking behaviors of spouses become more similar with longer marriages, suggesting that spouses have a strong influence on each other's smoking behavior.

The spouse also plays an important role in smoking cessation. Smokers who are married to nonsmokers or ex-smokers are more likely to quit and to remain abstinent (Price, Chen, & Cavallii, 1981). Support from the spouse is associated with successful smoking cessation. In particular, supportive behaviors involving cooperative participation, such as talking the smoker out of smoking a cigarette, and reinforcement, such as expressing pleasure at the smoker's efforts to quit, predict successful quitting. In contrast, negative behaviors such as nagging the smoker and complaining about the smoking predict relapse (Coppotelli & Orleans, 1985).

Thus research demonstrates that families influence most health-related behaviors, including smoking. The field of health promotion needs to stop thinking simply about healthy individuals and begin to think of healthy families and interventions directed at entire families rather than individuals.

### Vulnerability and Disease Onset/Relapse

Despite significant advances in our understanding of health and illness, we do not understand why some people become ill while others remain healthy when exposed to the same pathogens or risk factors. Part of the explanation comes from research demonstrating that psychosocial factors can affect an individual's susceptibility to disease. Studies of stress and social support have shown the most convincing evidence that psychosocial factors influence health. In addition, this work demonstrates that families are often the most important sources of both stress and social support.

Stress has become widely recognized by patients and health care professionals as influencing health. Patients often explain to their physicians that they are "under a lot of stress" and that their ulcer, back pain, or headache is "acting up." However, stress is difficult to define and study (Rabkin & Struening, 1976); yet one successful method has been to examine the relationship of stressful life events to illness. In 1967 Holmes and Rahe developed a life event scale by asking a random sample to rank how stressful they perceived each of 43 common life events to be. Most events on the Holmes and Rahe scale occur within families, and 10 of the 15 most stressful events are family events. Many retrospective and prospective studies using this scale have shown that an increase in the number of life events predicts the development of a wide range of diseases (F. Cohen, 1981).

Because children are likely to be affected by stress, a number of studies have looked at the relationship of family life events and child health. Meyer and Haggerty (1962) found that chronic stress was associated with higher rates of streptococcal pharyngitis and that 30% of the strep infections were preceded by a stressful family event. In a study of illness conducted in a day-care center, children who had experienced more stressful life events had longer, but not more frequent, respiratory illnesses (Boyce et al., 1977). A prospective study (Beautrais, Fergusson, & Shannon, 1982) of over 1,000 preschoolers found that family life events were strongly correlated with subsequent visits to the physician and hospital admissions for a wide range of conditions. Children from families with more than 12 life events during the 4-year study period were six times more likely to be hospitalized (Beautrais et al., 1982).

The death of a spouse is the most common stressful life event, and the health consequences of bereavement have been extensively studied (Osterweis, Solomon, & Green, 1984). Based on U.S. census data, Kraus and Lilienfeld (1959) found that young widowers had 10 times the normal death rate for many illnesses. In a classic prospective study, Parkes, Benjamin, and Fitzgerald (1969) followed London widowers for 9 years after the death of their spouses. The men had a 40% higher mortality rate during the first 6 months of bereavement when compared with the general population. A population study of 4,032 widowed persons (Helsing & Szklo, 1981) found that when potential confounding variables (especially smoking and socioeconomic status) were controlled, widowers, but not widows, had increased mortality rates, persisting throughout the 10 years of the study. However, widowers who remarried had a lower death rate than the control, nonwidowed group, suggesting that marriage had a protective effect on health. In a study of 95,647 widowed persons in Finland, death rates were highest, and twice the expected rate, during the first week of bereavement (Kaprio, Koskenvou, & Rita, 1987).

Divorce or marital separation is also an extremely stressful event, ranked second to the death of a spouse on the Holmes and Rahe scale. Several cross-sectional studies (Carter & Glick, 1970; Lynch, 1977; Verbrugge, 1977) have demonstrated that divorced persons have a higher death rate from all diseases than single, widowed, or married persons. However, research has also shown that chronic physical illness has an adverse effect on marital satisfaction (Bruhn, 1977; Klein, Dean, & Bogdanoff, 1968), which may eventually lead to divorce.

Recent research in psychoimmunology has suggested one of several possible biological mechanisms for the adverse health effects of bereavement and divorce. Studies in animals and humans have revealed that stress can lead to immunosuppression and an increase in illness (Ader, 1981;

Calabrese, Kling, & Gold, 1987). Two well-controlled studies demonstrated a decrease in cellular immunity (T-lymphocyte stimulation) during bereavement (Bartrop, Luckhurst, Lazarus, Kiloh, & Penny, 1977; Schleifer, Keller, Camerino, Thornton, & Stein, 1983). In another study, T-cell function was reduced only in those bereaved subjects who were clinically depressed (Linn, Linn, & Jensen, 1984). Divorced or separated women have significantly poorer immune function than sociodemographically matched married women (Kiecolt-Glaser et al., 1987). Among married women in the same study, poor marital quality correlated with both depression and decreased immunity. Immune function is also impaired in major depression, and leading researchers have suggested that changes that occur in the central nervous system during depression may be the final common pathway (Calabrese et al., 1987).

Although family stress can have harmful effects on health, family support can be beneficial. *Social support* can be defined as "the emotional, instrumental and financial aid that is obtained from one's social network" (Berkman, 1984, p. 415). An extensive body of research has demonstrated that social networks and supports can directly improve health as well as buffer the adverse effects of stress (S. Cohen & Syme, 1985). Furthermore, the family has been found to be the most important source of social support.

In a seminal study of over 6,000 adults, Berkman and Syme (1979) reported that social networks were a major predictor of mortality over a 9-year-period, independent of socioeconomic status, previous health status, or health practices. The most socially isolated adults had more than twice the mortality rate compared with the least isolated group. Marital status and contacts with relatives and friends were the most powerful predictors of health. In a 6-year follow-up study of 17,433 Swedish men and women, those with the fewest available social contacts had over three times the death rate compared with those with the most social contacts (Ortho-Gomer & Johnson, 1987).

Studies of social supports among the elderly have shown that the importance of different aspects of family support may change over the life span. Two studies (Blazer, 1982; Zuckerman, Kasl, & Osterfeld, 1984) found that older persons with impaired social supports have two to three times the death rate of those with adequate support systems. Unlike studies of younger populations, marital status was not associated with mortality. However, the presence and number of living children were the most powerful predictor of survival. This finding suggests that adult children become the most important source of social support to the elderly.

In an article in *Science,* sociologist House and colleagues (1988) reviewed the research on social support and health and concluded:

The evidence regarding social relationships and health increasingly approximates the evidence in the 1964 Surgeon General's report that established cigarette smoking as a cause or risk factor for mortality and morbidity from a range of diseases. The age-adjusted relative risk ratios are stronger than the relative risks for all cause mortality reported for cigarette smoking. (p. 543)

Thus social relationships deserve the same attention and study by public health specialists and policymakers as smoking has received.

These lines of research clearly demonstrate that family support and family stress, especially bereavement, have a powerful influence on overall mortality. An understanding of families and their potential sources of stress and support can provide health care professionals with ways to reduce family stress, bolster family supports, and improve health.

### Family Illness Appraisal

Most individuals who experience physical symptoms do not consult health professionals but instead manage these problems at home with family and friends. It is estimated that only 10%-30% of all health problems are brought to professional attention (Zola, 1972). Little is known about what factors influence whether an individual consults a physician or other health professional. Most research in this area has focused exclusively on individual factors such as the severity of the symptoms, individual's health beliefs, and access to health care services. However, there is considerable evidence that health care use and health appraisal are influenced by family factors and that there are distinct family patterns of health care use. These issues are critically important during this time of crisis and reform in the health care system. Understanding how families influence the appraisal of illness symptoms and the use of health care services will help health care reformers develop programs that most effectively use families' resources without being overburdened.

When an individual develops symptoms, he or she usually discusses the problem with those closest to him or her, that is, other family members. The health care decision-making process often involves the entire family. The symptom is assessed based upon its severity and potential for causing serious harm and upon the perceived likelihood that a health professional could help with the problem. This process is strongly influenced by the family's history with other health problems. For example, a family who has had a child with meningitis will be much more likely to seek care for febrile illnesses than other families. Astute clinicians will often ask patients who present with a particular symptom whether anyone else in their family or close friends have ever had similar symptoms. This information can help the provider assess the patient's level of anxiety and provide appropriate reassurance.

Not all family members have the same influence on this decision-making process. Many families have a "family health expert" (Doherty & Baird, 1983) who has been assigned and assumes the role of expert in health matters. Traditionally this role has been played by a female member of the family, often the wife or mother, but it can also be assumed by family members who are health professionals. From a clinical standpoint, it can be very helpful to identify the perceived health expert in the family and that individual's opinion regarding the symptoms. If a clinician contradicts or disagrees with the family health expert, the patient may be caught in a loyalty bind and be less likely to follow the health professional's recommendations.

The appraisal of a child's symptoms and the decision about whether to consult a physician are strongly influenced by the beliefs and level of stress experienced by the parents. Sometimes a child may serve as a surrogate patient who directly or indirectly expresses the stress and dysfunction within the family. A study of 500 families (Roghmann & Haggerty, 1973) found that family stress dramatically increased use of health services and that in one third of the visits there was no evidence of any physical symptoms. Another study (Turk, Litt, & Salovey, 1985) found that a family history of a similar symptom or problem was the strongest predictor of health care treatment for children's symptoms.

Other studies have shown that there are distinct family patterns of health care behavior and use. For example, many of the barriers to health care access such as lack of health insurance, money, transportation, or identified sources of health care are shared by family members. Thus, if one member of the family is unable to receive appropriate care, it is likely that other family members are in the same situation. Interventions to improve access to health care are likely to be more effective and cost efficient if they are directed at entire families rather than individuals who are not receiving health care. For example, one large study from the National Health Interview Survey found a strong association between mother and child use of physicians. The mother's health care use was a better predictor of the number of medical visits by the child than the child's own health status (Newacheck & Halfon, 1986). Osterweis, Bush, and Zuckerman (1979) found that an individual's use of medications was more strongly related to other family members' medication use than the individual's severity of symptoms or illness.

These studies suggest the important role of the family in health care decision making, but more quantitative and qualitative research is needed to better understand this process. Such information will be helpful not only to health care providers but to policymakers.

## Families' Acute Response to Illness

One of the most feared threats to family life is the development and diagnosis of a serious or life-threatening illness in a family member. Illness in the family ranks near the top of the Holmes and Rahe scale (Holmes & Rahe, 1967). This is demonstrated by the fact that many family members can remember the moment that they learned of a serious illness in their family.

The acute response by families to the diagnosis of a serious illness often follows a predictable course. There may be a period of denial or disbelief about the diagnosis, followed by rapid mobilization of resources and support within the family. During this crisis phase, most families will usually pull together and rally around the patient even when there's been a history of major conflicts, separation, or disengagement. This is the time that immediate family members are often deluged by casserole dishes and other offers of help from extended family and friends. During this acute phase, patients may even complain that they are getting too much attention and help from families and friends and have no time for privacy and rest. Unfortunately, if the acute illness is not resolved and becomes chronic, the support and assistance may decline over time. In the chronic phase (see below), patients and families may complain that they are no longer receiving help or support from extended families or friends and feel forgotten and isolated.

Studies of acutely ill patients have consistently shown that their spouses generally show higher levels of stress and anxiety than the patient (Oberst & James, 1985). Spouses often report high levels of physical symptoms sometimes similar to those experienced by the patient. They may also feel depressed and angry about the illness along with a sense of guilt about having those unacceptable feelings.

During the acute phase, family members report they often feel left out and uninformed, that what they need most from health professionals is more information about the patient's health problems. Traditionally, hospitals allow only limited contact with the patient when he or she is acutely ill. Most intensive care units allow family members to visit the patient for 5 to 10 minutes every 1 or 2 hours. These policies are based on the unfounded belief that family members will either interfere with ongoing medical treatments or tire the patient. Unfortunately, family members often experience enormous anxiety waiting outside intensive care units to receive information about their loved ones.

In summary, during the acute phase with a serious illness, many families experience shock and disbelief followed by acceptance. They usually pull together and feel more satisfied with their family relationships. Many families have difficulty talking about the illness and their fears and worries, often believing they need to protect the patient or other family members. Once the acute phase is over, family members may experience difficulties adapting to the long-term needs of chronic illness and the renegotiation of their roles and responsibilities.

### Family Adaptation to Illness and Recovery

Most families face chronic illness in a family member at some time during the life cycle. Chronic illness is increasing in prevalence and has replaced acute illness as the major cause of morbidity and mortality in the United States. Half of all people over age 65 and one fourth of those between ages 45 and 65 are limited in their activities by at least one chronic condition (U.S. Department of Commerce, 1980). As the elderly population increases, the burden of chronic illness increases and families must play even greater roles in the care of the elderly.

Families, not health care providers, are the primary caretakers for patients with chronic illness. Families help most with the physical demands of an illness, ranging from preparing special meals for a family member with heart disease, to assisting with insulin administration for a diabetic, to running a home dialysis machine. In addition, families are usually the major source of emotional and social support: someone to share the frustrations, discouragements, and despair of living with chronic illness.

Chronic illness affects all aspects of family life. Old and familiar patterns are changed forever, shared activities are forgone, and family roles and responsibilities change. Most patients and their families effectively cope with the stresses and demands of chronic illness and tend to pull together and become closer (Steinglass, Temple, Lisman, & Reiss, 1982). However, some families may become too close or enmeshed. By assuming too much responsibility and care for an ill family member, they may inhibit his or her autonomy and independence. Other families may collapse under the stress of chronic illness and even disintegrate through divorce (Sabbeth & Leventhal, 1984), institutionalization, or death. The spouses of chronically ill patients often have as much subjective distress as the patients (Klein et al., 1968). It is common for health care providers to focus on the "patient" and overlook the spouse's distress, not attending to his or her physical and emotional needs (Strong, 1988). The failure of health professionals to address the needs of family members can lead to a downward cycle: The family becomes more distressed and is less able to respond to the needs of the patient, who may then deteriorate physically and emotionally, resulting in more stress and demands on the family, leading finally to burnout.

Based on their work with different chronic illnesses, Steinglass and his colleagues have described four common characteristics of these families (Gonzales et al., 1989):

1. *The illness and its demands tend to dominate family life, and other family needs are neglected.* This response is initially adaptive as the family copes with the crisis but leads to family disruption over the long term.

2. *Family coalitions between the patient and one or more family members develop, or previous coalitions are intensified by the chronic illness.* For example, a mother may become overinvolved in the care of her ill child and the father may withdraw or be excluded (Penn, 1983).

3. *The family's coping response often becomes rigid, and the family fears that any change may have an adverse affect on their current adjustment.*

4. *Families tend to isolate themselves in coping with the demands of illness.* The primary task for families with chronic illness is to create a balance between the needs of the individual with the illness and those of the rest of the family.

With regard to chronic disease, especially heart disease, cancer, and diabetes, the family is an important source of support for complying with medical regimens. Based upon research on the influence of social and family support on compliance, the National Heart, Lung, and Blood Institute (1982) has recommended that all physicians use the following as one of three basic strategies for increasing compliance with antihypertensive regimens: "Enhance support from family members—identifying and involving one influential person, preferably someone living with the patients, who can provide encouragement, help support the behavior change and, if necessary, remind the patient about the specifics of the regimen" (p. xx).

Family members are the primary caregivers for people with chronic disabling health problems (Houlihan, 1987). Most elderly people with Alzheimer's disease or other incapacitating illnesses are cared for at home by adult children and are never institutionalized. The physical and emotional burden of this caregiving is enormous and can have serious adverse effects on the physical and mental health of the caregiver. Institutionalization of the elderly and chronically ill results more from caregiver "burnout" and poor health than from deterioration of the patient's condition. How well the family copes with the illness and supports the primary caregiver affects both the caregiver's and the patient's well-being.

In the past decade there has been an increasing number of studies focusing on the influence of the family on chronic illnesses, including research on asthma (Lask & Matthew, 1979), chronic renal failure (Steidl et al., 1980), heart disease (Ruberman, Weinblatt, Goldberg, & Chaudhary, 1984), and cancer (Horne & Picard, 1979). Research on diabetes has shown the most consistent relationship between family functioning and disease outcomes (Anderson & Auslander, 1980; Johnson, 1980). Adequate control of blood sugars in diabetes can prevent many of the long-term complications of disease but is difficult to achieve and maintain. Diabetic control is related both to intrinsic metabolic factors (as in the "brittle diabetic") and to compliance with insulin and diet. Several studies have shown that overall family dysfunction was strongly correlated with poor diabetic control (Grey, Genel, & Tamborlane, 1980; Koski & Kumento, 1977; Orr, Golden, Myers, & Marrerro, 1983). Most of the families of 30 poorly controlled diabetic children studied by White, Kolman, Wexler, Polin, and Winter (1984) had numerous "dysfunctional" psychosocial factors, including absent fathers, poor living conditions, inadequate parental functioning, chronic family conflict, and lack of family involvement with the diabetes. On the other hand, clear organization in the family has been associated with good metabolic control (Shouval, Ber, & Galatzer, 1982). High parental self-esteem is also associated with good control and is an important mediating factor between family functioning and diabetes (Grey et al., 1980).

The emotional closeness and cohesiveness of a family seems to be particularly important for the care of diabetes. Both low cohesion or disengagement and high cohesion or enmeshment have been associated with poor blood sugar control. In a carefully controlled study, Anderson, Miller, Auslander, and Santiago (1981) found that low cohesion and high conflict were associated with poor diabetic control. Parental indifference can result in the worst diabetic control and lead to depression in the diabetic child (Khurana & White, 1970). Thus, in emotionally distant or disengaged families, inadequate supervision and parental support can lead to noncompliance with treatment and poor diabetic control.

Minuchin and his colleagues (Minuchin, Rosman, & Baker, 1978; Minuchin et al., 1975) at the Philadelphia Child Guidance Clinic have studied poorly controlled diabetic children from families with high cohesion or enmeshment. Despite adherence to diet and insulin, these children had recurrent episodes of diabetic ketoacidosis. When hospitalized and removed from the family environment, their diabetes was easily managed. It appeared that stress and emotional arousal within the family directly affected the child's blood sugar. In studying these families and the families of children with severe asthma and anorexia nervosa, Minuchin discovered a specific pattern of interaction characterized by enmeshment (high cohesion), overprotectiveness, rigidity, and conflict avoidance. He called these families "psychosomatic families."

To determine how family interactions affect diabetes, Minuchin et al. (1978) studied the physiological responses of diabetic children to a stressful family interview. During the family interview, the children from psychosomatic families had a rapid rise in free fatty acids (a precursor to diabetic ketoacidosis) that persisted beyond the interview. The parents of these children also exhibited an initial rise in free fatty acids (FFA) levels, but these levels fell to normal when the diabetic child entered the room. Minuchin hypothesized that in psychosomatic families parental conflict is detoured or defused through the chronically ill child, and the resulting stress leads to exacerbations of the illness. In a larger sample of diabetic families, Cederblad, Helgesson, Larsson, and Ludvigsson (1982) demonstrated that high cohesion in the mother, rigidity in the father, and anxiety in the diabetic child were all associated with poor metabolic control. Minuchin and his colleagues (1975) have also reported the successful treatment of diabetics and their psychosomatic families by using structural family therapy to help disengage the diabetic and establish more appropriate family boundaries. In all 15 cases, the pattern of recurrent ketoacidosis ceased and insulin doses were reduced.

These studies suggest that the mechanisms by which families influence diabetic control depend on the style of family functioning, especially cohesion. Both high and low cohesion are associated with poor diabetic control. In enmeshed families, diabetic control is physiologically linked to emotional processes within the family. In disengaged families, inadequate family structure and support results in noncompliance. Optimal management of diabetes requires the support and supervision of the family along with respect for individuality and age-appropriate autonomy. Although these results suggest specific clinical interventions with each type of family, no controlled studies have been conducted at this time.

Research on the adaptation of families to chronic illness shows the enormous impact a chronic illness has on families and how they often reorganize themselves around the illness, sometimes developing new identities. Families' coping effectiveness will usually influence the course of the illness. When faced with the challenge of a chronic illness, some families prosper, become closer, and function better, whereas others disintegrate. Health providers and family professionals have a special opportunity to help families during this crisis.

## Implications for Family Professionals

This body of research demonstrates that every aspect of an individual's physical health influences and is influenced by the family. From health promotion to the treatment of life-threatening and terminal illness, families are the most important context for health and illness. Healthy and unhealthy behaviors develop and are maintained or changed within families. Families are the most important source of stress and social support, which have a profound effect on the development and course of physical illnesses. Family members are the primary caregivers for patients with chronic illness, and families suffer their own stresses and burdens, which are often neglected by health care professionals.

The most important implication of this research is the need for health professionals and health care planners to recognize family members as essential partners in the delivery of health care. Doherty and Baird (1983) have developed a useful concept, that is, the therapeutic triangle, in which the basic treatment system consists of the health care professional, the patient, and the family. Using this model, the health care professional cannot treat the patient in isolation but must develop an ongoing relationship with the patient's family.

When one accepts the importance of the family in health and illness and the need to involve the family in health care, it becomes apparent that most health care clinicians, educators, planners, and researchers are not knowledgeable about caring for families and thus require help from family professionals. There are at least four areas in which family professionals can play major roles in health care: clinical settings, education for health professionals, health care policy, and family and health research.

### Clinical Settings

Many physicians, nurses, and other clinicians have a basic understanding of families and can work effectively with them in different settings, providing education, support, and occasional counseling. However, families often present with problems that are beyond the expertise of the average clinician. These problems may be directly related to a health problem, such as the abuse or neglect of a handicapped child, depression resulting from a stroke or other disabling condition, a pathological grief reaction, or alcoholism. In addition, many patients consult their physicians about common family problems, such as marital conflicts, infidelity, parenting difficulties, substance abuse, or family violence. Most of these problems, whether they are intimately related to health problems, are beyond the expertise of medical providers and require referral to a family therapist or other mental health professional.

To effectively treat these families and their psychosocial problems, there must be close collaboration between medical professionals and family therapists (McDaniel et al., 1990). Family professionals and health care providers need to work together as a team to provide a comprehensive biopsychosocial approach and avoid a division between the physical and mental health care of the patient and family. This cooperation requires ongoing communication beginning at the time of referral. Physicians and therapists often complain that the other does not keep them informed about the patient's treatment and progress. For example, the therapist may suggest that the patient see a medical specialist about a health problem without speaking with the referring physician, or the physician may prescribe antidepressants or other psychotropic drugs without consulting the family therapist. Just as the health professional must form a partnership with the family to provide the best care for the patient, so must the family professional develop a partnership with the health professional to provide comprehensive care for the patient and family (McDaniel, Hepworth, & Doherty, 1992).

### Education for Health Professionals

As recognition of the importance of families in health care increases, there is a growing need to train physicians, nurses, and other health professionals to work with families. This training of medical providers about families is best done by family professionals teaching in collaboration with health professionals. A large number of family professionals, including family therapists and family social scientists, currently teach in family practice residency programs and have helped bring a family systems approach into family medicine. Many family professionals teach in medical schools, and some work in pediatric and internal medicine residencies. Teaching about families is most effective when family professionals work closely with physicians or other health professionals. Medicine has a unique culture with its own customs, rituals, and language, which usually take an extended period of time for family professionals to learn. Family professionals who use teaching methods they learned in graduate school to teach medical students or physicians-in-training are doomed to failure. It is impossible for the family professional alone to know what areas of family science are relevant to health care professionals.

Over the past 10 years, the author, a family physician, has taught family systems theory and practice with a family therapist. By working together, we have learned about each other's area of expertise and how best to teach in that area. This method of collaborative teaching is well worth the extra time and cost involved, to both the students and the instructors. Many family professionals who have tried to go it on their own in medical settings have "burned out" after several years of teaching.

Many resources are available to family professionals who are interested in teaching in medical settings. Over the past decade, numerous books have been written on family-oriented health care and family systems medicine providing basic curricula for teaching about families to health professionals (e.g., Christie-Seely, 1984; Doherty & Baird, 1983, 1987; McDaniel et al., 1990; Sawa, 1985). In addition, the Society of Teachers of Family Medicine has a working group devoted to teaching about families. This Group on the Family has published a monograph on curricula currently being taught in family medicine (STFM, 1989) and has a yearly conference devoted to families.

### Health Care Policy

The U.S. health care system is in a state of crisis and will go through enormous changes over the next decade. This situation offers an opportunity for family professionals to become involved in the reform of the health care system to make it more receptive to the needs of families. The current health care system is individually focused and does not address the needs of the entire family. Most health care services remain concentrated on hospital care and receive full reimbursement. Once the patient returns home, these services and their reimbursement are sharply curtailed. For example, the family caregivers of patients with chronic illnesses such as Alzheimer's disease often receive inadequate services and support in the home. However, there is a risk that, as hospital and other expensive health care services are reduced to save money, an increasing burden will be placed upon family members to provide these services in the home without adequate assistance.

Family professionals must make the needs of families known to health care policymakers. The Consortium of Family Organizations (1992) (which consists of the American Association of Marriage and Family Therapy, the American Home Economics Association, the National Council of Family Relations, Family Services of America, and Family Resource Coalition) has started this process by producing a "white paper" on family-centered health care policy, which has been distributed to politicians and policymakers in Washington, D.C. In addition, the National Council on Family Relations has recently published *Vision 2010: Family and Health* for use by educators and policymakers. These are useful primers for family professionals who wish to become involved in health care policy at the federal, state, or local level.

### Family and Health Research

Although a great deal of research on families and physical health has been conducted over the past two decades, more studies are needed to understand the relationships between family factors and physical health and the implications for health care practice and policy. By the very nature of the topic, this research should be interdisciplinary and involve health and family professionals. These fields do not have a sufficient understanding of each other to conduct needed research. For example, research conducted solely by family social scientists tends to have an oversimplified view of health and often uses crude and unvalidated measures of health status. The same is true for health professionals who are involved in studying families.

Family professionals can be particularly helpful in developing theories about how family interactions can influence health. Much of the current research on families and health is atheoretical and tends to be driven either by disease outcomes or by particular family assessment instruments. For example, there are many studies looking at the relationship between cohesion and adaptability as measured by the Family Adaptability and Cohesion Scale (FACES) and health outcomes such as blood sugar levels in diabetes. These studies are relatively easy to conduct and often show relationships between family and health variables. However, they lack an underlying theory of how families influence health, provide little rationale for choosing family variables, and do not explain how the interaction between health and families takes place. These studies rarely control potential confounding variables (e.g., socioeconomic status) or examine possible intervening variables, such as individual psychological states (depression or anxiety) or health-related behaviors.

Much of the research on families and health has tended to pathologize families and inadvertently blame them for causing health problems. For example, cross-sectional studies showing that some families with chronic illness, such as diabetes, tend to be overly close or enmeshed have been interpreted as demonstrating that enmeshment causes or can worsen chronic illness. It is equally plausible that families become closer in response to the illness and that this response may be quite functional. This focus on family pathology results both from early family therapy research that studied how family dysfunction could cause mental illness and from medical research that searches for pathogens and other "causative" factors. More recently, family social scientists have emphasized the strengths and resiliency of families. Family professionals can help bring this perspective to family and health research with studies examining the health promoting and enhancing functions of families.

Research on families and health is sufficiently advanced to begin to develop and test simple and practical family interventions in health care. Only when family intervention trials have demonstrated that a family approach is more effective or cost-effective than an individual approach will family-oriented health care become widely practiced. The most promising areas for family interventions are health promotion/disease prevention and management of chronic illness. As reviewed above, some studies have demonstrated that involving spouses in weight reduction programs results in better outcomes. This model could be extended to other health behaviors, such as smoking, dietary changes, and exercise. As part of the federal government initiative *Healthy People 2000,* there is considerable interest and funding for interventions to promote health.

There is also a need to develop interventions to assist family caregivers, particularly for Alzheimer's disease and other chronic degenerative illnesses. This interest comes partly from the recognition that Alzheimer's patients are usually institutionalized when their family caregivers "burn out." Much is currently understood about the processes and burdens of family caregiving, but interventions need to be developed to support caregivers, reduce the burden placed upon them, and help prevent premature nursing home placements. Family professionals can play an important role in developing and evaluating these interventions.

## Conclusion

The Chinese character for crisis includes two symbols—one that stands for danger and the other for opportunity. The current health care system with its emphasis on biomedical reductionism, overspecialization, high technology, and high costs is in a state of crisis. This crisis offers many new opportunities for family professionals to become involved in the health care field. Additional research is needed to demonstrate to clinicians, medical educators, and policymakers that families play a crucial role in all aspects of health and illness. This research must be methodologically sound and sophisticated with regard to health and family measures. Family professionals are needed to advocate for families at all levels of government so that new health care policies are "family friendly." Medical professionals need basic education and training about families at all levels, from medical and nursing school, to continuing education for practicing providers, and across all specialties. The education of physicians about families is currently primarily limited to family medicine with some family teaching occurring in pediatrics and general internal medicine. Oncologists, surgeons, cardiologists, and other specialists also need to have a basic understanding of how to work effectively with the families of their patients.

Perhaps most important, family professionals can use their own skills and knowledge gained from research on families and health to work collaboratively with health professionals in helping families who are struggling with health problems. It is at the clinical level, working with families and medical providers, that this new family-centered approach to health care will grow and prosper as its success is more widely recognized and implemented.

## References

Ader, R. (Ed.). (1981). *Psychoneuroimmunology*. New York: Academic Press.
Anderson, B. J., & Auslander, W. F. (1980). Research on diabetes management and the family: A critique. *Diabetes Care, 3,* 696-702.
Anderson, B. J., Miller, J. P., Auslander, W. F., & Santiago, J. V. (1981). Family characteristics of diabetic adolescents: Relationship to metabolic control. *Diabetes Care, 4,* 586-594.
Barbarin, O. A., & Tirado, M. (1984). Family involvement and successful treatment of obesity: A review. *Family Systems Medicine, 2,* 37-45.
Bartrop, R. W., Luckhurst, E., Lazarus, L., Kiloh, L. G., & Penny, R. (1977). Depressed lymphocyte function after bereavement. *Lancet, 1,* 834-836.

Beautrais, A. L., Fergusson, D. M., & Shannon, F. T. (1982). Life events and childhood morbidity: A prospective study. *Pediatrics, 70*, 935-940.

Berkman, L. F. (1984). Assessing the physical health effects of social networks and social support. *Annual Review of Public Health, 5*, 413-432.

Berkman, L. F., & Syme, S. L. (1979). Social networks, host resistance and mortality: A nine year follow-up study of Alameda County residents. *American Journal of Epidemiology, 109*, 186-204.

Bewley, B. R., & Bland, J. M. (1977). Academic performance and social factors relating to cigarette smoking by school children. *British Journal of Preventive and Social Medicine, 31*, 8-24.

Blazer, D. G. (1982). Social support and mortality in an elderly community population. *American Journal of Epidemiology, 115*, 684-694.

Boyce, W. T., Jensen, E. W., Cassel, J. C., Collier, A. M., Smith, A. H., & Ramey, C. T. (1977). Influence of life events and family routines on childhood respiratory illness. *Pediatrics, 60*, 609-615.

Bruhn, J. G. (1977). Effects of chronic illness on the family. *Journal of Family Practice, 4*, 1057-1060.

Bryan, M. S., & Lowenberg, M. E. (1958). The father's influence on young children's food preferences. *Journal of American Dietetic Association, 34*, 30-35.

Calabrese, J. R., Kling, M. A., & Gold, P. W. (1987). Alterations in immunocompetence during stress, bereavement and depression: Focus on neuroendocrine regulation. *American Journal of Psychiatry, 144*, 1123-1134.

Califano, J. A. J. (1979). *Healthy people: The surgeon general's report on health promotion and disease prevention* (DHEW [PHS] Publication No. 79-55071, Public Health Service). Washington, DC: Government Printing Office.

Campbell, T. L. (1986). Family's impact on health: A critical review and annotated bibliography. *Family Systems Medicine, 4*, 135-328.

Campbell, T. L., & Treat, D. F. (1990). The family's influence on health. In R. Rakel (Ed.), *Textbook of family practice* (pp. 101-110). Philadelphia: Saunders.

Carter, H., & Glick, P. C. (1970). *Marriage and divorce: A social and economic study.* Cambridge, MA: Harvard University Press.

Cederblad, M., Helgesson, M., Larsson, Y., & Ludvigsson, J. (1982). Family structure and diabetes in children. *Pediatric Adolescent Endocrinology, 10*, 94-98.

Christie-Seely, J. (Ed.). (1984). *Working with the family in primary care: A systems approach to health and illness.* New York: Praeger.

Cohen, F. (1981). Stress and bodily illness. *Psychiatric Clinics of North America, 4*, 269-285.

Cohen, S., & Syme, S. L. (Eds.). (1985). *Social support and health.* Orlando, FL: Academic Press.

Consortium of Family Organizations. (1992, Winter). Principals of family-centered health care: A health care reform white paper. *Family Policy Report, 2*(2), 1-15.

Coppotelli, H. C., & Orleans, C. T. (1985). Partner support and other determinants of smoking cessation among women. *Journal of Consulting and Clinical Psychology, 53*, 455-460.

Doherty, W. J., & Baird, M. A. (1983). *Family therapy and family medicine: Toward the primary care of families.* New York: Guilford.

Doherty, W. J., & Baird, M. A. (Eds.). (1987). *Family-centered medical care: A clinical casebook.* New York: Guilford.

Doherty, W. J., & Campbell, T. L. (1988). *Families and health.* Beverly Hills, CA: Sage.

Engel, G. L. (1977). The need for a new medical model: A challenge for biomedicine. *Science, 196,* 129-136.

Engel, G. L. (1980). The clinical application of the biopsychosocial model. *American Journal of Psychiatry,* 137, 535-544.

Goldstein, M. (1987). Psychological issues. *Schizophrenia Bulletin, 13,* 157-171.

Gonzales, S., Steinglass, P., & Reiss, D. (1989). Diabetes in children: Family responses and control. *Psychosomatics, 24,* 367-372.

Greene, H. L., Goldberg, R. J., & Ockene, J. K. (1988). Cigarette smoking: The physician's role in cessation and maintenance. *Journal of General Internal Medicine, 3,* 75-87.

Grey, M. J., Genel, M., & Tamborlane, W. V. (1980). Psychosocial adjustment of latency-age diabetics: Determinants and relationship to control. *Pediatrics, 65,* 69-73.

Heinzelman, F., & Bagley, R. W. (1970). Response to physical activity programs and their effects on health behavior. *Public Health Rep, 85,* 905-911.

Helsing, K. J., & Szklo, M. (1981). Mortality after bereavement. *American Journal of Epidemiology, 114,* 41-52.

Holmes, T. H., & Rahe, R. H. (1967). The social readjustment scale. *Journal of Psychosomatic Research, 39,* 413-431.

Horne, R. L., & Picard, R. S. (1979). Psychosocial risk factors for lung cancers. *Psychosomatic Medicine, 41,* 503-514.

Houlihan, J. P. (1987). Families caring for frail and demented elderly: A review of selected findings. *Family Systems Medicine, 5,* 344-356.

House, J. S., Landis, K. R., & Umberson, D. (1988). Social relationships and health. *Science, 241,* 540-545.

Johnson, S. B. (1980). Psychosocial factors in juvenile diabetes: A review. *Journal of Behavioral Medicine, 3,* 95-116.

Kaprio, J., Koskenvou, M., & Rita, H. (1987). Mortality after bereavement: A prospective study of 95,647 widowed persons. *American Journal of Public Health, 77,* 283-287.

Khurana, R., & White, P. (1970). Attitudes of the diabetic child and his parents towards his illness. *Postgraduate Medicine, 48,* 72-76.

Kiecolt-Glaser, J. K., Fisher, L. D., Ogrockl, P., Stout, J. C., Spelcher, C. E., & Glaser, R. (1987). Marital quality, marital disruption, and immune function. *Psychosomatic Medicine, 49,* 13-32.

Klein, R., Dean, A., & Bogdanoff, M. (1968). The impact of illness of the spouse. *Journal of Chronic Disease, 20,* 241-252.

Klesges, R. C., Coates, T. J., & Brown, G. (1983). Parental influences on children's eating behavior and relative weight. *Journal of Applied Behavior Analysis, 16,* 371-378.

Koski, M. L., & Kumento, A. (1977). The interrelationship between diabetic control and family life. *Pediatric Adolescent Endocrinology, 3,* 41-45.

Kraus, A. S., & Lilenfeld, A. M. (1959). Some epidemiological aspects of the high mortality rate in the young widowed group. *Journal of Chronic Disease, 10,* 207-217.

Lask, B., & Matthew, D. (1979). Childhood asthma: A controlled trial of family psychotherapy. *Archives of Diseases in Children, 54,* 116-119.

Linn, M. W., Linn, B. S., & Jensen, J. (1984). Stressful events, dysphoric mood, and immune responsiveness. *Psychological Report, 54,* 219-222.

Lynch, J. (1977). *The broken heart: The medical consequences of loneliness.* New York: Basic Books.

McDaniel, S., Campbell, T., & Seaburn, D. (1990). *Family-oriented primary care: A manual for medical providers.* New York: Springer-Verlag.

McDaniel, S. H., Hepworth, J., & Doherty, W. (1992). *Medical family therapy*. New York: Basic Books.

Meyer, R. J., & Haggerty, R. J. (1962). Streptococcal infections in families: Factors altering individual susceptibility. *Pediatrics, 29,* 539-549.

Minuchin, S., Baker, L., Rosman, B. L., Liebman, R., Milman, L., & Todd, T. C. (1975). A conceptual model of psychosomatic illness in children: Family organization and family therapy. *Archives of General Psychiatry, 32,* 1031-1038.

Minuchin, S., Rosman, B. L., & Baker, L. (1978). *Psychosomatic families*. Cambridge, MA: Harvard University Press.

National Heart, Lung, and Blood Institute. (1982). Management of patient compliance in the treatment of hypertension. *Hypertension, 4,* 415-423.

Newacheck, P. W., & Halfon, N. (1986). The association of mother's and children's use of physician services. *Medical Care, 24,* 415-423.

Oberst, M. T., & James, R. H. (1985, April). Going home: Patient and spouse adjustment following cancer surgery. *Topics in Clinical Nursing,* pp. 46-57.

Orr, D. P., Golden, M. P., Myers, G., & Marrerro, D. G. (1983). Characteristics of adolescents with poorly controlled diabetes referred to a tertiary care center. *Diabetes Care, 6,* 170-175.

Ortho-Gomer, K., & Johnson, J. V. (1987). Social network interaction and mortality: A six year follow-up study of a random sample of the Swedish population. *Journal of Chronic Disease, 40,* 949-957.

Osterweis, M., Bush, P. J., & Zuckerman, A. E. (1979). Family context as a predictor of individual medication use. *Social Science and Medicine, 13A,* 287-291.

Osterweis, M., Solomon, F., & Green, M. (Eds.). (1984). *Bereavement: Reactions, consequences, and care*. Washington, DC: National Academy.

Parkes, C. M., Benjamin, B., & Fitzgerald, R. G. (1969). Broken heart: A statistical study of increased mortality among widowers. *British Medical Journal, 1,* 740-743.

Penn, P. (1983). Coalitions and binding interactions in families with chronic illness. *Family Systems Medicine, 1,* 16-25.

Price, R. A., Chen, K. H., & Cavallii, S. L. (1981). Models of spouse influence and their applications to smoking behavior. *Social Biology, 28,* 14-29.

Public Health Service. (1990). *Health people 2000: National health promotion and disease prevention objective*. Washington, DC: U.S. Department of Health and Human Services.

Rabkin, J. G., & Struening, E. L. (1976). Life events, stress and illness. *Science, 194,* 1013-1020.

Roghmann, K. J., & Haggerty, R. J. (1973). Daily stress, illness and the use of health services in young families. *Pediatric Research, 7,* 520-526.

Ruberman, W., Weinblatt, E., Goldberg, J. D., & Chaudhary, B. S. (1984). Psychosocial influences on mortality after myocardial infarction. *The New England Journal of Medicine, 311,* 552-557.

Sabbeth, B., & Leventhal, J. M. (1984). Marital adjustment to chronic childhood illness: A critique of the literature. *Pediatrics, 73,* 762-768.

Sallis, J. F., & Nader, P. R. (1988). Family determinants of health behaviors. In D. S. Gochman (Ed.), *Health behavior*. New York: Plenum.

Sawa, R. J. (1985). *Family dynamics for physicians: Guidelines to assessment and treatment*. Lewiston, NY: Edwin Mellon.

Schleifer, S. J., Keller, S. E., Camerino, M., Thornton, J. C., & Stein, M. (1983). Suppression of lymphocyte stimulation following bereavement. *Journal of the American Medical Association, 250,* 374-377.

Shouval, R., Ber, R., & Galatzer, A. (1982). Family social climate and the health status and social adaptation of diabetic youth. *Pediatric Adolescent Endocrinology, 10,* 89-93.

Steidl, J. H., Finkelstein, F. O., Wexler, J. P., Feigenbaum, H., Kitsen, J., & Quinlan, D. M. (1980). Medical condition, adherence to treatment regime and family functioning: Their interaction in patients receiving long-term dialysis treatment. *Archives of General Psychiatry, 37,* 1025-1029.

Steinglass, P., Temple, S., Lisman, S., & Reiss, D. (1982). Coping with spinal cord injury: The family perspective. *General Hospital Psychiatry, 4,* 259-264.

STFM Family in Family Medicine Task Force. (1989). *The family in family medicine: Graduate curriculum and teaching strategies.* Kansas City, MO: Author.

Strong, M. (1988). *Mainstay: For the well spouse of the chronically ill.* Boston: Little, Brown.

Turk, D. C., Litt, M. D., & Salovey, P. (1985). Seeking urgent pediatric treatment: Factors contributing to frequency, delay, and appropriateness. *Health Psychology, 4,* 43-59.

U.S. Department of Commerce. (1980). *Statistical abstracts of the United States* (101s.d.IS.P.-25,N.802,888). Washington, DC: Government Printing Office.

Venters, M. H., Jacobs, D. R., Luepker, R. V., Maiman, L. A., & Gillum, R. F. (1984). Spouse concordance of smoking patterns: The Minnesota heart survey. *American Journal of Epidemiology, 120,* 608-616.

Verbrugge, L. M. (1977). Marital status and health. *Journal of Marriage and Family, 7,* 267-285.

Vitaliano, P. P., Becker, J., Russo, J., Magna-Amato, K., & Mariuvo, R. D. (1988). Expressed emotion in spouse caregivers of patients with Alzheimer's disease. *Journal of Applied Social Sciences, 13,* 215-220.

White, K., Kolman, M. L., Wexler, P., Polin, G., & Winter, R. J. (1984). Unstable diabetes and unstable families: A psychosocial evaluation of diabetic children with recurrent ketoacidosis. *Pediatrics, 73,* 749-755.

World Health Organization. (1976). *Statistical Indices of Family Health,* No. 589, p. 17 (New York).

Zola, I. K. (1972). Studying the decision to see a doctor. *Advances in Psychosomatic Medicine, 8,* 216-236.

Zuckerman, D. M., Kasl, S. V., & Osterfeld, A. M. (1984). Psychosocial predictors of mortality among the elderly poor: The role of religion, well-being, and social contact. *American Journal of Epidemiology, 119,* 410-423.

# 8

❀

# Mental Illness

## STEPHEN M. GAVAZZI

This chapter focuses on the ways in which family systems are affected by
the stressors and strains associated with the development of major mental
disorders in one or more family members. Hence a major goal of this
chapter is to incorporate a family-oriented perspective regarding mental
disorders. This perspective is in contrast with an individual-oriented perspective regarding mental disorders, which constitutes an enormous and
well-established body of literature concerning mental disorders.

As will be discussed, it is almost impossible to explain the development
of mental disorders (i.e., etiology) without addressing family factors. What
then is meant by the taking of an individually oriented perspective? Apart
from describing the origins of the disorder as a function of an individual's biological makeup, personality traits, and so on, much of the literature concerning mental disorders focuses on assessment, treatment, and
research issues at the level of the individual (i.e., "How does an individual
display symptoms that relate to a particular mental disorder?" "How do we
treat such an individual?" and "What is the effect of the mental disorder
and/or its treatment on this individual?").

More recent and less conspicuous in volume and attention is the body of
literature using a family-oriented perspective on mental disorders. Here,
issues concerning assessment, treatment, and research focus on the entire
family. By adopting a family systems perspective, information is gained
about all family members, that is, how they interact as a system in the

context of coping with one or more of their members suffering from a mental disorder. Such information would otherwise be overlooked by a focus solely upon the individual with the mental disorder. From a family systems perspective, questions regarding assessment, treatment, and research are reformulated within a family systems framework (i.e., "What do interaction patterns look like in families that contain a member or members suffering from a mental disorder?" "How do we help such families?" and "What is the effect of the mental disorder and/or its treatment on this family?").

Following a demographic and historical overview of the literature focused on mental disorders, the remainder of the chapter will focus on the study of stress and coping within the family system in response to the development of a mental disorder in one or more family members. Where necessary, the family-oriented perspective will be compared and contrasted with the individually oriented perspective.

## Demographic Factors and
## Historical Background in the United States

### Demographic Factors

It is estimated that approximately 15.5% of all adult men and women in this country suffer from some form of mental disorder (Regier et al., 1988). Other studies have indicated estimates of between 17% and 23% of all U.S. adults (Smith, 1989). In addition, at least 7.5 million (or approximately 12%) of American children and adolescents are estimated to be similarly affected (National Institute of Mental Health, 1991). Of course, the percentage of the population affected by mental disorders would increase exponentially if these figures were calculated to include family members.

The economic costs of the treatment and care of mental disorders are staggering. It has been reported that health care costs in this country total approximately $640 billion annually, representing over 11% of the total gross national product (GNP) of the United States (Smith, 1989). Of this amount, the economic costs directly related to mental health concerns are currently estimated to be approximately $70 billion annually (Shore, Lash, Hadley, Wagman, & Schulz, 1990), which represents over 10% of total U.S. health care costs.

Rising expenditures linked to mental disorders are frequently reported in the popular literature. For instance, a recent cover story in *Time* magazine stated that the total annual cost of mental disorders to the U.S. economy was approximately $129 billion. *Time* magazine obtained a much-higher figure because the staff used a variety of figures not always factored into studies on the economic impact of mental disorders. Their $129 billion figure included the combined costs of such things as payments to physicians, psychopharmaceutical expenditures, billing for hospitalization, legal fees, and lost income ("Pills for the Mind," 1992).

There are thought to be significant sex differences with regard to the prevalence of specific disorders. For instance, males have been found to display higher rates of antisocial personality disorders, whereas females are significantly more likely to display affective and anxiety disorders (Regier et al., 1988). Further, there is an interaction effect between sex and marital status. A variety of studies consistently have found married women and unmarried men (single, widowed, or divorced) to be significantly more likely to experience mental disorders than single women (single, widowed, or divorced) and married men (Balcom & Healey, 1990; Gove, 1972; Gurin, Veroff, & Feld, 1960). It should be noted that a feminist-informed perspective suggests that close attention be paid to the dominance of male-oriented definitions of mental health and dysfunction, which include terminology and theoretical frameworks of professionals operating with a family systems-oriented perspective (Bograd, 1990). Furthermore, certain factors related to the outpatient care given to individuals with mental disorders following their hospitalization discharge (Thurer, 1983) may be contributing to the feminization of deinstitutionalizing patients.

The literature suggests that older individuals are less susceptible to mental disorders than are younger people, with the exception of disorders related to severe cognitive impairment (Regier et al., 1988). However, there are also studies that have reported that approximately 85% of nursing home patients (Goldfarb, 1962) suffer from some sort of mental disorder (Rovner & Rabins, 1985, report that more recent studies have placed that figure closer to 50%). One explanation of these apparently contradictory findings regarding age and mental health status would be to conclude that nursing homes are being used as a "dumping ground" for elderly family members who display psychiatric symptomatology. This practice would greatly inflate the rate of nursing home residents suffering from mental disorders. However, because there is evidence suggesting that the total number of physical and psychological complaints increases with advanced age (Brody & Kleban, 1983; Watson & Wright, 1984), and that nursing home patient numbers are now estimated to be on the order of 1.2 million Americans (Rovner & Rabins, 1985), in actuality it may be that a significant portion of mental disturbance in older people goes undetected in the general elderly population.

Although the reported frequencies of minority populations and poverty-stricken individuals suffering from various mental disorders vary widely, there is general agreement in the literature regarding the greater vulnerability of these populations to mental illness. In large part, one of the primary reasons for these widely varying figures seems to be the general lack of effort given by researchers to disentangling the combined effects of ethnicity and socioeconomic status.

Sandua's (1985) review of the literature on mental disorders describes the significant impact of both ethnicity and socioeconomic factors on such variables as antecedent influences, family interaction styles, and attitudes toward mental illness itself. Despite such evidence, the majority of studies focusing on mental disorders have disregarded the importance of these issues. Such a failure to account for ethnicity and socioeconomic variations results in findings that are extremely limited (Sandua, 1985).

Lefley (1985) notes that there is a great need to understand how the literature on mental disorders is culturally determined. Such issues as chronicity of the disorder, medication used in treatment planning, actual diagnosis, and treatment outcome are all thought to be suffused with the prevailing views of the dominant culture (Lefley, 1990). Further, Jansen (1982) warns against the oversimplifications that can result from failure to account for the detrimental impact of larger societal forces on families. For example, Lawson (1986) notes the consequences of such larger societal factors as racial discrimination and prejudicial labeling on the overall adaptation of African American families containing a member suffering from a mental disorder; these are often translated into constraints on their daily lives as parents, marital partners, employees, and so on.

*Historical Background*

Historically, definitions regarding mental disorders—invariably including such labels as "madness," "insanity," and the like—included a wide range of disabilities and behaviors that were perceived to be deviant from the norms and expectations of society (Scheflen, 1981). Attempts to classify mental disorders can be dated back as far as 2600 B.C. (Webb, DiClemente, Johnstone, Sanders, & Perley, 1981). Freud and other early pioneers in the study and treatment of mental disorders began to develop typologies that would aid in the diagnosis of an individual's mental health status and the subsequent prognosis for treatment. However, it was only with the establishment and further development of nosologies such as the *Diagnostic and Statistical Manual of Mental Disorders (DSM,* American Psychiatric Association, 1952; *DSM-II,* American Psychiatric Association, 1968; *DSM-III,* American Psychiatric Association, 1980) that a comprehensive and methodologically sophisticated classification system became available to the mental health field.

The most recent version of the *Diagnostic and Statistical Manual of Mental Disorders (DSM-III-R,* American Psychiatric Association, 1987) continues to reflect a largely individual-oriented perspective with regard to the multiaxial classification (multidimensional) and diagnosis of mental disorders, because there is a great deal of attention given to biological, psychological, and/or behavioral symptoms displayed *by individuals.* Such symptoms are categorized on Axes I, II, and III of this classification system. Each axis becomes the representation of a set of core variables, which, when combined with the other axes, in effect create a definition of what is considered to be a mental disorder.

> All clinical syndromes (i.e., Schizophrenia, Affective Disorders and Mental Retardation) plus other conditions that are not mental disorders but are a focus of attention or treatment (i.e., Uncomplicated Bereavement, Parent Child Problems, Malingering), as well as no disorder or condition, are coded on Axis I. Personality Disorders and Specific Developmental Disorders are coded on Axis II. . . . [Axis III] permits the clinician to document any physical conditions or disorders that are potentially relevant to the understanding or management of the individual. Any other significant physical findings (e.g., soft neurological signs) may also be listed on Axis III. (Webb et al., 1981, p. 10)

Unlike its predecessors, both versions of *DSM-III* now also take into account certain psychosocial stressors, life events, and the adaptive functioning of the individual within an *interpersonal and social realm,* which are categorized on Axes IV and V of this classification system.

> [Axis IV] permits the clinician to identify and evaluate the psychosocial stressors relevant to the assessment and treatment of the individual. The clinician takes note of the number and the severity of life events that are judged significant in the development or exacerbation of the current disorder. . . . [Axis V] permits the clinician to indicate his/her judgement of the peak level of adaptive functioning that an individual has been able to maintain for a period of time the previous year. A composite of three major areas denotes *DSM-III's* concept of adaptive functioning: social relations, occupational functioning, and the use of leisure time. (Webb et al., 1981, pp. 10-11)

Unfortunately, the use of Axes IV and V in current diagnostic and assessment efforts and the ethical considerations related to the incorporation of the entire *DSM* classification system within a family system framework are debatable points of contention (Denton, 1989, 1990). It is hoped that the new version of the *Diagnostic and Statistical Manual of Mental Disorders—DSM-IV,* with an estimated printing date of 1994—will be more compatible with a systems-oriented perspective (Millon & Klerman, 1986).

## Etiology

As mentioned in the introductory paragraph of this chapter, it is extremely difficult to discuss the literature on the etiology of mental disorders without mentioning the role of family or at the very least one parent (mother and/or father) because even molecular, genetic-based research studies on mental disorders have at their core the implication of family heritage. In fact, the only nonfamilial factors discussed in the literature seem to be various accounts of how environmental toxins and circumstances of "community hysteria" (Cooper, 1986) or socially related psychoses (Al-Issa, 1977) contribute in comparatively rare and isolated ways to the development of mental disorders.

Thus the majority of writings on the etiology of mental disorders focus on the linkage between the development of mental disorders and certain behaviors occurring inside of the family domain. According to Kendler (1988), "a long tradition in psychiatry has advocated the importance of intrafamilial factors in the etiology of psychiatric illness. A particular focus has been the behavioral characteristics in parents that predispose to psychiatric disorders in their offspring" (p. 657). Kendler also notes that the resulting etiological accounts incorporate either "direct vertical cultural transmission" or "indirect vertical cultural transmission" explanatory models. In the "direct" model, family environmental traits are thought to be identical to the resulting mental disorder (i.e., parents displaying depressive symptomatology result in depressed offspring). The "indirect" model holds that the critical predisposing family environmental traits bear little or no characterological resemblance to the resulting mental disorder.

Alternately, Fristad and Clayton (1991) discuss the family-oriented literature regarding mental disorders with a different set of categories, reporting on both (a) those studies that attempt to define a genetic link between parents' mental disorder and the mental health risk to their offspring and (b) those studies linking mental disorders in children to characteristics of their families. These authors note that few of these studies use variables representing *both* of these family-oriented dimensions, despite research evidence supporting their combined usage in both assessment and intervention efforts (Fristad & Clayton, 1991).

A great deal of evidence concerning genetic linkage exists in the present literature, as we shall see in the review of research findings. From the use of multigenerational data gathering strategies to the mapping of DNA polymorphisms (Spence, 1987), a variety of sophisticated methodologies have created the explanatory notion that mental disorders have distinct biological origins. Such efforts often have led to a rapid return to the more individually oriented perspective regarding mental disorders, especially if present family system characteristics are not assessed.

Much of our early understanding of family stress and coping responses to mental disorders evolved from research by family therapists on families that contained a member with a major mental disorder—usually schizophrenia. Examples of these research programs included the work of such family therapy pioneers as Bateson, Jackson, Haley, Weakland, and Satir at the twin Palo Alto, California, projects known as "The Project for the Study of Schizophrenia" and "The Mental Research Institute (MRI)"; Boszormenyi-Nagy at the Eastern Pennsylvania Psychiatric Institute (EPPI) in Philadelphia; Wynne and Bowen at the National Institute of Mental Health (NIMH) in Washington, D.C.; and Lidz at Yale University (see Broderick & Schrader, 1981; Hoffman, 1981; Nichols & Schwartz, 1991, for extensive review of these works).

From this work, several themes developed as explanations concerning the etiology of mental disorders within a family-oriented perspective. In general, many of these themes focused on family environment variables with emphasis on family communication patterns. For instance, the two Palo Alto groups were very interested in the concept of "double bind" communications in their research and therapy with families containing schizophrenic members (Bateson, Jackson, Haley, & Weakland, 1956). In somewhat oversimplified fashion, the double bind hypothesis held that mental disorders were the result of conflicting messages given to a family member, who in turn was expected to act on both messages simultaneously. Work on the double bind theory led to the advancement of a significant line of research and therapy regarding the communication patterns of families with mentally ill family members (see Berger, 1978; Jackson, 1968a, 1968b; Sluzki & Ransom, 1976).

More recently, research and therapy efforts have been advanced through a focus on other types of communication patterns such as "communication deviance" and "expressed emotion." Communication deviance (CD) refers to the dysfunctional patterns of communication displayed by parents with schizophrenic sons or daughters. Such dysfunctional interaction patterns are thought to be of two basic types: *fragmented* (in which family communications are described in ways such as erratic, disruptive, and awkward) and *amorphous* (in which family communications are labeled in ways such as vague, confused, and intrusive) communications (Singer & Wynne, 1963, 1965a, 1965b). CD has been hypothesized to lie on a continuum, with the available evidence suggesting that parents of "disturbed" (i.e., schizophrenic) offspring display significantly more CD than parents of "normal" (i.e., nonschizophrenic) offspring (Doane, 1978). Currently, Wynne (1987) has expanded the conceptualization and empirical work surrounding this construct to include measures of healthy communication patterns, which are seen as "related to but not simply the inverse of CD" (p. 59).

The work on expressed emotion (see Brown, Birley, & Wing, 1972; Brown, Monck, Carstairs, & Wing, 1962) now greatly influences thinking about the family-oriented perspective on mental disorders. Expressed emotion (EE) is a concept that has been used to describe both (a) the level of emotional (over)involvement between family members and (b) the degree to which families display critical comments in their communications about the family member with the mental disorder (Vaughn & Leff, 1976a, 1976b). This body of research largely has been directed toward the study of how higher levels of expressed emotion are related to relapse rates following the hospitalization of a family member as well as how EE levels vary according to type of mental disorder and marital quality indicators (Hooley, 1987).

## Assessment

Understanding the impact of mental disorders from a family-oriented perspective requires that professionals working with families begin any intervention strategies with a thorough assessment of stressors and strains. Often, these stressors and strains are discussed as "burdens" associated with having a family member suffering from a mental disorder. Hoenig and Hamilton (1966) have categorized the burdens faced by family members as being both subjective and objective. Although far from universal in actual usage (Bailey & Garralda, 1987), subjective burdens generally have to do with perceptions about the illness, whereas objective burdens are centered on observable and countable stressors related to mental disorders (Maurin & Boyd, 1990).

Objective burdens are usually discussed in terms of the economic hardships faced by families. These burdens usually are calculated on the basis of a family's outright payment or copayment for expenses incurred through contact with the medical system as well as lost wages suffered as the result of having to provide functional assistance to the member with the mental disorder. Franks (1990) argues that many other family efforts regarding the care and treatment of members—providing transportation, food, clothing, payment of insurance, and so on—should be calculated into figures regarding objective burdens. In fact, for progressive policy reasons, the argument is made that all family efforts related to helping a family member with a mental disorder should be seen not as a burden but as a "resource contribution," in effect making families one of many service providers in the mental health delivery system (Franks, 1990). However, such a viewpoint must be tempered with the expressed needs and desires of families themselves. In particular, the reframing of families as resource providers may be counterproductive if it were to lead to policymaking decisions that increased the objective and subjective burdens experienced by families (Hatfield, 1987; Lefley, 1989).

By far, one of the most severe subjective burdens on family members is the stigma attached to mental disorders.

> Stigma—an ugly word and an ugly reality for many patients and their families. The stigma of mental illness is often as painful and disabling as the symptoms of major psychiatric disorders. . . . Stigma is a prison that separates the mentally ill from our society and keeps them apart from their fellow citizens. (Flynn, 1987, p. 53)

The generally negative public perceptions of mental disorders are heightened by the media's continued propagation of inaccurate and stereotypical descriptions of individuals with mental disorders (Flynn, 1987), which serve to reinforce family members' sense of alienation from their social context. Psychological burdens related to the stigma of mental disorders include lower self-esteem levels, reduced social contacts, job loss, and family relationship difficulties (Fuchs, 1986; Leete, 1987; Mittleman, 1985; Wahl & Harman, 1989). In addition, these individuals and families must interact with a mental health system that is organized in ways that are often antithetical to proper and efficient care delivery, especially in regard to chronic mental disorders (Hatfield, 1987; Klein, 1987; Meyerson & Herman, 1987). Family members must also interact with mental health professionals who typically operate within a generally negative set of attitudes about individuals with mental disorders and their families (Lefley, 1989; Manis, Hunt, Brewer, & Kercher, 1965; Minkoff, 1987; Mirabi, Weinman, Magnetti, & Keppler, 1985; Morrison, 1979).

## Theoretical Perspectives and Summary of Research Findings

### Theoretical Perspectives

According to Hahlweg and Goldstein (1987), much of the current family-oriented research on mental disorders follows the "vulnerability-stress model," which they credit as originally being articulated by Rosenthal (1970) and subsequently advanced by Zubin and Spring (1977).

> According to this model, a predisposition to a disorder, such as schizophrenia, is inherited and forms the basis for various indices of vulnerability to the disorder. This vulnerability is modified by all life events that increase or decrease the likelihood that a major psychiatric disorder, such as schizophrenia, will emerge in early adulthood. The stress-vulnerability model is also applicable to the post-onset stage of psychiatric disorder because vulnerability continues to be modified in association with variations in remission from the acute phase of the disorder, and this vulnerability interacts with various intercurrent life events, within and outside of the family, to modify the risk for subsequent episodes of the disorder. (Hahlweg & Goldstein, 1987, p. 2)

It should be noted that the "diathesis-stress" model is also used interchangeably to describe this theoretical framework. Hahlweg and Goldstein (1987) note the need for researchers to examine the relationship between family interaction processes and specific mental disorders to generate critical information regarding both "protective" and "adversive" family contexts that either decrease or increase family members' vulnerability levels with regard to specific disorders.

The present review of studies using a family-oriented perspective on mental disorders is organized into three categories thought to address research implications. The first category includes those studies that have examined how the presence of a mental disorder in a parent puts that parent's offspring at risk of also developing a mental disorder (genetic linkage research). The second category reviews studies that assess the relationship between various family environment factors and the subsequent mental health status of family members. Finally, the third category examines those studies that attempt to combine aspects of both genetic linkage and family context in the development of mental disorders.

## Genetic Linkage Research

Genetic linkage research usually takes the form of exploring the relationship between the presence of a mental disorder in one family member and concurrent or eventual manifestation of mental health difficulties in other family members. Predominant in this line of research are those studies assessing the connection between parental mental health status and the "high genetic risk" status of their offspring (Mednick & Schulsinger, 1968). Goodman's (1984) review of this literature compartmentalizes the research foci into six distinct categories: psychophysiological-neurological functioning, cognitive-intellectual functioning, attentional processes, social-interpersonal functioning, clinical-affective functioning, and obstetrical complications. In such studies, the outcome of high-risk status is usually viewed from the perspective of the offspring of a mentally ill parent developing either the same or a similar mental disorder and/or developing other adjustment difficulties. The literature review conducted by Goodman (1984) contains widespread examples of studies that have generated empirical support of this perspective.

### Research on Family Environment

A great deal of the research on family environment factors related to the development of mental disorders has used either the communication deviance (CD) or expressed emotion (EE) constructs. Studies examining CD mainly used projective tests (such as the Rorschach) in an attempt to discern differences between families of disturbed and normal offspring. Doane (1978) has reported that a consistent pattern of results emerges from many of these studies. Specifically, families with disturbed members displayed greater amounts of CD than did families with nondisturbed members, and the amount of CD found among families with different types of mental disorders was significantly related to the degree of psychopathological severity levels (Doane, 1978).

Studies examining EE have historically relied on use of the Camberwell Family Interview (Vaughn & Leff, 1981; Vaughn, Snyder, Jones, Freeman, & Falloon, 1984), although there have been two recent attempts to construct self-report instruments, that is, the Level of Expressed Emotion Scale (Cole & Kazarian, 1988) and the Family Emotional Involvement and Criticism Scale (Shields, Franks, Harp, McDaniel, & Campbell, 1992). Hooley (1987) has used an attribution theoretical model in the service of reviewing EE-related studies. From this perspective, it is asserted first and foremost that studies have generated face validity evidence for the EE construct, in essence supporting the use of both emotional involvement and levels of family criticism as differentiating variables in the study of mental disorders. Also, the research evidence shows that EE levels vary according to how severely impaired an individual is by a given mental disorder as well as through the use of psychoeducationally based treatment strategies (to be discussed), at least with certain types of families (Hooley, 1987).

It should be noted that there have been a number of efforts to unite the CD and EE constructs in research on mental disorders and the family. Many of these studies are either cited or reproduced in a compilation of theoretical and empirical papers edited by Hahlweg and Goldstein (1987). Finally, it should be noted that CD and EE research does not constitute the entire scope of efforts to examine the relationship between family environment and mental disorders. Several other contributions have been made throughout this literature's development, including work on family typologies (Epstein, Baldwin, & Bishop, 1983; Lewis, Beavers, Gossett, & Phillips, 1976) and the work on family evaluation strategies done by Reiss and colleagues (Oliveri & Reiss, 1982; Reiss, 1971).

### Combining Genetic Linkage and Family Environment Efforts

Fristad and Clayton (1991) provide a review of those studies attempting to combine genetic linkage and family environment variables. These include Wynne's (1987) work on CD in families where risk status was defined through a parent's prior hospitalization experience, a study of stressful interactions in families with a mother diagnosed with an affective disorder (Hammen et al., 1987), research on family system functioning in adoptive families differentiated by the presence or absence of a schizophrenic mother (Tienari et al., 1987), and Goldstein's (1987) longitudinal work predicting eventual onset of major mental disorders in the offspring of families displaying varying levels of CD, EE, and affective style as well as the presence or absence of a family member with a diagnosed mental disorder.

Other research efforts combining genetic linkage and family environment factors reviewed by Fristad and Clayton (1991) include a study of children's personal adjustment as affected by family functioning and the presence or absence of affective disorders in a biological parent (Keller et al., 1986) as well as the Billings and Moos (1986) research on offspring of currently depressed, previously depressed, or never-depressed parents. Fristad and Clayton's (1991) own research looked at mental disorder diagnoses in children in relation to family functioning levels and the prevalence of mental disorders in prior family generations.

## Interventions

### *Therapy*

As previously noted, the family therapy profession has greatly influenced the family-oriented perspective regarding mental disorders. Unfortunately, much of this work either directly or indirectly has been used to blame families for "causing" the mental disorder of one of its members. Such blaming attitudes can be seen, for instance, in a particular school of family therapy known as the Milan model (Selvini Palazzoli, Boscolo, Cecchin, & Prata, 1978), a theoretical descendent of work done with the double bind hypothesis by the MRI research and therapy teams cited above. One version of the Milan model (it has undergone a series of splits and permutations since its original inception; see Campbell, Draper, & Crutchley, 1991) currently holds that much of the blame for mental disorders in individuals resides in the "dirty games" that family members play with each other in the course of their interactions (Selvini Palazzoli & Prata, 1989). From this perspective, therapeutic interventions are designed to disrupt these unhealthy family interactions to eliminate the symptoms of the mental disorder.

Alternately, however, many family therapists have moved away from positions of blame. Most illustrative of this trend are those family therapists using a "psychoeducational approach" to work with mental disorders in a family context (McFarlane, 1991). Within this approach, family members are encouraged to learn all that they can about the family member's mental disorder—in effect becoming fully educated about the facts surrounding assessment and treatment concerns. As opposed to therapeutic approaches designed to eliminate a particular disorder, the psychoeducational approach largely seeks to prevent the *return* of the disorder as well as to alleviate the pain and suffering of family members involving the individual with the mental disorder (Falloon, 1988).

Debate surrounding these discrepant approaches within the family-oriented literature on mental disorders continues. On one hand, family pathology-based theories and therapies have been criticized regarding, among other things, causing new problems in their attempt to understand and alleviate the initial problems brought to the therapist. Such negative outcomes are thought to include the therapist directly communicating to family members that they are "crazymaking" and thus are to blame for the mental disorder (Goldstein, 1981) as well as communicating messages that are paradoxical and impossible to respond to by family members (Lefley, 1989). In contrast, the psychoeducational approach has been criticized for having provided at best a limited view of what possibilities for change exist and at worst a framework that guarantees continued dysfunctional interactions among family members (Nichols & Schwartz, 1991). The literature does contain attempts to synthesize the best of both standpoints, most notably in the work of Anderson and colleagues (see Anderson, Reiss, & Hogarty, 1986).

The debate on the relative merits of these approaches is far from over, however. For example, a recent case study presented by Selvini (1992) on working with families containing a schizophrenic member serves as evidence that the field still contains a great deal of emotionality about these treatment approaches. Further evidence of this passionate debate exists in subsequent letters to the editor that followed this case study's publication. Other dialogues in the literature underscore this point as well (see Falloon, 1986; Hatfield, 1986).

### Social Policy

Perhaps the most powerful impact on social attitudes and policymaking decisions surrounding mental disorders has come as the result of the growth of such grassroots organizations as the National Alliance for the Mentally Ill (NAMI) and its related affiliates. NAMI has a dual focus of both advocating for patient (and family) rights and attempting to provide general public education (Howe & Howe, 1987). The efforts of NAMI have resulted in a number of important issues being brought to the forefront, including quality of care and other mental health service consumer concerns, treatment difficulties associated with dual diagnosis and involuntary hospitalization, and outreach to other self-help organizations and advocacy groups.

Professional groups also have played a role in social policy efforts. In particular, the Group for the Advancement of Psychiatry has proffered a great deal of literature aimed at educating both professional and lay audiences about critical issues associated with mental disorders and families. Perhaps most notable in this regard is a book published in cooperation with "Dear Abby" columnist Abigail van Buren that covers many of the problems and concerns of families in the initial and advanced stages of dealing with a family member diagnosed with a mental disorder (Group for the Advancement of Psychiatry, 1986).

## Future Directions

The future of both research and intervention strategies regarding the family-oriented perspective on mental disorders may be best served by models that attend to the factors of stress and coping dealt with throughout the chapters of this book. In particular, a focus on variations in perceptions, available resources, and the cumulative stressors and strains faced by families, in combination with attention to cognitive, emotional, and behavioral coping strategies employed by these families (Lefley, 1987), allows for the most sophisticated assessment of a family's adaptation to mental disorders. This viewpoint has been advanced by several scholars in the field, including Hatfield and Lefley (1987), who have encouraged a respectful climate between clinicians, researchers, and families. In effect, then, future efforts must include further advancement of both research models and clinical frameworks that move beyond positions of blame and toward continued collaboration (Johnson, 1986). This is especially true in regard to issues of family empowerment (Chamberlin, Rogers, & Sneed, 1989; Spaniol, Zipple, & FitzGerald, 1984).

One very important ramification of collaborative ventures focuses on professional training issues. In essence, the training of mental health professionals should include a dissemination of information leading to an understanding of the particular stresses, coping styles, and subsequent adaptation levels of families dealing with the presence of mental disorders (Lefley, 1988). Information also will need to be continually disseminated regarding how these families historically have perceived and evaluated the services of mental health professionals (Holden & Lewine, 1982). Further, given the increasingly successful use of support groups that focus directly on the impact of mental disorders on family members, clinicians also would do well to strengthen their knowledge of and collaborative ties with the self-help community (Barbee, Kasten, & Rosenson, 1991; Wintersteen & Young, 1988). Finally, various attempts to "build bridges" between professionals and families (Backer & Richardson, 1989) may include the adoption of more collaborative labels—such as that of "family consultant" (Bernheim, 1989)—and collaborative descriptions for the work that they are doing with individuals and families dealing with mental disorders. In sum, the family-oriented perspective regarding mental disorders is gaining increased attention among mental health professionals. At the same time that the mental health field is becoming sophisticated enough to develop models of collaborative care, however, we now live in an era in which health insurance companies are seeking to deal with health care's skyrocketing costs by severely restricting (or in some cases totally eliminating) mental health benefits. As a result, therapists in the United States increasingly are finding their hands tied professionally by managed health care plans that seek to micromanage the mental health treatment given to their subscribers. If the family-oriented perspective regarding mental disorders is seen as a nonessential component of mental health care delivery, treatment models sensitive to this approach may be among the first casualties of this restrictive environment.

## References

Al-Issa, I. (1977). Social and cultural aspects of hallucination. *Psychological Bulletin, 84,* 570-587.

American Psychiatric Association. (1952). *Diagnostic and statistical manual of mental disorders.* Washington, DC: Author.

American Psychiatric Association. (1968). *Diagnostic and statistical manual of mental disorders* (2nd ed.). Washington, DC: Author.

American Psychiatric Association. (1980). *Diagnostic and statistical manual of mental disorders* (3rd ed.). Washington, DC: Author.

American Psychiatric Association. (1987). *Diagnostic and statistical manual of mental disorders* (3rd ed., rev.). Washington, DC: Author.

Anderson, C. M., Reiss, D., & Hogarty, B. (1986). *Schizophrenia and the family.* New York: Guilford.

Backer, T. E., & Richardson, D. (1989). Building bridges: Psychologists and families of the mentally ill. *American Psychologist, 44,* 546-550.

Bailey, D., & Garralda, M. E. (1987). The use of the social stress and support interview in families with deviant children: Methodological issues. *Social Psychiatry, 22,* 209-215.

Balcom, D. A., & Healey, D. (1990). The context for couples treatment of wife abuse. In M. P. Mirkin (Ed.), *The social and political contexts of family therapy* (pp. 121-137). Boston: Allyn & Bacon.

Barbee, J. G., Kasten, A. M., & Rosenson, M. K. (1991). Toward a new alliance: Psychiatric residents and family support groups. *Academic Psychiatry, 15,* 40-49.

Bateson, G., Jackson, D. D., Haley, J., & Weakland, J. H. (1956). Toward a theory of schizophrenia. *Behavioral Science, 1,* 251-264.

Berger, M. M. (1978). *Beyond the double bind: Communication and family systems, theories,
and techniques with schizophrenics.* New York: Brunner/Mazel.

Bernheim, K. F. (1989). Psychologists and families of the severely mentally ill: The role of
family consultation. *American Psychologist, 44,* 561-564.

Billings, A. G., & Moos, R. H. (1986). Children of parents with unipolar depression: A controlled 1-year follow-up. *Journal of Abnormal Child Psychiatry, 14,* 949-955.

Bograd, M. (1990). Scapegoating mothers: Conceptual errors in systems formulations. In M. P.
Mirkin (Ed.), *The social and political contexts of family therapy* (pp. 69-87). Boston: Allyn
& Bacon.

Broderick, C. B., & Schrader, S. S. (1981). The history of professional marriage and family
therapy. In A. S. Gurman & D. P. Kniskern (Eds.), *Handbook of family therapy* (pp. 5-35).
New York: Brunner/Mazel.

Brody, E. M., & Kleban, M. H. (1983). Day-to-day mental and physical health symptoms of
older people: A report on health logs. *The Gerontologist, 23,* 75-85.

Brown, G. W., Birley, J. L. T., & Wing, J. K. (1972). Influence of family life on the course of
schizophrenic disorders: A replication. *British Journal of Psychiatry, 121,* 241-258.

Brown, G. W., Monck, E. M., Carstairs, G. M., & Wing, J. K. (1962). Influence of family life
on the course of schizophrenic disorders. *British Journal of Preventive and Social Medicine,
16,* 55-68.

Campbell, D., Draper, R., & Crutchley, E. (1991). The Milan systemic approach to family
therapy. In A. S. Gurman & D. P. Kniskern (Eds.), *Handbook of family therapy* (Vol. 2,
pp. 325-362). New York: Brunner/Mazel.

Chamberlin, J., Rogers, J. A., & Sneed, C. S. (1989). Consumers, families, and community
support systems. *Psychosocial Rehabilitation Journal, 12,* 93-106.

Cole, J. D., & Kazarian, S. S. (1988). The Level of Expressed Emotion Scale: A new measure
of expressed emotion. *Journal of Clinical Psychology, 44,* 392-397.

Cooper, B. (1986). Epidemiology and clinical psychiatry. *Acta Psychiatria, 86,* 340-348.

Denton, W. H. (1989). DSM-III-R and the family therapist: Ethical considerations. *Journal of
Marital and Family Therapy, 15,* 367-378.

Denton, W. H. (1990). A family systems analysis of DSM-III-R. *Journal of Marital and Family
Therapy, 16,* 113-126.

Doane, J. A. (1978). Family interaction and communication deviance in disturbed and normal
families: A review of research. *Family Process, 17,* 357-376.

Epstein, N. B., Baldwin, L. M., & Bishop, D. S. (1983). The McMaster Family Assessment
Device. *Journal of Marital and Family Therapy, 9,* 171-180.

Falloon, I. R. H. (1986). Response to Agnes B. Hatfield. *Schizophrenia Bulletin, 12,* 334-336.

Falloon, I. R. H. (1988). Prevention of morbidity in schizophrenia. In I. R. H. Falloon (Ed.),
*Handbook of behavioral family therapy* (pp. 316-349). New York: Guilford.

Flynn, L. M. (1987). The stigma of mental illness. In A. B. Hatfield (Ed.), *Families of the
mentally ill: Meeting the challenges* (pp. 53-60). San Francisco: Jossey-Bass.

Franks, D. D. (1990). Economic contribution of families caring for persons with severe and
persistent mental illness. *Administration and Policy in Mental Health, 18,* 9-18.

Fristad, M., & Clayton, T. L. (1991). Family dysfunction and family psychopathology in child
psychiatry outpatients. *Journal of Family Psychology, 5,* 46-59.

Fuchs, L. (1986). First person account: Three generations of schizophrenia. *Schizophrenia
Bulletin, 12,* 744-747.

Goldfarb, A. (1962). Prevalence of psychiatric disorders in metropolitan old age and nursing homes. *Journal of the American Gerontological Society, 10*, 77-84.

Goldstein, M. J. (1981). *New developments in interventions with families of schizophrenics.* San Francisco: Jossey-Bass.

Goldstein, M. J. (1987). Family interaction patterns that antedate the onset of schizophrenia and related disorders: A further analysis of data from a longitudinal study. In K. Hahlweg & M. J. Goldstein (Eds.), *Understanding major mental disorders: The contribution of family interaction research* (pp. 11-32). New York: Family Process.

Goodman, S. H. (1984). Children of disturbed parents: The interface between research and intervention. *American Journal of Community Psychiatry, 12*, 663-687.

Gove, W. (1972). The relationship between sex roles, marital status, and mental illness. *Social Forces, 51*, 38-44.

Group for the Advancement of Psychiatry. (1986). *A family affair: Helping families cope with mental illness.* New York: Brunner/Mazel.

Gurin, G., Veroff, J., & Feld, S. (1960). *Americans view their mental health.* New York: Basic Books.

Hahlweg, K., & Goldstein, M. J. (1987). *Understanding major mental disorders: The contribution of family interaction research.* New York: Family Process.

Hammen, C., Gordon, D., Burge, D., Adrian, C., Jaenicke, C., & Hiroto, D. (1987). Communication patterns of mothers with affective disorders and their relationship to children's status and social functioning. In K. Hahlweg & M. J. Goldstein (Eds.), *Understanding major mental disorders: The contribution of family interaction research* (pp. 103-119). New York: Family Process.

Hatfield, A. B. (1986). Semantic barriers to family and professional collaboration. *Schizophrenia Bulletin, 12*, 325-333.

Hatfield, A. B. (1987). The expressed emotion theory: Why families object. *Hospital and Community Psychiatry, 38*, 341.

Hatfield, A. B., & Lefley, H. P. (1987). *Families of the mentally ill: Coping and adaptation.* New York: Guilford.

Hoenig, J., & Hamilton, M. W. (1966). The schizophrenic patient in the community and his effect on the household. *The International Journal of Social Psychiatry, 12*, 165-176.

Hoffman, L. (1981). *Foundations of family therapy.* New York: Basic Books.

Holden, D. F., & Lewine, R. R. (1982). How families evaluate mental health professionals, resources, and effects of illness. *Schizophrenia Bulletin, 8*, 626-633.

Hooley, J. M. (1987). The nature and origins of expressed emotion. In K. Hahlweg & M. J. Goldstein (Eds.), *Understanding major mental disorders: The contribution of family interaction research* (pp. 176-194). New York: Family Process.

Howe, C. W., & Howe, J. W. (1987). The National Alliance for the Mentally Ill: History and ideology. In A. B. Hatfield (Ed.), *Families of the mentally ill: Meeting the challenges* (pp. 23-42). San Francisco: Jossey-Bass.

Jackson, D. D. (1968a). *Communication, family, and marriage: Human communication* (Vol. 1). Palo Alto, CA: Science and Behavioral Books.

Jackson, D. D. (1968b). *Therapy, communication, and change: Human communication* (Vol. 2). Palo Alto, CA: Science and Behavioral Books.

Jansen, H. A. M. (1982). The nuclear family as a mediator between class and mental disturbance in children. *Journal of Comparative Family Studies, 23*, 155-170.

Johnson, D. L. (1986). Professional-family collaboration. In A. B. Hatfield (Ed.), *Families of the mentally ill: Meeting the challenges* (pp. 73-79). San Francisco: Jossey-Bass.

Keller, M. B., Beardslee, W. R., Dorer, D. J., Lavori, P. W., Samuelson, H., & Klerman, G. R. (1986). Impact of severity and chronicity of parental affective illness on adaptive functioning and psychopathology in children. *Archives of General Psychiatry, 43*, 930-937.

Kendler, K. S. (1988). Indirect vertical cultural transmission: A model for nongenetic parental influences on the liability to psychiatric illness. *American Journal of Psychiatry, 145*, 657-665.

Klein, J. I. (1987). Resistances to care of the chronic patient: A lawyer's contribution. In A. T. Meyerson (Ed.), *Barriers to treating the mentally ill* (pp. 87-93). San Francisco: Jossey-Bass.

Lawson, W. B. (1986). Chronic mental illness and the black family. *The American Journal of Social Psychology, 6*, 57-61.

Leete, E. (1987). A patient's perspective on schizophrenia. In A. B. Hatfield (Ed.), *Families of the mentally ill: Meeting the challenges* (pp. 81-90). San Francisco: Jossey-Bass.

Lefley, H. P. (1985). Families of the mentally ill in cross-cultural perspective. *Psychosocial Rehabilitation Journal, 8*, 57-75.

Lefley, H. P. (1987). The family's response to mental illness in a relative. In A. B. Hatfield (Ed.), *Families of the mentally ill: Meeting the challenges* (pp. 3-21). San Francisco: Jossey-Bass.

Lefley, H. P. (1988). Training professionals to work with families of chronic patients. *Community Mental Health Journal, 24*, 338-357.

Lefley, H. P. (1989). Family burden and family stigma in major mental illness. *American Psychologist, 44*, 556-560.

Lefley, H. P. (1990). Culture and chronic mental illness. *Hospital and Community Psychiatry, 41*, 277-286.

Lewis, J. M., Beavers, W. R., Gossett, J. T., & Phillips, V. A. (1976). *No single thread: Psychological health in family systems.* New York: Brunner/Mazel.

Manis, M., Hunt, C. L., Brewer, M., & Kercher, L. (1965). Public and psychiatric conceptions of mental illness. *Journal of Health and Social Behavior, 6*, 48-55.

Maurin, J. T., & Boyd, C. B. (1990). Burden of mental illness on the family: A critical review. *Archives of Psychiatric Nursing, 4*, 99-107.

McFarlane, W. R. (1991). Family psychoeducational treatment. In A. S. Gurman & D. P. Kniskern (Eds.), *Handbook of family therapy* (Vol. 2, pp. 363-395). New York: Brunner/Mazel.

Mednick, S. A., & Schulsinger, F. (1968). Some premorbid characteristics related to breakdown in children with schizophrenic mothers. In D. Rosenthal & S. Kety (Eds.), *The transmission of schizophrenia* (pp. 469-475). New York: Pergamon.

Meyerson, A. T., & Herman, G. H. (1987). Systems resistance to the chronic patient. In A. T. Meyerson (Ed.), *Barriers to treating the mentally ill* (pp. 21-33). San Francisco: Jossey-Bass.

Millon, T., & Klerman, G. L. (1986). *Contemporary directions in psychopathology: Toward the DSM-IV.* New York: Guilford.

Minkoff, K. (1987). Resistance of mental health professionals to working with the chronic mentally ill. In A. T. Meyerson (Ed.), *Barriers to treating the mentally ill* (pp. 3-19). San Francisco: Jossey-Bass.

Mirabi, M., Weinman, M., Magnetti, S., & Keppler, K. (1985). Professional attitudes toward the mentally ill. *Hospital and Community Psychiatry, 36*, 404-405.

Mittleman, G. (1985). First person account: The pain of parenthood of the mentally ill. *Schizophrenia Bulletin, 11*, 300-303.

Morrison, J. (1979). Attitudes of community gatekeepers and psychiatric social workers toward mental illness. *Journal of Community Psychology, 7,* 147-150.

National Institute of Mental Health. (1991). *Implementation of the national plan for research on child and adolescent mental disorders* (PA-91-46). Washington, DC: U.S. Department of Health and Human Services.

Nichols, M. P., & Schwartz, R. C. (1991). *Family therapy: Concepts and methods* (2nd ed.). Boston: Allyn & Bacon.

Oliveri, M. E., & Reiss, D. (1982). Family styles of construing the social environment: A perspective on variation among nonclinical families. In F. Walsh (Ed.), *Normal family processes* (pp. 94-114). New York: Guilford.

"Pills for the mind." (1992). *Time, 140*(1), 52-60.

Regier, D. A., Boyd, J. H., Burke, J. D., Rae, D. S., Myers, J. K., Krmaer, M., Robins, L. N., George, L. K., Karno, M., & Locke, B. Z. (1988). One month prevalence of mental disorders in the United States. *Archives of General Psychiatry, 45,* 977-986.

Reiss, D. (1971). Varieties of consensual experience: I. A theory for relating family interaction to individual thinking. *Family Process, 10,* 1-28.

Rosenthal, D. (1970). *Genetic theory and abnormal behavior.* New York: McGraw-Hill.

Rovner, B. W., & Rabins, P. V. (1985). Mental illness among nursing home patients. *Hospital and Community Psychiatry, 36,* 119-128.

Sandua, V. D. (1985). The family and sociocultural factors of psychopathology. In L. L'Abate (Ed.), *The handbook of family psychology and therapy* (pp. 847-875). Homewood, IL: Dorsey.

Scheflen, A. E. (1981). *Levels of schizophrenia.* New York: Brunner/Mazel.

Selvini, M. (1992). Schizophrenia as a family game: Posing a challenge to biological psychiatry. *Family Therapy Networker, 16,* 81-83.

Selvini Palazzoli, M., Boscolo, L., Cecchin, G., & Prata, G. (1978). *Paradox and counterparadox.* New York: Jason Aronson.

Selvini Palazzoli, M., & Prata, G. (1989). *Family games: General models of psychotic processes in the family.* New York: Norton.

Shields, C. G., Franks, P., Harp, J. J., McDaniel, S. H., & Campbell, T. L. (1992). Development of the Family Emotional Involvement and Criticism Scale (FEICS): A self-report scale to measure expressed emotion. *Journal of Marital and Family Therapy, 18,* 395-407.

Shore, D., Lash, L., Hadley, S., Wagman, A., & Schulz, S. C. (1990). National Institute of Mental Health Clinical Research Career Opportunities. *Academic Psychiatry, 14,* 1-8.

Singer, M., & Wynne, L. (1963). Differentiating characteristics of parents of childhood schizophrenics, childhood neurotics, and young adult schizophrenics. *American Journal of Psychiatry, 120,* 234-243.

Singer, M., & Wynne, L. (1965a). Thought disorder and family relations of schizophrenics. III: Methodology using projective techniques. *Archives of General Psychiatry, 12,* 187-200.

Singer, M., & Wynne, L. (1965b). Thought disorder and family relations of schizophrenics. IV: Results and implications. *Archives of General Psychiatry, 12,* 201-212.

Sluzki, C. E., & Ransom, D. C. (1976). *Double bind: The foundation of the communicational approach to the family.* New York: Grune & Stratton.

Smith, W. (1989). *A profile of health and disease in America: Mental illness and substance abuse.* New York: Facts on File.

Spaniol, L., Zipple, A., & FitzGerald, S. (1984). How professionals can share power with families: Practical approaches to working with families of the mentally ill. *Psychosocial Rehabilitation Journal, 8,* 77-84.

Spence, M. A. (1987). Genetic linkage: Sampling issues and multipoint mapping. *Journal of Psychiatric Research, 21,* 631-637.

Thurer, S. L. (1983). Deinstitutionalization and women: Where the buck stops. *Hospital & Community Psychiatry, 34,* 1162-1163.

Tienari, P., Lahti, I., Sorri, A., Naarala, M., Wahlberg, K., Ronkko, T., Moring, J., & Wynne, L. (1987). The Finnish adoptive family study of schizophrenia: Possible joint effects of genetic vulnerability and family interaction. In K. Hahlweg & M. J. Goldstein (Eds.), *Understanding major mental disorders: The contribution of family interaction research* (pp. 33-54). New York: Family Process.

Vaughn, C. E., & Leff, J. P. (1976a). The influence of family and social factors on the course of psychiatric illness: A comparison of schizophrenic and depressed neurotic patients. *British Journal of Psychiatry, 129,* 125-137.

Vaughn, C. E., & Leff, J. P. (1976b). The measurement of expressed emotion in the families of psychiatric patients. *British Journal of Social and Clinical Psychology, 15,* 157-165.

Vaughn, C. E., & Leff, J. P. (1981). Patterns of emotional response in the relatives of schizophrenic patients. *Schizophrenia Bulletin, 7,* 43-44.

Vaughn, C. E., Snyder, K. S., Jones, S., Freeman, W. B., & Falloon, I. R. (1984). Family factors in schizophrenic relapse: Replication in California of British research on expressed emotion. *Archives of General Psychiatry, 41,* 1169-1177.

Wahl, O. F., & Harman, C. R. (1989). Family views of stigma. *Schizophrenia Bulletin, 15,* 131-139.

Watson, W. L., & Wright, L. M. (1984). The elderly and their families: An interactional view. In E. I. Coppersmith (Ed.), *Families with handicapped members* (pp. 75-87). Rockville, MD: Aspen.

Webb, L. J., DiClemente, C. C., Johnstone, E. E., Sanders, J. L., & Perley, R. A. (1981). *DSM-III training guide.* New York: Brunner/Mazel.

Wintersteen, R. T., & Young, L. (1988). Effective professional collaboration with family support groups. *Psychosocial Rehabilitation Journal, 12,* 19-31.

Wynne, L. C. (1987). Parental psychopathology and family system variables as predictors of child competence. In K. Hahlweg & M. J. Goldstein (Eds.), *Understanding major mental disorders: The contribution of family interaction research* (pp. 55-90). New York: Family Process.

Zubin, J., & Spring, B. J. (1977). Vulnerability: A new view of schizophrenia. *Journal of Abnormal Psychology, 86,* 103-126.

# 9

# Death, Dying, and Bereavement

### COLLEEN I. MURRAY

Death has been viewed as the experience that "poses the most painful adaptational challenges for families" (Walsh & McGoldrick, 1991, p. 25). Annually, approximately 8 million Americans experience the death of an immediate family member (Burnell & Burnell, 1989). Death of an immediate member is a crisis that *all* families will encounter and is recognized as *the* most stressful life event that families face (Dohrenwend & Dohrenwend, 1974; Holmes & Rahe, 1967). However, death may be the last taboo issue in family science and family therapy (Dickenson & Fritz, 1981; Walsh & McGoldrick, 1991).

## Etiology of "Invisible Death" and Its Consequences

Historically, death was viewed as natural and inevitable (DeSpelder & Strickland, 1992). A movement to deny the realities of death occurred during the eighteenth and early nineteenth centuries, and by the twentieth century a lack of firsthand familiarity with death fostered an attitude of "invisible death" (Aries, 1974, 1985).

Factors contributing to our lack of familiarity with death include increased life expectancy (U.S. Bureau of the Census, 1975, 1992), changes in leading causes of death from communicable diseases to chronic and degenerative diseases, redistribution of death from the young to old (Olshansky & Ault, 1986), and decreased mortality rates (U.S. Bureau of the Census, 1975, 1992). Geographic mobility results in reduced intergenerational contact and less opportunity to participate in the death-related experiences of family members. The use of life-extending technologies has (a) confined dying to an institution rather than one's home (Kastenbaum, 1980; Lerner, 1980), (b) resulted in care dominated by efforts to delay death by all means available, (c) questioned our definitions of what constitutes life and death, and (d) confronted families with decisions of prolonging dying or terminating life.

The overall effect of these changes has been to increase the potential stress families experience when coping with death. Death, dying, and bereavement are not viewed as normal experiences throughout the life span, and death has become compartmentalized, with children frequently excluded from the experience (Feifel, 1977; E. Jackson, 1965; Walsh & McGoldrick, 1991). Adapting to loss has been hampered by a lack of cultural supports that could assist families in "integrating the fact of death with ongoing life" (Walsh & McGoldrick, 1991, p. 2). For many Americans a minimum of rituals exist surrounding death; the roles of the chronically ill or bereaved are not clearly defined; and geographic distance hinders the completion of "unfinished business."

Although the death of a family member is a normal experience, and grieving is a normal process (Paul & Paul, 1982), there can be physical, psychological, and social consequences for surviving family members that can be viewed as stressor experiences (Burnell & Burnell, 1989). Bereavement can result in negative consequences for physical health (Elliot & Eisdorfer, 1982), including physical illness, aggravation of existing medical conditions, increased use of medical facilities, and presence of new symptoms and complaints (Burnell & Burnell, 1989; Parkes, 1988). Immune system functioning also may be impaired during bereavement (Hall & Goldstein, 1986; Schleifer, Keller, Camerino, Thornton, & Stein, 1983).

A limitation of epidemiological bereavement studies is that they cannot assess a direct causal relationship but can only present bereavement as an antecedent of disease (Stroebe, Stroebe, Gergen, & Gergen, 1981). Many conditions leading to increased morbidity and mortality rates may result from self-damaging or neglectful behaviors that can occur during bereavement (Jacobs & Ostfeld, 1977; Zisook & Shuchter, 1986). In addition, most studies on morbidity and mortality rates are limited to bereaved spouses (e.g., Osterweis, Solomon, & Green, 1984; Parkes, 1972; Parkes,

Benjamin, & Fitzgerald, 1969), with some attention to bereaved parents (Huygen, van den Hoogen, van Eijk, & Smits, 1989). The consequences of bereavement as a stressor for mental health also are difficult to assess (Parkes, 1988). Many of the characteristics typically associated with the emotion of grief are ones that would evoke concern in other circumstances. High rates of depression, insomnia, suicides, and anorexia reported by the bereaved may exist in conjunction with increased consumption of drugs, alcohol, and tobacco (Clayton, 1974).

Individuals identify bereavement as a social stressor (Burnell & Burnell, 1989) and report a lack of role clarity and social or familial support (Rando, 1986). Factors that may accompany the death, such as change in the survivor's social status, loss of roles or conflicts in identity (Lopata, 1973), conflict over family inheritance, and loss of income or retirement funds, can contribute to a sense of social isolation.

## Theories of Grieving

Theories of grieving include those focused on the individual's experience as a family member and those based on the family system.

### Individual-Based Theories

Scholars have proposed a variety of developmental theories focusing on stages or trajectories for the dying person (e.g., Kubler-Ross, 1969; Pattison, 1977) and survivors (e.g., Parkes, 1986; Rando, 1988; Raphael, 1983; Worden, 1982). Such theories generally are derived from the works of Freud (1917) or Bowlby (1969, 1980). These theories differ in the number of stages proposed, but each assumes grieving follows three basic phases (DeSpelder & Strickland, 1992): (a) shock, denial, and disorganization; (b) intense separation pain, volatile emotions, and active grief work; and (c) resolution, acceptance, and (for the bereaved) withdrawal of energy from the deceased and reinvestment into the world of the living.

Critics of individual theories question the definition of "normal" grief and many of the assumptions about how people should respond to death, such as the following: (a) intense emotional distress or depression is inevitable; (b) failure to experience distress is indicative of pathology; (c) it is important to work through loss—intense distress will not last forever, and there will be recovery; and (d) by working through loss, individuals can achieve a state of resolution including intellectual acceptance (Wortman & Silver, 1989).

Stage theories have been criticized for presenting the image that progress toward adjustment is linear. Critics contend that progress is unsteady, not always forward, and there may be no definite ending to the process of grieving (Glick, Weiss, & Parkes, 1974; Rosenblatt, 1983; Wortman & Silver, 1989). Another concern deals with viewing grief as passive, with "little choice of paths through the process" (Attig, 1991, p. 386). Critics contend that grieving is active and presents challenges, choices, and opportunities.

Also questioned is the necessity of "grief work"—traditionally viewed as a cognitive process of confronting loss, which is essential for adjustment (Bowlby, 1969, 1980; Freud, 1917; Lindemann, 1944; Parkes, 1988). Pathological grief is seen as the failure to undergo or complete grief work. Recently, Stroebe (1992) suggested that grief work is not a universal concept; its definitions and operationalizations are problematic; and few studies have yielded substantial conclusions.

### Family Theories of Coping With Death

Much of what has been written about coping with loss focuses on dying or bereaved individuals or occasionally on the dyadic relationship between the bereaved and the deceased (e.g., Pinkus, 1974; Schiff, 1977; Viorst, 1986). Yet individuals do not deal with death and dying in isolation (Pattison, 1977). Family stress and family systems theories can facilitate understanding of the complexity of the death of a family member.

*Family stress theory.* Family stress theory (see Chapter 1) conceptualizes the family's response to the dynamic processes of dying and bereavement through an examination of the nature of the event, meanings families give to loss, available resources, and coping strategies. One version, the Typology Model of Family Adjustment and Adaptation (McCubbin & McCubbin, 1989), can be used to understand differing amounts of crisis/disorganization families experience in relation to loss by isolating characteristics of the individual, family unit, and community/society (Boss, 1987; Hill, 1949). The three basic *adjustment* coping strategies (i.e., avoidance, elimination, and assimilation) (McCubbin & Patterson, 1983) are often inadequate long-term responses in cases of chronic illness or bereavement (McCubbin & McCubbin, 1989).

*Family systems theory.* Systems theory focuses on dynamics and provides concepts for describing relationships (e.g., Bertalanffy, 1968;

D. Jackson, 1965; Kantor & Lehr, 1975). The following premises of systems theory can be useful in examining families' adaptation to death:

1. A family reacts to loss as a system. Although we grieve as individuals, the family system has qualities beyond those of the individual members (D. Jackson, 1965), and all members participate in mutually reinforcing interactions (Walsh & McGoldrick, 1991).

2. The reactions of one family member affect the others.

3. Death of a member disrupts a family system's equilibrium, modifies the structure, and requires reorganization of the system in its feedback processes, distribution of roles, and functions (Bowen, 1976; Buckley, 1967; D. Jackson, 1965).

4. Death may produce an emotional shock wave, that is, a series of serious life events that can occur anywhere in the extended family following a death (Bowen, 1976). Waves exist in an environment of denied emotional dependence and may seem unrelated to the death.

5. There is no single outcome from the death of a family member that characterizes all family systems. Various family characteristics, such as feedback processes (D. Jackson, 1965) and family paradigm (Reiss & Oliveri, 1980), influence the outcome.

Although family systems theory appears well suited for examining the adaptation of a family to death, it has not often been applied. Instead, loss has traditionally been identified as a historical, individual, or content issue and inappropriate for systems work (which tends to focus on process, current interaction, and the present) (Madanes & Haley, 1977; Walsh & McGoldrick, 1991).

## Factors Related to
## Family Adaptation to Death

### Characteristics of the Loss

Various factors have been identified as related to death itself and how society's interpretation of the loss influences family adaptation. These include the following:

*Timing of illness or death.* When the duration of time before the actual death is far longer (Rando, 1984) or shorter than expected, or the sequence of death differs from expected societal order, problems may occur. The elderly are assumed to experience "timely" deaths (Feifel,

1977). Early parental loss, death of a young spouse, and death of a child or grandchild of any age are considered tragic (Craig, 1977; Ponzetti & Johnson, 1991) and evoke rage and a search for an explanation (Counts & Counts, 1991; Ramsden, 1991).

*Nature of death.* Initial grief reaction to a sudden or unexpected death is more intense (Bowlby, 1980). In these cases, unfinished business is more likely to remain, with no opportunity to experience "anticipatory grief" (Lindemann, 1944), that is, a period that may allow family members to experience a series of small losses (e.g., loss of a healthy family member, loss of family life as it had been) (Kupst et al., 1982; Rando, 1986). Violence such as homicide and suicide often constitutes a sudden death (Figley, 1983, 1989). Loss perceived as senseless is especially difficult for families to bear, particularly when survivors believe that justice has not prevailed (Walsh & McGoldrick, 1991).

Deaths following protracted illness can also be particularly stressful. In the case of such illness, family members have experienced a series of stressors before the death. These can include increased time commitments for caring, loss of financial well-being as a result of the costs of care and lost employment, emotional exhaustion, interruption of career and family routines, sense of social isolation, and lack of time for self or other family members (Kalnins, Churchill, & Terry, 1980; McCubbin & McCubbin, 1989). Although research findings on the existence and role of anticipatory grief are inconsistent, protracted illness appears associated with secondary morbidity—that is, difficulties in physical, emotional, cognitive, and social functioning of those closely involved with the terminally ill person (Sherwood, Kastenbaum, Morris, & Wright, 1988). Deaths following chronic illness may still be perceived as sudden or unexpected by surviving adults who are not yet "ready" and by children whose developmental stage inhibits their understanding that death is inevitable.

*Losses unacknowledged by society.* Recently, attention has been devoted to unrecognized and unsanctioned grief (Pine et al., 1990) or disenfranchised grief (Doka, 1989), that is, grief that exists although society does not recognize one's "need, right, role, or capacity to grieve" (Doka, 1989, p. 3). Examples of unrecognized family relationships and unacknowledged losses (i.e., ones not recognized as significant) include grief over (a) former spouses, lovers, cohabitors, and extramarital lovers; (b) foster children/parents; (c) stepparents/stepchildren; (d) coworkers; (e) partners in gay/lesbian relationships;

(f) deaths related to pregnancy (i.e., miscarriage, elective abortion, stillbirth, or neonatal death); (g) loss of a companion animal; or (h) the grief of professional caretakers. Bereaved grandparents, men in general (Gilbert, in press), and families of deceased addicts may also be disenfranchised. In addition, some people are seen as incapable of grief (Doka, 1989; Kauffman, 1993). These include young children, older adults, and mentally disabled persons.

*Stigmatized losses.* People who are grieving as a result of various types of death report they feel their grief has been stigmatized (Froman, 1992; Schiff, 1977). They feel the discomfort of others who distance themselves from the griever and experience direct or indirect social pressure to become "invisible mourners" (Rosaldo, 1989). Disenfranchised grief often results from stigmatized losses, particularly when there is a fear of contagion, such as with AIDS- or cancer-related deaths (Sontag, 1988). AIDS-related deaths also are stigmatized in this society because of their concentration in the homosexual community or poor inner-city neighborhoods (Froman, 1992; Klein & Fletcher, 1986). Surviving companions of gay relationships frequently deal with a lack of legal standing, denial of death benefits, and isolation.

Suicide may be the most painful death for families (Cain, 1972; Dunne, McIntosh, & Dunne-Maxim, 1988). It is both violent and stigmatized, in addition to provoking feelings of anger and guilt (Miles & Demi, 1992). Resulting secrecy and blame can distort family communication, isolate family members, and diminish social support (Walsh & McGoldrick, 1991).

### Factors Affecting Family Vulnerability

*Timing and concurrent stressors in the family life cycle.* Families may have additional difficulty adapting to loss in the presence of other stressors. When normative events associated with the stages of the family life cycle (e.g., new marriage, birth of child, or adolescent's move toward increased independence) are concurrent with illness or death, they may pose incompatible tasks (Brown, 1989; Gonzalez & Reiss, 1981; McGoldrick & Walsh, 1991).

*Function and position of a person prior to his or her death.* The centrality of the individual's functional role and degree of the family's emotional dependence on the individual influence adaptation (Brown, 1989; McGoldrick & Walsh, 1983). Shock waves rarely follow deaths of well-liked people who played peripheral roles or of dysfunctional members unless the dysfunction played a central role in maintaining family equilibrium (Bowen, 1976).

*Conflicted relationship with the deceased.* Although conflict exists in all family relationships, when there is ambivalence, estrangement, or conflict that is intense and continuous, there is potential for complications in adaptation (Walsh & McGoldrick, 1991). In the case of life-threatening illness, there may be time to repair estranged relationships. However, family members may hesitate, fearing that confrontations may increase the risk of death.

### Family Resources, Capabilities, and Strengths

Resources that assist in meeting demands may be tangible (e.g., money or health) or intangible (e.g., friendship, self-esteem, or a sense of mastery) (McCubbin & McCubbin, 1989). The amount of disruption a bereaved family experiences is also related to its degree of openness (Brown, 1989) and mediated by the intensity and chronicity of family stress. Although all family systems are open to some degree, adaptation is facilitated by "the ability of each family member to stay nonreactive to the emotional intensity in the system and to communicate his or her feelings to the others without expecting the others to act on them" (Brown, 1989, p. 472).

Social support appears to be one of the best buffers for dealing with stress (Eckenrode, 1991; Gottlieb, 1983). Yet availability of formal or informal networks does not guarantee support, especially in a society in which the expression of emotions surrounding loss is expected to be confined. In response, some bereaved family members turn to self-help groups, composed of persons who have experienced a similar type of loss (Klass, 1984). However, the rules of some family systems discourage sharing intimate information and feelings with persons outside the family.

### Family Belief System, Definition, and Appraisal

*Family paradigm.* To fully understand how a family perceives a death or the coping strategies it uses, it is necessary to determine the family's view of the world (Boss, 1987). One common paradigm (Lerner, 1971; Lerner & Simmons, 1966) is the "belief in a just world." This perspective values control and mastery and assumes that there is a fit between one's efforts and outcomes; underlying this view is the belief that one gets what one deserves. Such a view is functional only when something can be done to change a situation. For example, it can lead to chronically ill persons being blamed for their conditions and lack of recovery and to linking adolescent deaths to drug use or reckless behavior as a way of affirming "it can't happen to my child."

*Death's legacy.* Family history and experiences with death provide a legacy (a way of looking at loss that has been received from ancestors) that is related to how the family will adapt to subsequent loss (McGoldrick, 1991). Particularly in relation to several traumatic untimely deaths, there can be either a legacy of empowerment (in which family members see themselves as survivors who can be hurt, but not defeated) or a legacy of trauma (with a feeling of being "cursed" and unable to rise above the losses)—both of which can inhibit openness of the system. Families may not recognize transgenerational anniversary patterns or the concurrence of a death with other life events, and members may have a lack of memory or discrepant memories regarding a death (Brown, 1989).

### Boundary Ambiguity

*Boundary ambiguity* refers to the confusion a family experiences when it is not clear who is in and who is out of the family system (Boss, 1987, 1991). Ambiguity rises when (a) facts surrounding a death are unclear, (b) a person is missing but it is unclear whether death has occurred, or (c) the family denies the loss. Degree of boundary ambiguity, rather than specific coping skills or resources, may better explain adaptation and coping. Both denial (Hamburg & Adams, 1967) and boundary ambiguity may be initially functional because they give a family time to deny the loss and then cognitively accept the fact that it is real. If a high degree of ambiguity exists over time, the family is at risk for maladaptation.

### Factors of Diversity

*Gender.* Societal expectations are that women should be responsible for the social and emotional tasks related to bereavement, including caregiving for the chronically ill and surviving family members (Walsh & McGoldrick, 1991). Women display more sorrow and depression than men (DeFrain, Ernst, Jakub, & Taylor, 1991; DeFrain, Martens, Stork, & Stork, 1990), and support outside of the family is primarily directed toward women (Gilbert, 1989). Men are socialized to manage instrumental tasks, such as those related to the funeral, burial, finances, and property (Bach-Hughes & Page-Lieberman, 1989). Whether such distributions are influenced by biology is under debate (see Moir & Jessel, 1991). However, gender-related differences are influenced by expectations and socialization patterns (Schatz, 1986) and may be a result of diverse activities performed in relation to illness and death (Littlewood, 1992).

It is thought that men may have unspecified problems that exist because their socialization interferes with active grief work (Staudacher, 1991, p. 9). Their response to grief typically includes coping styles that mask fear and insecurity, including remaining silent; taking physical or legal action in order to express anger and exert control; immersion in work, domestic, recreational, or sexual activity; engaging in solitary or secret mourning; and exhibiting addictive behavior, such as alcoholism. Cook (1988) identified a double bind that men experience: Societal expectations are that they will contain their emotions in order to protect and comfort their wives but that they cannot heal their own grief without the sharing of feelings. Our understanding of men's mourning process is limited because the grief-loss models are based on the experience of women (Cook, 1988). As such, Lindemann's (1944) concept of grief work may not be relevant for men.

*Cultural, religious, and ethnic factors.* Through immigration and contact between different groups, mourning patterns of groups in the United States continue to change (McGoldrick, Almedia, et al., 1991). Yet group differences in values and practices continue to exist and present a wide range of normal responses to death (McGoldrick, 1989). General areas in which differences exist include variation in (a) the extent of ritual (e.g., the importance of attending funerals, types of acceptable emotional displays, and the degree to which these affairs should be costly); (b) the need to see the dying relative; (c) openness and type of display of emotion; (d) emphasis on verbal expression of feelings and public versus private (namely, solitary or family) expression of grief; (e) appropriate length of mourning; (f) the importance of anniversary events; (g) roles of men and women; (h) role of the extended family; (i) beliefs about what happens after death, particularly related to the ideas of suffering, fate, and destiny; and (j) whether certain deaths are stigmatized (McGoldrick et al., 1991).

## Specific Losses

### Death of a Child

The death of one's child may be the most difficult loss to experience, for it is contrary to the expected developmental progression and thrusts one into a marginal social role that has unclear role expectations (Klass & Marwit, 1988). From an Eriksonian perspective, young-adult parents grapple with death-related issues of identity as parents and intimacy with the spouse; middle-aged parents deal with loss of generativity with a child's death (Kalish, 1989); and elderly parents deal with loss in terms of ego integrity versus despair. Klass and Marwit (1988) suggest that attachment and psychoanalytic models are inadequate. Instead, they propose a model that accounts for the uniqueness of the (a) parent-child attachment and (b) grief experienced with the death of a child.

Society expects spouses to provide support and comfort during times of stress; however, this may not be possible for bereaved parents who are both experiencing intense grief as a result of the death of a child. They grieve as individuals, with unique timetables, and may not be "in sync" (Rando, 1986). Sexual expression can serve as a reminder of the child and elicit additional distress.

Death of an adult child may be very disturbing even though there is likely to be a degree of separation between the child and parent (Raphael, 1983). This untimely death can provoke survivor guilt for the older parent and mean the loss of a major caregiver.

### Death of a Sibling

Most research on sibling death is recent, and it tends to focus on children and adolescents (see Balk, 1990, 1991; Donnelly, 1988; Hogan, 1988). Prior examination of sibling loss was generally confined to clinical studies. Sibling grief reactions are not uniform, nor are they the same as those experienced by bereaved parents (Hankoff, 1975; Rando, 1988). Such reactions can be best understood in relation to individual characteristics (e.g., sex, developmental stage, relationship to the sibling).

Common reactions of siblings of all ages include (a) fear and insecurity from seeing the family foundation shaken (Schiff, 1977), (b) a sense that parents are unreachable, and (c) a frightening sense of abandonment (Hare-Mustin, 1979). Guilt as a result of sibling interactions and rivalry prior to the death is common and persists even when siblings can recognize the irrationality of such beliefs (Cain, Fast, & Erickson, 1964; Murray, 1982). Survivor guilt and anger also are common (Rando, 1988). However, rarely is anger directed toward parents, for they are perceived to be vulnerable and hence to need protection from any additional pain.

Surviving siblings in a triangulated position may feel a need to fulfill the roles the deceased child played for the parents, or they may act in an opposite manner from the sib in an attempt to show that they are different (Bank & Kahn, 1975).

### Death of a Parent

Each year an estimated 5% of Americans experience the death of a parent (Pearlin & Lieberman, 1979). Children's reactions vary and are influenced by emotional and cognitive development, closeness to the deceased parent, and responses of/interactions with the surviving parent (Kubler-Ross, 1983; Rando, 1988).

Death of a parent is the most common form of loss in middle age (Moss & Moss, 1989). Adult response to the death of a parent is influenced by the meaning of the relationship and the roles the parent played at the time of death (Rando, 1988). It may create a "developmental push"—a realization of responsibilities as they become the oldest generation in the family (Osterweis et al., 1984).

### Death of a Spouse

Death of a spouse has been the most intensively studied adulthood loss (e.g., Clayton, 1974, 1979; Glick et al., 1974; Lopata, 1973, 1979; Parkes & Weiss, 1983). Yet little attention has been given (a) to the death of a spouse in early or middle adulthood, (b) to widowed parents with dependent children (Demi, 1989), (c) to committed homosexual couples (DeSpelder & Strickland, 1992), or (d) to experiences of widowers (Clark, Siviski, & Weiner, 1986).

Loneliness is often seen as the single greatest concern of spouses who lose a companion and a source of emotional support (Clark et al., 1986). The couple orientation of middle-class America contributes to a feeling of isolation (Osterweis et al., 1984; Rando, 1988). The death of a spouse can be especially difficult for individuals whose relationship assumed a sharp division of traditional sex roles (Lopata, 1972, 1973; Rando, 1988), leaving them unprepared to assume the range of tasks required to maintain a household. Death of one's spouse brings up issues of self-definition and prompts the need for developing a new identity. Despite these problems, many bereaved spouses adjust very well. Some even derive pleasure and independence from their new lifestyle, feeling more competent than when married (Rando, 1988).

## Interventions

### Clinical

Before family clinicians successfully intervene, they need to come to terms with the experiences of death and loss in their own lives. This may include examining the fears, reactions, and beliefs they hold as influenced by their gender socialization and ethnic/religious background and exploring what "healthy mourning" entails.

McGoldrick (1991) has identified several goals to facilitate adaptation of bereaved family members. These goals include shared acknowledgment of the reality of death, shared experience, putting the death in context, reorganization of the family system, and reinvestment in other relationships or interests (pp. 54-55). Some specific suggestions include the following:

1. Use a multigenerational perspective to attend to the legacies of past losses. Genograms can provide insight into family experiences with death, loss, and ambiguity (Brown, 1989; McGoldrick & Gerson, 1985; Rolland, 1987), coping, the family's belief system, and its hardiness (McGoldrick, 1991; Rolland, 1991).

2. Develop a knowledge of the normative developmental tasks for each stage of the family life cycle. Death provokes particular issues in relation to how life-cycle tasks are disrupted.

3. Attend to the impact of anticipated losses as well as those that have occurred in the past few years. Help families establish functional patterns before a loss (Rolland, 1991).

4. Develop an awareness of beliefs, rituals, and roles related to death and bereavement for the ethnic, religious, or socioeconomic groups your practice serves. Differences also exist in the time required to create trust in a therapeutic relationship.

5. Explore with families their use of rituals (i.e., presence, changes in, rigidity, or absence) and plans for subsequent rituals as potential indicators of family functioning (McGoldrick et al., 1991). When appropriate, thera-

pists should assist in designing rituals to facilitate healing (Imber-Black, 1991).

6. When warranted, suggest self-help group participation and individual psychotherapy *in conjunction with* family therapy (Videka-Sherman & Lieberman, 1985).

7. Use creative methods to bring grief out into the open so it can be dealt with as part of normal life experiences. Audio- and videotape confrontations, split-screen imaging of the client with a photo of the deceased, letters, literature, or film clips can be used to help feelings surface (Paul, 1976; Paul & Paul, 1982, 1989).

8. Identify the overall circumstances and demands on family members as related to specific types of loss. For example, caregivers of persons with AIDS may be simultaneously dealing with their own illness and that of a number of friends or family members who are at various stages of the HIV/AIDS spectrum, therefore experiencing different stages of anticipatory loss (Rolland, 1991).

9. Deal openly with questions related to loss to avoid reinforcement of the "invisible community of the bereaved" (Rosaldo, 1989).

### Public Policy/Education

Education regarding various aspects of death, dying, and bereavement is necessary before public policy can be instituted that will facilitate individuals and their families in dealing with loss. Topics may include the following:

1. *Death, dying, and bereavement as normal and natural experiences throughout the life span.* Issues covered would include varying reactions as related to type of loss, cultural factors, and characteristics of the family or survivor, with no single appropriate response or time line. This information should sensitize policymakers and practitioners to (a) the normality of the grief, (b) individual differences in grief, and (c) the needs of individuals and families as they cope with grief.

2. *Planning for loss, including preparation and discussion of living wills.* Family members are increasingly confronted with the dilemma over whether and how long to maintain life support efforts for a person with a protracted illness or injury in which there is virtually no hope of recovery. They are caught in the controversy over the patient's right to die, family rights and expenses, medical ethics, religious beliefs, and criminal prosecution. Preplanning also can encourage individuals to

pursue efforts to encourage the courts, hospitals, and politicians to rethink policies in light of technological advances.

3. *Rethinking the current approach to dealing with difficulty, which suggests that personal responsibility and effort are the way to improve health and postpone death* (see Siegel, 1986; Simonton, Mathews-Simonton, & Creighton, 1978). This approach places blame on the individual, resulting in a sense of shame and failure. Such an experience can alter a family's paradigm for several generations (Rolland, 1991). This is not to say that it is unimportant for families to believe they have some control over their circumstances but that control can be perceived in various nuances of the situation—not limited to controlling health and death.

4. *Education in relation to stigmatized losses, such as suicide or AIDS-related deaths.* The belief that AIDS is a proper atonement for immoral behavior ignores the worldwide demographic characteristics of the people who contract HIV. Such attitudes foster a family context of secrecy and isolation and increase the chance of unresolved grief complicated by guilt or shame (Froman, 1992; Rolland, 1991). Stigmatizing beliefs also inhibit research and clinical trials aimed at curing or slowing the progression of disease.

### Future Directions

There are many directions that research and intervention strategies dealing with death can take. For research, a shift from the examination of bereavement as an individual experience to viewing it within a family systems context could yield needed information. As part of this approach, instruments need to be developed that address the multigenerational legacy of loss. This instrumentation would be particularly useful in examining the paradigms of families with children living in inner cities, in which child development occurs amid chronic community violence, terror, and death (Garbarino, Dubrow, Kostelny, & Pardo, 1992).

Interventions with the bereaved could benefit from an integration of developmental and systems theories, particularly in relation to family tasks at each phase of the life cycle (Brown, 1989; Walsh & McGoldrick, 1991). Past losses can provide valuable information about current paradigms and coping strategies. Also needed is a shift away from viewing the bereaved as passive victims to seeing them as survivors, engaged in an active bereavement process, and capable of self-determination (Reynolds, 1993).

Rosen (1986) indicated that we have come to view bereavement as a form of pathology. As such, we know more about the problems of coping than about the process of coping, and we know more about factors that inhibit grieving than about those that facilitate it. Both researchers and clinicians could benefit from structuring work around the premise that bereavement is natural and functional.

## Conclusions and Summary

Dealing with death involves a process, not an event. It is an experience that all families *will* encounter. "Bereavement is complex, for it reaches to the heart of what it means to be human and what it means to have a relationship" (Klass, 1987, p. 31). Despite its importance in the experiences of individuals and families, death still appears to be a taboo subject. Research and theory have focused on the experiences of the dying individual or on the dyadic relationship of the bereaved and deceased. A multigenerational approach to family systems theory is well suited to address issues of loss and needs further application to research and clinical practice. Families' adaptation to death varies; factors that influence the process include characteristics of the death, family vulnerability, the history of past losses, incompatible life-cycle demands, resources, and belief systems.

Although loss is a normal experience, it has been treated by theorists and researchers as a problem. At this point, more work needs to focus on processes and strengths, such as the process of coping (rather than problems) and factors that facilitate growth from loss (rather than those that inhibit growth). In so doing, we may begin to identify the positive factors that emerge from mourning, such as creativity (Pollock, 1989) or spiritual development (Dershimer, 1990).

## References

Aries, P. (1974). *Western attitudes toward death: From the Middle Ages to the present.* Baltimore, MD: Johns Hopkins University Press.

Aries, P. (1985). *Images of man and death.* Cambridge, MA: Harvard University Press.

Attig, T. (1991). The importance of conceiving of grief as an active process. *Death Studies, 15,* 385-393.

Bach-Hughes, C., & Page-Lieberman, J. (1989). Fathers experiencing a perinatal loss. *Death Studies, 13,* 537-556.

Balk, D. E. (1990). The self-concepts of bereaved adolescents: Sibling death and its aftermath. *Journal of Adolescent Research, 5,* 112-132.

Balk, D. E. (1991). Sibling death, adolescent bereavement, and religion. *Death Studies, 15,* 1-20.

Bank, S., & Kahn, M. D. (1975). Sisterhood-brotherhood is powerful: Sibling sub-systems and family therapy. *Family Process, 14,* 311-337.

Bertalanffy, L. von. (1968). *General systems theory.* New York: George Braziller.

Boss, P. (1987). Family stress. In M. B. Sussman & S. K. Steinmetz (Eds.), *Handbook of marriage and the family* (pp. 695-723). New York: Plenum.

Boss, P. (1991). Ambiguous loss. In F. Walsh & M. McGoldrick (Eds.), *Living beyond loss* (pp. 164-175). New York: Norton.

Bowen, M. (1976). Family reaction to death. In P. J. Guerin (Ed.), *Family therapy: Theory and practice.* New York: Gardner.

Bowlby, J. (1969). *Attachment and loss: Vol. 1. Attachment.* New York: Basic Books.

Bowlby, J. (1980). *Attachment and loss: Vol. 3. Loss: Sadness and depression.* New York: Basic Books.

Brown, F. H. (1989). The impact of death and serious illness on the family life cycle. In B. Carter & M. McGoldrick (Eds.), *The changing family life cycle* (2nd ed., pp. 457-482). Needham Heights, MA: Allyn & Bacon.

Buckley, W. (1967). *Sociology and modern systems theory.* Englewood Cliffs, NJ: Prentice Hall.

Burnell, G. M., & Burnell, A. L. (1989). *Clinical management of bereavement: A handbook for healthcare professionals.* New York: Human Sciences.

Cain, A. (Ed.). (1972). *Survivors of suicide.* Springfield, IL: Charles C Thomas.

Cain, A. C., Fast, I., & Erickson, M. E. (1964). Children's disturbed reactions to the death of a sibling. *American Journal of Orthopsychiatry, 34,* 741-752.

Clark, P. G., Siviski, R. W., & Weiner, R. (1986). Coping strategies of widowers in the first year. *Family Relations, 35,* 425-430.

Clayton, P. (1974). Mortality and morbidity in the first year of widowhood. *Archives of General Psychiatry, 125,* 747-750.

Clayton, P. (1979). The sequelae and non-sequelae of conjugal bereavement. *American Journal of Psychiatry, 136,* 1530-1543.

Cook, J. A. (1988). Dad's double binds: Rethinking fathers' bereavement from a men's studies perspective. *Journal of Contemporary Ethnography, 17,* 285-308.

Counts, D. R., & Counts, D. A. (1991). Conclusions: Coping with the final tragedy. In D. R. Counts & D. A. Counts (Eds.), *Coping with the final tragedy: Cultural variation in dying and grieving* (pp. 277-291). Amityville, NY: Baywood.

Craig, Y. (1977). The bereavement of parents and their search for meaning. *British Journal of Social Work, 7,* 41-54.

DeFrain, J., Ernst, L., Jakub, D., & Taylor, J. (1991). *Sudden infant death: Enduring the loss.* Lexington, MA: Lexington Books.

DeFrain, J., Martens, L., Stork, J., & Stork, W. (1990). The psychological effects of a stillbirth on surviving family members. *Omega, 22,* 81-108.

Demi, A. S. (1989). Death of a spouse. In R. A. Kalish (Ed.), *Midlife loss: Coping strategies* (pp. 218-248). Newbury Park, CA: Sage.

Dershimer, R. A. (1990). *Counseling the bereaved.* New York: Pergamon.

DeSpelder, L. A., & Strickland, A. L. (1992). *The last dance: Encountering death and dying* (3rd ed.). Mountain View, CA: Mayfield.

Dickenson, G. E., & Fritz, J. L. (1981). Death in the family: An overlooked area in marriage and family textbooks. *Journal of Family Issues, 2,* 379-384.

Dohrenwend, B. S., & Dohrenwend, B. P. (Eds.). (1974). *Stressful life events: Their nature and effects.* New York: John Wiley.

Doka, K. J. (Ed.). (1989). *Disenfranchised grief.* Lexington, MA: Lexington Books.

Donnelly, K. F. (1988). *Recovering from the loss of a sibling.* New York: Dodd, Mead.

Dunne, E., McIntosh, J., & Dunne-Maxim, K. (1988). *Suicide and its aftermath.* New York: Norton.

Eckenrode, J. (Ed.). (1991). *The social context of coping.* New York: Plenum.

Elliot, G. R., & Eisdorfer, C. (Eds.). (1982). *Stress and human health: A study by the Institute of Medicine, National Academy of Sciences.* New York: Springer.

Feifel, H. (1977). *New meanings of death.* New York: McGraw-Hill.

Figley, C. R. (1983). Catastrophes: An overview of family reactions. In C. R. Figley & H. I. McCubbin (Eds.), *Stress and the family: Coping with catastrophe* (pp. 3-20). New York: Brunner/Mazel.

Figley, C. R. (1989). *Helping traumatized families.* San Francisco: Jossey-Bass.

Freud, S. (1917). Mourning and melancholies. In J. Strachey (Ed. and Trans.), *The standard edition of the complete psychological works of Sigmund Freud* (Vol. 14, pp. 243-258). London: Hogarth.

Froman, P. K. (1992). *After you say goodbye: When someone you love dies of AIDS.* San Francisco: Chronicle Books.

Garbarino, J., Dubrow, N., Kostelny, K., & Pardo, C. (1992). *Children in danger: Coping with the consequences of community violence.* San Francisco: Jossey-Bass.

Gilbert, K. R. (1989). Interactive grief and coping in the marital dyad. *Death Studies, 13,* 605-626.

Gilbert, K. R. (in press). Family loss and grief. In R. D. Day, K. R. Gilbert, B. Settles, & W. R. Burr (Eds.), *Advanced family science.* Belmont, CA: Brooks/Cole.

Glick, I., Weiss, R., & Parkes, C. (1974). *The first year of bereavement.* New York: John Wiley.

Gonzales, S., & Reiss, D. (1981). *Families and chronic illness: Technical difficulties in assessing adjustment.* Paper presented at the Research and Theory Construction Workshop, annual meeting of the National Council on Family Relations, Milwaukee, WI.

Gottlieb, B. H. (1983). *Social support strategies: Guidelines for mental health practice.* Beverly Hills, CA: Sage.

Hall, N. R., & Goldstein, A. L. (1986). Thinking well: The chemical links between emotions and health. *The Sciences, 26,* 34-40.

Hamburg, D. A., & Adams, J. E. (1967). A perspective on coping: Seeking and utilizing information in major transitions. *Archives of General Psychiatry, 17,* 277-284.

Hankoff, L. D. (1975). Adolescence and the crisis of dying. *Adolescence, 10,* 373-387.

Hare-Mustin, R. T. (1979). Family therapy following the death of a child. *Journal of Marital and Family Therapy, 5,* 51-59.

Hill, R. (1949). *Families under stress.* New York: Harper & Row.

Hogan, N. S. (1988). The effects of time on the adolescent sibling bereavement process. *Pediatric Nursing, 14,* 333-335.

Holmes, T. H., & Rahe, R. H. (1967). The social readjustment rating scale. *Journal of Psychosomatic Research, 11,* 213-218.

Huygen, F. J. A., van den Hoogen, H. J. M., van Eijk, J. Y. M., & Smits, A. J. A. (1989). Death and dying: A longitudinal study of their medical impact on the family. *Family Systems Medicine, 7,* 374-384.

Imber-Black, E. (1991). Rituals and healing process. In F. Walsh & M. McGoldrick (Eds.), *Living beyond loss* (pp. 207-224). New York: Norton.

Jackson, D. (1965). The study of the family. *Family Process, 4,* 1-20.

Jackson, E. N. (1965). *Telling a child about death.* New York: Hawthorn.

Jacobs, S., & Osfeld, A. (1977). An epidemiological review of the mortality of bereavement. *Psychosomatic Medicine, 39,* 344-357.

Kalish, R. A. (Ed.). (1989). *Midlife loss: Coping strategies.* Newbury Park, CA: Sage.

Kalnins, I., Churchill, M. P., & Terry, G. (1980). Concurrent stresses in families with a leukemic child. *Journal of Pediatric Psychology, 5,* 81-92.

Kantor, D., & Lehr, W. (1975). *Inside the family.* San Francisco: Jossey-Bass.

Kastenbaum, R. (1980). Death, dying, and bereavement in old age: New developments and their possible implications for psychosocial care. In *Annual editions: Aging* (pp. 200-207). Guilford, CT: Dushkin.

Kauffman, J. (1993). Mourning and retardation. *The Forum, 18*(2), 1, 12-13.

Klass, D. (1984). Bereaved parents and The Compassionate Friends: Affiliation and healing. *Omega, 15,* 353-373.

Klass, D. (1987). John Bowlby's model of grief and the problems of identification. *Omega, 18,* 13-21.

Klass, D., & Marwit, S. J. (1988). Toward a model of parental grief. *Omega, 19,* 31-50.

Klein, S., & Fletcher, W. (1986). Gay grief: An examination of the uniqueness brought to light by the AIDS crisis. *Journal of Psychosocial Oncology, 4,* 15-25.

Kubler-Ross, E. (1969). *On death and dying.* New York: Macmillan.

Kubler-Ross, E. (1983). *On children and death.* New York: Collier.

Kupst, M. J., Tylke, L., Thomas, L., Mudd, M., Richardson, L., & Schulman, J. L. (1982). Strategies of intervention with families of pediatric leukemia patients: A longitudinal perspective. *Social Work in Health Care, 8*(2), 31-47.

Lerner, M. (1971). Justice, guilt, and veridical perception. *Journal of Personality and Social Psychology, 20,* 127-135.

Lerner, M. (1980). When, why, and where people die. In E. S. Schneidman (Ed.), *Death: Current perspectives* (pp. 87-106). Palo Alto, CA: Mayfield.

Lerner, M., & Simmons, C. (1966). Observers' reactions to the innocent victim: Compassion or rejection? *Journal of Personality and Social Psychology, 14,* 203-210.

Lindemann, E. (1944). Symptomology and management of acute grief. *American Journal of Psychiatry, 101,* 141-148.

Littlewood, J. (1992). *Aspects of grief: Bereavement in adult life.* London: Tavistock/Routledge.

Lopata, H. (1972). *Widowhood in an American city.* Cambridge, MA: Schenkman.

Lopata, H. (1973). Self-identity in marriage and widowhood. *The Sociological Quarterly, 14,* 407-418.

Lopata, H. (1979). *Women as widows: Support systems.* New York: Elsevier.

Madanes, C., & Haley, J. (1977). Dimensions of family therapy. *Journal of Nervous and Mental Disease, 165,* 88-98.

McCubbin, M. A., & McCubbin, H. I. (1989). Theoretical orientations to family stress and coping. In C. R. Figley (Ed.), *Treating stress in families* (pp. 3-43). New York: Brunner/Mazel.

McCubbin, H. I., & Patterson, J. (1983). Family transitions: Adaptation to stress. In H. I. McCubbin & C. R. Figley (Eds.), *Stress and the family: Vol. 1. Coping with normative transitions* (pp. 5-25). New York: Brunner/Mazel.

McGoldrick, M. (1989). Ethnicity and the family life cycle. In B. Carter & M. McGoldrick (Eds.), *The changing family life cycle* (2nd ed., pp. 69-90). Boston: Allyn & Bacon.

McGoldrick, M. (1991). Echoes from the past: Helping families mourn their losses. In F. Walsh & M. McGoldrick (Eds.), *Living beyond loss* (pp. 50-78). New York: Norton.

McGoldrick, M., Almeida, R., Hines, P. M., Garcia-Preto, N., Rosen, E., & Lee, E. (1991). Mourning in different cultures. In F. Walsh & M. McGoldrick (Eds.), *Living beyond loss* (pp. 176-206). New York: Norton.

McGoldrick, M., & Gerson, R. (1985). *Genograms in family assessment.* New York: Norton.

McGoldrick, M., & Walsh, F. (1983). A systemic view of family history and loss. In M. Aronson & L. Wolberg (Eds.), *Group and family therapy* (pp. 252-270). New York: Brunner/Mazel.

McGoldrick, M., & Walsh, F. (1991). A time to mourn: Death and the family life cycle. In F. Walsh & M. McGoldrick (Eds.), *Living beyond loss* (pp. 30-49). New York: Norton.

Miles, M. S., & Demi, A. S. (1992). A comparison of guilt in bereaved parents whose children died by suicide, accident, or chronic disease. *Omega, 24,* 203-215.

Moir, A., & Jessel, D. (1991). *Brain sex.* New York: Carol.

Moss, M. S., & Moss, S. Z. (1989). The death of a parent. In R. Kalish (Ed.), *Midlife loss* (pp. 89-114). Newbury Park, CA: Sage.

Murray, C. I. (1982). Bereaved parent-adolescent interaction: A need for understanding. In K. M. Campbell (Ed.), *Proceedings of the 1982 Ohio Council on Family Relations Annual Meeting* (pp. 33-44). Columbus: Ohio Council on Family Relations.

Olshansky, S. J., & Ault, A. B. (1986). The fourth stage of the epidemiologic transition: The age of delayed degenerative diseases. *The Millbank Quarterly, 64,* 355-391.

Osterweis, M., Solomon, F., & Green, M. (Eds.). (1984). *Bereavement: Reactions, consequences, and care.* Washington, DC: National Academy Press.

Parkes, C. M. (1972). *Bereavement: Studies of grief in adult life.* New York: International Universities Press.

Parkes, C. M. (1986). *Bereavement: Studies of grief in adult life* (3rd ed.). New York: International Universities Press.

Parkes, C. M. (1988). Research: Bereavement. *Omega, 18,* 365-377.

Parkes, C. M., Benjamin, B., & Fitzgerald, R. G. (1969). Broken heart: A statistical study of increased mortality among widowers. *British Medical Journal, 1,* 740-743.

Parkes, C. M., & Weiss, R. S. (1983). *Recovery from bereavement.* New York: Basic Books.

Pattison, E. M. (1977). *The experience of dying.* Englewood Cliffs, NJ: Prentice Hall.

Paul, N. (1976). Cross-confrontation. In P. Guerin (Ed.), *Family therapy: Theory and practice* (pp. 520-529). New York: Gardner.

Paul, N., & Paul, B. (1982). Death and changes in sexual behavior. In F. Walsh (Ed.), *Normal family processes* (pp. 325-410). New York: Guilford.

Paul, N., & Paul, B. (1989). *A marital puzzle.* Boston: Allyn & Bacon.

Pearlin, L., & Lieberman, M. (1979). Social sources of distress. In R. Simons (Ed.), *Research in community and mental health* (pp. 217-248). Greenwich, CT: JAI.

Pine, V. R., Margolis, O. S., Doka, K., Kutscher, A. H., Schaefer, D. J., Siegel, M., & Cherico, D. J. (Eds.). (1990). *Unrecognized and unsanctioned grief: The nature and counseling of unacknowledged loss.* Springfield, IL: Charles C Thomas.

Pinkus, L. (1974). *Death and the family: The importance of mourning.* New York: Pantheon.

Pollock, G. H. (1989). *The mourning-liberation process* (Vol. 1). Madison, CT: International Universities Press.

Ponzetti, J. J., & Johnson, M. A. (1991). The forgotten grievers: Grandparents' reactions to the death of grandchildren. *Death Studies, 15,* 157-167.

Ramsden, P. G. (1991). Alice in the afterlife: A glimpse in the mirror. In D. R. Counts & D. A. Counts (Eds.), *Coping with the final tragedy: Cultural variation in dying and grieving* (pp. 27-41). Amityville, NY: Baywood.

Rando, T. A. (1984). *Grief, dying, and death: Clinical interventions for caregivers*. Champaign, IL: Research Press.

Rando, T. A. (Ed.). (1986). *Parental loss of a child*. Champaign, IL: Research Press.

Rando, T. A. (1988). *Grieving: How to go on living when someone you love dies*. Lexington, MA: Lexington Books.

Raphael, B. (1983). *The anatomy of bereavement*. New York: Basic Books.

Reiss, D., & Oliveri, M. (1980). Family paradigm and family coping: A proposal for linking the family's intrinsic adaptive capacities to its response to stress. *Family Relations, 29,* 431-444.

Reynolds, J. (1993). Grief and the culture of victimization. *The Forum, 18*(2), 9, 11.

Rolland, J. S. (1987). Chronic illness and the life cycle: A conceptual framework. *Family Process, 26,* 203-221.

Rolland, J. S. (1991). Helping families with anticipatory loss. In F. Walsh & M. McGoldrick (Eds.), *Living beyond loss* (pp. 144-163). New York: Norton.

Rosaldo, R. (1989). *Culture and truth: The remaking of social analysis*. Boston: Beacon.

Rosen, H. (1986). *Unspoken grief*. Lexington, MA: Lexington Books.

Rosenblatt, P. (1983). *Bitter, bitter tears: Nineteenth century diarists and twentieth century grief theorists*. Minneapolis: University of Minnesota Press.

Schatz, W. H. (1986). Grief of fathers. In T. A. Rando (Ed.), *Parental loss of a child* (pp. 293-302). Champaign, IL: Research Press.

Schiff, H. (1977). *The bereaved parent*. New York: Crown.

Schleifer, S. J., Keller, S. E., Camerino, M., Thornton, J. C., & Stein, M. (1983). Suppression of lymphocyte stimulation following bereavement. *Journal of the American Medical Association, 250,* 374-377.

Sherwood, S., Kastenbaum, R., Morris, J. N., & Wright, S. M. (1988). The first months of bereavement. In V. Mor, D. S. Greer, & R. Kastenbaum (Eds.), *The hospice experiment* (pp. 149-150). Baltimore, MD: Johns Hopkins University Press.

Siegel, B. S. (1986). *Love, medicine, and miracles*. New York: Harper & Row.

Simonton, C., Mathews-Simonton, S., & Creighton, J. (1978). *Getting well again*. Los Angeles: Jeremy Tarcher.

Sontag, S. (1988). *AIDS and its metaphors*. New York: Farrar, Straus, & Giroux.

Staudacher, C. (1991). *Men and grief*. Oakland, CA: New Harbinger.

Stroebe, M. (1992). Coping with bereavement: A review of the grief work hypothesis. *Omega, 26,* 19-42.

Stroebe, M. S., Stroebe, W., Gergen, K. J., & Gergen, M. (1981). The broken heart: Reality or myth? *Omega, 12,* 87-106.

U.S. Bureau of the Census. (1975). *Historical statistics, colonial times to 1970*. Washington, DC: Government Printing Office.

U. S. Bureau of the Census. (1992). *Statistical abstract of the United States 1992*. Washington, DC: Government Printing Office.

Videka-Sherman, L., & Lieberman, M. (1985). The effects of self-help and psychotherapy intervention on child loss: The limits of recovery. *American Journal of Orthopsychiatry, 55,* 70-82.

Viorst, J. (1986). *Necessary losses*. New York: Simon & Schuster.

Walsh, F., & McGoldrick, M. (1991). Loss and the family: A systems perspective. In F. Walsh & M. McGoldrick (Eds.), *Living beyond loss* (pp. 1-29). New York: Norton.

Worden, W. (1982). *Grief counseling and grief therapy.* New York: Springer.

Wortman, C. B., & Silver, R. C. (1989). The myths of coping with loss. *Journal of Consulting and Clinical Psychology, 57,* 349-357.

Zisook, S., & Shuchter, S. R. (1986). The first four years of widowhood. *Psychiatric Annals, 16,* 288-298.

# PART II

# Situational Stressors

# 10

❀

# Divorce

DAVID H. DEMO
LAWRENCE H. GANONG

Divorce is widely viewed as a serious problem confronting American families. The word *divorce* conjures up images of divided families, vulnerable children, separated couples, failed marriages, forgotten commitments, long and expensive legal battles, resentment, hostility, bitterness, and economic hardship. These images are reflected and perpetuated in popular prime-time television shows, in numerous best-selling books on how to survive divorce, and in television and radio talk shows. It is understandable that people do not attach a positive value to divorce. Children do not grow up dreaming that one day they will be divorced. Nor do most children hope that one day their parents will divorce and reside in separate households. One objective of this chapter is to offer new perspectives for thinking about divorce and to challenge some unquestioned assumptions about how families are affected by divorce. For example, one common assumption is that children and adults experience severe and long-term postdivorce adjustment problems. Although studies of small clinical samples tend to support this assumption (e.g., Wallerstein & Blakeslee, 1990), careful studies of larger and more representative populations suggest moderate and short-term effects, both for adults (Booth & Amato, 1991) and for children

AUTHORS' NOTE: We thank the editors and Katherine Allen for their many helpful comments and suggestions on an earlier version of this chapter.

(Demo & Acock, 1988). As researchers continue to explore the mechanisms by which divorce influences family members, attention is being focused on a number of previously unasked questions, suggesting new interpretations of these and other findings.

In addition, there is increasing emphasis on conceptualizing divorce as a process (rather than a discrete event) that occurs within the life course of children, adolescents, and adults. Therefore a second objective of this chapter is to describe the life course of divorce and to address the issue of how divorce is a social and/or personal problem and how it may serve as a safety valve or potential solution to a series of individual and family problems.

A third objective of this chapter is to illustrate the highly variable nature of adjustment to divorce. As feminist family researchers emphasize, family life is perceived, defined, and experienced differently by each family member (e.g., Baca Zinn, 1990; Ferree, 1990; Glenn, 1987). Rather than one unitary or "core" family reality, there are multiple and sometimes conflicting family realities predivorce, during divorce, and postdivorce. Women and men typically have sharply contrasting experiences, perceptions, and outcomes of divorce, and it is common for siblings to adjust differently to their parents' divorce. Understanding divorce thus requires us to understand the multiple perspectives of family members regarding their pre- and postdivorce family histories, relationships, and experiences.

The last objective of this chapter is to describe various interventions that may facilitate adjustment to divorce. Because divorce is a process that occurs within larger social, legal, and cultural systems, it is important to consider possible changes in prevailing systems that may ease the experience of divorce and provide greater support for individuals and families. In particular, we consider changes in child support guidelines and enforcement, family life education, and therapy.

## History and Context

Divorce is an increasingly common experience for American families. Although it is commonly believed that the divorce rate was quite low through the 1950s and then soared in the past few decades, historical analyses indicate that the divorce rate increased steadily from the mid-nineteenth century through the 1970s (Cherlin, 1992). The divorce rate then stabilized at a historically high level in the 1980s. Approximately half of all first marriages formed in the past decade will end in divorce, and if current trends continue, the divorce rate may climb as high as 60% for recent marriages (Bumpass, 1990).

Through the 1960s and 1970s, American society experienced a steadily increasing emphasis on individualism, often over familism. This emphasis led to new experiences, experimentation with different lifestyles, more impulsive behaviors, new ways of thinking about oneself, and greater self-awareness. Singlehood, cohabitation, childlessness, and premarital and extramarital sexual relations became more acceptable while opposition to abortion and divorce weakened (Thornton, 1989).

For many adults, concerns with self-development, self-fulfillment, and careers have fostered a declining commitment to others, including spouses and children, rendering marriage and other intimate relationships fragile and vulnerable (Bellah, Sullivan, Swidler, & Tipton, 1985; Schnaiberg & Goldenberg, 1989). Other factors also have contributed to rising divorce rates. Changing work patterns, diminished occupational opportunities, and massive unemployment and underemployment have created uncertainties and led to domestic upheaval for families of many diverse types, cultures, and social backgrounds (Stacey, 1991).

The growing acceptance of nontraditional lifestyles also has been influential in that there are more alternatives available to individuals in unhappy or unfulfilling relationships (Cherlin, 1992). Many individuals, especially women, recognized that marriage was not meeting their personal needs, or, as Jessie Bernard (1972) observed, that "her" marriage was less attractive than "his." Women in unhappy, oppressive, or violent marriages found it easier and more acceptable to end such marriages through legal divorce. But perhaps one of the most insidious factors undermining marital satisfaction and longevity is that individuals enter into marriage with unrealistic, idealistic, and romanticized notions about marriage. The coexistence of these conditions—personal fulfillment being strongly valued, lofty expectations not being satisfied, and the perception that desirable alternatives are available—increases the probability of divorce.

The reality is that the divorce rate in the United States is high and is likely to remain high. This raises two important questions. First, what makes some marriages more (or less) vulnerable to divorce than others, and, second, what are the consequences of divorce for family members and for society?

## Proneness to Divorce

The reasons that some couples stay together, while others do not, are much more complicated than distinctions between happy and unhappy marriages. There is consistent evidence that several demographic and life course factors contribute to a higher probability of divorce, including early age at marriage, premarital childbearing, childlessness during marriage, and lower income and socioeconomic status (White, 1990). Among the important factors protecting or insulating marriages from divorce are shared leisure time (Hill, 1988), presence of children (Thornton, 1977), paternal involvement in child rearing (Morgan, Lye, & Condran, 1988; Seecombe & Lee, 1987), marital happiness (Booth, Johnson, & Edwards, 1983), and accumulation of assets (Booth, Johnson, White, & Edwards, 1986).

Unfortunately, we know little about how family processes and relationships relate to the likelihood of divorce (White, 1990). Hill (1988), drawing on exchange theory (e.g., Lewis & Spanier, 1979) and the new "home economics" (e.g., Becker, Landes, & Michael, 1977), hypothesized that frequent and pleasurable shared leisure time provides short-term benefits for spouses by drawing the couple together and provides long-term benefits by preventing marital breakup. She found that couples with higher levels of shared recreational and leisure time were more likely to be together over the 5-year time of the study.

Hill's (1988) study also clarified the multiple and counteracting mechanisms by which children influence marital stability. On one hand, children may facilitate marital stability because parents may want to stay together "for the sake of the children," and parents fear that divorce would reduce their involvement with their children and weaken parent-child bonds. On the other hand, the presence of children restricts couples' leisure time and time alone, undermining marital happiness and destabilizing the marriage. Hill found that, compared with couples with no children, those with children spend an average of 7 to 10 fewer hours per week in shared leisure time. Thus, somewhat paradoxically, children both contribute to and detract from marital stability.

From a social exchange perspective, shared leisure time is one of the many rewards marriage may provide. Others include social status, emotional gratification, sexual pleasure, and the accumulation of physical property and economic assets. Costs of the marital relationship include time and energy invested in household labor, wage labor, emotional labor, and child care. According to social exchange theory, low marital quality occurs when the marriage ceases to be profitable, that is, when the costs exceed the rewards. When the marriage is not profitable, and when outcomes fall below the level that could be obtained in some other relationship, one or both parties may choose to end the marriage. Thus the current relationship is judged in the context of the rewards and costs it generated in the past, the anticipated rewards and costs of that relationship in the future (Lewis

& Spanier, 1979), and the attractiveness of alternatives to the current relationship.

Another interesting but underused approach for uncovering the causes of divorce is to ask divorced people "what went wrong" in their marriages. One of the themes that emerges from studies using this method is that wives report more dissatisfaction with marriage than do husbands (Kitson & Sussman, 1982; Spanier & Thompson, 1983). Common complaints by wives include husband's authoritarianism, mental cruelty, verbal and physical abuse, excessive drinking, lack of love, neglect of children, emotional and personality problems, and extramarital sex (Bloom, Niles, & Tatcher, 1985; Cleek & Pearson, 1985; Kitson, 1985; Kitson & Sussman, 1982; Thurnher, Fenn, Melichar, & Chiriboga, 1983). Significantly more men than women describe themselves as having a problem with alcohol, drugs, or physical abuse that contributed to the divorce (Bloom, Niles, et al., 1985; Cleek & Pearson, 1985). It is also common for divorced women and men to share the view that communication problems, basic unhappiness, and incompatibility led to the divorce.

The accounts of formerly married people reveal reasons for divorce that are often overlooked in large-scale historical or demographic studies. These accounts also illustrate how differently women and men perceive and experience marriage and family life. Former spouses' descriptions of their marriages underscore that gender differentiation and power imbalances in marriage, work, and parenthood often have undesirable, even harsh, consequences for family members.

### Divorce and Its Aftermath

Although public disapproval of divorce has softened, divorced individuals still confront stigma. Gerstel (1990) interviewed 102 separated and divorced women and men and found that, although most divorced individuals do not think their friends or family disapprove of their divorce, they nonetheless experience social and emotional fallout. Friends are lost, rejection is felt as friends and others assess and attribute blame, elaborate "accounts" are developed to explain the divorce to self and to others, and many married people exclude the divorced from social gatherings and friendship networks.

The broader structure of predivorce and postdivorce social networks provides illustrations of gender-based beliefs, expectations, opportunities, and constraints. Both during marriage and following divorce, women are expected to be familistic and to be "kinkeepers," while men are encouraged to be independent and generally have social networks that are dominated by ties with friends (Milardo, 1987). Compared with men, women interact more frequently with both consanguineous and affinal kin during marriage, and they are more likely to sustain these ties postdivorce. Although both women's and men's social networks generally become smaller and less dense following divorce (Rands, 1988), women typically have fewer friends and lower levels of social participation postdivorce (Hetherington, Cox, & Cox, 1977). To an important degree, these patterns impair the ability of social support networks to provide support for women and men coping with, and adjusting to, divorce. Men are disadvantaged because they are less likely than women to have intimate friends and less likely to receive support from kin and nonkin (Spanier & Thompson, 1984). On the other hand, lower levels of contact with kin also means men have less social interference (Milardo, 1987). For women, it is precisely their heavier involvement with and commitment to their families that precludes them from enjoying higher levels of social participation and recreation.

### Economic Consequences

The economic consequences of divorce also tend to be different for women than for men, with women typically more disadvantaged. Of course, some women and men fare better than others, and predivorce family standard of living is an important consideration in measuring economic decline postdivorce. But the clear pattern is that, although the economic well-being of divorced women (and their dependent children) plunges in comparison with predivorce levels, their former husbands often enjoy a *better* financial situation postdivorce (Burkhauser & Duncan, 1989; Weitzman, 1985).

For a significant portion of women, including many heading mother-only families, the economic result of divorce is poverty. Using two measures of poverty, the official poverty threshold and a "near-poor" level that captures families living "on the edge" of poverty, Morgan (1989) found that over one fourth of divorced women fall into poverty during the 5 years following the end of their marriage. Postdivorce poverty is especially common among women who had lower family incomes while married (Holden & Smock, 1991), but the *degree of change* in family income is most severe for women who were relatively well-off during marriage. Women with the highest predivorce family incomes experience a 55% to 71% decline in family income following divorce, whereas women with the lowest predivorce family incomes experience declines averaging 23% to 29% (Weiss, 1984; Weitzman, 1985).

Unfortunately, women's economic plight following divorce is not short-lived. Despite high levels of female employment prior to separation and higher levels postseparation, economic hardship typically extends for at least 5 years following divorce (R. Peterson, 1989; Weiss, 1984). Duncan and Hoffman (1985) report that, at the fifth year postdivorce, women's family income is still only 71% of predivorce income. Although economic recovery is faster for women with higher than average predivorce family incomes, the evidence is compelling that the only way most women can restore their economic situation is through remarriage (Duncan & Hoffman, 1985; R. Peterson, 1989).

For most men, by contrast, divorce has only short-term economic costs and usually contributes to an *improved* standard of living within a short period of time. One year after divorce, men's income is 90% of their predivorce income (Duncan & Hoffman, 1985). Examining a national sample, Duncan and Hoffman found that men's income-to-needs ratio improves 13% over predivorce levels by the first year postdivorce and improves to 24% over predivorce levels by the second year following divorce.

Why are the economic costs of divorce so much greater for women? First, most marriages and divorces involve children, and mothers continue to devote substantially more time than fathers to caring for children (Demo, 1992). The time women invest in child care and other unpaid family labor restricts their educational and occupational opportunities as well as their income. Women are less likely to work if they have young children (Moen, 1985), and family demands prompt many employed women to reduce time spent in paid work (Berk, 1985). Further, most children reside with their mothers postdivorce. One of the major reasons, however, is that, although child support is awarded in most divorce cases, full compliance by fathers is rare. In 1985 only half of those mothers entitled to child support received full payment; one fourth received irregular or incomplete payments; and one fourth received no payments (U.S. Bureau of the Census, 1989). Even when fathers comply fully and make regular payments, child support awards are typically too low to meet the costs of rearing children, and the awards are not indexed for inflation.

Institutionalized sexism and gender-based discrimination in the wage workplace also contribute to women's sustained postdivorce economic decline. Most employment opportunities for women are limited to low-paying or temporary work, jobs that offer no future of advancement. Women's lower earnings relative to men's, when combined with the inadequacies of child support payments and the lack of affordable day care, doom most women and their families to long periods of economic hardship following divorce.

## Psychological Adjustment

In some cases, it is fairly straightforward to think of changes associated with divorce as *consequences* of divorce, such as postdivorce changes in the size or composition of friendship networks or in individual or family income. Of course, even here, some of the changes may predate the divorce. But other changes are even more difficult to assess.

Although several studies have examined the course of adult mental health following divorce, most studies involve cross-sectional designs, rely on clinical or convenience samples, or fail to include control groups. Still, there are some interesting and consistent findings. In a rare longitudinal study, Coysh, Johnston, Tschann, Wallerstein, and Kline (1989) examined a predominantly white, middle- and higher-income sample of divorced women and men that varied in their custody arrangements. Two thirds of the families involved mothers' sole physical custody and one third had joint physical custody. They found that an important predictor of both women's and men's postdivorce psychological adjustment was their *pre*divorce level of adjustment. For both women and men, better coping and emotional functioning prior to divorce were associated with more effective coping and less anger and emotional distress following divorce. Preseparation communication and shared decision making regarding child rearing also were associated with more cooperative involvement between parents after divorce.

Coysh and colleagues (1989) also found important differences in the ways women and men responded to family experiences preceding and following divorce. Although both women and men who were involved in relationships with new partners were doing much better psychologically and emotionally than others without such relationships, women were bothered more by pre- and postdivorce family issues, tensions, and conflicts. The researchers' clinical data suggest that, for men, "new relationships were able to undo, with surprising rapidity, the narcissistic injury engendered by the divorce" (Coysh et al., 1989, p. 68). In contrast, "women appear to be more affected by the residual hostility from the past marriage and problematic relations between partners and children in their new marriages or relationships" (p. 68).

White women also appear to be more severely affected by divorce than African American women (Gove & Shin, 1989). The evidence on race differences in adjustment to divorce is limited, but it appears that, compared with their white counterparts, African American women receive more social support postdivorce (Cherlin, 1992). Kitson (1992) suggests that, although African Americans view divorce as regrettable, the higher divorce rate among African Americans prompts greater acceptance and less stigma. For those who remarry, there are few and small differences in the psychological adjustment of whites and African Americans (Fine, McKenry, Donnelly, & Voydanoff, 1992).

There are a number of explanations for these findings. Women, in general, are more deeply committed to marriage, parenthood, and family life than men are; women devote substantially more time and energy to these activities than men do; they tend to be more expressive, affectionate, and emotional in marriage than men; and "women's well-being seems to be tied more closely to the emotional make-up of marriage" (Thompson & Walker, 1989, p. 846). Having invested more in the relationship, it is reasonable that the dissolution of the relationship inflicts greater emotional pain for women than for men. Other factors certainly contribute to women's postdivorce distress, including their worsened economic position and the chronic stresses associated with coordinating employment and single parenting (Thompson & Ensminger, 1989).

As bleak a picture as this paints for many divorced women, there is considerable evidence to suggest that divorce is a short-term crisis, with stress increasing during the divorce process and subsiding as life is reorganized and individuals adjust to new routines and lifestyles. Booth and Amato (1991) found that levels of unhappiness and psychological stress rise and reach peak levels during the predivorce period, then subside within 2 years following divorce to levels experienced by married persons (Booth & Amato, 1991). Consistent with other studies (Coysh et al., 1989), Booth and Amato found that predivorce well-being is an important factor in the adjustment process. Many divorced women may feel that, even with the economic, parental, and other demands placed on them, they prefer their current situation to the lives they had when they were married. In an analysis of a nationally representative sample of divorced mothers, Acock and Demo (in press) found that more than four out of five divorced mothers said they are happier or much happier than before they separated. In addition, nearly three out of five report they have more leisure time and better career opportunities than when they were married, and two thirds rate their social lives as better or much better. More than half judge their housing situation and sex life to be better than before the separation. Consistent with the evidence previously discussed, two of five divorced mothers report their finances are worse or much worse than before they separated, nearly one in five report they are "doing about the same" financially, and the remaining two fifths report they are doing better financially.

### Children's Adjustment

Perhaps no issue surrounding divorce generates more concern or stirs more controversy than children's adjustment to divorce. The research literature on the subject is voluminous, and the reader is referred to several recent publications that review and assess the available evidence (e.g., Allen, 1993; Amato, 1993; Demo, 1993; Demo & Acock, 1988; Emery, 1988). Our main purpose is to briefly summarize what we know about how children are influenced by divorce, and processes associated with divorce, and to offer some explanations for these patterns.

As is the case for most adults who experience divorce, the evidence suggests that most children and adolescents suffer emotional problems for 1 to 2 years during the period leading up to and immediately following parental separation and divorce (Hetherington, Cox, & Cox, 1982). This is usually the period when marital and family conflict intensifies, legal battles are fought, and relationships with residential and nonresidential parents are restructured and renegotiated. On average, however, the adjustment of children and adolescents in postdivorce families is only marginally lower than that of their counterparts in continuously intact two-parent families. Differences in children's psychological well-being *within* family types tend to be far greater than differences *between* family types. For example, on measures of self-esteem, some children in two-parent families score near the top of the scale, some in the middle, and some near the bottom. But, on average, their scores are very similar to the scores of children living in single-parent families. Also, adolescents appear to adjust more readily to parental divorce than younger children (Demo & Acock, 1988).

There are further similarities in the adjustment processes of children and adults. As with adults, the nature of legal custody arrangements does not appear to affect children's well-being (Furstenberg & Cherlin, 1991). More important to children's postdivorce adjustment are the provision of economic resources, the maintenance (or development) of positive, nurturing relationships with both parents, and low levels of interparental and family conflict (Demo, 1992; Emery, 1988). Children's predivorce adjustment is also influential in shaping the course of their well-being through the dissolution and postdissolution process (Emery, 1988).

It is widely speculated that reduced involvement with nonresidential parents (usually fathers) is damaging to children's well-being. Heightening this concern are studies showing that only a small percentage of nonresidential fathers maintain regular contact with their children, that in most cases paternal involvement following divorce is infrequent (Furstenberg, Morgan, & Allison, 1987), and that fathers' contact typically diminishes over time (Maccoby & Mnookin, 1992). But the broader picture is much more complex. Some nonresidential fathers (especially African American fathers) maintain regular contact with their children (Mott, 1990), many children change residences (some several times) to live with a different parent, and children living with their fathers typically have relatively frequent contact with nonresidential mothers (Maccoby & Mnookin, 1992). At a minimum, these patterns demonstrate that traditional definitions of family structure (e.g., father-present or father-absent) often obscure and distort temporal and cultural variations in residential and visitation processes (Mott, 1990).

There is also evidence that the frequency of contact with the nonresidential parent has little effect on children's well-being following divorce (Emery, 1988; Furstenberg & Cherlin, 1991). One plausible explanation for this is that the frequency of parental visitation or contact may be unrelated to the history and/or quality of the relationship. For example, although low levels of paternal involvement appear to be the norm for children in mother-only families, for some children this means seeing less of a nurturing and supportive father while for others it means seeing less of a detached or abusive father. On the other hand, it seems that the *quality* of children's relationships with parents—both residential and nonresidential—affects children's adjustment to divorce. One study found that children are much more likely to report a close relationship with nonresidential mothers than with nonresidential fathers (Peterson & Zill, 1986), but research linking the quality of these relationships to children's well-being is sparse and inconclusive. There is consistent evidence, however, that children's adjustment is enhanced if they have a good relationship with at least one of their parents (Emery, 1988).

A serious problem confronting many children following divorce is prolonged economic hardship. Although children's postdivorce residential arrangements are widely variable and change over time, most children (roughly two thirds) live with their mothers, 10% live with their fathers, and the remainder have dual residence or live in other arrangements (Maccoby & Mnookin, 1992). As we have seen, most women and their children experience a sharp and long-term decline in their standard of living. Economic hardship is associated with lowered parental well-being, less effective and less supportive parenting, inconsistent and harsh discipline, and distress and impaired socioemotional functioning in children (Elder, Nguyen, & Caspi, 1985; McLoyd, 1990). It should be clear, however, that these adverse effects are not inevitable consequences of divorce. They are products of chronic financial stress and, as such, they are experienced by children in divorced and nondivorced families alike.

## Interventions

The last two decades have seen the rise of what has been called the "divorce industry," professionals from a variety of fields that focus on divorce (Bohannan, 1984). The divorce industry has led to the development of new professions such as family mediation and to expanded opportunities for attorneys, therapists, school counselors, family life educators, and social workers, among others. In this section we will examine interventions executed by those in the divorce industry and consider societal-level changes designed to facilitate postdivorce adjustment.

### Individual and Family Interventions

*Individual counseling and therapy.* Because children are seen as the primary victims of divorce, therapy for "children of divorce" has become a major focus of intervention efforts (Emery, 1988; Hodges, 1986). There are a number of intervention programs for children whose parents are divorced/divorcing (e.g., Kalter, Pickar, & Leskowitz, 1984; Pedro-Carrol & Cowen, 1985). Many of these are school-based programs that focus on helping children adapt socially and emotionally: becoming aware of their feelings about themselves, their parents, and the divorce; expressing feelings in appropriate ways; learning to cope with frustration; learning to get along with others; and enhancing self-esteem. There is some evidence that these group interventions are effective (Pedro-Carrol & Cowen, 1985; Stolberg & Garrison, 1985). However, few programs have been adequately evaluated in controlled studies, and findings from the evaluation studies that have been conducted are not clear-cut. Too often these are pilot or demonstration projects of short duration, precluding assessment of long-term benefits. Another criticism of these programs is that there is little overlap between research on children's adjustment to divorce and interventions (Grych & Fincham, 1992).

Divorce therapy, with the goal of helping adults adapt to the dissolution of the spousal relationship, was developed in the 1970s as a subspecialty of marital therapy (Sprenkle & Storm, 1983). Most evaluations of divorce therapy have not been adequately designed (Sprenkle & Storm, 1983), and divorce therapy has been criticized as therapy in a "contextual vacuum" (Lund, 1990). Much of the divorce therapy literature has ignored the different experiences of men and women, treating the experience for males and females as similar, even though there are well-documented gender differences in power, role changes, social support, values, and meanings attached to divorce (Lund, 1990). Divorce therapists may be guilty of ignoring gender inequalities in nuclear family ideology, perhaps unintentionally perpetuating inequalities for women and children postdivorce.

*Family life education.* A number of prevention and intervention programs for divorcing parents have been established in recent years (e.g., Bloom, Hodges, Kern, & McFaddin, 1985; Buehler, Betz, Ryan, Legg, & Trotter, 1992; Stolberg & Garrison, 1985). In general, their goals have been broad: facilitating parents' emotional adjustment to divorce, helping parents learn ways to coparent with former spouses, teaching parents what to expect from their children as they adjust to postdivorce family life, and handling finances and legal issues. The programs typically last for several sessions and are usually offered for parents who are recently divorced or who are facing an imminent divorce. Perhaps because of the breadth of topics covered in these programs, or perhaps because they are offered so near to the legal divorce, the success of these programs varies (Buehler et al., 1992; Stolberg & Garrison, 1985). As with other areas of family life education, assessment efforts have been relatively few, and more evaluation research of these programs is needed.

A new trend in family life education with divorcing adults has been "divorce classes" mandated by judges or districts (Lawson, 1992). The goals of these programs include increasing parents' awareness of their children's developmental needs and responses to divorce and guiding them in thinking about how to coparent (Bradburn-Stern, 1992). As with other postdivorce parenting classes, these mandated programs share child development information with parents so that they can assess whether children are adjusting "normally." Unlike other family life education offerings, however, these court-ordered classes typically last one or two sessions and are more narrowly focused on children's reactions. Little evaluation of the effectiveness of these programs has been done, but they are rapidly being implemented across the country. Such programs have political and intuitive appeal, so it is likely that the absence of evaluation will not deter their widespread implementation.

*Mediation.* Mediation has grown as an alternative to adjudicated divorces. Mediation allows the divorcing couple to maintain control of decisions about child support, parenting, and financial settlements. Although more research is needed on the effects of mediation on the psychological well-being of all family members, there are indications that: (a) compliance with mediated agreements is greater than compliance with adjudicated agreements (Pearson & Thoennes, 1988); (b) mediation may be less costly than litigation (Kelly, 1990); (c) mediation may be more efficient than litigation, because settlements can be made in less time (Emery, Matthews, & Wyer, 1991); (d) fewer mediated agreements return to court after the legal divorce than other types of agreements (Pearson & Thoennes, 1988); and (e) nonresidential parents are more likely to remain in contact with children, child support is more likely to be paid, and parents are more satisfied with postdivorce arrangements (Grych & Fincham, 1992; Kelly, 1991). Couples who mediate tend to be more satisfied with decisions surrounding the divorce and with the divorce process (Emery et al., 1991; Kelly, 1989), although men are generally more satisfied than women (see Menzel, 1991, for a review of fairness in mediation).

Despite the evidence supporting mediation as a way to settle divorces, the practice of mediation is not without critics. One concern is that power imbalances that put women at a disadvantage in negotiating are ignored or minimized (e.g., threats of physical violence by men, uneven access to financial resources). In addition, some couples may not be able to mediate because of personality or relational problems. These are important areas for future research. Of particular concern is the issue of gender inequity, because trends to make legal aspects of divorce gender-neutral have resulted in severe economic problems for divorced women (Buehler, in press; Price & McKenry, 1988).

## Interventions at the System Level

The social systems that most directly interact with families (i.e., schools, religious organizations, and health care agencies) have been criticized for being poorly prepared to interact with divorced families (Ahrons & Rodgers, 1987). These systems, through policies and organizational structures, at best ignore divorced families and at worst make life more difficult for them.

*Normalizing divorce.* One societal-level change that may help parents and children experiencing divorce would be to redefine divorce as a normative process with a range of outcomes rather than as an "unscheduled" event that is inherently traumatic (Ahrons & Rodgers, 1987; Price & McKenry, 1988; Veevers, 1991). Accepting the possibility of divorce may encourage individuals to construct their relationships differently, to live in ways that would make marriage a more satisfying experience as well as reduce problems related to dissolution of the marriage. Normalizing divorce may reduce stigma and may allow people to consider the possibility that divorces may have outcomes that strengthen family members (Veevers, 1991). Family policy surrounding divorce would likely differ from what it is now if divorces were seen as predictable, normative experiences.

*Schools.* Because almost all divorced families come in contact with school systems, school interventions have the potential of facilitating the postdivorce adjustment of children and their parents. Support groups are the most widespread school-based intervention for children whose parents are divorced. Although such programs are useful for some children, this illustrates the prevailing view among school personnel that all children of divorce are at risk, an overgeneralization that stigmatizes children with divorced parents and may lead to inappropriate teacher-student and parent-school interactions (Guttmann & Broudo, 1989).

School personnel should be educated about the range of effects of divorce on children, and they should receive training to help them be more sensitive when interacting with children and parents from postdivorce families. School practices that ignore the diversity of children's families should be abolished or revised.

## Legal Interventions in Divorce

*Divorce settlements: Child support awards and enforcement.* For over two decades, changes have been made in the legal divorce process aimed at reducing the negative effects of divorce on families and on society; attention has been focused primarily on reforms designed to offset the financial problems facing divorced mothers and their children

(Emery, 1988). Solutions have focused on developing stricter child support laws (Ramsey & Masson, 1985). The Federal Child Support Enforcement Act of 1984 (P.L. 98-378) required all states to set quantitative guidelines for awarding child support because (a) too often child support awards were too low, (b) child support awards did not always treat persons with similar income levels the same, and (c) there was a high level of noncompliance with support orders (Rowe, 1991). In this act, each state was allowed to set guidelines, which were advisory rather than binding. Consequently, considerable judicial discretion was allowed, and guidelines differed greatly (Christensen & Rettig, 1991). States used different approaches to establishing awards; some of these varied widely in the amounts awarded to families with identical situations (Rowe, 1989).

There is evidence that P.L. 98-378 has not succeeded in making awards more equitable or in providing adequate income levels for children (Christensen & Rettig, 1991; Stafford, Jackson, & Seiling, 1990). Ongoing problems with child support orders include the following: Few include cost of living increases; few recognize changes in child-rearing costs as children get older; mechanisms for changing orders are sometimes difficult and expensive; and most support orders end when a child reaches age 18 (Rowe, 1991). Disagreements also exist over some of the values and assumptions underpinning these guidelines (Rettig, Christensen, & Dahl, 1991; Salt, 1991).

The Family Support Act of 1988 attempted to address the discrepancies in child support awards by requiring all states to have mandatory guidelines that would be applied consistently (Buehler, in press). Mandatory wage withholding for all support payments must be in place by 1994, provisions were made for increased interstate enforcement, and tighter judicial restrictions were established (Buehler, in press). It is too early to tell if this effort to improve child support payments will be effective, although projections are that child support income will be increased substantially for many single parents (Garfinkel, Oellerich, & Robins, 1991).

*Child custody.* Traditional rules of custody give control over children to one parent in the "best interests of the child" (Emery, 1988). Although there have been attempts to make legal divorce decisions gender-free (Buehler, in press), child custody awards are more often made to mothers. Shared, or joint, custody has achieved widespread attention, if not acceptance, in the belief that children need to continue to relate to both parents following divorce (Grych & Fincham, 1992). Research findings on the effects of different types of custody on postdivorce adjustment have been mixed (Emery, 1988; Grych & Fincham, 1992), and many moderating variables in custody arrangements (e.g., economic levels, coparental hostility) need to be considered before evaluations of joint custody are definitive. It should be noted that no study has found joint custody to be harmful.

## Conclusions

Perhaps there are more important questions than why the divorce rate is so high, or why children and adults experience postdivorce problems adjusting to their new lifestyles and relationships. Recent evidence suggests that the divorce process needs to be rethought. To more fully understand it, family professionals, social scientists, and policymakers may profit by focusing attention on, and directing resources to, several more pressing and more important questions. For example, why are the economic consequences of divorce substantially worse for women than for men, and how long can this continue given the harmful consequences for women and their dependent children? What can be done to facilitate greater paternal involvement in child rearing and family life? At least within the context of heterosexual, monogamous marriage, paternal involvement has a variety of benefits for fathers as well as for mothers and children. One benefit is a reduced risk of marital dissolution. But should divorce occur, a history of sustained and supportive predivorce paternal involvement increases the likelihood that fathers will continue to provide emotional and financial resources for their children in the years postdivorce. Without the disruption of resources, the severity of the stresses is reduced and any potential crisis may be averted.

Another important question is how wage work and unpaid domestic work can be reorganized and better balanced so that women and men divide labor equitably. Eliminating discrimination women face in wage work, enhancing employment opportunities for women and men, emancipating men from the pressures and strains of work absorption, and coordinating family work so that it is divided equitably are viable avenues and formidable challenges for strengthening marriages and families. These questions broaden the narrow focus on divorce as a social problem to a comprehensive concern with how society and families can be changed to attach greater importance to, and provide more support for, mutually fulfilling intimate relationships such as marriage.

Interventions for children and adults could be made more effective in several ways. First, the content of programmed interventions needs to be connected more closely to empirically identified problems related to divorce. Second, there need to be more carefully controlled studies of the efficacy of divorce interventions. Studies are needed to evaluate both individual and family-level interventions and broader-based, social policy interventions. Finally, practitioners should widen the lens they use to view postdivorce families: (a) Consideration should be made of ways to normalize the divorce experience; (b) family life educators and family therapists should be aware of gender-related discrepancies in divorce experiences; and (c) efforts should be made to resist assuming that divorce has uniform effects on children or on women and men.

## References

Acock, A. C., & Demo, D. H. (in press). *Family structure and family relations*. Newbury Park, CA: Sage.

Ahrons, C. A., & Rodgers, R. H. (1987). *Divorced families: A multidisciplinary developmental view*. New York: Norton.

Allen, K. R. (1993). The dispassionate discourse of children's adjustment to divorce. *Journal of Marriage and the Family, 55*, 46-50.

Amato, P. (1993). Children's adjustment to divorce: Theories, hypotheses, and empirical support. *Journal of Marriage and the Family, 55*, 23-38.

Baca Zinn, M. (1990). Family, feminism and race in America. *Gender and Society, 4*, 68-82.

Becker, G. S., Landes, E. M., & Michael, R. T. (1977). An economic analysis of marital instability. *Journal of Political Economy, 85*, 1141-1187.

Bellah, R. N., Sullivan, W. M., Swidler, A., & Tipton, S. M. (1985). *Habits of the heart: Individualism and commitment in American life*. New York: Harper & Row.

Berk, S. F. (1985). *The gender factory: The apportionment of work in American households*. New York: Plenum.

Bernard, J. (1972). *The future of marriage*. New York: World.

Bloom, B. L., Hodges, W. F., Kern, M. B., & McFaddin, S. C. (1985). A preventive intervention program for the newly separated: Final evaluation. *American Journal of Orthopsychiatry, 55*, 9-26.

Bloom, B. L., Niles, R. L., & Tatcher, A. M. (1985). Sources of marital dissatisfaction among newly separated persons. *Journal of Family Issues, 6*, 359-373.

Bohannan, P. (1984). *All the happy families: Exploring the varieties of family life*. New York: McGraw-Hill.

Booth, A., & Amato, P. (1991). Divorce and psychological stress. *Journal of Health and Social Behavior, 32*, 396-407.

Booth, A., Johnson, D., & Edwards, J. N. (1983). Measuring marital instability. *Journal of Marriage and the Family, 45*, 387-394.

Booth, A., Johnson, D., White, L., & Edwards, J. N. (1986). Divorce and marital instability over the life course. *Journal of Family Issues, 7*, 421-442.

Bradburn-Stern, B. (1992). *Children cope with divorce*. Paper presented at the Fifth International Family Therapy Conference, Jerusalem, Israel.

Divorce                                                                      215

Buehler, C. (in press). Divorce law in the United States. *Marriage and Family Review.*

Buehler, C., Betz, P., Ryan, C. R., Legg, B. H., & Trotter, B. B. (1992). Description and evaluation of the Orientation for Divorcing Parents: Implications for postdivorce prevention programs. *Family Relations, 41,* 154-162.

Bumpass, L. L. (1990). What's happening to the family? Interactions between demographic and institutional change. *Demography, 27,* 483-498.

Burkhauser, R. V., & Duncan, G. J. (1989). Economic risks of gender roles: Income loss and life events over the life course. *Social Science Quarterly, 70,* 3-23.

Cherlin, A. J. (1992). *Marriage, divorce, and remarriage* (rev., enlarged ed.). Cambridge, MA: Harvard University Press.

Christensen, D. H., & Rettig, K. D. (1991). Standards of adequacy for child support awards. In C. A. Everett (Ed.), *The consequences of divorce: Economic and custodial impact on children and adults* (pp. 19-47). New York: Haworth.

Cleek, M., & Pearson, T. (1985). Perceived causes of divorce: An analysis of interrelationships. *Journal of Marriage and the Family, 47,* 179-183.

Coysh, W. S., Johnston, J. R., Tschann, J. M., Wallerstein, J. S., & Kline, M. (1989). Parental postdivorce adjustment in joint and sole physical custody families. *Journal of Family Issues, 10,* 52-71.

Demo, D. H. (1992). Parent-child relations: Assessing recent changes. *Journal of Marriage and the Family, 54,* 104-117.

Demo, D. H. (1993). The relentless search for effects of divorce: Forging new trails or tumbling down the beaten path? *Journal of Marriage and the Family, 55,* 42-45.

Demo, D. H., & Acock, A. C. (1988). The impact of divorce on children. *Journal of Marriage and the Family, 50,* 619-648.

Duncan, G. J., & Hoffman, S. D. (1985). Economic consequences of marital instability. In M. David & T. Smeeding (Eds.), *Horizontal equity, uncertainty, and economic well-being* (pp. 427-467). Chicago: University of Chicago Press.

Elder, G. H., Nguyen, T., & Caspi, A. (1985). Linking family hardship to children's lives. *Child Development, 56,* 361-375.

Emery, R. E. (1988). *Marriage, divorce, and children's adjustment.* Newbury Park, CA: Sage.

Emery, R., Matthews, S. G., & Wyer, M. M. (1991). Child custody mediation and litigation: Further evidence on the differing views of mothers and fathers. *Journal of Consulting and Clinical Psychology, 59,* 410-418.

Ferree, M. M. (1990). Beyond separate spheres: Feminism and family research. *Journal of Marriage and the Family, 52,* 866-884.

Fine, M. A., McKenry, P. C., Donnelly, B. W., & Voydanoff, P. (1992). Perceived adjustment of parents and children: Variations by family structure, race, and gender. *Journal of Marriage and the Family, 54,* 118-127.

Furstenberg, F. F., Jr., & Cherlin, A. J. (1991). *Divided families: What happens to children when parents part.* Cambridge, MA: Harvard University Press.

Furstenberg, F. F., Morgan, P., & Allison, P. D. (1987). Paternal participation and children's well-being after marital dissolution. *American Sociological Review, 52,* 695-701.

Garfinkel, I., Oellerich, D., & Robins, P. K. (1991). Child support guidelines: Will they make a difference? *Journal of Family Issues, 12,* 404-429.

Gerstel, N. (1990). Divorce and stigma. In C. Carlson (Ed.), *Perspectives on the family: History, class, and feminism* (pp. 460-478). Belmont, CA: Wadsworth.

Glenn, E. N. (1987). Gender and the family. In B. B. Hess & M. M. Ferree (Eds.), *Analyzing gender: A handbook of social science research* (pp. 348-380). Newbury Park, CA: Sage.

Gove, W. R., & Shin, H. (1989). The psychological well-being of divorced and widowed men and women: An empirical analysis. *Journal of Family Issues, 10,* 122-144.

Grych, J. H., & Fincham, F. (1992). Interventions for children of divorce: Toward greater integration of research and action. *Psychological Bulletin, 111,* 434-454.

Guttmann, J., & Broudo, M. (1989). The effect of children's family type on teachers' stereotypes. *Journal of Divorce, 12,* 315-328.

Hetherington, E. M., Cox, M., & Cox, R. (1977). The aftermath of divorce. In J. H. Stevens & M. Mathews (Eds.), *Mother-child, father-child relations* (pp. 95-135). Washington, DC: National Association for the Education of Young Children.

Hetherington, E. M., Cox, M., & Cox, R. (1982). Effects of divorce on parents and children. In M. E. Lamb (Ed.), *Nontraditional families* (pp. 233-288). Hillsdale, NJ: Lawrence Erlbaum.

Hill, M. S. (1988). Marital stability and spouses' shared time: A multidisciplinary hypothesis. *Journal of Family Issues, 9,* 427-451.

Hodges, W. F. (1986). *Interventions for children of divorce: Custody, access, and psychotherapy.* New York: John Wiley.

Holden, K. C., & Smock, P. J. (1991). The economic costs of marital dissolution: Why do women bear a disproportionate cost? *Annual Review of Sociology, 17,* 51-78.

Kalter, N., Pickar, J., & Leskowitz, M. (1984). School based developmental facilitation groups for children of divorce: A preventive intervention. *American Journal of Orthopsychiatry, 54,* 613-623.

Kelly, J. B. (1989). Mediated and adversarial divorce: Respondents' perceptions of their processes and outcomes. *Mediation Quarterly, 24,* 71-88.

Kelly, J. B. (1990). Is mediation less expensive? Comparison of mediated and adversarial divorce costs. *Mediation Quarterly, 8,* 15-26.

Kelly, J. B. (1991). Parent interaction after divorce: Comparison of mediated and adversarial divorce processes. *Behavioral Science and the Law, 9,* 387-398.

Kitson, G. C. (1985). Marital discord and marital separation: A county survey. *Journal of Marriage and the Family, 47,* 693-700.

Kitson, G. C. (1992). *Portrait of divorce: Adjustment to marital breakdown.* New York: Guilford.

Kitson, G. C., & Sussman, M. (1982). Marital complaints, demographic characteristics, and symptoms of mental distress in divorce. *Journal of Marriage and the Family, 44,* 87-101.

Lawson, C. (1992, January 23). Requiring divorce classes for the sake of the child. *The New York Times,* pp. B1, B3.

Lewis, R. A., & Spanier, G. B. (1979). Theorizing about the quality and stability of marriage. In W. R. Burr, R. Hill, F. I. Nye, & I. L. Reiss (Eds.), *Contemporary theories about the family* (pp. 268-294). London: Free Press.

Lund, K. (1990). A feminist perspective on divorce therapy for women. *Journal of Divorce, 13,* 57-67.

Maccoby, E. E., & Mnookin, R. H. (1992). *Dividing the child: Social and legal dilemmas of custody.* Cambridge, MA: Harvard University Press.

McLoyd, V. C. (1990). The impact of economic hardship on black families and children: Psychological distress, parenting, and socioemotional development. *Child Development, 61,* 311-346.

Menzel, K. E. (1991). Judging the fairness of mediation: A critical framework. *Mediation Quarterly, 9,* 3-20.

Milardo, R. M. (1987). Changes in social networks of women and men following divorce: A review. *Journal of Family Issues, 8,* 78-96.

Divorce                                                                              217

Moen, P. (1985). Continuities and discontinuities in women's labor force activity. In G. H.
Elder, Jr. (Ed.), *Life course dynamics: Trajectories and transitions, 1968-1980* (pp. 113-
155). Ithaca, NY: Cornell University Press.
Morgan, L. A. (1989). Economic well-being following marital termination: A comparison of
widowed and divorced women. *Journal of Family Issues, 10,* 86-101.
Morgan, S. P., Lye, D., & Condran, G. (1988). Sons, daughters, and the risk of marital dis-
ruption. *American Journal of Sociology, 94,* 110-129.
Mott, F. L. (1990). When is a father really gone? Paternal-child contact in father-absent homes.
*Demography, 27,* 499-517.
Pearson, J., & Thoennes, N. (1988). Divorce mediation research results. In J. Folberg & A.
Milne (Eds.), *Divorce mediation: Theory and practice* (pp. 429-452). New York: Guilford.
Pedro-Carrol, J. L., & Cowen, E. L. (1985). The children of divorce intervention project: An
investigation of the efficacy of a school-based prevention program. *Journal of Consulting
and Clinical Psychology, 53,* 603-611.
Peterson, J. L., & Zill, N. (1986). Marital disruption, parent-child relationships, and behavior
problems in children. *Journal of Marriage and the Family, 48,* 295-307.
Peterson, R. R. (1989). *Women, work, and divorce.* Albany: State University of New York Press.
Price, S., & McKenry, P. (1988). *Divorce.* Newbury Park, CA: Sage.
Ramsey, S., & Masson, J. (1985). Stepparent support of stepchildren: A comparative analysis
of policies and problems in the American and English experience. *Syracuse Law Review,
36,* 659-714.
Rands, M. (1988). Changes in social networks following marital separation and divorce. In
R. M. Milardo (Ed.), *Families and social networks* (pp. 127-146). Newbury Park, CA: Sage.
Rettig, K. D., Christensen, D. H., & Dahl, C. M. (1991). Impact of child support guidelines on
the economic well-being of children. *Family Relations, 40,* 167-175.
Rowe, B. R. (1989). Child support guidelines: Economic theory and policy considerations.
*Lifestyles: Family and Economic Issues, 10,* 345-369.
Rowe, B. R. (1991). The economics of divorce: The findings from seven states. In C. A. Everett
(Ed.), *The consequences of divorce: Economic and custodial impact on children and adults*
(pp. 5-17). New York: Haworth.
Salt, R. (1991). Child support in context: Comments on Rettig, Christensen, and Dahl. *Family
Relations, 40,* 175-178.
Schnaiberg, A., & Goldenberg, S. (1989). From empty nest to crowded nest: The dynamics of
incompletely-launched young adults. *Social Problems, 36,* 251-266.
Seecombe, K., & Lee, G. (1987). Female status, wives' autonomy, and divorce: A cross-cultural
study. *Family Perspective, 20,* 241-249.
Spanier, G. B., & Thompson, L. (1983). Relief and distress after marital separation. *Journal
of Divorce, 7,* 31-49.
Spanier, G. B., & Thompson, L. (1984). *Parting: The aftermath of separation and divorce.*
Beverly Hills, CA: Sage.
Sprenkle, D., & Storm, C. (1983). Divorce therapy outcome research: A substantive and meth-
odological review. *Journal of Marital and Family Therapy, 9,* 239-258.
Stacey, J. (1991). *Brave new families.* New York: Basic Books.
Stafford, K., Jackson, G., & Seiling, S. (1990). The effects of child support guidelines: An
analysis of the evidence in court records. *Lifestyles: Family and Economic Issues, 11,*
361-381.
Stolberg, A. L., & Garrison, K. M. (1985). Evaluating a primary prevention program for
children of divorce. *American Journal of Community Psychology, 13,* 111-124.

Thompson, L., & Walker, A. J. (1989). Gender in families: Women and men in marriage, work, and parenthood. *Journal of Marriage and the Family, 51,* 845-871.

Thompson, M. S., & Ensminger, M. E. (1989). Psychological well-being among mothers with school age children: Evolving family structures. *Social Forces, 67,* 715-730.

Thornton, A. (1977). Children and marital stability. *Journal of Marriage and the Family, 39,* 531-540.

Thornton, A. (1989). Changing attitudes toward family issues. *Journal of Marriage and the Family, 51,* 873-893.

Thurnher, M., Fenn, C. B., Melichar, J., & Chiriboga, D. A. (1983). Sociodemographics: Perspectives on reasons for divorce. *Journal of Divorce, 6,* 25-35.

U.S. Bureau of the Census. (1989). Child support and alimony: 1985 (Supplemental Report). In *Current population reports* (P-23, No. 154). Washington, DC: Government Printing Office.

Veevers, J. E. (1991). Traumas versus strengths: A paradigm of positive versus negative divorce outcomes. *Journal of Divorce and Remarriage, 15,* 99-126.

Wallerstein, J. S., & Blakeslee, S. (1990). *Second chances: Men, women, and children a decade after divorce.* New York: Ticknor and Fields.

Weiss, R. (1984). The impact of marital dissolution on income and consumption in single-parent households. *Journal of Marriage and the Family, 46,* 115-127.

Weitzman, L. (1985). *The divorce revolution: The unexpected social and economic consequences for women and children in America.* New York: Free Press.

White, L. K. (1990). Determinants of divorce: A review of research in the eighties. *Journal of Marriage and the Family, 52,* 904-912.

# 11

# Remarriage and Recoupling

## MARGARET CROSBIE-BURNETT

### Demographic Factors

Remarriage and the creation of stepfamilies have been common practices for centuries. However, until the dramatic rise in the divorce rate in the 1970s, nearly all remarriages occurred after the death of a spouse. Today, almost all remarriages occur after divorce; 72% of divorced women and 80% of divorced men remarry (Glick, 1989a). Women are not only less likely to remarry, but they also remarry less quickly in all age groups. The mean length of time between divorce and remarriage is 3.6 years for men and 3.9 years for women. Rates of remarriage decline with age for both men and women; rates of remarriage for divorced women peaked in 1965 and then declined steadily until 1985 (Glick, 1989a). Of the 1½ million divorced men and women who do remarry each year, 61% marry divorced, 35% marry single, and 4% marry widowed partners. Nearly 5% of remarriages (twice the percentage of first marriages) are interracial, including all racial combinations. When we examine remarriages as a subset of all marriages, we find that 49% of European American (white) and 40% of African American marriages are a remarriage for one or both partners (Wilson & Clarke, 1992).

Contrary to popular myth, the divorce rate for remarriages (49%) is only slightly higher than the divorce rate for first marriages (47%) (Martin &

Bumpass, 1989). Therefore it is not surprising that remarrieds and first
marrieds have reported comparable levels of marital satisfaction (Vemer,
Coleman, Ganong, & Cooper, 1989). However, wives in both groups report
less marital satisfaction than husbands (Ihinger-Tallman & Pasley, 1987)
even though sex roles are more egalitarian in second marriages than in first
(Ishii-Kuntz & Coltrane, 1992).

It should be noted that remarriage is *not* synonymous with the creation
of stepfamily households. Only one half of the 11 million households of
remarrieds include minor children and are therefore defined as stepfamilies
by the U.S. Bureau of the Census. However, most of the other half of
remarried households include step-relationships. These households include
homes with stepchildren who have reached majority age and may or may
not be living at home, and they include noncustodial homes that minor
children visit. In addition to the stepfamilies formed by the remarriage of
one or two parents, an increasing number of stepfamilies are created when
unmarried mothers marry for the first time, and a small number of stepfamilies are formed when gay and lesbian parents recouple. It is estimated
that, in the United States, 3 million gay men and lesbians are parents (Harvard Law Review Association, 1990); an unknown percentage of these
parents cohabit with a same-sex partner, forming either custodial or noncustodial stepfamily households.

If we examine the stepfamily demographic statistics from the child's
perspective, we find that, in any one year, 7% of minor children (nearly 6
million) live with a legally married parent and stepparent, and another 2.5%
live with a parent who is cohabiting with a partner (Sweet, 1991). These
percentages do not include young adult stepchildren who are living in the
parental home or children who visit a stepfamily household formed by the
noncustodial parent's recoupling. In addition, another 5% of minor children live in stepfamilies but were born to the remarried couple (Glick,
1989b). Projections suggest that about 30% of today's children will live in
a stepfamily before they reach the age of 18 (Glick, 1979), and about 45%
of these children will be either a stepchild or a stepparent during their lives
(Ganong & Coleman, 1988).

*Definitions*

The rest of this chapter addresses the stepfamilies formed by the recoupling of parents. It will not include the recoupling of childless adults. It is
the presence of step-relationships that makes stepfamilies different from

other two-parent families. Although nearly all of the research on stepfamilies has been done with samples of legally remarried European American
spouses, the term *recoupling* is used because it is more inclusive than remarriage. Recoupling includes heterosexual and homosexual cohabitors
and first marriages of parents.

*Stepfamily* is defined as a family in which at least one of the recoupling
adults has one or more children from a prior relationship and the children
spend time in the adult's household. *Extended stepfamily network* is defined as the households that are linked together by traditional extended
family *and* by biological ties between children and their nonresidential
parent.

### Costs and Benefits

There are costs and benefits to recoupling at both the societal level and
the individual level. Economically, recoupling with a wage earner usually
means a higher standard of living (Hill, 1992), particularly for women and
their children. However, the recoupling of one's noncustodial father is
likely to mean less financial and emotional support from him (Ahrons &
Wallisch, 1987).

Unfortunately, stepfamilies have a higher incidence of spouse abuse
(Kalmuss & Seltzer, 1986) and child abuse and neglect than biological
families (Daly & Wilson, 1991). Although research results are not totally
consistent, having a stepfather in the home appears to have a positive effect
for boys, but girls do not fair as well as boys in stepfather or in stepmother
families (Emery, 1988). Family theorists are struggling to find explanations
for these findings, but hypotheses include the interruption of close parent-
daughter relationships and sexual tension between stepfathers and stepdaughters.

### A Family Stress Theory of Recoupling

In this chapter a model of family stress and coping that has both sociological and psychological components will be used to integrate the theory
and research on stepfamilies and to suggest interventions that can promote adjustment to recoupling and stepfamily living (see Figure 11.1).
The model is based on the Double ABC-X Model (McCubbin & Patterson,
1983a) and the Contextual Model of family stress (Boss, 1987).

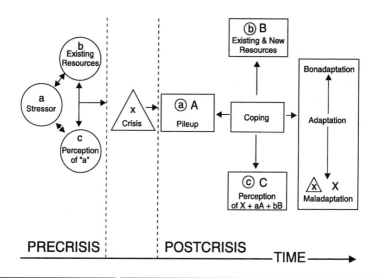

| a + aA (Hardships & Pileups) | b + bB (Resources) | c + cC (Perception) |
|---|---|---|
| 1. Combining two family cultures or integrating new member<br>2. Redistribution of resources<br>3. Boundary ambiguity<br>4. Role ambiguity<br>5. Loyalty & Jealousy<br>6. Conflicting lifestyle stages<br>7. Sexual tension<br>8. Geographic move<br>9. Emotional exhaustion<br>10. Unresolved emotional issues from loss of first family<br>11. Problems developed as single-parent family<br>12. Developmental changes<br>13. Birth of baby<br>14. Children changing households<br>15. Stresses from social institutions | 1. Individual<br>  a. Health & Intelligence<br>  b. Education & job skill<br>  c. Money & possessions<br>  d. Self-esteem<br>  e. Sense of mastery<br>  f. Openness to change<br>  g. Alternatives to present family<br>2. Stepfamily<br>  a. Realistic expectations<br>  b. Communication skills<br>  c. Cooperation & collective goals<br>  d. Common interests & values<br>  e. Flexibility & agreement regarding role structure<br>  f. Feelings of unity & belonging<br>  g. Economic & emotional interdependence<br>3. Extended stepfamily network, friends, and community<br>  a. Networks and social support<br>  b. Bartering goods and services<br>  c. Stepfamily support groups<br>  d. Children's support groups<br>  e. Stepfamily newsletters<br>  f. Role models of healthy stepfamilies in the community and media<br>  g. Counselors & therapists with stepfamily training | 1. Second chance at marriage and/or having a family<br>2. "Reconstitution" vs. pioneering a new family form<br>3. Rescuing or being rescued<br>4. Intrusion of stepparent (& stepchildren) & threat to prior family structure<br><br>x + xX (Crisis & Adaptation)<br><br>1. Maladaptation<br>  a. Demand-capability imbalance<br>  b. Inability to integrate new member(s) in manner acceptable to family members<br>  c. Avoidance—denial of negative feelings & problems<br>  d. Redivorcing<br>  e. Extrusion of children from the home prematurely<br>2. Bonadaptation<br>  a. Demand-capability balance<br>  b. Successful integration of new family members<br>  c. Establishment of family identity<br>  d. Permeable boundaries with other households |

**Figure 11.1.** The Double ABC-X Model as a Guide for the Assessment of Stepfamilies, Intervention With Stepfamilies, and Policy Change in Support of Stepfamilies

SOURCE: Based on the Double ABC-X Model (McCubbin & Patterson, 1983a) and the Contextual Model of family stress (Boss, 1987).

# The Stressor Event

Recoupling (see "a" in Figure 11.1) can be defined as a normative developmental stressor event (McCubbin & Patterson, 1983b) because it changes the family boundary by adding one or more new family members to the family group (the prior single-parent household), and because recoupling is now being conceptualized by some (Carter & McGoldrick, 1988; Crosbie-Burnett, 1989) as a normal part of a family's life cycle. Recoupling also creates pressure to change the structure of the family, allowing for the stepparent to have an adult role and, possibly, integrating stepsiblings into the subsystem of children with concomitant changes in birth order and/or sex ratio.

## Hardships Associated With the Stressor

*New family member(s).* The addition of a partner for the biological parent forces a reorganization of roles and relationships. First, the biological parent shares the family leadership role (to varying degrees) with the new adult. This means a redistribution of family power (Crosbie-Burnett & Giles-Sims, 1987), which often includes a displacement of an older child, who may have been a coleader in the single-parent household, by the new stepparent. The entry of a new partner for the biological parent is also reported to threaten the relationships between that parent and the children (Visher & Visher, 1979). Thus both parties can experience the stepparent as "coming between" the biological parent and children, disrupting a bond that predated the recoupling. When two families are joined by a recoupling, two family cultures are brought together with the potential for discrepant values, habits, and interests. Integrating two family cultures requires negotiation and the creation of new family rituals and traditions. Family rituals and traditions have been identified as a characteristic of healthy families (McCubbin & McCubbin, 1987), and, by definition, new families have few or none.

*Redistribution of resources.* A variety of resources—money, space, time, and affection—must be redistributed among family members, if the family is to meet the needs of new, as well as original, family members. Stepchildren report that the acquisition of stepsiblings, which 40%-50% of stepchildren experience (Bumpass, 1984), is a source of stress (Lutz, 1983). The distribution of money within the stepfamily and between households in the extended stepfamily network is a commonly reported source of stress for stepfamilies (Albrecht, 1979; Fishman,

1983; Goetting, 1982). Money-related stress is exacerbated because many couples are reluctant to discuss this delicate issue before recoupling (Dolan & Lowen, 1985).

*Boundary ambiguity.* The ambiguity of boundaries between households that have biological parent-child ties linking them together suggests a third source of stress for these families (Boss & Greenberg, 1984). For example, is a nonresidential father with joint legal custody a member of the stepfamily? He has decision-making power that influences the functioning of the stepfamily.

To complicate matters further, stepfamily members may disagree among themselves on who is and who is not part of their family (Pasley, 1987). It is clear that there is an inherent boundary ambiguity for stepfamilies and an inherent tension between the new stepfamily's need for boundary definition to enhance group cohesion and unity and the needs of biological parents and children separated by households to include each other in "family" and to have permeable boundaries through which to maintain emotional ties.

*Stepparent role ambiguity.* Stepparent role ambiguity is a major source of stress (Giles-Sims, 1984; Schwebel, Fine, & Renner, 1991). There are few social norms for the stepparent role, especially when the nonresidential biological parent is active in the child's life. Consequently, family members have their own individual (usually unspoken) expectations for the stepparent role, adding to the probability of conflict between members of the stepfamily and the entire extended stepfamily network. Disagreement about the amount and nature of nurturance and discipline of children that the stepparent "should" perform is a notorious source of stress for stepfamilies (Cherlin, 1978; Ihinger-Tallman & Pasley, 1987; Visher & Visher, 1983). Family role flexibility (Boss, 1980) may be a crucial factor in the stepfamily's adjustment when there are a variety of roles to be filled, a variety of adults to fill them, and no clear role prescriptions delineating the division of labor (Crosbie-Burnett & Lewis, 1993). Our society adds to the ambiguity of the stepparent role by, for example, denying stepparents legal parental rights yet including stepparent income in computing Aid to Families with Dependent Children and college financial aid.

*Stepchild role ambiguity and loyalty conflicts.* The stepchild role is also ambiguous; children do not know how they are *supposed* to relate to a stepparent, especially if their nonresidential biological parent is part of their lives. Yet the relationship between the stepparent and stepchild appears to be a key factor in stepfamily happiness (Crosbie-Burnett,

1984) and stepchild adjustment (Furstenberg, Nord, Peterson, & Zill, 1983).

Having a biological parent and a stepparent of the same sex has been identified as a source of stress caused by recoupling in heterosexual families. For example, children report feeling guilty for liking a stepparent better than the same-sex biological parent (Lutz, 1983).

Jealousy and competition between the same-sex parents can heighten loyalty conflicts for children (Wallerstein & Kelly, 1980) and biological parents, who may be trying to coparent with a former spouse while building a marriage with a new spouse. It is not unusual for the nonresidential parent (and the relatives on that side of the extended stepfamily network) to be threatened by the recoupling and harass family members in the remarrying couple's household in a variety of ways, including relitigating and demanding demonstrations of loyalty from the children.

*Conflicting life-cycle stages.* Recoupling can bring together individuals who are in different life-cycle stages; this can cause stress and conflict. For example, the newlyweds need time alone, whereas children demand attention. The couple may want to create family cohesion by doing family activities, whereas adolescents are individuating and desiring more time with peers. A mature stepfather who has reared one set of children and is ready to be finished with major parenting responsibilities may find himself with a new baby. The new couple may wish to purchase a home, but college tuition bills for stepchildren may need to be paid.

*Sexual tension.* Recoupling often brings together children, adolescents, and adults of the opposite sex without benefit of the incest taboo. This potential for sexual tension is hypothesized to be the reason that girls are reporting more family-related stress than boys (Lutz, 1983), why they are reported by their residential mothers to have poorer well-being than boys (Crosbie-Burnett, 1988a), and why some studies are finding stepdaughters to have worse relations than stepsons with stepfathers (Clingempeel, Ievoli, & Brand, 1984; Clingempeel & Segal, 1986; Peterson & Zill, 1986; Santrock, Warshak, Lindbergh, & Meadows, 1982). This delicate subject can be threatening to couples and children.

### Resources

Resources (see "b" in Figure 11.1) are a combination of individual family members' strengths and assets, the family's capabilities of resistance vis-à-vis the stressor, and extrafamilial resources (McCubbin, 1979). They include health, intelligence, education, job skills, money and possessions, a spirit of cooperation, relationship skills, and networks and social support (Boss, 1987). A family's use of resources is a measure of its ability to cope with the stressor.

*Individual.* In addition to the above assets that individuals can bring to the stepfamily, individual resources that are particularly important in times of transition are self-esteem and a sense of control or mastery (Pearlin & Schooler, 1978), openness to change, and self-efficacy in successful adaptation. In recoupling, the addition of a second wage earner is particularly important because it usually improves the standard of living for the family, particularly for mothers and their children (Folk, Graham, & Beller, 1992; Hill, 1992). For stepchildren, having a nonresidential parent's household for either temporary or permanent "escape" also can be a resource.

*Family.* Family stress research has identified factors that promote the family resources of cohesion and integration (Olson & McCubbin, 1982) and are considered to help the family buffer the hardships associated with a stressor: common interests and values, agreement on role structure, affection, feelings of unity, collective as opposed to personal goals, and economic interdependence. By definition, many of these resources are missing in new stepfamilies: Bringing together two family cultures and individuals at different stages in family life cycles lessens the probability of common interests and values and collective goals. Role and boundary ambiguity are a threat to feelings of unity and agreement on role structure. Sharing affection in the step-relationship takes time and can be awkward for stepfamilies, particularly those with adolescents. The flow of monies between households in the extended stepfamily network may diminish economic interdependence within the stepfamily household by providing alternative sources of support.

Family stress research has identified additional resources that have been associated with successful adaptation. These resources may be especially crucial for stepfamilies: open communication, shared power and flexibility in the authority and status structure, and successful experience coping with past stressors like divorce or poverty.

*Extended family and community.* Even in our mobile society, extended family is still an important source of emotional support and other helping behavior (McCubbin, Joy, Cauble, Patterson, & Needle, 1980; Unger & Powell, 1980). This appears to be true for stepfamilies as well (Booth & Edwards, 1992; Pasley & Ihinger-Tallman, 1982). A well-functioning extended stepfamily network can expand this traditional resource by sharing resources, such as child care, children's clothing, emotional energy, and skills, across the households of coparents as well as the households of extended biological kin.

Friends are, of course, an important source of social support (McCubbin, 1979). However, this may be an underused source of support in new stepfamilies. In addition to the potential loss of this support associated with a divorce and with geographic moves at recoupling, there is a desire on the part of many remarried couples to "gloss over" problems in an effort to ward off a much-feared second divorce and to appear successfully "reconstituted" to friends and family.

*Community resources* refers to the solutions that the community provides to support the family under stress. The adequacy of these solutions depends upon the fit between the family and the community (Hansen & Hill, 1964; Mechanic, 1974). Unfortunately, the fit between stepfamilies and the community is often awkward at best and is more likely to be a hardship than a resource at the present time. This problem is multiplied for gay and lesbian stepfamilies and sometimes for families of color, depending upon their community.

Cherlin (1978) hypothesized that the basis of stresses in stepfamilies is a function of the lack of institutionalization of remarriage and recoupling in the society. This idea is supported by studies reporting not only a lack of norms for behavior for remarrieds (Goetting, 1980) but a bias against stepfamily members (Bryan, Coleman, Ganong, & Bryan, 1986; Bryant, Coleman, & Ganong, 1988; Coleman & Ganong, 1987). This bias adds to the pressure for a stepfamily to "pass" as an intact, nuclear family.

On the more positive side, community resources are becoming more available as the numbers of stepfamilies increase and therefore the family form becomes normative. Stepfamily associations, newsletters, and support groups for remarrieds are becoming more prevalent. Mental health professionals are becoming more aware of the need for special training in the unique aspects of stepfamilies. Schools are beginning to recognize the need to respond to stepparents more positively; some schools now offer postdivorce support groups for children of divorce and recoupling.

### Perception of Recoupling

The subjective definition that the family makes of the stressor and its concomitant hardships (see "c" in Figure 11.1) is a reflection of the family members' values, histories, culture(s), religion(s), economics, and developmental stages. However, the definition or meaning given to a recoupling may be quite discrepant across family members. Discrepant perceptions must be added to the list of hardships, because they add stress to the family.

*Biological parent.* The biological parent may perceive the change as a "reconstitution"—a chance to become a legitimate family again. It is also a second (or subsequent) chance to have a good marriage or partnership. The recoupling also may mean help with child rearing and an increase in standard of living.

*Stepparent.* Some stepparents see themselves as rescuers of single parents and children and therefore anticipate appreciation. On the contrary, other stepparents see themselves as gaining a spouse but have no intention of parenting stepchildren, and this may be in conflict with a biological parent's expectation that he or she is gaining a helpmate with parenting.

Previously single stepparents are entering their first coupling and are more likely to view the situation with all of the idealism of first marrieds. There is preliminary evidence that previously single stepfathers try to perform a more traditional father role than stepfathers who had a prior family (Crosbie-Burnett, 1988a). Also, stepparents who are unable to have biological children of their own may anticipate being a "mom" or "dad."

For previously married stepparents, the recoupling can have a similar meaning to that of the biological parent—a second chance. For stepparents who have "lost" their biological children through loss of custody, geographic mobility, and so on, the recoupling can mean being part of a family again.

*Stepchildren.* The largest discrepancies in the meaning of the recoupling may be found between adults and children. Understandably, children are anxious about the meaning of the recoupling for life in their own household(s) and for relationships with biological parents, grandparents, and other extended family. Some stepchildren, of course, anticipate the recoupling with the same optimism for a better life as the adults. Others perceive the recoupling as a threat to family stability and see the stepparent as an intruder; this is especially true for the child who is being displaced as the single parent's confidant and helpmate in the household (Visher & Visher, 1979). Children who are not in poverty and who have a nonresidential parent who is active in their lives may perceive no need for a stepparent. Adolescents appear to be especially resistant to integrating a stepparent into the family. For children who gain stepsiblings through the recoupling, it may mean a change in birth order, which children can find disconcerting (Ihinger-Tallman, 1987).

*Crisis*

A crisis response of disequilibrium (see "x" in Figure 11.1) so acute that the family system is immobilized, incapacitated, and unable to restore stability is likely to occur if the recoupling, interacting with the family's resources and the family members' meaning of the recoupling, is not accompanied by a major change in family structure and patterns of interaction. The stress of this change does not have to reach crisis proportions. A crisis response is likely if there is resistance by members of the prior single-parent family or if the integration of the stepparent inappropriately places him or her into an "instant parent that the children will love and obey" role. In a crisis state, the stepparent will have no appropriate role, and the family rules will not have changed or changed too suddenly to accommodate the needs of all family members.

Typical signs of resistance to appropriate structural change in stepfamilies are (a) outright conflict; (b) avoidance, that is, denial of negative feelings and denial of problems, especially by the adults, and literal avoidance of the stepparent by the children; and (c) elimination—redivorcing, which keeps the prior single-parent family structure intact. A variation on elimination in stepfamilies is removing a particularly resistant child from the home (White & Booth, 1985) by sending him or her to live with the other biological parent or elsewhere, but this also means a change in family structure.

If these initial attempts at adjustment do not eliminate the crisis, the family begins to move into the adaptation phase by restructuring—changing roles, rules, goals, and patterns of interaction—and consolidation, in which family members must make the subsequent changes that are needed to accomplish a shared lifestyle, to compromise, and to meet individuals' needs. This is discussed below.

*Pileup*

*Pileup* (see "aA" in Figure 11.1) refers to additional demands on the family that are related to the initial stressor—prior strains, normative developmental changes, consequences of the family's attempt to cope with the initial stressor, and/or ambiguity about the family situation. Stepfamilies often experience many pileup demands.

*Initial stressor.* Additional demands directly related to the recoupling often include the biological parent's feeling caught in the middle as she or he attempts to facilitate the integration of the stepparent. Also, recoupling sometimes requires a geographic move and the concomitant stresses associated with loss of peer group, change of school or work, and the like for the moving adult and children.

*Prior strains.* Most individuals in stepfamilies have experienced prior loss of the first family. There are often unresolved emotional issues related to that experience for both children and adults. For example, children who have been abandoned by a nonresidential parent may find it hard to trust a new stepparent.

There may also be pileup from a single-parent stage of the family. An overworked single parent may have not had the time or emotional energy to supervise children and adolescents, who may now be in trouble in school or with the law. Wallerstein and Kelly (1980) and Wallerstein and Blakeslee (1989) have documented how the family crisis of divorce can hamper children's normal development. Furthermore, the strain of poverty experienced by many single-mother families can leave financial and emotional problems that are not cured by a recoupling alone. If the recoupling was an effort to cope with an unhappy situation of a single parent, it too would be considered pileup.

*Normative developmental changes.* Difficulties of combining conflicting life-cycle stages at the time of recoupling are frequent. As children continue to mature, they reach the stage of searching for their own identities; one common developmental issue for stepadolescents is a desire to know the nonresidential parent better. This has potential for placing new demands on the stepfamily, especially if relationships with the other parent are strained or nonexistent.

The birth of a baby is a major transition for any family (LaRossa & LaRossa, 1981). Furthermore, in stepfamilies a baby is symbolically important because he or she is the only family member who is biologically related to everyone in the household. However, there is no evidence that the birth of a new baby strengthens the bonds between stepfamily members (Ganong & Coleman, 1988).

*Consequences of attempts to cope with the stressor.* One common maladaptive coping mechanism in stepfamilies is lack of acknowledgment of negative feelings, apparently because of the fear that showing these feelings will cause redivorce (Visher & Visher, 1983). Stepparents who have tried to "instantly" love their stepchildren in an effort to "reconstitute" a nuclear family, and cannot do so, report feeling guilty. Another maladaptive coping mechanism used by stepparents is to become increasingly more authoritarian or more distant, causing more problems and alienation of the stepchildren or of the stepparent, depending upon the biological parent's alliance (White & Booth, 1985). Resistant children may choose or be sent to live with the other biological parent. This can cause a pileup of demands on the family if the child or either biological parent is unhappy with the change. The nonresidential parent who is unsupportive of the recoupling can be a source of continual pileup of hardships by creating problems with respect to visitation, child support, and/or relitigation.

*Ambiguity about the situation.* Social ambiguity (McCubbin & Patterson, 1983a) is a chronic stress for stepfamilies as they look for models of realistic, healthy stepfamily functioning in the society and find virtually none. Our social institutions are based on nuclear families. Society's ambivalence toward stepfamilies is evidenced in the inconsistencies in law and policy and the invisibility of healthy stepfamilies, who are camouflaged as "regular" two-parent families.

### Family Adaptive Resources

Existing resources are those resources that the family still has available over time as it moves into the adaptation phase. Expanded family resources are those resources that are strengthened or developed in response to the stressor, crisis, and/or pileup. (See "bB" in Figure 11.1.) In stepfamilies, these might include venting emotions and "getting the cards on the table," increased communication within and between households, use of literature on recoupling, and assistance from counselors, support groups, or social agencies.

### Family Definition and Meaning

The meaning (see "cC" in Figure 11.1) the family gives to the total situation—the crisis, pileup, and existing and new resources—is crucial in stepfamilies. For example, if children continue to see the recoupling as an invasion by the stepparent or stepsiblings, or either adult perceives the recoupling as a move into an overwhelming situation and is feeling "worn down," *bonadaptation* (positive adaptation) is unlikely. On the other hand, if family members continue to try to make the recoupling a "reconstitution" of a nuclear family and deny the need for functioning differently, bonadaptation is also unlikely. If the stepfamily can reevaluate their "failure" to make the family run smoothly, let go of self- and other-blaming, and perceive themselves as pioneers in a new family form, the stepfamily may be open to the opportunity for growth.

### Adaptation

The Double ABC-X Model has three units of analysis: the individual family member, the family unit, and the community. For stepfamilies, one might add the extended stepfamily network and a second community, if children spend time in the homes of parents who live in different communities. Assessment of all units is crucial to understanding the family's process in response to the stressor and to predicting outcomes (see "xX" in Figure 11.1). According to the model, each unit has demands and capabilities, and bonadaptation occurs through these reciprocal relationships when the demand of one unit is met by the capabilities of another. When this happens, balance is achieved. *Maladaptation* occurs when a demand-capability imbalance exists. Assessment of each unit's demands and a search for a unit capable of meeting those demands would minimize imbalances and promote bonadaptation. There are imbalances to which stepfamilies are particularly vulnerable; these will be discussed below.

*Balance between individual and family.* A stepparent may have capabilities that are being underused if he or she is not an integral part of the family. Alternatively, the addition of a stepparent with high demands may drain the already strained resources of the prior single-parent household. Individual developmental needs, especially of children, may go unmet because they are in conflict with the life cycle of a new marriage. The demands of a new stepmother to be "woman of the house" may be met with the family's inability to move a daughter out of that role. Alternatively, a study of changes in labor force participation of new stepmothers and remarrying biological mothers found that those women who decreased their participation had much lower levels of marital satisfaction than those women who did not (Crosbie-Burnett, 1988b). This suggests that trading in one's role at a workplace for an increased mother/wife role takes its toll on women's marital happiness.

*Balance between stepfamily and other households in the extended stepfamily network.* A joint custody, nonresidential parent may have demands on the stepfamily with respect to decision-making power that the new stepfamily may be incapable of giving because of the demands of the new stepparent to be "in charge." The adults in the stepfamily may want to move geographically to improve employment or living conditions, but this may mean decreasing a stepchild's visits with a nonresidential parent and/or grandparents.

*Balance between family and community.* The community and its institutions (health care, school, workplace, government, and so on) make demands on families with the assumption that the families are intact, nuclear families. The culture still defines stepfamilies as outside of the norm (Coleman & Ganong, 1987). These demands threaten family pride and cohesion. The stepfamily may turn to the community for support and understanding but too often find misunderstanding or, even worse, prejudice and discrimination.

*Bonadaptation and maladaptation.* In stepfamilies, bonadaptation is characterized by an integration of the new family member(s) into the family by restructuring roles and rules and changing interaction patterns. The stepfamily may begin to experience a sense of unity by having a family identity of its own yet have permeable boundaries to allow for visitation. Children will have permission to enjoy all households of which they are a part. Family members will be able to resume developmental tasks and get their needs for a sense of control and affection met. These changes are facilitated by an important modification in the family's paradigm (Reiss & Oliveri, 1980), giving up the hope for "reconstitution of a nuclear family," and the adoption of a new, more realistic perspective on their family.

Maladaptation is characterized by divorce or separation, exclusion of children, or a disorganization of the family such that individuals cannot get their needs met and are therefore unable to proceed developmentally. Also, it is possible for some family members (e.g., the couple) to have bonadaptation following recoupling, whereas others (e.g., children) may be experiencing maladaptation (Brand & Clingempeel, 1987; White & Booth, 1985). Psychosomatic or behavioral symptoms of distress may appear. Given the many hardships and pileup demands, the lack of community resources, and the potential for problems with respect to perception of the recoupling, it is no wonder that stepfamilies experience a high rate of distress. Yet the combined Double ABC-X Model and Contextual Model, combined with the empirical and clinical literature, suggest directions for maximizing the probability of bonadaptation and minimizing the probability of maladaptation for stepfamilies.

### Cultural Variations

Nearly all of the findings reported above are based on dominant-culture stepfamilies. The few studies with ethnic minorities have focused on comparisons between African Americans and European Americans in terms of remarriage rates (Smock, 1990; Wilson & Clarke, 1992), redivorce rates

(Aguirre & Parr, 1982; Teachman, 1986), child support awards (Beller & Graham, 1986), mother-daughter relationships (Fox & Inazu, 1982), and adjustment of stepfamily members (Fine et al., 1992). The Fine et al. study found similar levels of adjustment of parents and children in the two sub-samples, suggesting that findings of studies of *adjustment* with dominant-culture stepfamilies may be generalizable to African American stepfamilies. However, this study does not suggest that family *processes* in these two groups are similar.

Noteworthy exceptions to these comparison studies are a study of inter-actions among family members in a variety of African American family structures (Barnes, 1985) and a clinician's report of racially intermarried stepfamilies in therapy (Baptiste, 1984). Perhaps this lack of research on family processes related to stress and coping in stepfamilies of color is a result of the small numbers of family scholars of color and of the domi-nant culture's conceptualization and definition of "stepfamily," which is based on the legal definition of "stepparent." Many types of ethnic minority families function in ways that are different from the way family functioning is conceptualized in the legal system (Crosbie-Burnett & Lewis, 1993).

The sparce literature on gay and lesbian stepfamilies is limited to clini-cal observations of these families (Baptiste, 1987a, 1987b), an empirical study of relationship quality in lesbian couples with and without children (Koepke, Hare, & Moran, 1992), and an empirical study of both social support and the correlates of couple and family happiness in gay male stepfamilies with adolescents (Crosbie-Burnett & Helmbrecht, 1993). In general these writings suggest that homosexual stepfamilies must cope with the same stresses as heterosexual stepfamilies as well as the additional stresses of homophobia and closeting.

## Implications of the Model
## for Assessment, Intervention, and Policy

### *Assessment and Intervention*

According to the Double ABC-X Model, assessment of stepfamily ad-justment should cover the basic issues included under Hardships and Pile-ups, Resources, and Perception in order to understand the stepfamily's level of adaptation to the recoupling. (See Figure 11.1.) The identification of hardships, used and untapped resources, and adaptive and maladaptive perceptions and attributions can then direct therapeutic or preventive interventions. For example, if the assessment of all family members reveals that the adolescent and the biological parent have very different role expectations for the stepparent than the stepparent has (a), then basic communication skills to share expectations and negotiate new roles and rules for interaction should decrease the hardship associated with displacement of a child by the stepparent. Also, simply listing all of the resources (b) that individuals bring to the stepfamily can be an empowering experience for the stepfamily. Finding stepfamily support groups for family members could increase use of community resources (b), just as helping the stepfamily toward a "pioneering" perception of itself and away from the maladaptive "reconstitution" myth could generate a more realistic and optimistic meaning (c) of the family's situation.

*Policy*

The model also identifies possibilities for change in policy at many levels. At the national level, educational campaigns might reduce the negative connotation of "step-" in our society and raise the public's awareness of stepfamily issues, including presenting healthy models of coping. Research on extended stepfamily networks could become a funding priority. Federal guidelines for student financial aid, aid to families with dependent children (AFDC), and children's health care need to be modified to reduce the financial burden of stepparents. At the state level, laws could be modified to reflect stepparents' contributions to our children (Fine & Fine, 1992) by giving them some level of parental rights. At the local level, support groups and helping professionals trained in stepfamily issues could be identified and publicized. Free educational workshops for remarrying couples could prepare couples to cope with the hardships that are necessarily part of recoupling (e.g., role ambiguity) and help them to avoid others that are not (e.g., jealousy). Many of the policies and procedures of schools and colleges, and the attitudes of school personnel, are not supportive of stepchildren and their parents; these need to be modified (Crosbie-Burnett, in press). Universities that train helping professionals should offer coursework in this family form or integrate the information into current coursework. Churches and temples should encourage their ministers and rabbis to receive training in recoupling so that their premarital counseling would be more appropriate for this group.

## Future Directions

### Research

A decade of research with stepfamilies has taught us much about European American custodial stepfamily households. But the research should move from comparisons between recoupled families and other family structures to identification of family processes that promote healthy stepfamily coping. This search for an understanding of adaptive outcomes calls for increased use of qualitative research methods with well-functioning stepfamilies because qualitative methods may identify new, salient variables in the functioning of stepfamilies. This should lead to the creation of theories based on stepfamilies rather than on intact families. These new theories can then serve as the basis for therapeutic interventions, the effectiveness of which would be tested. Intervention research with stepfamilies is nonexistent at present. In addition, examination of family functioning in other cultures can shed light on how others have successfully answered the needs of family members in nonnuclear structures (Crosbie-Burnett & Lewis, 1993).

The topics of stepfamily research should expand in a variety of directions—across social institutions, across types of stepfamily households, and across age ranges. For example, the institutions of education and the law are being influenced by the growing numbers of stepfamilies. The stepfamily households of recoupled noncustodial parents, of gay and lesbian stepfamilies, and of first-married mothers—about whom virtually nothing is known—should receive attention from researchers. Stepfamily relationships between adult children and elderly parents, and between stepchildren and (step)grandparents, are only beginning to be explored.

### Interventions

As more is learned about healthy stepfamily coping, educational and preventive programs and related literature should increase for both children and adults. Support groups for stepchildren in schools are already increasing. As therapists become more knowledgeable about the unique aspects of stepfamilies, both through initial training in graduate schools and through continuing education workshops, more appropriate therapeutic interventions should replace inappropriate interventions that were designed for traditional nuclear families.

*Summary*

The numbers of stepfamilies are increasing because of remarriage after divorce, first marriage of parents, and cohabitation of heterosexual and homosexual parents. About 10% of minor children live in stepfamilies. Family stress theory was used in this chapter as a framework for integrating the empirical research and clinical reports on stepfamilies. Given our increasing knowledge of stepfamilies, directions for change in the law, education, and therapy are becoming clear. The present model could be used as a basis for a comprehensive prevention and remediation program for the benefit of helping stepfamilies cope with stressors.

# References

Aguirre, B. E., & Parr, W. C. (1982). Husband's marriage order and the stability of first/second marriages of white and black women. *Journal of Marriage and the Family, 44,* 605-620.

Ahrons, C. R., & Wallisch, K. (1987). Parenting in the binuclear family: Relationships between biological and stepparents. In K. Pasley & M. Ihinger-Tallman (Eds.), *Remarriage and stepparenting: Current research and theory* (pp. 225-256). New York: Guilford.

Albrecht, S. (1979). Correlates of marital happiness among the remarried. *Journal of Marriage and the Family, 41,* 857-867.

Baptiste, D. A. (1984). Marital and family therapy with racially/culturally intermarried stepfamilies: Issues and guidelines. *Family Relations, 33,* 373-380.

Baptiste, D. A. (1987a). The gay and lesbian stepparent family. In F. Bozett (Ed.), *Gay and lesbian parenting* (pp. 112-137). New York: Praeger.

Baptiste, D. A. (1987b). Psychotherapy with gay/lesbian couples and their children in "stepfamilies": A challenge for marriage and family therapists. *Journal of Homosexuality, 14,* 223-238.

Barnes, A. S. (1985). *The black middle class family: A study of black subsociety, neighborhood, and home in interaction.* Bristol, IN: Wyndham Hall.

Beller, A. H., & Graham, J. W. (1986). Child support awards: Differentials and trends by race and marital status. *Demography, 23,* 231-245.

Booth, A., & Edwards, J. (1992). Why remarriages are more unstable. *Journal of Family Issues, 13,* 179-194.

Boss, P. (1980). The relationship of psychological father presence, wife's personal qualities, and wife/family dysfunction in families of missing fathers. *Journal of Marriage and the Family, 42,* 541-549.

Boss, P. (1987). Family stress. In M. Sussman & S. Steinmetz (Eds.), *Handbook of marriage and the family* (pp. 695-723). New York: Plenum.

Boss, P., & Greenberg, J. (1984). Family boundary ambiguity: A new variable in family stress theory. *Family Process, 23,* 535-546.

Brand, E., & Clingempeel, W. (1987). Interdependencies of marital and stepparent-stepchild relationships and children's psychological adjustment: Research findings and clinical implications. *Family Relations, 36,* 140-145.

Bryan, L., Coleman, M., Ganong, L., & Bryan, H. (1986). Person perception: Family structure as a cue for stereotyping. *Journal of Marriage and the Family, 48,* 169-174.

Bryant, Z. L., Coleman, M., & Ganong, L. (1988). Race and family structure stereotyping: Perceptions of black and white nuclear and stepfamilies. *Journal of Black Psychology, 15,* 1-16.

Bumpass, L. (1984). Some characteristics of children's second families. *American Journal of Sociology, 90,* 608-623.

Carter, B., & McGoldrick, M. (Eds.). (1988). *The changing family life style* (2nd ed.). New York: Gardner.

Cherlin, A. (1978). Remarriage as an incomplete institution. *American Journal of Sociology, 84,* 634-650.

Clingempeel, W., Ievoli, R., & Brand, E. (1984). Structural complexity and the quality of stepfather-stepchild relationships. *Family Process, 23,* 547-560.

Clingempeel, W., & Segal, S. (1986). Stepparent-stepchild relations and the psychological adjustment of children in stepmother and stepfather families. *Child Development, 57,* 474-484.

Coleman, M., & Ganong, L. (1987). The cultural stereotyping of stepfamilies. In K. Pasley & M. Ihinger-Tallman (Eds.), *Remarriage & stepparenting: Current research & theory* (pp. 19-41). New York: Guilford.

Crosbie-Burnett, M. (1984). The centrality of the step relationship: A challenge to family theory and practice. *Family Relations, 33,* 459-463.

Crosbie-Burnett, M. (1988a). Impact of joint versus maternal legal custody, sex and age of adolescent, and family structure complexity on adolescents in remarried families. *Conciliation Courts Review, 26,* 47-52.

Crosbie-Burnett, M. (1988b). Relationship between marital satisfaction and labor force participation in remarrying couples. *Family Perspective, 22,* 347-359.

Crosbie-Burnett, M. (1989). Application of family stress theory to remarriage: A model for assessing and helping stepfamilies. *Family Relations, 38,* 323-331.

Crosbie-Burnett, M. (in press). The interface between stepparent families and schools: Research, theory, policy, and practice. In K. Pasley & M. Ihinger-Tallman (Eds.), *Stepparenting: Issues in theory, research, and practice* (pp. 348-383). New York: Greenwood.

Crosbie-Burnett, M., & Giles-Sims, J. (1987). Marital power in stepfather families. *Journal of Family Psychology, 4,* 484-495.

Crosbie-Burnett, M., & Helmbrecht, L. (1993). A descriptive empirical study of gay male stepfamilies. *Family Relations, 42*(3), 256-262.

Crosbie-Burnett, M., & Lewis, E. (1993). Use of African-American family structure and functioning to address the challenges of European-American post-divorce families. *Family Relations, 42*(3), 243-248.

Daly, M., & Wilson, M. (1991). A reply to Gelles: Stepchildren are disproportionately abused, and diverse forms of violence can share causal factors. *Human Nature, 2,* 419-426.

Dolan, E., & Lowen, J. (1985). Remarried family: Challenges and opportunities. *Journal of Home Economics, 77,* 36-44.

Emery, R. E. (1988). *Marriage, divorce, and children's adjustment.* Newbury Park, CA: Sage.

Fine, M. A., & Fine, D. R. (1992). Recent changes in laws affecting stepfamilies: Suggestions for legal reform. *Family Relations, 41,* 334-340.

Fine, M. A., McKenry, P. C., Donnelly, B. W., & Voydanoff, P. (1992). Perceived adjustments of parents and children: Variations by family structure, race, and gender. *Journal of Marriage and the Family, 54*(1), 118-127.

Fishman, B. (1983). The economic behavior of stepfamilies. *Family Relations, 32,* 359-366.

Folk, K. F., Graham, J. W., & Beller, A. H. (1992). Child support and remarriage implications for the economic well-being of children. *Journal of Family Issues, 13,* 142-157.

Fox, G. L., & Inazu, J. K. (1982). The influence of mother's marital history on the mother-daughter relationship in black and white households. *Journal of Marriage and the Family, 44,* 143-153.

Furstenberg, F., Nord, C., Peterson, J., & Zill, N. (1983). The life course of children of divorce: Marital disruption and parental contact. *American Sociological Review, 48,* 656-668.

Ganong, L., & Coleman, M. (1988). Do mutual children cement bonds in stepfamilies? *Journal of Marriage and the Family, 50,* 687-698.

Giles-Sims, J. (1984). The stepparent role: Expectations, behavior, and sanctions. *Journal of Family Issues, 5,* 116-130.

Glick, P. (1979). Future American families. *The Washington COFO MEMO, 2,* 2-5.

Glick, P. (1989a). The family life cycle and social change. *Family Relations, 38,* 123-129.

Glick, P. (1989b). Remarried families, stepfamilies, and stepchildren: A brief demographic profile. *Family Relations, 38,* 24-27.

Goetting, A. (1980). Former spouse—current spouse relationships: Behavioral expectations. *Journal of Family Issues, 1,* 58-80.

Goetting, A. (1982). The six stations of remarriage: Developmental tasks of remarriage after divorce. *Family Relations, 31,* 213-222.

Hansen, D., & Hill, R. (1964). Families under stress. In H. Christensen (Ed.), *Handbook of marriage and the family* (pp. 782-819). Chicago: Rand McNally.

Harvard Law Review Association. (1990). *Sexual orientation and the law.* Cambridge, MA: Harvard University Press.

Hill, M. S. (1992). The role of economic resources and remarriage in financial assistance for children of divorce. *Journal of Family Issues, 13,* 158-178.

Ihinger-Tallman, M. (1987). Sibling and stepsibling bonding in stepfamilies. In K. Pasley & M. Ihinger-Tallman (Eds.), *Remarriage & stepparenting: Current research & theory* (pp. 164-184). New York: Guilford.

Ihinger-Tallman, M., & Pasley, K. (1987). *Remarriage.* Newbury Park, CA: Sage.

Ishii-Kuntz, M., & Coltrane, S. (1992). Remarriage, stepparenting, and household labor. *Journal of Family Issues, 13,* 215-233.

Kalmuss, D., & Seltzer, J. A. (1986). Continuity of marital behavior in remarriage: The case of spouse abuse. *Journal of Marriage and the Family, 48,* 113-120.

Koepke, L., Hare, J., & Moran, P. B. (1992). Relationship quality in a sample of lesbian couples with children and child-free lesbian couples. *Family Relations, 41*(2), 224-229.

LaRossa, R., & LaRossa, M. M. (1981). *Transition to parenthood: How infants change families.* Beverly Hills, CA: Sage.

Lutz, P. (1983). The stepfamily: An adolescent perspective. *Family Relations, 32,* 367-375.

Martin, T., & Bumpass, L. (1989). Recent trends in marital disruption. *Demography, 26,* 37-51.

McCubbin, H. I. (1979). Integrating coping behaviors into family stress theory. *Journal of Marriage and the Family, 41,* 237-244.

McCubbin, H. I., Joy, C., Cauble, A., Patterson, J., & Needle, R. (1980). Family stress, coping, and social support: A decade review. *Journal of Marriage and the Family, 42,* 855-871.

McCubbin, H. I., & McCubbin, M. A. (1987). Family stress theory and assessment: The T-Double ABCX Model of family adjustment and adaptation. In H. McCubbin & A. Thompson (Eds.), *Family assessment inventories for research and practice* (pp. 3-34). Madison: University of Wisconsin Press.

McCubbin, H. I., & Patterson, J. M. (1983a). The family stress process: The Double ABCX Model of adjustment and adaptation. In H. I. McCubbin, M. B. Sussman, & J. M. Patterson (Eds.), *Social stress and the family: Advances and developments in family stress theory and research* (pp. 7-37). New York: Haworth.

McCubbin, H. I., & Patterson, J. M. (1983b). Family transitions: Adaptation to stress. In H. I. McCubbin & C. R. Figley (Eds.), *Stress and the family* (Vol. 1, pp. 5-25). New York: Brunner/Mazel.

Mechanic, D. (1974). Social structure and personal adaptation: Some neglected dimensions. In G. Coehlo, D. Hamburg, & J. Adams (Eds.), *Coping and adaptation* (pp. 32-44). New York: Basic Books.

Olson, D. H., & McCubbin, H. I. (1982). The Circumplex Model of Marital and Family Systems VI: Application of family stress and crisis intervention. In H. I. McCubbin, A. E. Cauble, & J. M. Patterson (Eds.), *Family stress, coping, and social support*. Springfield, IL: Charles C Thomas.

Pasley, K. (1987). Family boundary ambiguity: Perceptions of adult stepfamily family members. In K. Pasley & M. Ihinger-Tallman (Eds.), *Remarriage & stepparenting: Current research & theory* (pp. 206-224). New York: Guilford.

Pasley, K., & Ihinger-Tallman, M. (1982). Remarried family life: Supports and constraints. In N. Stinnett, J. DeFrain, H. Lingren, G. Rowe, S. VanZandt, & R. Williams (Eds.), *Building family strengths: Vol. 4. Positive support systems* (pp. 367-383). Lincoln: University of Nebraska Press.

Pearlin, L., & Schooler, C. (1978). The structure of coping. *Journal of Health and Social Behavior, 19,* 2-21.

Peterson, J., & Zill, N. (1986). Marital disruption, parent-child relationships, and behavior problems in children. *Journal of Marriage and the Family, 48,* 295-307.

Reiss, D., & Oliveri, M. (1980). Family paradigm and family coping: A proposal for linking the family's intrinsic adaptive capacities to its responses to stress. *Family Relations, 29,* 431-444.

Santrock, J., Warshak, R., Lindbergh, C., & Meadows, L. (1982). Children's and parents' observed social behavior in stepfather families. *Child Development, 53,* 472-480.

Schwebel, A., Fine, M., & Renner, M. (1991). A study of perceptions of the stepparent role. *Journal of Family Issues, 12,* 43-57.

Smock, P. J. (1990). Remarriage patterns of black and white women: Reassessing the role of educational attainment. *Demography, 27,* 467-473.

Sweet, J. A. (1991, November). *The demography of one-parent and step-families: Changing marriage, remarriage, and reproductive patterns.* Paper presented at the Fifth Annual Wingspread Conference on Remarriage, Denver.

Teachman, J. D. (1986). First and second marital dissolution: A decomposition exercise with whites and blacks. *Sociological Quarterly, 27,* 571-590.

Unger, D., & Powell, D. (1980). Supporting families under stress: The role of social networks. *Family Relations, 29,* 566-574.

Vemer, E., Coleman, M., Ganong, L., & Cooper, H. (1989). Marital satisfaction in remarriage: A meta-analysis. *Journal of Marriage and the Family, 51,* 713-725.

Visher, E., & Visher, J. (1979). *Stepfamilies: A guide to working with stepparents and stepchildren.* New York: Brunner/Mazel.

Visher, E., & Visher, J. (1983). Stepparenting: Blending family. In H. I. McCubbin & C. R. Figley (Eds.), *Stress and the family* (Vol. 1, pp. 133-148). New York: Brunner/Mazel.

Wallerstein, J., & Blakeslee, S. (1989). *Second chances: Men, women, and children a decade after divorce.* New York: Ticknor and Fields.

Wallerstein, J., & Kelly, J. (1980). *Surviving the breakup.* New York: Basic Books.

White, L., & Booth, A. (1985). The quality and stability of remarriages: The role of stepchildren. *American Sociological Review, 50,* 689-698.

Wilson, B. F., & Clarke, S. C. (1992). Remarriages: A demographic profile. *Journal of Family Issues, 13,* 123-141.

# 12

❁

# Drug and Alcohol Abuse

ROBERT A. LEWIS
IRWANTO

## A Historical Perspective on Drugs and Alcohol

Most observers of families view drugs and alcohol as serious stressors on families. Drug and alcohol use, however, has played an interesting role in American history. Alcohol and drugs have been perceived by some as "positive" symbols of freedom and self-determination but by others as negative, evil substances and even symbols of anarchy and perverse immorality. Some historians have observed increases and decreases in drug and alcohol use especially during and following important stressful events in American history, especially wars, such as the American Revolution, the Civil War, the civil rights movement, and the Vietnam war (Buchanan, 1992; Musto, 1991; Rorabough, 1979).

Some historians and sociologists, as well as social conservators, have suggested that societal change may result in increased drug and alcohol use by producing stress in families. No systematic analysis, however, has been conducted to assess the association between recent social and demographic changes in American families and trends in drug abuse. However, some trends in families and drug use do appear to be similar. For example, there was a dramatic increase in the abuse of all kinds of drugs during the early 1970s and early 1980s for all age groups in the United States. Although some trends in adolescents' drug use seem to have plateaued in the 1980s, such as dropping significantly in 1988 especially among youth aged 12 to 17 years, drug abuse among the addicted remains a very serious social problem.

In terms of family changes, Glick (1988) has detailed how during the past 50 years American families have undergone significant and stressful transformations. Overall, social acceptance of various forms of families has steadily replaced the older, normative definition of families as including two parents and their children, the father as a breadwinner and the mother as a homemaker. Especially in the 1960s and 1970s, decades of social revolution, Americans witnessed increasing numbers of cohabiting couples, families being maintained by single parents, and many adults living alone. As a result of increasing alternative family forms, divorce, single-parenthood, childlessness, gay/lesbian orientation, and living alone have become more socially acceptable.

Significant transformation also has occurred in gender attitudes, which have moved toward greater egalitarianism. Increased percentages of both young men and women are critical of patriarchy and seek freedom from traditionally defined gender roles (Lewis, 1986; Thornton, 1989). By 1987 a quarter of all children under 18 years of age no longer lived with both of their parents: 83% of these children lived with stepfathers, whereas only 18% lived with stepmothers. Of interest, the late 1980s and early 1990s seem to reflect a period of some stabilization, in which many of these trends have flattened (Glick, 1988; Thornton, 1989).

As we have suggested, these parallel changes in family structure and drug use in the last three decades do not necessarily indicate that changes in attitudes toward families and changes in family structures and forms have directly caused current trends in drug use. These parallel changes may imply, however, that the instability of families either allows or imposes greater stresses upon individuals and society. Similarly, the stabilization of families may provide more secure environments for family members, who consequently may more effectively cope without the abuse of substances.

## The Incidence and Prevalence of Drug Use

As previously indicated, the use of alcohol and some other drugs has become somewhat normative in the United States, whereas abuse of illicit drugs has become rampant within certain levels and cohorts of American society. In fact, young adult Americans' involvement with illicit, addictive drugs is currently greater than that found in any other industrialized nation—and it may still be growing. For example, one national survey indicated that during 1975 to 1982 the lifetime use of illicit drugs by high school seniors rose from 55.2% to 65.8%. Similarly, the prevalence of lifetime use of marijuana rose from 47.3% in 1975 to 60.4% in 1979 (Buchanan, 1992; Johnston, O'Malley, & Bachman, 1988). However, lifetime abuse of any illicit drugs by high school seniors dropped somewhat to 44.1% in 1991, and the abuse of marijuana/hashish dropped to 36.5% in 1991. Nevertheless, drug addictions are still widespread throughout society, and their consequences are very serious for families and society.

## Social Costs

This somewhat optimistic recent decline in the use of many illicit drugs by high school students, however, represents only a small part of the entire picture. It is estimated that 100,000 Americans die every year as a result of drug use. Furthermore, alcohol, drug abuse, and nicotine abuse are still numbered among the most serious health problems in America, especially among young people.

Overall life expectancy in the United States has steadily risen over the last 75 years in all age groups except for those Americans between the ages of 15 and 24 years. Most of the deaths of adolescents and young adults are from injuries, accidents, and disappearances often related to substance abuse. Persons who are addicted to substances are also at higher risk for a variety of other health problems, such as lower immunity to infections, short-term memory impairment, and even malnutrition.

The relatively high prevalence of drug and alcohol abuse in the United States, especially after the Vietnam war, has exacted extremely high costs in economic and human resources. For example, in 1985 it was estimated that Americans paid approximately $44.1 billion to deal with the problems of drug abuse, including drug treatment, drug-related crimes, law enforcement, loss of health, and decreased productivity on the job. This amount increased to $58.3 billion in 1988. The IRS has estimated that the value of the illicit drug trade is between $25 and $30 billion each year.

Each year an estimated 2 million individuals are hospitalized, and three fourths of these are persons aged 15 to 44 years (Rice, Kelman, & Miller, 1991). Approximately 100,000 Americans die each year as the result of drug abuse; these numbers, unfortunately, will increase with the spread of

AIDS. Each loss of adult life is about equal to $400,000, or 35 productive-person-years lost (Rice et al., 1991).

Between 1985 and 1988, cocaine-related hospital emergencies more than tripled. Although decreasing since 1989, these cases remain more than double what they were in 1985. The cost of treating one infant born to a cocaine-addicted woman can be as high as $125,000, and it is estimated that tens of thousands of "cocaine-babies" are born each year.

The long-term psychological effects of many drugs also have been documented in increasing work- and school-related difficulties for all age groups. Higher drug use is associated with low social and intellectual skills, such as poor problem solving and impaired social relationships. Depression, hostility, and anxiety are among the many results of long-term substance abuse. However, because so many Americans are addicted to the so-called soft and/or legal drugs (alcohol and nicotine), they are reluctant to call their own use of addictive substances "drug abuse." Such attitudes of denial impede the necessary diagnosis and treatment of many addictions for Americans.

## Some Explanations of Drug Addictions

Although there are many theories about the causes of alcohol and drug abuse, the drug abuser's family looms large in many of these explanations (Volk, Edwards, Lewis, & Sprenkle, 1989). For example, there are theories that (a) disrupted families cause alcohol and substance abuse in children (broken home hypothesis); (b) overprotective mothers, with or without ineffectual fathers, such as enmeshed parents and children, produce substance abuse; (c) substance abuse is reinforced by changes made in the family's interaction (functional hypothesis); and (d) family disengagement or distance produces drug addiction (Volk et al., 1989).

One major debate in the area of families and drug abuse continues to be whether dysfunctional family life creates drug addiction or whether drug addiction produces dysfunctional families (Lewis, 1989). In other words, are alcoholism and other drug addictions "diseases of individuals" or are they products of disorganized families and other social systems? The former "individual-focused" view is more often held by medical practitioners and drug counselors who favor self-help groups such as Alcoholics Anonymous (AA), Al-Anon, and Narcotics Anonymous (NA). The latter "systemic" view is held by family therapists and family practitioners who prefer to treat drug addictions by working with the families to change family systems into more healthy environments (Lewis, 1989).

## Family Predictors of Drug Abuse

Because drug and alcohol use have a long established intergenerational pattern, both genetics and family socialization have been claimed as causes of drug and alcohol abuse. Some documentation has recently fallen on the side of behavioral genetics, especially as a predictor of alcoholism. Yet it should be noted that only 20% of the children of alcoholics become alcoholics themselves, and more than half of alcoholics do not have a family history of alcoholism (Hawkins, Lishner, Catalano, & Howard, 1986; Searles, 1990, 1991).

Most sociologists and family scientists give greater credence to the role of family socialization (Barnes, 1990; Barnes & Farrell, 1992; Bennett & Wolin, 1990; Jacob, 1992). For example, Barnes (1990) argues, instead, that biological vulnerability does not (yet) offer adequate explanations regarding the strong associations between alcohol abuse, illicit drug use, and other problem behaviors.

Steinglass, Bennett, Wolin, and Reiss (1987) contend that the disruption of the functional properties of the family systems (e.g., family rituals, problem-solving strategies) would in return provide an environment conducive to greater drug use and abuse by members of subsequent generations. Another argument is that drug use in a family increases risks of all kinds of abuse, especially sexual and physical abuse (Barnes, 1990; Leonard & Jacob, 1988), which in turn contributes as a causative factor in adolescent drug abuse. Searles (1990, 1991), however, has suggested that future research should pay more attention to how the family environment, such as parenting styles, uniquely influences individual members of a family.

### Family Structure

Parental composition, family size, and birth order are the most commonly studied variables in drug and family research. Although these factors seem to help us understand the etiology (causes) of drug abuse, some caution should be exercised regarding the interpretation of the findings.

Currently, approximately 50% of American children born in the late 1970s to early 1980s will experience changing family structures, especially parental composition; for example, they are more likely to live with a divorced parent than was true of the previous generations. Many children will live in female-headed homes under subsistence conditions and have higher risks for engaging in socially undesirable behavior. The ability of parents to supervise and monitor their children has consistently been found to deter initiation into drug experimentation and other delinquent behaviors (Dishion & Loeber, 1985; Dishion, Patterson, & Reid, 1988; Selnow, 1987). Dishion and Loeber (1985) found statistical associations between living in a single-parent family, poor parental monitoring, adolescent involvement with drug abusing peers, and early drug exploration; these results were replicated in 1988 (Dishion et al., 1988). A recent study of 1,082 high school freshmen (Smart, Chibucos, & Didier, 1990) obtained similar results; significantly higher percentages of adolescents from single-parent families were using alcohol and tobacco than those from two-parent families.

Stanton and Todd (1979) and Hawkins et al. (1987a), however, state that caution should be used in the interpretation of these findings. They maintain that family structural factors do not add much to our understanding of the etiology of drug abuse. A meta-analysis of the impact of family structure on delinquency (Wells & Rankin, 1991), for instance, found very limited support for the association between family disorganization and delinquency. It seems that more important risks lie in certain family processes and the quality of family environments. A large study by Barnes and Farrell (1992) indicated that, after controlling for race, family structure did not predict regular drinking and deviance in adolescents. They concluded that being in a single-parent family may not be as crucial for adolescent outcomes as are parenting practices per se, such as support and monitoring behaviors.

Variations in family size impose certain restrictions and opportunities for the use of family resources (e.g., parental support, finances). In his review, Glynn (1984) indicated that "only children" were the least at risk and that drug use was more prevalent in families of five to seven children. Most studies, however, have not found any meaningful association between family size and drug use (e.g., Hawkins et al., 1987a; Piercy, Volk, Trepper, Sprenkle, & Lewis, 1991).

Birth order exposes each child to different opportunities for social learning and behavioral expectations. Research on the family and drug abuse has not yet yielded any consistent relationship between birth order and drug abuse. There are, however, some data that suggest that firstborns are the least at risk, compared with subsequent children, especially the youngest child, for experimenting with illicit drugs (Glynn, 1984; Glynn & Haenlein, 1988;

Hawkins et al., 1987a). Searles (1990, 1991) has argued that future research should focus more attention on birth order, especially the way in which it may play an important role in how the family environment is perceived by each child—something that may lead to very different behavioral outcomes.

*Family History*

There is some well-established evidence that drug use by any member of the family is somehow related to drug use by other members. In couple relationships, female partner initiation to illicit drug use and progression toward drug dependency are related to patterns of drug use in the male partner, whereas male illicit drug use is more independent of spousal drug use (Weiner, Wallen, & Zankowski, 1990). Parental and sibling drug use has been consistently found to be associated with adolescent drug abusing behavior (Hawkins et al., 1986). However, the means of transmitting the problem behavior is perceived differently by scholars.

Although there is an increasing fascination with genetic explanations, as previously mentioned, more research is needed to validate genetic assumptions (Cadoret, 1990; Searles, 1990, 1991). Furthermore, research on the family clustering of opiate and alcohol abuse indicates that a purely genetic explanation is inadequate, considering that the community or environment affects the choice of the substance of dependence (Maddux & Desmond, 1989).

A systemic (family) approach presents more compelling explanations. Research focusing on the role of parental attitudes and values has revealed a high congruence between parents' and adolescents' perceptions of the use and abuse of drugs (Barnes, 1990). When parents use drugs such as cigarettes and alcohol, it indicates to children that those behaviors are allowed, if not actually expected, in their family.

Heavy drug use in the family, especially by parents, also disrupts functional properties of the family system (e.g., care and support, problem solving), which, in turn, provides a conducive environment for drug use and abuse by other members of subsequent generations (Steinglass et al., 1987). Dishion and Loeber (1985) have argued that parental drug use diminishes parental ability to exert effective monitoring and supervision. Such parenting allows children to mingle with peers who abuse drugs frequently. Clinical observation also suggests that parental drug use blocks effective communication, alters modes of interpersonal relations, and is associated with all kinds of child abuse (Barnes, 1990; Leonard & Jacob, 1988).

*Family Processes and Family Climates*

There are at least two broad dimensions of family life: (a) support and (b) control; and there is one facilitating dimension—communication (Barber, 1992; Rollins & Thomas, 1979). The support dimension refers to positive, affective experiences associated with relationships in the family such as acceptance, encouragement, security, and love. The control dimension pertains to the extent to which children's behavior is or is not restricted by the caregiver(s), ranging from establishing rules and discipline to varieties of physical coercion (e.g., hitting and yelling).

*Family support.* Family support is usually conceptualized as a unidimensional variable; that is, it may have different behavioral manifestations, but they are all linearly related to adolescent behavioral outcomes (Barber, 1992; Barnes & Farrell, 1992). Family support has been found to be the most robust variable in the prevention of most deviant behaviors of adolescents (Baumrind, 1991; Gecas & Seff, 1990; Hill, 1987). Although different aspects of support have been identified, such as general support, physical affection, companionship, and sustained contact (Gecas & Seff, 1990), all of them are negatively associated with socially unacceptable behaviors. Coombs and Landsverk (1988), for example, found consistent evidence that maintaining rewarding parent-child relationships deters substance abuse during childhood and adolescence. Parental praise and encouragement, involvement and attachment or perceived closeness, trust, and help with personal problems are all characteristics of families with drug abstainers. Parental rejection, conflicts, and manipulative relationships are all related to the earlier onset of drug experimentation and further use of illicit substances.

A study involving 152 drug-using adolescents and their families (Lewis, Piercy, Sprenkle, & Trepper, 1990; Piercy et al., 1991; Volk et al., 1989) indicated that the more closeness perceived by each member of the family, the less likely the adolescents were to use harder drugs. Similar results were found by Smart et al. (1990). Andrews, Hops, Ary, Lichtenstein, and Tildesley (1991) found that girls who use harder drugs reported their families as significantly less cohesive, and that they had more conflicts with their parents, than girls using soft drugs; the parents' perception of family cohesion was also lower. These researchers concluded that poor relationships in the family were a risk factor for the transition to harder drugs for both boys and girls. Finally, in a longitudinal study, Baumrind (1991) found that mutual attachment, observed between parents and children as early as 4 years old, is an effective buffer against more severe drug use. She also found that parents of heavy drug users were typically and frequently absent from the home, did not provide positive structures for growth, and were nonsupportive, and as a result the children were alienated.

*Family control.* The second dimension, the control dimension of family processes, is somewhat more complicated. Control is usually seen as multidimensional with its association to adolescent behavioral outcomes depending more on the consistency, types, and degree of control attempts (Barber, 1992; Baumrind, 1991; Rollins & Thomas, 1979). Basically, there are two broad categories of control: behavioral and psychological (Barber, 1992), and each is related differently to behavioral outcomes.

Lack of consistent behavioral control, such as careful supervision and monitoring, has repeatedly been found to be associated with early experimentation with drugs, involvement with drug-using peers, and progression toward the use of harder drugs (Baumrind, 1988, 1991; Dishion & Loeber, 1985; Dishion et al., 1988). Some current research in the area of adolescent delinquency (Steinberg, 1987) suggests that parental permissiveness, even when combined with warmth and perceived closeness, is a powerful predictor of adolescent immaturity and peer susceptibility, especially in early and midadolescence. For example, parents' knowledge of their adolescents' whereabouts was associated with lower drug use (Fors & Rojek, 1983).

Too much behavioral control, however, such as cruel and harsh discipline that may involve physical punishment, is also characteristic of parents of depressives and alcoholics (Barber, 1992; Holmes & Robins, 1987). Baumrind (1988, 1991) found that relationships of abstainers with their parents were characterized by moderate behavioral control combined with warmth and effective communication. These parents were more directive and consistent in the management of their adolescents' behaviors.

Psychological control is concerned with the extent to which one's individuality is acknowledged in the family (Barber, 1992). Concepts such as independence, autonomy, and individual freedom are related to this type of control (Barber, 1992; Baumrind, 1987; Gecas & Seff, 1990; Grotevant & Cooper, 1986). Authoritarian parenting (Baumrind, 1987), rigid rule practices, and parent-child overinvolvement were extreme types of psychological control and were consistently found to be associated with social withdrawal, lack of social competence, and drug abuse in adolescence (Glynn & Haenlein, 1988; Maccoby & Martin, 1983; Smart et al., 1990; Volk et al., 1989).

There are controversies, however, with regard to the role of overinvolved parents in the etiology of adolescent drug use. Clinical observations yield the impression that the family of adolescent drug users is characterized by overly involved or enmeshed relationships between adolescents and their mothers and strained relationships with fathers (Glynn & Haenlein, 1988; Hawkins et al., 1987a; Kaufman, 1981; Stanton et al., 1982). This overly "tight" relationship seems to prevent the adolescents from developing their own identity, whereas drugs are used by adolescents to reach out for autonomy or to act "as if" they were in control of their own behaviors. Because clinical observations yield the impression that drug use also creates other types of dependency on parents and other members of the family, this process of individuation is often called "pseudoindividuation" (Stanton et al., 1982).

Some self-report studies, however, have obtained contrary results (Friedman, Utada, & Morrissey, 1987; Piercy et al., 1991; Smart et al., 1990; Volk et al., 1989). Friedman et al. (1987), for example, found that members of families of drug abusing adolescents perceived their families as "disengaged," whereas their family therapists tended to see the families as "enmeshed." In another study (Volk et al., 1989), hard drug abusers also tended to perceive their families as more disengaged than did the soft drug users. Other studies likewise have found that lack of perceived closeness and involvement in daily activities is consistently correlated with early drug experimentation and progression to harder drug use (Baumrind, 1988; Bry, 1988; Hawkins et al., 1987a; Kandel, Kessler, & Margulies, 1978). A very recent study, using family conversations as well as standardized instrumentation, suggests that the families of hard drug users conveyed more "distancing messages" than did families of the soft drug users (Irwanto, 1992); however, "closeness messages" were often used by parents of hard drug users to induce behavioral and emotional changes in their adolescents regarding the family.

*Family communication.* To provide support or effectively exert control, family members usually rely upon communication. Watzlawick, Beavin, and Jackson (1967) argue that, whenever one communicates with another, one defines the relationship with the other person. The authors also maintain that, to communicate well, communicants should be able to understand the other's perceptions regarding the things they talk about and their relationship. In the families of drug abusers, however, studies have consistently found that communication is fraught with misperceptions and exchanges of negative affection. These studies also indicate that communication in these families is blocked either by the use of drugs or by feelings of just not being understood (Hawkins et al., 1987a; Jurich, Polson, Jurich, & Bates, 1985; Piercy et al., 1991).

## Gender and Ethnic Variations

Gender and ethnicity mediate the meaning of the use and abuse of certain drugs and how the families cope with their problems (Kaufman & Borders, 1988). The Irish, for instance, view the drinking of alcohol as a way of proving their Irishness. Mexican males often use alcoholic beverages to facilitate their male bonding (Kaufman & Borders, 1988). Among Native Americans, the Navajo Indians accept drinking and tolerate episodic drunkenness, whereas the Hopis condemn drinking and intoxication as threats to cosmic harmony (Young, 1992). Italians and Jews practice drinking behavior in their religious ceremonies; these highly controlled circumstances for drinking alcohol have resulted in an overall lower prevalence of drunkenness and alcoholism in these two communities (Kaufman & Borders, 1988).

There have also been some observed gender differences in the initiation of drug use and drug use careers. Tyler and Thompson (1980), for example, have indicated that heroin is the most abused drug by women who initially use drugs at the age of 19 to 20 years. In a survey of 567 heroin users, Hser, Anglin, and McGlothin (1987) found that males were the initiators of both male and female users. Women were commonly introduced to illicit drugs by a male sexual partner. Women also have been found to use prescribed drugs (for medical reasons) more frequently than males (Clayton, Voss, Robbins, & Skinner, 1986). Finally, Hser, Anglin, and Booth (1987) have found that women have shorter addiction careers than men.

Although we have some information regarding ethnic and gender variations in drug and alcohol abuse, knowledge with reference to the way in which those variations mediate family coping behaviors is lacking. Future research should focus on the interlinkage of culture, gender, drug use, and various family coping behaviors. These specifications of knowledge should better guide treatment, prevention, and social policies.

## The Family and Other Social Systems

When the adolescent member of a family is involved in drug abuse, his or her peer group and school are two other systems that should be considered. These systems intervene with parenting practices because they provide much of the environment for learning values, attitudes, and norms, which may or may not be shared by one's family.

It is well known that most new drug users are introduced to various drugs by peers and that peers help maintain patterns of use including greater dependent use. To assess the influence of peers, one should assess the following indicators: (a) time spent with peers, (b) the degree of attachment to peers, and (c) the extent of peer delinquency or drug use (Agnew, 1991).

Although researchers find consistent evidence regarding the relationship between dropping out, low performance, and underachievement in school and drug abuse, it is not known when school factors become salient as possible predictors of drug abuse (Hawkins et al., 1986). Some research indicates that a low grade point average (GPA) and dropping out of school are strongly associated with children's involvement with drug-abusing peers. It is clear, on the other hand, that parental involvement in children's school-work and activities reduces the chances of a child's being seriously involved with drug use.

Hawkins et al. (1987a) has also documented the association between drug use and social isolation of the family. For example, the 1990 National Household Survey indicated that current drug users are especially concentrated within families of lower social economic status and within communities of color—both groups that may be more likely to be isolated from the mainstream of society.

## Interventions

*Prevention*

Drug abuse education and prevention programs in both schools and community agencies are often more successful in increasing knowledge about the effects of drugs than in altering adolescents' behaviors and attitudes toward drugs. Generalized drug programs, especially, have been shown to be the least effective because students often begin to abuse alcohol and other drugs for various reasons. Programs that have only one focus (e.g., improving self-esteem) may miss the other causes of drug abuse. More successful drug programs, therefore, should be designed for specific at-risk groups as defined by known social-psychological and demographic risk factors.

Unfortunately, many national and international efforts have been directed toward the control of the distribution of addictive substances rather than the control of the addictions themselves. More attention and resources have been provided for the enforcement of laws punishing drug distribution rather than solving the problems and causes of drug addictions, that is, the demand for drugs.

In the last 10 to 15 years, drug prevention efforts have relied upon knowledge that (a) the most effective prevention programs are multilevel, (b) targeting youth aged 12 and younger is the most cost-effective, (c) the family is the most influential context, especially with younger and female drug users, and (d) life-skills rather than knowledge-oriented programs are more effective in preventing drug abuse.

### Treatment Through Families

Contemporary drug treatments come in many kinds and varieties, such as pharmacological treatment, psychotherapy (both individual and group), therapeutic communities, and self-help groups (e.g., AA, NA, Al-Anon). Most of these treatments can be divided into either inpatient treatment or outpatient treatment, depending upon whether it is 24-hour-a-day treatment and done within a residential or agency setting, such as a therapeutic community. Some treatments focus primarily on the individual drug addict either in one-on-one counseling or within a group. Some drug treatments are very extensive and may take many years (e.g., psychoanalysis), whereas other models are rather brief (e.g., solution-oriented therapy), where treatment may last less than 20 sessions.

There is a growing awareness, however, in much of the treatment field that no matter whether treatment is inpatient or outpatient, long term or brief, the direct involvement of the drug abuser's family is integral for any eventual success. Therefore some of the more promising models of adolescent, as well as adult, drug treatment now contain both an individual focus and a family focus (Lewis, 1989). The "individual treatment" centers on the teaching of social skills and strategies for abstinence and better coping with stress, whereas the family portion concentrates on helping the parents (or spouses) with their own parenting and nurturing skills, thereby helping the addict prevent relapse.

As described earlier, dysfunctional family life is one potential contributor to the development of drug addictions in young family members. The reciprocal nature of addictions and disorganized families, however, is evident in that not only may dysfunctional families produce addictive behaviors in their members, but these addictions, in turn, may affect the quality of family life. That is, addictions may negatively affect the behavior of family members and devitalize or fracture family relationships. The most demoralizing aspect of this reciprocity is that drug addictions are often passed from one generation to the next unless there is successful treatment or intervention.

Until about 15 years ago, very few drug treatment programs directly used spouses, parents, or other family members in their treatment of the identified patient. However, family involvement is currently the "treatment of choice" for most drug abusers, especially in the area of alcoholism treatment. There is also a growing body of research indicating that family-centered drug interventions are very effective in getting family members off and keeping them off drugs (Lewis & McAvoy, 1984). There is evidence, for example, that family groups given "systemic" family interventions have a higher treatment success rate, such as decreased drug dependence and less recidivism (Stanton et al., 1982). In contrast, if an adolescent is treated individually and his or her family system has not changed, the adolescent often returns home to continue in the same roles and behaviors that earlier fostered his or her addictive behaviors. The inclusion of other family members in an adolescent's drug treatment adds to the complexity of drug treatment. Yet this addition often gives a family therapist greater opportunity for sustained and successful drug treatment (Lewis & McAvoy, 1984) because of the drug abuser's wish to maintain family love relationships. Therefore strengthening family relationships may help to reduce or eliminate an individual's addictive behaviors.

The most effective drug treatment, however, may lie in a combined treatment (Lewis, 1989), in which the "individual treatment" focuses on the teaching of social skills and strategies for coping with stress, while the "family treatment" component strives to increase the nurturance and parenting skills of the other family members.

### Advocacy and Other Policy Issues

Although more funding and attention seem to be given to drug treatment, the advocacy of drug-free environments is also important. Some drug prevention programs—that is, educating young people in school about the many dangers of drug use—appear to be working somewhat, as evidenced by recent national surveys. Not only are very young children "saying no to drugs," but a growing number of older children and adolescents are becoming convinced that even experimenting with crack and cocaine is exceedingly dangerous. For example, according to the "Monitoring the Future" study conducted yearly at the University of Michigan, drug education in and outside of schools is working because it is reducing the demand for drugs among adolescents.

Therefore, because reducing the demand for drugs is possible, more federal funding could profitably be directed toward drug education and drug treatment programs and perhaps less to law enforcement and the interdiction of drugs. The effects of drug education and treatment could be continuing effects, whereas use of legal procedures alone will probably be only temporary and ineffectual.

Drug use among the already addicted groups in American society is not decreasing but is holding steady and even increasing, sometimes at an epidemic rate. Federal resources will be continually needed to adequately fund more and better treatment centers, discover more effective treatment programs, and increase the all too few patient slots for those who are seriously addicted to drugs, especially for addicted, pregnant women.

Drug addictions and the numerous societal consequences of these addictions for Americans in terms of physical and emotional health, economic losses, and increasing crime are threatening society as we know it. There is therefore a serious need for community involvement and changes in societal attitudes toward the use of addictive substances. An all-out war against the abuse of drugs is necessitated to curb the current drug and alcohol epidemic, which is related to ever-increasing crime, declining worker productivity, and increases in juvenile delinquency, teen pregnancy, AIDS, and other venereal diseases.

The media should be discouraged from portraying the abuse of illegal and legal drugs as sexy, romantic, masculine, and/or adult behavior in alcohol and tobacco advertisements. Instead, constructive alternatives to drug use should be portrayed by the media.

Preventive programs must receive priority action. School systems should be continually funded and empowered to provide programs from preschool/ kindergarten through 12th grade to help teachers recognize the signs of drug use among their students. Better school- and community-based programs must be designed and evaluated to provide more effective drug prevention programs, especially those that will provide the means of raising students' self-esteem. Parents should be offered and encouraged to attend their own educational programs on drug use and prevention.

## Summary

This chapter has explored some of the evidence for the reciprocal effects between drug and alcohol abuse and family stress and dysfunction. According to this perspective, family members' abuse of drugs and alcohol may produce stressful changes within their families, changes that often are dysfunctional. In turn, these dysfunctional families may help to continue the transmission of drug and alcohol addictions from generation to generation. Conversely, individuals may use drugs and alcohol to cope with stress in their families. Regardless of the direction of the relationship between drug and alcohol use and family stress, families and society suffer a wide range of social costs.

A number of family predictors of drug abuse have been identified, relating to certain family structures, family histories, and family processes, such as lack of family support and parental monitoring. Some of the more affective forms of intervention have been focused on changing family interaction. Because of the enormity of the problem, many policy issues at the societal level need to be addressed, including prevention, access to treatment, and change of attitudes toward the consumption of alcohol and drugs.

## References

Agnew, R. (1991). The interactive effects of peer variables on delinquency. *Criminology, 29,* 47-72.

Andrews, J. A., Hops, H., Ary, D., Lichtenstein, E., & Tildesley, E. (1991). The construction, validation and use of Guttman scale of adolescent substance use: An investigation of family relationships.

Barber, B. K. (1992). Family, personality, and adolescent problem behavior. *Journal of Marriage and the Family, 54,* 69-79.

Barnes, G. M. (1990). Impact of family on adolescent drinking patterns. In R. L. Collins, K. E. Leonard, & J. S. Searles (Eds.), *Alcohol and the family: Research and clinical perspectives* (pp. 137-161). New York: Guilford.

Barnes, G. M., & Farrell, M. P. (1992). Parental support and control as predictors of adolescent drinking, delinquency, and related problem behaviors. *Journal of Marriage and the Family, 54,* 763-776.

Baumrind, D. (1987). A developmental perspective on adolescent risk taking behavior in contemporary America. In W. Damon (Ed.), *New direction for child development: Adolescent health and social behavior,* 93-126.

Baumrind, D. (1988). Familial antecedent of adolescent drug use: A developmental perspective. In C. L. Jones & R. J. Battjes (Eds.), *Research analysis and utilization system: Etiology of drug abuse, implication for prevention* (Research Monograph Series 56, pp. 13-44). Rockville, MD: NIDA.

Baumrind, D. (1991). The influence of parenting style on adolescent competence and substance use. *Journal of Early Adolescence, 11,* 56-95.

Bennett, L. A., & Wolin, S. J. (1990). Family culture and alcoholism transmission. In R. L. Collins, K. E. Leonard, & J. S. Searles (Eds.), *Alcohol and the family: Research and clinical perspectives* (pp. 194-219). New York: Guilford.

Bry, B. H. (1988). Family-based approaches to reducing adolescent substance use: Theories, techniques, and findings. In E. R. Rahdert & J. Grabowski (Eds.), *Adolescent drug abuse:*

*Analyses of treatment research* (Research Monograph Series 77, pp. 39-68). Rockville, MD: NIDA.

Buchanan, D. R. (1992). A social history of American drug use. *The Journal of Drug Issues, 22,* 31-52.

Cadoret, R. J. (1990). Genetics of alcoholism. In R. L. Collins, K. E. Leonard, & J. S. Searles (Eds.), *Alcohol and the family: Research and clinical perspectives* (pp. 114-127). New York: Guilford.

Clayton, R. R., Voss, H. L., Robbins, C., & Skinner, W. F. (1986). Gender differences in drug use: An epidemiological perspective. In B. A. Ray & M. C. Braude (Eds.), *Women and drugs: A new era for research* (pp. 80-99). Rockville, MD: NIDA.

Coombs, R. H., & Landsverk, J. (1988). Parenting styles and substance use during childhood and adolescence. *Journal of Marriage and the Family, 50,* 473-482.

Dishion, T. J., & Loeber (1985). Male adolescent marijuana and alcohol use: The role of parents and peers revisited. *Journal of Alcohol and Substance Abuse, 11,* 11-25.

Dishion, T. J., Patterson, G. R., & Reid, J. R. (1988). Parent and peer factors associated with sampling in early adolescence: Implications for treatment. In E. R. Rahdert & J. Grabowski (Eds.), *Adolescent drug abuse: Analyses of treatment research* (pp. 69-93). Rockville, MD: NIDA.

Fors, S. W., & Rojek, D. G. (1983). The social demographic correlates of adolescent drug use patterns. *Journal of Drug Education, 13,* 205-222.

Friedman, A. S., Utada, A., & Morrissey, M. R. (1987). Families of adolescent drug abusers are "rigid": Are these families either "disengaged" or "enmeshed" or both? *Family Process, 26,* 131-147.

Gecas, V., & Seff, M. A. (1990). Families and adolescents: A review of the 1980s. *Journal of Marriage and the Family, 52,* 941-958.

Glick, P. C. (1988). Fifty years of family demography: A record of social change. *Journal of Marriage and the Family, 50,* 861-873.

Glynn, T. J. (1984). Adolescent drug use and the family environment: A review. *Journal of Drug Issues, 14,* 272-295.

Glynn, T. J., & Haenlein, M. (1988). Family theory and research on adolescent drug use: A review. In R. H. Coombs (Ed.), *The family context of adolescent drug use* (pp. 39-55). New York: Haworth.

Grotevant, H. D., & Cooper, C. R. (1986). Individuation in family relationships. *Human Development, 29,* 82-100.

Hawkins, J. D., Lishner, D., & Catalano, R. F. (1987a). Childhood predictors and the prevention of adolescents substance abuse. In C. L. Jones & R. J. Battjes (Eds.), *Research analysis and utilization system: Etiology of drug abuse, implication for prevention* (Research Monograph Series 56, Vol. 9, pp. 75-126). Rockville, MD: NIDA.

Hawkins, J. D., Lishner, D. M., Catalano, R. F., & Howard, M. O. (1986). Childhood predictors of adolescent substance abuse: Toward empirically grounded theory. *Journal of Children in Contemporary Society, 18,* 11-48.

Hawkins, J. D., Lishner, D. M., Jenson, J. M., & Catalano, R. F. (1987b). Delinquents and drugs: What the evidence suggests about prevention and treatment programming. In B. Brown & A. Mills (Eds.), *Youth at high-risk for substance abuse.* Rockville, MD: NIDA.

Hill, J. (1987). Research on adolescents and their families: Past and prospect. In W. Damon (Ed.), *New direction for child development: Adolescent health and social behavior, 37,* 93-126.

Holmes, S. J., & Robins, L. N. (1987). The influence of childhood disciplinary experience on the development of alcoholism and depression. *Journal of Child Psychology and Psychiatry, 28,* 399-415.

Hser, Y. I., Anglin, M. D., & Booth, M. W. (1987). Sex differences in addict careers: 3. Addiction. *American Journal of Drug and Alcohol Abuse, 13,* 231-251.

Hser, Y. I., Anglin, M. D., & McGlothin (1987). Sex differences in addict careers: 1. Initiation of use. *American Journal of Drug and Alcohol Abuse, 13,* 33-57.

Irwanto. (1992). *Relational dynamics of families with drug abusing adolescents: A qualitative analysis of conversations.* Unpublished doctoral dissertation, Purdue University, West Lafayette, IN.

Jacob, T. (1992). Family studies of alcoholism. *Journal of Family Psychology, 5,* 319-338.

Johnston, L. D., O'Malley, P. M., & Bachman, J. G. (1988). *Drug use among high school students, college students, and other young adults: National trends through 1987.* Washington, DC: Government Printing Office.

Jurich, A. P., Polson, C. J., Jurich, J. A., & Bates, R. A. (1985). Family factors in the life of drug users and abusers. *Adolescence, 20,* 143-159.

Kandel, D. B., Kessler, R. C., & Margulies, R. Z. (1978). Antecedents of adolescent initiation into stages of drug abuse: A developmental analysis. *Journal of Youth and Adolescence, 7,* 13-40.

Kaufman, E. (1981). Family structures of narcotic addicts. *The International Journal of the Addictions, 16,* 273-282.

Kaufman, E., & Borders, L. (1988). Ethnic family differences in adolescent substance use. In R. H. Coombs (Ed.), *The family context of adolescent drug use* (pp. 99-122). New York: Haworth.

Leonard, K. E., & Jacob, T. (1988). Alcohol, alcoholism, and family violence. In V. B. van Hasselt, R. L. Morrison, A. L. Bellack, & M. Hersen (Eds.), *Handbook of family violence* (pp. 383-406). New York: Plenum.

Lewis, R. A. (1986). What men get out of marriage and parenthood. In R. A. Lewis & R. E. Salt (Eds.), *Men in families* (pp. 11-25). Newbury Park, CA: Sage.

Lewis, R. A. (1989). The family and addiction: An introduction. *Family Relations, 38,* 254-257.

Lewis, R. A., & McAvoy, P. (1984). Improving the quality of relationships: Therapeutic intervention with opiate abusing couples. In S. W. Duck (Ed.), *Personality relationships: Repairing personal relationships* (pp. 5, 89-102). London: Academic Press.

Lewis, R. A., Piercy, F. P., Sprenkle, D. H., & Trepper, T. S. (1990). Family-based interventions for helping drug-abusing adolescents. *Journal of Adolescent Research, 5,* 82-95.

Maccoby, E. E., & Martin, J. A. (1983). Socialization in the context of the family: Parent-child interaction. In E. M. Hetherington (Ed.), *Handbook of child psychology: Vol. 4. Socialization, personality, and social development* (pp. 1-101). New York: John Wiley.

Maddux, J. F., & Desmond, D. P. (1989). Family and environment in the choice of opioid dependence or alcoholism. *American Journal of Drug and Alcohol Abuse, 15,* 117-134.

Musto, D. (1991). Opium, cocaine, and marijuana in American history. *Scientific American, 265,* 40-47.

Piercy, F. P., Volk, R. J., Trepper, T., Sprenkle, D. H., & Lewis, R. A. (1991). The relationships of family factors to patterns of substance abuse. *Family Dynamics of Addiction Quarterly, 1,* 41-54.

Rice, D. P., Kelman, S., & Miller, L. (1991). Economic costs of drug abuse. In W. S. Cartwright & J. M. Kaple (Eds.), *Economic costs, cost-effectiveness, financing, and community-based drug treatment* (pp. 10-32). Rockville, MD: NIDA.

Rollins, B. C., & Thomas, D. L. (1979). Parental support, power, and control techniques in socialization of children. In W. R. Burr, F. I. Nye, & I. L. Reiss (Eds.), *Contemporary theories about the family* (Vol. 1, pp. 317-364). New York: Free Press.

Rorabough, W. J. (1979). *The alcoholic republic.* New York: Oxford University Press.

Searles, J. S. (1990). The contribution of genetic factors to the development of alcoholism: A critical review. In R. L. Collins, K. E. Leonard, & J. S. Searles (Eds.), *Alcohol and the family: Research and clinical perspectives* (pp. 3-38). New York: Guilford.

Searles, J. S. (1991). The genetics of alcoholism: Impacts on family and sociological models of addiction. *Family Dynamics of Addiction Quarterly, 1,* 8-21.

Selnow, G. A. (1987). Parent-child relationships and single and two parent families: Implications for substance usage. *Journal of Drug Education, 17,* 315-326.

Smart, L. S., Chibucos, T. R., & Didier, L. A. (1990). Adolescent substance use and perceived family functioning. *Journal of Family Issues, 11,* 208-227.

Stanton, M. D., & Todd, T. C. (1979). Structural family therapy with drug addicts. In E. Kaufman & P. Kaufman (Eds.), *Family therapy of drug and alcohol abuse* (pp. 46-62). New York: Garner.

Stanton, M. D., Todd, T. C., and associates (1982). *The family therapy of drug addiction.* New York: Guilford.

Steinberg, L. (1987). Familial factors in delinquency: A developmental perspective. *Journal of Adolescence Research, 2,* 255-268.

Steinglass, P., Bennett, L. A., Wolin, S. J., & Reiss, D. (1987). *The alcoholic family.* New York: Basic Books.

Thornton, A. (1989). Changing attitudes toward family issues in the United States. *Journal of Marriage and the Family, 51,* 873-893.

Tyler, J., & Thompson, M. (1980). Patterns of drug abuse among women. *The International Journal of Addictions, 15,* 309-321.

Volk, R. J., Edwards, D. W., Lewis, R. A., & Sprenkle, D. H. (1989). Family system of adolescent substance abusers. *Family Relations, 38,* 266-272.

Watzlawick, P., Beavin, J. H., & Jackson, D. D. (1967). *Pragmatics of human communications.* New York: Norton.

Weiner, H. D., Wallen, M. C., & Zankowski, G. L. (1990). Culture and social class as intervening variables in relapse prevention with chemically dependent women. *Journal of Psychoactive Drugs, 22,* 239-248.

Wells, L. E., & Rankin, J. H. (1991). Families and delinquency: A meta-analysis of the impact of broken homes. *Social Problems, 38,* 71-93.

Young, T. J. (1992). Substance abuse among Native American youth. In G. W. Lawson & A. W. Lawson (Eds.), *Adolescent substance abuse: Etiology, treatment, and prevention* (pp. 381-390). Gaithersburg, MD: Aspen.

## Suggested Readings

Bush, P. J., & Iannotti, R. J. (1987). The development of children's health orientation and behaviors: Lessons for substance use prevention. In C. L. Jones & R. J. Battjes (Eds.), *Research analysis and utilization system: Etiology of drug abuse, implication for prevention* (Research Monograph Series 56, pp. 45-74). Rockville, MD: NIDA.

Compas, B. E., & Wagner, B. M. (1991). Psychological stress during adolescence: Intraper-
sonal and interpersonal processes. In M. E. Colten & S. Gore (Eds.), *Adolescent stress:
Causes and consequences*. New York: Aldine de Gruyter.

Conger, R. D., Lorenz, F. P., Elder, G. H., Melby, J. N., Simons, R. L., & Conger, K. J. (1991).
A process model of family economic pressure and early adolescent alcohol use. *Journal of
Early Adolescence, 11*, 430-449.

Gerstein, D. R., & Harwood, H. J. (Eds.). (1990). *Treating drug problems, I*. Washington, DC:
National Academy Press.

Kaufman, E. (1985). Family systems and family therapy of substance abuse: An overview of
two decades of research and clinical experience. *International Journal of the Addictions,
20*, 897-916.

Lewis, R. A., et al. (1988). Purdue Brief Family Therapy Model for adolescent substance
abusers. In T. Todd & M. Selekman (Eds.), *Family therapy approaches with adolescent
substance abusers*. New York: Gardner.

Sessa, F. M., & Steinberg, L. (1991). Family structure and the development of autonomy during
adolescence. *Journal of Early Adolescence, 11*, 38-55.

Zimmerman, S., & Zimmerman, A. M. (1990). Genetic effects of marijuana. *The International
Journal of the Addiction, 25*, 19-33.

# 13

❁

# Family Violence, Abuse, and Neglect

RICHARD J. GELLES

In our society, people are more likely to be killed and physically assaulted, abused and neglected, and sexually assaulted and molested in their own homes and by other family members than anywhere else or by anyone else. Family life and the home traditionally have been viewed as warm, intimate, stress reducing—the place to which people flee for safety. In reality, the family is often the site of significant interpersonal and social stress that can lead to conflict and often to violence.

## Historical Patterns of Family Violence

Women and children have been subjected to physical violence throughout the history of society. In ancient times, infants had no rights until the "right to live" was bestowed upon them, typically as part of some formal cultural ritual carried out by their fathers (Radbill, 1980). When the right to live was withheld, infants were abandoned or left to die. Although we do not know how often children were killed or abandoned, we do know that infanticide was widely accepted among ancient and prehistoric cultures. Infanticide continued through the eighteenth and nineteenth centuries; even today illegitimate children continue to run the greatest risk of infanticide.

Killing children was not the only form of abuse inflicted by generations of parents. Since prehistoric times, children have been mutilated, beaten, and maltreated. Such treatment was not only condoned but often promoted as the most appropriate child-rearing method (Greven, 1991).

The subordinate status of women in the United States and in most of the world's societies is well documented. Because physical force and violence is the last resort in keeping subordinate groups in their place, the history of women in many societies has been one in which women have been victims of physical assault. A husband in ancient Rome could chastise, divorce, or kill his wife. Blackstone's codification of English common law in 1768 asserted that husbands had the right to "physically chastise" an errant wife, provided that the stick was no thicker than his thumb; thus the "rule of thumb" was born (Davidson, 1978; Pleck, 1987).

Siblings have also been the victims of family violence. The first case of family violence described in the Bible is Cain killing Abel. There has been less historical and current interest in sibling violence or violence toward men compared with concern about violence toward children and women in families. In part, this is because social concern for victims of family violence is tied to the perceived powerlessness and helplessness of the victims. Thus there is greater social concern for violence toward infants and young children than violence toward adolescents or adult men.

### Estimates of the
### Current Incidence and Frequency

Until the early 1960s, violence between family members was perceived to be rare and committed only by mentally ill or otherwise disturbed and defective individuals. Only the most sensational and lurid cases received public attention, and there was a general belief that, even though family violence was a significant problem, it was not widespread.

There are various forms of family violence, including the abuse and neglect of children, the sexual abuse of children, violence between spouses, abuse and neglect of the elderly, violence between siblings, and courtship violence and abuse. Various techniques have been used in attempts to achieve an accurate estimate of abuse and neglect in families in the United States. Researchers have examined official reports of child maltreatment, other official records, including police reports and clinical case records, and, finally, self-report survey data. Because of the various definitions of abuse and neglect, and the differing methodologies used to examine incidence and frequency, there are no definitive data on the extent of abuse and neglect in families. The following section briefly reviews some of the data for each of the major forms of family violence.

*Child maltreatment.* The National Center on Child Abuse and Neglect has conducted two surveys designed to measure the national incidence of reported and recognized child maltreatment (Burgdorf, 1980; NCCAN, 1988). A total of 1,025,900 maltreated children were identified by the agencies surveyed in 1988.

A second source of data on the extent of child maltreatment comes from the National Study of Child Neglect and Abuse Reporting conducted by the American Association for Protecting Children (1988, 1989). During 1987, the last year the survey was conducted, 2,178,384 children were reported to state agencies for suspected child abuse and neglect. Of these, it is estimated that 686,000 reports were substantiated by state Child Protective Service agencies.

The National Family Violence Surveys interviewed two nationally representative samples of families—2,146 family members in 1976 and 6,002 family members in 1985 (Gelles & Straus, 1987, 1988; Straus & Gelles, 1986; Straus, Gelles, & Steinmetz, 1980). Violence and abuse were measured by asking respondents to report on their own behavior toward their children in the previous 12 months. Milder forms of violence, violence that most people think of as physical punishment, were, of course, the most common. However, even the rates of severe violence were surprisingly high. Abusive violence was defined as acts that had a high probability of injuring the child. These included kicking, biting, punching, hitting or trying to hit a child with an object, beating up a child, burning or scalding, and threatening or using a gun or a knife. Slightly more than 2 parents in 100 (2.3%) admitted to engaging in one act of abusive violence during the year prior to the 1985 survey. Seven children in 1,000 were hurt as a result of an act of violence directed at them by a parent in the previous year. Projecting the rate of abusive violence to all children under the age of 18 years of age who live with one or both parents means that 1.5 million children experience acts of abusive physical violence each year, and 450,000 children are injured each year as a result of parental violence.

*Sexual abuse of children.* Among the most dramatic changes taking place over the last few decades has been the increased attention to child sexual abuse. In a comprehensive review of studies on the incidence and prevalence of child sexual abuse, Peters, Wyatt, and Finkelhor (1986) report that estimates of prevalence range from 6% to 62% for females and from 3% to 31% for males. They point out that this variation may be accounted for by a number of methodological factors, such as differences in definitions of abuse, sample characteristics, interview format (e.g., in-person versus phone interview), and number of questions used to elicit information about abuse experiences. However, even the most conservative estimates indicate that sexual abuse is a problem that affects large numbers of children.

*Child homicide.* Homicide is one of the five leading causes of death for children between the ages of 1 and 18 years. More than 1,300 children are killed by their parents or caretakers each year (Daro, 1992). Even with an estimate this high, researchers believe that homicides of infants are probably underrecorded in health statistics (Jason, Gilliland, & Tyler, 1983). Infants (from 1 week to 1 year of age) are most likely to be killed by a parent.

*Dating and courtship violence.* The virtues of romantic love, a phenomenon considered synonymous with American dating patterns, have been extolled in poems, songs, romance novels, television soap operas, and folklore. Sadly, along with the moonlight cruises, the first kiss, the flirtations, and affection, violence also is very much a part of American dating patterns. Studies that examine the possibility of violence in dating and courtship have found that between 10% and 67% of dating relationships involve violence (Sugarman & Hotaling, 1989). Researchers have found that the rate of severe violence among dating couples ranged from about 1% to 27% each year (Arias, Samios, & O'Leary, 1987; Lane & Gwartney-Gibbs, 1985; Makepeace, 1983).

*Spouse abuse.* The National Family Violence Surveys also examined violence between husbands and wives (Gelles & Straus, 1988; Straus & Gelles, 1986). In 16% of the homes surveyed, some kind of violence between spouses had occurred in the year prior to the survey. More than one in four (28%) of the couples reported marital violence at some point in their marriages. As with violence toward children, the milder forms of violence were the most common. More than 3 in 100 women were victims of abusive violence during the 12-month period prior to the interview in 1985. Wife beating is a pattern—not a single event in most violent households. On average, a woman who is a victim of wife abuse is abused three times each year.

*Homicide of intimates.* Researchers generally report that intrafamilial homicides account for between 20% and 40% of all murders (Curtis, 1974). About 680 husbands and boyfriends are killed by their wives and girlfriends each year, whereas more than 1,300 wives and girlfriends are slain by their husbands or boyfriends (U.S. Department of Justice, 1991).

*Elder abuse.* Pillemer and Finkelhor (1988) interviewed 2,020 community dwelling (noninstitutionalized) elderly persons in the Boston metropolitan area. Overall, 32 elderly persons per 1,000 reported experiencing physical violence, verbal aggression, and/or neglect in the past year. The rate of physical violence was 20 per 1,000 individuals. Although the conventional view of elder abuse is that of middle-aged children abusing and neglecting their elderly parents, Pillemer and Finkelhor found that spouses were the most frequent abusers of the elderly and that roughly equal numbers of men and women were victims. Women, however, were the victims of the most serious forms of abuse, such as punching, kicking, beating, and choking.

*Hidden violence: Siblings and parents.* Although parent-to-child and marital violence has received the most public attention, physical fights between brothers and sisters are by far the most common form of family violence. It is, however, rare that parents, physicians, or social workers consider sibling fighting as a problematic form of family violence. Violence between siblings often goes far beyond so-called normal violence; for example, at least 109,000 children use guns or knives in fights with siblings each year (Straus, Gelles, & Steinmetz, 1980).

Parents are also hidden victims of family violence. Each year, according to Straus and Gelles's national surveys, between 750,000 to 1 million parents experience violent acts against them by their teenage children (Cornell & Gelles, 1982).

### The Costs of Family Violence

Physical harm is but one consequence of violence in the home. There are emotional and social consequences as well. Widom (1989) reports that abused and neglected children have a higher likelihood of arrest for delinquency, adult criminality, and violent criminal behavior than children who were not abused and neglected.

Researchers have found that abused and neglected children have social and emotional deficits, including communication problems, poor performance in school, and learning disabilities (Starr, 1988). As adults, abused children have higher rates of drug and alcohol abuse, criminal behavior, and psychiatric disturbances (Smith, Hansen, & Nobel, 1973).

For women victims of domestic assault, the consequences also extend beyond physical injury. Research consistently reports a high incidence of depression and anxiety among samples of battered women as well as an increased risk of suicide attempts (Christopoulos et al., 1987; Gelles & Harrop, 1989; Hilberman, 1980; Schechter, 1983).

The consequences of family violence for society include days lost from work by victims of spouse abuse, medical care that victims require, and investment of time by social and criminal justice agencies. Domestic disturbance calls constitute the single largest category of police calls (Parnas, 1967).

## Factors Associated With Family Violence

The early thinking and writing on family violence was dominated by a mental illness model (Gelles, 1973). Abuse and neglect were thought to be caused by certain personality factors, such as immaturity or impulsiveness, or psychopathology. The assumption was that no psychologically normal person would physically abuse a wife or child. There are a number of problems with the psychopathological or mental illness model of family violence and abuse. First, most of the conclusions about the causes of family violence are based on studies of a limited number of cases, typically without comparison groups, that draw conclusions after the data are collected rather than testing hypotheses developed prior to data collection. Second, such an explanation results in the viewpoint that people who abuse their children or spouses have to be mentally ill because they would not have committed an outrageous act of violence or abuse if they were not mentally ill. A third problem is that the psychopathological model ignores the fact that certain societal factors are related to family violence. The remainder of this section examines those societal factors.

### Gender

Outside the American family, violent men clearly outnumber violent women. In the home, women are frequently as, or even more, violent than men. Not surprisingly, research on child abuse often finds that mothers are slightly more likely than fathers to abuse children (Gil, 1970; Parke & Collmer, 1975; Straus et al., 1980; Wolfner & Gelles, 1993). Of course, one obvious explanation for this gender difference is that mothers spend more time with their children than do fathers; thus they have more opportunity to be violent and abusive. Moreover, regardless of the amount of time parents spend with children, mothers tend to be the ones who have the greatest responsibility for child rearing. Margolin (1992) found that when one controls for the amount of responsibility mothers and fathers have for child care, males were more likely to be abusive.

There is considerable debate about the comparative rates of husband and wife violence. Although some investigators report that the rate of wife-to-husband violence is about the same as the rate of husband-to-wife violence (Straus & Gelles, 1986), others explain that women are the disproportionate victims of family violence (Dobash & Dobash, 1979; Dobash, Dobash, Wilson, & Daly, 1992). If one goes by how much harm is done, who initiates the violence, and how easy it is for a victim to escape violence, women clearly are the disproportionate victims of domestic violence.

Boys are the more violent siblings and offspring. Mothers and sisters are the more frequent targets of the young or adolescent boys' family violence.

### Social Characteristics

There are two persistent myths concerning the relationship between social class and family violence. The first is that violence is *confined* to lower-class families. Because the poor are more likely to go to emergency rooms or clinics, they are more likely to come to the attention of the authorities if their child is bruised or battered. Similarly, clinics or emergency rooms are the most likely source of medical aid for lower-class battered women.

The second myth, virtually the opposite of the first, is that family violence cuts evenly across the society. There is, of course, a grain of truth to this. Family violence does occur in virtually every social category, *but* the distribution is far from even. Gelles (1992) found that the rate of severe or abusive violence toward children was 30 per 1,000 children in families with incomes above the official poverty line, whereas for children in families with incomes below the poverty line, the rate was 105 per 1,000 children. Similarly, the rate of abusive husband-to-wife violence was twice as high among those couples with below poverty incomes compared with couples with incomes above the poverty line (Gelles, 1993).

Rates of family violence also vary by race. The rates of violence toward children and between husbands and wives are highest among Hispanics compared with blacks and whites, and higher among blacks compared with whites (Hampton & Gelles, 1991; Hampton, Gelles, & Harrop, 1989; Straus & Smith, 1990). For spouse abuse, the higher rates in Hispanic families reflect the economic deprivation, youthfulness, and urban residence of Hispanics, because when these factors are controlled, there is no statistically significant difference between Hispanics and non-Hispanic whites. However, in regard to violence toward children, the differences between Hispanics, blacks, and whites persist even when demographic and socioeconomic factors are controlled.

Rates of family violence are highest for urban families, people with no religious affiliation, people with some high school education, blue-collar workers, people under the age of 30, and in homes where the husband is unemployed (Gelles & Straus, 1988; Straus et al., 1980).

## Stress

The finding that homes where husbands are unemployed are the most likely to be violent suggests that stress is related to domestic assault. Financial problems, being a single parent, being a teenage mother, and sexual difficulties are all factors that are related to stress (Gelles, 1989; Gelles & Straus, 1988; Parke & Collmer, 1975; Straus et al., 1980).

## Social Isolation

People who are socially isolated from neighbors and relatives are more likely to be violent in the home. One major source of stress reduction and an insulator to family violence is being able to call on friends and family for help, aid, and assistance. The more a family is integrated into the community, the more groups and associations they belong to, the less likely they are to be violent (Milner & Chilamkurti, 1991; Straus et al., 1980).

## The Cycle of Violence

The notion that abused children grow up to be abusing parents and violent adults has been widely expressed in the child abuse and family violence literature (Gelles, 1980). Kaufman and Zigler (1987) reviewed the literature that tested the intergenerational transmission of violence hypothesis and concluded that the best estimate of the rate of intergenerational transmission appears to be 30% (plus or minus 5%). Although a rate of 30% intergenerational transmission is substantially less than the majority of abused children, the rate is considerably more than the rate of abuse of between 2% and 4% found in the general population (Straus & Gelles, 1986).

Evidence from studies of parental and marital violence indicate that, although experiencing violence in one's family of origin is often correlated with later violent behavior, such experience is not the sole determining factor. When the cycle of violence occurs, it is likely the result of a complex set of social and psychological processes.

## Factors Associated With Sexual Abuse of Children

There has been a great deal of research on the characteristics of sexual abusers, but current research has failed to isolate characteristics, especially demographic, social, or psychological characteristics, that discriminate between sexual abusers and nonabusers (Quinsey, 1984).

One of the key questions raised in discussions about sexual abuse is whether all children are at risk for sexual abuse or whether some children, because of some specific characteristic (e.g., age or poverty status), are at greater risk than others. In their review of studies on prevention, Finkelhor and Baron (1986) conclude that it is currently not clear what factors increase children's risk for sexual abuse. It appears that girls are at greater risk, although boys are also victimized. Girls are more likely to be victimized if they have sometime been separated from their mothers (e.g., ever lived away from mother, mother ill or disabled) or if they report poor relationships with their mothers. As the researchers note, these factors may be consequences of sexual abuse as much as risk factors. The data suggest the importance of mothers in protecting children from sexually aggressive men.

## Theoretical Perspectives

A number of sociological and psychological theories may help explain the causes of family violence. They include the following.

### Social Learning Theory

Social learning theory proposes that individuals who have experienced violence are more likely to use violence in the home than those who have experienced little or no violence. Children who either experience violence themselves or witness violence between their parents are more likely to use violence when they grow up. This finding has been interpreted to support the idea that family violence is learned. The family is the institution and social group in which people learn the roles of husband and wife, mother and father. The home is the prime location where people learn how to deal with various stresses, crises, and frustrations. In many instances, the home is also the site where a person first experiences violence. Not only do people learn violent behavior, but they learn how to justify being violent. For example, hearing a father say "this will hurt me more than it will hurt you," or a mother say, "you have been bad, so you deserve to be spanked," contributes to how children learn to justify violent behavior.

## Social Situation/Stress and Coping Theory

Social Situation/Stress and Coping Theory explains why violence is used in some situations and not others. The theory proposes that abuse and violence occur because of two main factors. The first is structural stress and the lack of coping resources in a family. For instance, the association between low income and family violence indicates that an important component in violence is inadequate financial resources. The second factor is the cultural norm concerning the use of force and violence. In contemporary American society, as well as many other societies, violence in general, and violence toward children in particular, is normative (Straus et al., 1980). Thus individuals learn to use violence both expressively and instrumentally as a means of coping with a pileup of stressor events.

## Resource Theory

Resource theory assumes that all social systems (including the family) rest to some degree on force or the threat of force. The more resources— social, personal, and economic—a person can command, the more force he or she can muster. However, the fewer resources a person has, the more he or she will actually use force in an open manner. Thus a husband who wants to be the dominant person in the family but has little education, has a job low in prestige and income, and lacks interpersonal skills may choose to use violence to maintain the dominant position. In addition, family members (including children) may use violence to redress a grievance when they have few alternative resources available. Thus wives who have few social resources or social contacts may use violence toward their husbands to protect themselves.

## Ecological Theory

Garbarino (1977) proposed an ecological model to explain the complex nature of child maltreatment. The ecological model proposes that violence and abuse arise out of a mismatch of parent to child or family to neighborhood and community. For example, parents who are under a great deal of social stress and have poor coping skills may have a difficult time meeting the needs of a child who is hyperactive. The risk of abuse and violence increases when the functioning of the children and parents is limited and constrained by developmental problems, such as children with learning disabilities and social or emotional handicaps, and when parents are under considerable stress or have personality problems, such as immaturity or impulsiveness. Finally, if there are few institutions and agencies in the community to support troubled families, then the risk of abuse is further increased.

## *Exchange Theory*

Exchange theory proposes that wife abuse and child abuse are governed by the principle of costs and benefits. Abuse is used when the rewards are greater than the costs (Gelles, 1983). The private nature of the family, the reluctance of social institutions and agencies to intervene—despite mandatory child abuse reporting laws—and the low risk of other interventions reduce the costs of abuse and violence. The cultural approval of violence as both expressive and instrumental behavior raises the potential rewards for violence. The most significant reward is social control or power.

## *Sociobiology Theory*

A sociobiological, or evolutionary, perspective on family violence suggests that violence toward human or nonhuman primate offspring is the result of the reproductive success potential of children and parental investment. The theory's central assumption is that natural selection is the process of differential reproduction and reproductive success (Daly & Wilson, 1980). For example, males and females can be expected to invest in offspring when there is some degree of parental certainty (how confident the parent is that the child is his or her own genetic offspring). Parents recognize their offspring and avoid squandering valuable reproductive effort on someone else's offspring. Children not genetically related to the parent (e.g., stepchildren, adopted, or foster children) or children with low reproductive potential (e.g., handicapped or retarded children) are at the highest risk for infanticide and abuse (Burgess & Garbarino, 1983; Daly & Wilson, 1980; Hrdy, 1979). Large families can dilute parental energy and lower attachment to children, thus increasing the risk of child abuse and neglect (Burgess, 1979).

Smuts (1992) applied an evolutionary perspective to male aggression against females. Smuts (1992), Daly and Wilson (1988), and Burgess and Draper (1989) argue that male aggression against females often reflects male reproductive striving. Both human and nonhuman male primates are postulated to use aggression against females to intimidate females so that they will not resist future male efforts to mate with them and to reduce the likelihood that females will mate with other males. Thus males use aggression to control female sexuality to the males' reproductive advantage. The frequency of male aggression varies across societies and situations depending on the strength of female alliances, the support women can receive from their families, the strength and importance of male alliances, the degree of equality in male-female relationships, and the degree to which males control the economic resources within a society. Male aggression toward females, both physical violence and rape, is high when female alliances are weak, when females lack kin support, when male alliances are strong, when male-female relationships are unbalanced, and when males control societal resources.

### Feminist Theory

Feminist theorists (e.g., Dobash & Dobash, 1979; Pagelow, 1984; Yllo, 1983, 1988) see wife abuse as a unique phenomenon that has been obscured and overshadowed by what they refer to as a "narrow" focus on domestic violence. The central thesis of feminist theory is that economic and social processes operate directly and indirectly to support a patriarchal (male-dominated) social order and family structure. Patriarchy is seen as leading to the subordination of women and causing the historical pattern of systematic violence directed against wives (see Chapter 2, "Issues of Gender," for a more comprehensive review of this perspective).

### A Model of Sexual Abuse

Finkelhor (1984) reviewed research on the factors that have been proposed as contributing to sexual abuse of children and has developed what he calls a "Four Precondition Model of Sexual Abuse." His review suggests that all the factors relating to sexual abuse can be grouped into one of four preconditions that need to be met before sexual abuse can occur. The preconditions are as follows:

1. A potential offender needs to have some motivation to abuse a child sexually.
2. The potential offender has to overcome internal inhibitions against acting on that motivation.
3. The potential offender has to overcome external impediments to committing sexual abuse.
4. The potential offender or some other factor has to undermine or overcome a child's possible resistance to sexual abuse.

## Interventions

### *Protecting Children*

By the late 1960s all 50 states had enacted mandatory reporting laws for child abuse and neglect. These laws require certain professionals (or, in some states, all adults) to report cases of suspected abuse or neglect. When a report comes in, state protective service workers investigate to determine if the family is in need of help or assistance. Although a wide array of options are available to public social workers, they typically have two basic ways of protecting victims of child abuse: (a) removing the children and placing them in a foster home or institution or (b) providing the family with social support, such as counseling, food stamps, or day-care services.

Neither solution is ideal, and there are risks in both. For instance, children may not understand why they are being removed from the home. Children who are removed from abusive homes may well be protected from physical damage but still suffer emotional harm. The emotional harm arises from the fact that abused children still love and have strong feelings for their parents and do not understand why they have been removed from their parents and homes. Often, abused children feel that they are responsible for their own abuse. Abused children frequently require special medical and/or psychological care, and it is difficult to find a suitable placement for them. They could well become a burden for foster parents or institutions that have to care for them. Therefore the risk of abuse might be even greater in a foster home or institution than in the home of the natural parents.

Leaving children in an abusive home and providing social services involves another type of risk. Most protective service workers are overworked, undertrained, and underpaid. Family services, such as crisis day care, financial assistance, suitable housing, and transportation services, are often limited. This can lead to cases in which children who were reported as abused, investigated by state agencies, and supervised by state agencies are killed during the period the family was supposedly being monitored. Half of all children who are killed by caretakers are killed *after* they have been reported to child welfare agencies.

Only a handful of evaluations have been made of prevention and treatment programs for child maltreatment. In Rochester, New York, Olds, Henderson, Tatelbaum, and Chamberlin (1986) evaluated the effectiveness of a family support program during pregnancy and for the first 2 years after birth for low-income, unmarried, teenage first-time mothers. Of a sample of poor unmarried teenage girls who received no services during their pregnancy period, 19% were reported for subsequent child maltreatment. However, of those children of poor, unmarried, teenage mothers who were provided with the full complement of nurse "home visits" during the mother's pregnancy and for the first 2 years after birth, 4% had confirmed cases of child abuse and neglect reported to the state child protection agency.

Daro and Cohn (1988) reviewed evaluations of 88 child maltreatment programs that were funded by the federal government between 1974 and 1982. They found that there was no noticeable correlation between a given set of services and the likelihood of further maltreatment of children. In fact, the more services a family received, the worse the family got and the more likely children were to be maltreated. Lay counseling, group counseling, and parent education classes resulted in more positive treatment outcomes. The optimal treatment period appeared to be between 7 and 18 months. The projects that were successful in reducing abuse accomplished this by separating children from abusive parents, either by placing them in foster homes or by requiring the maltreating adult to move out of the house.

## Protecting Women

There are a number of options available to women who want either to escape violence or to force their husbands to cease abusing them. One option is to call the police. The best-known assessment of intervention into marital violence is the Minneapolis Police Experiment (Sherman & Berk, 1984). This study was designed to examine whether arresting husbands for wife beating would decrease the risk of further abuse. This study called for the police to randomly assign incidents of misdemeanor family assaults to one of three treatments: arrest, separation, or advice/mediation. Those households receiving the arrest intervention had the lowest rate (10%) of recidivism (relapse into violent behavior) and those who were separated had the highest (24%).

Replications of the Minneapolis study, however, found that, contrary to the evidence from Minneapolis, arrest had no more effect in deterring future arrests or complaints of violence than did separation or counseling (Berk, Campbell, Klap, & Western, 1992; Dunford, Huizinga, & Elliott, 1990; Pate & Hamilton, 1992; Sherman & Smith, 1992). The replications did find that men who were employed when they were arrested were less likely to be violent after arrested compared with men who were not arrested. However, men who were unemployed when they were arrested were actually more likely to be violent after they were arrested compared with unemployed men who were not arrested.

A second possibility is for the wife to go to a shelter or safe house. *If* a shelter is nearby, *if* the woman knows how to get to it, and *if* there is room, shelters provide physical protection, social support, counseling, legal aid, and even occupational counseling. Shelters are the most cost-efficient form of intervention into wife battering. Researchers find that the effects of shelters seem to depend on the attributes of the victims. When a victim is actively engaged in taking control of her life, a shelter stay can dramatically reduce the likelihood of new violence. For some victims, a shelter stay may have no impact, whereas for others, it may actually lead to an escalation of violence when they return home (Berk, Newton, & Berk, 1986). Bowker (1983) talked to women who had been beaten and who managed to get their husbands to stop being violent. Among the things these women did were to talk to friends and relatives, threaten their husbands, aggressively defend themselves from their husbands, go to shelters, call social service agencies, call the police, and various other actions. No one action worked best. Bowker concluded that, ultimately, the crucial factor was the woman taking a stand and showing her determination that the violence had to stop.

Researchers have also evaluated group programs developed for violent men. Dutton (1986) reports that 50 men enrolled in a court-mandated program and followed for up to 3 years had recidivism rates as low as 4%. Gondolf (1987) reports that men who complete voluntary programs show nonviolence rates of two thirds to three quarters. Results of assessments of men's groups must be read cautiously because such groups tend to have low recruitment rates and high attrition rates (Pirog-Good & Stets, 1986). The more optimistic findings typically apply only to those men who complete counseling programs.

### Prevention

At present, the vast majority of programs, such as shelters, crisis daycare centers, police intervention programs, and parents support groups, aimed at dealing with family violence are treatment programs that are implemented *after* the abusive incident. What is needed, and what has not been attempted on any large scale, are services that would prevent violence and abuse before they begin. But such prevention programs require sweeping changes in both the society and the family. After the conclusion of their national survey of family violence, Straus et al. (1980) proposed the following steps for the *prevention of violence*:

1. Eliminate the norms that legitimize and glorify violence in the society and the family.
2. Reduce violence-provoking stress created by society.
3. Integrate families into a network of kin and community.
4. Change the sexist character of society.
5. Break the cycle of violence in the family.

In summary, violence, abuse, and neglect in families can be reduced by policies and programs that are directed at reducing stress in families, providing increased resources and sources of social support to help families cope with stress, and eliminating cultural norms that support the use of violence toward intimates as a coping mechanism.

## References

American Association for Protecting Children. (1988). *Highlights of official child neglect and abuse reporting, 1986*. Denver, CO: American Humane Association.

American Association for Protecting Children. (1989). *Highlights of official child neglect and abuse reporting, 1987*. Denver, CO: American Humane Association.

Arias, I., Samios, M., & O'Leary, K. D. (1987). Prevalence and correlates of physical aggression during courtship. *Journal of Interpersonal Violence, 2*, 82-90.

Berk, R. A., Campbell, A., Klap, R., & Western, B. (1992). The deterrent effect of arrest incidents of domestic violence: A Bayesian analysis of four field experiments. *American Sociological Review, 57*, 698-708.

Berk, R. A., Newton, P., & Berk, S. F. (1986). What a difference a day makes: An empirical study of the impact of shelters for battered women. *Journal of Marriage and the Family, 48*, 481-490.

Bowker, L. H. (1983). *Beating wife beating*. Lexington, MA: Lexington Books.

Burgdorf, K. (1980). *Recognition and reporting of child maltreatment*. Rockville, MD: Westat.

Burgess, R. L. (1979). *Family violence: Some implications from evolutionary biology*. Paper presented at the annual meetings of the American Society of Criminology, Philadelphia.

Burgess, R. L., & Draper, P. (1989). The explanation of family violence: The role of biological, behavioral, and cultural selection. In L. Ohlin & M. Tonry (Eds.), *Family violence: Crime and justice: A review of research* (Vol. 11, pp. 59-116). Chicago: University of Chicago Press.

Burgess, R. L., & Garbarino, J. (1983). Doing what comes naturally? An evolutionary perspective on child abuse. In D. Finkelhor, R. Gelles, M. Straus, & G. Hotaling (Eds.), *The dark side of the families: Current family violence research* (pp. 88-101). Beverly Hills, CA: Sage.

Christopoulos, C., Cohn, D. A., Shaw, D. S., Joyce, S., Sullivan-Hanson, J., Kraft, S. P., & Emery, R. (1987). Children of abused women: Adjustment at time of shelter residence. *Journal of Marriage and the Family, 49,* 611-619.

Cornell, C. P., & Gelles, R. J. (1982). Adolescent to parent violence. *Urban Social Change Review, 15,* 8-14.

Curtis, L. (1974). *Criminal violence: National patterns and behavior.* Lexington, MA: Lexington Books.

Daly, M., & Wilson, M. (1980). Discriminative parental solicitude: A biosocial perspective. *Journal of Marriage and the Family, 42,* 277-288.

Daly, M., & Wilson, M. (1988). *Homicide.* New York: Aldine de Gruyter.

Daro, D. (1992). *Current trends in child abuse reporting and fatalities: NCPCA's 1991 Annual Fifty State Survey.* Chicago: National Committee for Prevention of Child Abuse.

Daro, D., & Cohn, A. H. (1988). Child maltreatment evaluations efforts: What have we learned? In G. T. Hotaling, D. Finkelhor, J. T. Kirkpatrick, & M. A. Straus (Eds.), *Coping with family violence: Research and policy perspectives* (pp. 275-287). Newbury Park, CA: Sage.

Davidson, T. (1978). *Conjugal crime: Understanding and changing the wifebeating pattern.* New York: Hawthorn.

Dobash, R. E., & Dobash, R. (1979). *Violence against wives.* New York: Free Press.

Dobash, R. P., Dobash, R. E., Wilson, M., & Daly, M. (1992). The myth of sexual symmetry in marital violence. *Social Problems, 39,* 71-91.

Dunford, F. W., Huizinga, D., & Elliott, D. S. (1990). The role of arrest in domestic assault: The Omaha Police Experiment. *Criminology, 28,* 183-206.

Dutton, D. G. (1986). The outcome of court-mandated treatment for wife assault: A quasi-experimental evaluation. *Violence and Victims, 1,* 163-176.

Finkelhor, D. (1984). *Child sexual abuse: New theory and research.* New York: Free Press.

Finkelhor, D., & Baron, L. (1986). High risk children. In D. Finkelhor (Ed.), *A sourcebook on child sexual abuse* (pp. 60-88). Beverly Hills, CA: Sage.

Garbarino, J. (1977). The human ecology of child maltreatment. *Journal of Marriage and the Family, 39,* 721-735.

Gelles, R. J. (1973). Child abuse as psychopathology: A sociological critique and reformulation. *American Journal of Orthopsychiatry, 43,* 611-621.

Gelles, R. J. (1980). Violence in the family: A review of research in the seventies. *Journal of Marriage and the Family, 42,* 873-885.

Gelles, R. J. (1983). An exchange/social control theory. In D. Finkelhor, R. Gelles, M. Straus, & G. Hotaling (Eds.), *The dark side of families: Current family violence research* (pp. 151-165). Beverly Hills, CA: Sage.

Gelles, R. J. (1989). Child abuse and violence in single parent families: Parent-absence and economic deprivation. *American Journal of Orthopsychiatry, 59,* 492-501.

Gelles, R. J. (1992). Poverty and violence toward children. *American Behavioral Scientist, 35,* 258-274.

Gelles, R. J. (1993). *Husband to wife violence by income.* Unpublished mimeograph.

Gelles, R. J., & Harrop, J. W. (1989). Violence, battering, and psychological distress among women. *Journal of Interpersonal Violence, 4,* 400-420.

Gelles, R. J., & Straus, M. A. (1987). Is violence towards children increasing? A comparison of 1975 and 1985 national survey rates. *Journal of Interpersonal Violence, 2,* 212-222.

Gelles, R. J., & Straus, M. A. (1988). *Intimate violence.* New York: Simon & Schuster.

Gil, D. G. (1970). *Violence against children: Physical child abuse in the United States.* Cambridge, MA: Harvard University Press.

Gondolf, E. W. (1987). Evaluating progress for men who batter: Problems and prospects. *Journal of Family Violence, 2,* 95-108.

Greven, P. (1991). *Spare the child: The religious roots of punishment and the psychological impact of physical abuse.* New York: Knopf.

Hampton, R. L., & Gelles, R. J. (1991). A profile of violence toward black children. In R. L. Hampton (Ed.), *Black family violence* (pp. 21-34). Lexington, MA: Lexington Books.

Hampton, R. L., Gelles, R. J., & Harrop, J. W. (1989). Is violence in black families increasing: A comparison of 1975 and 1985 national survey rates. *Journal of Marriage and the Family, 51,* 969-980.

Hilberman, E. (1980). Overview: "The wife-beater's wife" reconsidered. *American Journal of Psychiatry, 137,* 1336-1346.

Hrdy, S. B. (1979). Infanticide among animals: A review classification, and examination of the implications for reproductive strategies of females. *Ethology and Sociobiology, 1,* 13-40.

Jason, J., Gilliland, J., & Tyler, C., Jr. (1983). Homicide as a cause of pediatric mortality in the United States. *Pediatrics, 72,* 191-197.

Kaufman, J., & Zigler, E. (1987). Do abused children become abusive parents? *American Journal of Orthopsychiatry, 57,* 186-192.

Lane, K. E., & Gwartney-Gibbs, P. A. (1985). Violence in the context of dating and sex. *Journal of Family Issues, 6,* 45-59.

Makepeace, J. M. (1983). Life events stress and courtship violence. *Family Relations, 32,* 101-109.

Margolin, L. (1992). Beyond maternal blame: Physical child abuse as a phenomenon of gender. *Journal of Family Issues, 13,* 410-423.

Milner, J. S., & Chilamkurti, C. (1991). Physical child abuse perpetrator characteristics: A review of the literature. *Journal of Interpersonal Violence, 6,* 345-366.

National Center on Child Abuse and Neglect. (1988). *Study findings: Study of national incidence and prevalence of child abuse and neglect: 1988.* Washington, DC: U.S. Department of Health and Human Services.

Olds, D. L., Henderson, C. R., Jr., Tatelbaum, R., & Chamberlin, R. (1986). Preventing child abuse and neglect: A randomized trial of nurse home visitation. *Pediatrics, 77,* 65-78.

Pagelow, M. (1981). *Women battering: Victims and their experiences.* Beverly Hills, CA: Sage.

Pagelow, M. (1984). *Family violence.* New York: Praeger.

Parke, R. D., & Collmer, C. W. (1975). Child abuse: An interdisciplinary analysis. In M. Hetherington (Ed.), *Review of child development research* (Vol. 5, pp. 1-102). Chicago: University of Chicago Press.

Parnas, R. (1967). The police response to domestic disturbance. *Wisconsin Law Review, 914,* 914-960.

Pate, A. M., & Hamilton, E. E. (1992). Formal and informal social deterrents to domestic violence: The Dade County Spouse Assault Experiment. *American Sociological Review, 57,* 691-697.

280                                                                      Situational Stressors

Peters, S. D., Wyatt, G. E., & Finkelhor, D. (1986). Prevalence. In D. Finkelhor (Ed.), *A sourcebook on child sexual abuse* (pp. 15-59). Beverly Hills, CA: Sage.

Pillemer, K., & Finkelhor, D. (1988). The prevalence of elder abuse: A random sample survey. *The Gerontologist, 28,* 51-57.

Pirog-Good, M. A., & Stets, J. (1986). Programs for abusers: Who drops out and what can be done. *Response, 9,* 17-19.

Pleck, E. (1987). *Domestic tyranny: The making of American social policy against family violence from colonial times to the present.* New York: Oxford University Press.

Quinsey, V. L. (1984). Sexual aggression: Studies of offenders against women. In D. N. Weisstub (Ed.), *Law and mental health: International perspectives* (Vol. 1, pp. 84-121). New York: Pergamon.

Radbill, S. A. (1980). A history of child abuse and infanticide. In R. Helfer & C. Kempe (Eds.), *The battered child* (3rd ed., pp. 3-20). Chicago: University of Chicago Press.

Schechter, S. (1983). *Women and male violence.* Boston: South End.

Sherman, L. W., & Berk, R. A. (1984). The specific deterrent effects of arrest for domestic assault. *American Sociological Review, 49,* 261-272.

Sherman, L. W., & Smith, D. A. (1992). Crime, punishment, and stake in conformity: Legal and informal control of domestic violence. *American Sociological Review, 57,* 680-690.

Smith, S., Hansen, R., & Nobel, S. (1973). Parents of battered babies: A controlled study. *British Medical Journal, 5,* 388-391.

Smuts, B. (1992). Male aggression against women: An evolutionary perspective. *Human Nature, 3,* 1-44.

Starr, R. H., Jr. (1988). Physical abuse of children. In V. B. Van Hasselt, R. L. Morrison, A. S. Bellack, & M. Hersen (Eds.), *Handbook of family violence* (pp. 119-155). New York: Plenum.

Straus, M. A., & Gelles, R. J. (1986). Societal change and change in family violence from 1975 to 1985 as revealed in two national surveys. *Journal of Marriage and the Family, 48,* 465-479.

Straus, M. A., Gelles, R. J., & Steinmetz, S. K. (1980). *Behind closed doors: Violence in the American family.* New York: Doubleday/Anchor.

Straus, M. A., & Smith, C. (1990). Violence in Hispanic families in the United States: Incidence rates and structural interpretations. In M. A. Straus & R. J. Gelles (Eds.), *Physical violence in American families: Risk factors and adaptations in 8,145 families* (pp. 341-367). New Brunswick, NJ: Transaction.

Sugarman, D. B., & Hotaling, G. T. (1989). Dating violence: Prevalence, context, and risk factors. In M. A. Pirog-Good & J. E. Stets (Eds.), *Violence in dating relationships* (pp. 3-32). New York: Praeger.

U.S. Department of Justice. (1991). *Uniform crime reports for the United States, 1991.* Washington, DC: U.S. Department of Justice, Federal Bureau of Investigation.

Widom, C. S. (1989). The cycle of violence. *Science, 244,* 160-166.

Wolfner, G., & Gelles, R. J. (1993). A profile of violence toward children. *Child Abuse and Neglect: The International Journal, 17,* 197-212.

Yllo, K. (1983). Using a feminist approach in quantitative research. In D. Finkelhor, R. Gelles, M. Straus, & G. Hotaling (Eds.), *The dark side of families: Current family violence research* (pp. 277-288). Beverly Hills, CA: Sage.

Yllo, K. (1988). Political and methodological debates in wife abuse research. In K. Yllo & M. Bograd (Eds.), *Feminist perspectives on wife abuse* (pp. 28-50). Newbury Park, CA: Sage.

# 14

# Homelessness

ELIZABETH W. LINDSEY

During the 1980s, homelessness emerged as a major social problem. Historically, homeless persons were primarily men who were invisible to society because they generally lived in "Skid Row" areas. By the early 1980s, a "new homeless group" became visible as people began sleeping in such public places as streets, doorways, and railroad or bus stations (Rossi, 1989). One of the most striking aspects of this new homeless population was the increasing prevalence of homeless women and entire families (Rossi, 1989).

Estimates of the prevalence of homelessness have ranged from 250,000 (U.S. Department of Housing and Urban Development, 1984) to 3 million (Hoombs & Snyder, 1982). Using a national probability sampling of urban homeless households, Burt and Cohen (1989) estimated that 500,000-600,000 people were homeless on a single day in March 1987. Of these households, 73% were single men, 9% were single women, and 9% were women accompanied by children. Burt and Cohen estimated that 37% of all shelter beds were being used by homeless family members—a figure that is similar to the most recent HUD estimate of 36% (U.S. Department of Housing & Urban Development, 1989).

Annual surveys of 28 large cities indicate that the percentage of the homeless population comprising families is rising rapidly. Between 1985 and 1989, the percentage of homeless families increased from 25% to 36%

of the total homeless population (Reyes & Waxman, 1986, 1989b). Shelter requests by families rose by 32% in 1987 and by 22% in 1988, whereas overall requests for shelter only rose by 21% and 13%, respectively (Reyes & Waxman, 1989a).

Approximately 80% of all homeless families are headed by single parents, primarily women, although there are regional differences (Reyes & Waxman, 1989a). In the East, a majority of homeless families are headed by women (e.g., Bassuk, Rubin, & Lauriat, 1986; Ryan, Goldstein, & Bartelt, 1989), whereas there tend to be more two-parent families in the West (e.g., Reyes & Waxman, 1989b; van Ry, 1993; Wood, Valdez, Hayashi, & Shen, 1990). Two-parent families also constitute the majority of homeless families in some rural areas (Patton, 1988, Appendix C), although little is known about these families as most studies have been conducted in urban areas. According to Mihaly (1991), families with children currently make up the fastest growing segment of the homeless population.

This chapter will review the literature on homeless female-headed families, including characteristics of mothers and children, housing histories, precipitants of homelessness, its impact on family life, and services for homeless families. Theories that have been suggested to explain homelessness among this population will also be discussed.

## Characteristics of Homeless Mothers

Studies of homeless mothers have focused on demographic characteristics, work history, and personal problems that may be related to homelessness. Although primarily descriptive in nature, some studies imply that certain characteristics of the mothers constitute causal factors leading to homelessness.

### Demographic Characteristics

The average homeless mother is in her late twenties (Bassuk et al., 1986; Dail, 1990; McChesney, 1987; Shinn, Knickman, & Weitzman, 1991) and has two children (Burt & Cohen, 1989; Dail, 1990; Goodman, 1991a). Many of these women became mothers as teenagers. Homeless women are also more likely to be pregnant or to have had a child in the last year than low-income housed women (Shinn et al., 1991).

Female heads of homeless families tend to be single, divorced, or separated from their husbands. Reports of single marital status have ranged from 70% (Goodman, 1991a) to 28% (Anderson, Boe, & Smith, 1988), but most studies report the majority of mothers are either single or never married (Bassuk & Rosenberg, 1988; Burt & Cohen, 1989; Mills & Ota, 1989; Shinn et al., 1991). Estimates of women who are divorced or separated range from 64% (Anderson et al., 1988) to 18% (Burt & Cohen, 1989).

The racial distribution of homeless families tends to reflect the percentage of poor persons in a given location (Bassuk, 1990), with some studies finding predominantly white samples (Dail, 1990; Goodman, 1991a) and others finding a majority of African Americans (Johnson & Kreuger, 1989; Mills & Ota, 1989; Shinn et al., 1991). In their national probability sample, which may be less prone to some of the regional racial biases of other studies, Burt and Cohen (1989) found that 83% of homeless women with children were nonwhite. However, because this study includes only urban areas, it probably overrepresents poor people who live in inner cities and does not account for rural homeless families.

Homeless mothers tend to have limited education. High school graduation rates for homeless female heads of household range from 25% to 43% (Bassuk & Rosenberg, 1988; Burt & Cohen, 1989; Goodman, 1991a; Shinn et al., 1991). Homeless women who became mothers as teenagers are likely to have completed fewer years of school than women who became mothers for the first time after their teen years (Bassuk et al., 1986; Mills & Ota, 1989).

### Work History and Income Sources

Many homeless mothers have highly inconsistent work histories. Bassuk et al. (1986) found that only one third of their sample had held a job for longer than 1 month. Goodman (1991a) found that 30% of respondents had worked less than 2 years and 56% for over 5 years. Burt and Cohen (1989) found that 51% of homeless mothers had been jobless for 2 or more years, with a mean of 46 months of joblessness.

The inconsistent work records of these mothers are reflected in their sources of income. Homeless women with children are less likely than single homeless men or women to rely on earned income and more likely to rely on public assistance. Burt and Cohen (1989) reported that 69% of homeless female heads of household received either AFDC or General Assistance, and 53% received food stamps. Other studies have found similarly high proportions of homeless mothers relying on public assistance (Bassuk et al., 1986; Goodman, 1991a; Mills & Ota, 1989).

*Substance Abuse and Mental Illness*

Estimates of substance abuse rates among homeless mothers range from 9% to 25% (Anderson et al., 1988; Bassuk et al., 1986; Mills & Ota, 1989; Weitzman, Knickman, & Shinn, 1990), and estimates of psychiatric problems range from 4% to 18% (Anderson et al., 1988; Bassuk et al., 1986; Mills & Ota, 1989; Weitzman et al., 1990). One study involving actual psychiatric evaluations rather than self-reports found that 27% of homeless mothers suffered from a major psychiatric syndrome (Bassuk & Rosenberg, 1988; Bassuk et al., 1986), but only 24% of these women had current contact with the mental health system. Goodman (1991a) found no difference between low-income housed and homeless mothers on a clinical depression assessment, but the rate was 68% for the entire sample, indicating that low-income women, in general, are at high risk for depression.

However, mental illness and substance abuse do not appear to be present among homeless mothers to the extent they do in the larger homeless population. Johnson and Kreuger (1989) found that homeless mothers were significantly less likely to have been treated for mental illness or to have been told they have a drinking problem than were women without children. Burt and Cohen (1989) found substantially higher rates of psychiatric disturbance and substance abuse among single men, single women, and women with children than in the general population. However, among these three groups, women with children had the lowest rates of chemical dependency treatment, psychiatric hospitalization, and attempted suicide. Homeless mothers scored highest on measures of clinical depression, but all three groups scored more than double the mean for American adults, which the authors in general attribute to the psychologically distressing state of being homeless.

*History of Family Disruptions and Physical or Sexual Abuse*

Many homeless women have had extremely traumatic childhoods and/or adult relationships. Homeless mothers are more likely than housed low-income women to report six traumatic experiences in childhood: (a) lived in foster care, (b) lived in a group home or institution, (c) lived on the street or other public place, (d) ran away from home for a week or more, (e) was physically abused, and (f) was sexually abused (Shinn et al., 1991). Bassuk et al. (1986) found that 33% of homeless mothers had never known their fathers and that more than 66% had experienced at least one major family disruption during childhood; 50% of these disruptions were a result of separation or divorce of parents, and the rest were a result of death, mental illness, alcoholism of parent, or abuse resulting in placement outside the home. One third reported physical abuse by their parents, and 11% reported having been sexually abused as a child. In their comparison of the sample of homeless mothers with a group of housed poor mothers, Bassuk and Rosenberg (1988) found similar proportions of housed (57%) and homeless (69%) women reporting a major family disruption, although childhood abuse was more frequently reported by homeless women.

    Anderson et al. (1988) reported similar findings in their study of homeless women in Portland: 69% (a majority of whom had children living with them) had been physically abused at some point in their lives—19% as children and 53% as adults—and 48% reported having been sexually abused—28% as children (many were victims of incest) and 22% as adults (many having been raped by their husbands). Another study found no difference in rates of childhood physical or sexual abuse between low-income housed and homeless mothers, although housed women were more likely to have been sexually abused as adults (Goodman, 1991a). However, only 11% of the entire sample had not been physically or sexually abused at some point in their lives, leading Goodman (1991a) to conclude that "women who are poor are unlikely to escape some form of physical violation" (p. 497).

    In summary, homeless female heads of household tend to be young mothers with two or three children. They are poorly educated and have inconsistent work records, relying primarily on public assistance rather than earned income. A large percentage of these mothers have never been married. The racial composition of homeless families reflects the racial composition of the poverty population in the geographic area studied. Although many of these mothers experience substance abuse and psychiatric problems, these are at a lower rate than the general homeless population. There is a high rate of prevalence of sexual and physical abuse among these mothers, both as children and as adults. Many of the problems homeless mothers face are similar to those of housed low-income mothers, and the nature of a possible causal relationship between these problems and homelessness is still undetermined.

## Characteristics of Homeless Children

    Children form the largest growing segment of the homeless population (Reyes & Waxman, 1989b). The average age of children in female-headed homeless families is around 6 years (Dail, 1990) with a majority of children of preschool age (Bassuk & Rubin, 1987; Burt & Cohen, 1989; Hall & Maza, 1990; Johnson, 1989). These children are at grave risk for various health, developmental, psychological, and educational problems.

## Health Problems

Health problems for homeless children begin before birth. Only 60% of homeless women in a New York City sample received even minimal prenatal care as compared with 85% of housed poor women (Chavin, Kristal, Seabron, & Guigli, 1987). These women were more likely to have low birth weight babies and had an infant mortality rate of 25 per 1,000 live births as compared with 17 per 1,000 live births for housed low-income women.

Homeless children suffer from malnutrition (Molnar, Rath, & Klein, 1990), elevated lead levels (Alperstein, Rappaport, & Flanigan, 1988; Bernstein, Alperstein, & Fierman, 1988), and iron deficiencies (Acker, Fierman, & Dreyer, 1987) and are less likely to be immunized than other children (Alperstein et al., 1988; Miller & Lin, 1988; Redlener, 1988). Rates of pregnancy, alcoholism, substance abuse, and psychiatric disorders are higher for homeless teenagers (Wright, 1990). Homeless children suffer from common childhood disorders such as upper respiratory infections and ear infections at a much higher rate than in the general population and have higher rates of chronic physical disorders such as cardiac disease, anemia, and neurological disorders (Wright, 1990). Factors that contribute to these health problems include inadequate diet, poor facilities for personal hygiene, exposure to the elements, communal sleeping and bathing arrangements, and lack of health insurance.

## Developmental Problems

Serious developmental delays have been found in preschool-age homeless children. In one sample, 50% showed evidence of developmental lags in such areas as language skills, personal/social development, gross motor skills, and fine motor coordination (Bassuk & Rubin, 1987). Other studies have documented poor cognitive and language abilities (Wagner & Menke, 1990; Whitman, Stretch, & Accardo, 1987).

Studies that compare homeless and low-income housed preschoolers report significant differences between the two groups in some aspects of development, but not in others (Molnar et al., 1990; Rescorla, Parker, & Stolley, 1991). However, Bassuk and Rosenberg (1988) found that 54% of homeless preschoolers manifested at least one developmental lag compared with 16% of housed children.

While poverty is a key mediator of developmental delays in both poor housed and homeless children, the condition of homelessness itself contributes to the delays. Inadequate shelter conditions, lack of access to quality day care or other stimulation programs, instability in child-care arrangements, and the effects of homelessness on parents are mediators of developmental problems in homeless children (Rafferty & Shinn, 1991).

*Psychological Problems*

The most frequently reported psychological problems for homeless children are anxiety, depression, and behavioral problems, but the findings are somewhat inconsistent. High levels of anxiety and depression have been reported, with 50% of the children in three samples in need of psychiatric evaluation and/or treatment (Bassuk, 1990; Bassuk et al., 1986; Wagner & Menke, 1990). Although 25% of homeless children in one study were reported by their mothers as having emotional problems, only 9% were in therapy (Bassuk & Rubin, 1987). Wagner and Menke (1990) found that 35% of homeless children aged 7 to 12 were clinically depressed (boys being somewhat more depressed than girls). Molnar (1988) found serious behavior problems among a sample of homeless preschoolers, including short attention span, withdrawal, and aggression.

Some comparison studies of low-income housed and homeless children reported no significant differences between the two groups on depression (Masten, 1990) or parental reports of behavior problems (Masten, 1990; Molnar et al., 1990; Wood, Hayashi, Schlossman, & Valdez, 1989). Other studies have found only minor or statistically insignificant differences between the two groups (Bassuk & Rosenberg, 1988; Rescorla et al., 1991).

Inconsistencies in these findings may be a result of small sample sizes, lack of adequate comparison groups, and other methodological problems (Rafferty & Shinn, 1991). However, it is clear that both poor and homeless children are at risk for anxiety, depression, and behavioral problems. Homeless children are at even greater risk than housed poor children because homelessness makes it even more difficult for them to secure adequate health care, nutrition, and shelter, all of which affect psychological health. Furthermore, homeless mothers often are not equipped to handle their children's psychological problems.

*Education*

Homeless children often manifest serious difficulties in school. Estimated school attendance rates range from 43% (National Coalition for the

Homeless, 1987) to 57% (Hall & Maza, 1990) to 70% (U.S. Department of Education, 1989). Homeless children have poorer attendance than housed children at all grade levels, and attendance declines more rapidly for homeless children as grade level increases (Rafferty & Rollins, 1989).

When homeless children do attend school, often they do not perform well academically. Only 42.3% of homeless children in grades 3-10 scored at or above grade level in reading compared with 68% of all New York City students (Rafferty & Rollins, 1989). The comparable figures for math were 28% for homeless children and 57% for the general student population. Shaffer and Caton (1984) reported that 50% of their sample of 10- to 17-year-olds scored 1 standard deviation below the norm in reading. Bassuk et al. (1986) found that 25% of homeless children were in special education programs, compared with 10.9% of all U.S. students enrolled in special education classes (Hallahan & Kauffman, 1988).

Poor performance often leads to school failure. Estimates of grade retention among homeless children range from 30% (Hall & Maza, 1990) to 43% (Bassuk et al., 1986; Rafferty & Rollins, 1989), with boys somewhat more likely to be retained than girls (Shaffer & Caton, 1984). Several studies have found homeless children more likely to have been retained than housed poor children (Masten, 1990; Wood et al., 1989), but Rescorla et al. (1991) found similar retention rates among housed and homeless children.

Rafferty and Shinn (1991) cited several barriers to education for homeless children. These included residency and guardianship requirements, problems in obtaining school records, and lack of transportation, clothes, supplies, and health services.

In conclusion, homeless children are at risk for developing health, developmental, psychological, and educational problems. These risk factors are all related, and problems in one area are likely to lead to or compound problems in another area. The fact that children who are at risk for such serious problems compose the fastest growing segment of the homeless population poses a serious challenge for society at large and, more specifically, for institutions responsible for child education and welfare.

## Housing Histories

Female-headed homeless families tend to have unstable housing histories. Bassuk et al. (1986) found that most families had moved more than three times in the year before becoming homeless, with an average of six moves in the past 5 years. For many families, the condition of homelessness is not a one-time experience. Estimates of families who have had multiple shelter experiences range from 34.3% (Shinn et al., 1991) to 60% (van Ry, 1993) to 67% (Bassuk & Rosenberg, 1988).

Applying for entrance to a shelter is usually a last resort—a step only taken when mothers have exhausted other resources such as family or friends. Bassuk and Rosenberg (1988) found only 14% of female-headed families were living independently just prior to requesting shelter. Dail (1990) reported that 50% of her sample had been living in an apartment or home prior to coming into shelter, whereas the remaining 50% had been living with friends or relatives for up to a year. Bassuk et al. (1986) found that 85% of families had been "doubled or tripled up" with family or friends before becoming homeless.

Women with children tend to have shorter current episodes of homelessness than single women or men (Burt & Cohen, 1989). For example, 70% of families were homeless 12 months or less, compared with 64% of single women and 49% of single men. Women with children were homeless for an average of 15 months.

## Events Leading to Homelessness

Precipitants of homelessness fall into several categories: (a) economic events such as eviction, inability to pay rent, or job loss; (b) relationship events including women leaving abusive situations and disagreements with friends or relatives with whom they were living; and (c) unsafe living conditions such as a house fire, drug use or sales, condemned structures, or lack of heat or electricity. In a Detroit study, the most frequently cited precipitant was eviction or inability to pay rent (47.1%), followed by domestic conflict (21.8%), and unsafe living conditions (20.7%) (Mills & Ota, 1989). Hall and Maza (1990) reported that the main reason for homelessness among their sample of St. Louis families applying for assistance to Traveler's Aid was loss of job (44% of these families were single-parent families). Bassuk et al. (1986) reported that 57% of families in their sample became homeless as a result of eviction, nonpayment of rent, condominium conversion, or overcrowding. A third of this sample cited an interpersonal precipitant such as the end of a relationship with a man, battering, death or illness in mother's nuclear family, or inability to get along with others in shared domestic arrangements. McChesney (1987) found that 40% of families became homeless as a result of economic events (including both one-

and two-parent families), 26% because of relationship events (usually single mothers with children leaving abusive relationships), and 33% because of economic difficulties during migration to find work (these were mainly two-parent families).

Weitzman et al. (1990) discovered that the pathways by which families become homeless differ according to their living situation prior to seeking shelter. Families who had been primary tenants experienced a rapid descent into homelessness after losing their own residence because of an eviction, rent-related problems, or building problems. These mothers tended to be older and to have fewer problems. The second group experienced a "slow slide from primary tenancy to homelessness" (Weitzman et al., 1990, p. 133) as their housing grew more marginal over time. They had left their own place of residence at least a year earlier and had lived with others for most of that time. These mothers generally became literally homeless because of problems related to "doubling up" or because of relationship problems. These women were more likely to have had substance abuse and mental problems and to have open protective services cases. For the third group of families, who had never had a stable residence of their own, doubling up in crowded apartments with relatives or friends was a permanent way of life. Of these, 68% cited problems with the primary tenant as the main reason they became homeless. Also, 60% of these women had parents who had received public assistance. This group had the least education and work experience of the three groups.

Families become homeless for a variety of reasons. However, an overriding theme is poverty and women's inability to access adequate housing when current living situations are threatened, whether by interpersonal or economic crises.

## Effect of Homelessness on Family Life

Very little is known about the impact of homelessness on family relationships and family life. What is known focuses on the disruption to daily family life and the difficulties mothers experience in carrying out their parental responsibilities.

### Daily Life

When families become homeless, mothers become preoccupied with basic human needs such as food, shelter, employment, and health (Merves,

1986). Once in a shelter, the family loses control over much of its daily schedule. Residents must wait in line to use rest rooms and have no control over what they eat or when they go to bed or get up (Merves, 1986). Many shelters have poor sanitation, and children may be exposed to illness as well as alcohol and drug use (Kozol, 1988). During the day, families must leave the shelter. Mothers may search for jobs or housing or visit social service agencies. Often they must take preschool-age children with them, as child care is rarely available. School-age children's lives are often disrupted when they are no longer able to attend their previous school.

### Parent-Child Relationships

According to Ziefert and Brown (1991), "the parenting role disintegrates quickly when a family becomes homeless. . . . Family boundaries are often fragmented and parent roles abdicated . . . [or] parent roles are rigidly conceived and performed" (p. 217). While entry into a shelter ensures that certain basic needs are met, shelter life may actually be antithetical to parent-child relationships.

In a study of mother-child interaction in a shelter, Boxill and Beaty (1990) found two major themes related to the mothers' behavior: "public mothering" and the "unraveling of the mother role." *Public mothering* refers to absence of privacy for family interactions: "Every aspect and nuance of the mother/child relationship occurs and is affected by its public and often scrutinized nature" (Boxill & Beaty, 1990, p. 58). Thus discipline, expressions of love and caring, as well as family frustrations are acted out in full public view. *Unraveling of the mother role* refers to the fact that mothers seemed to abdicate parental responsibilities to older children, generally teenage girls, who often bathed, fed, and disciplined younger siblings. The authors contended that, in fact, the mothers had not abdicated their responsibilities, but that they "were being soothed by the efforts of their older children. In an unkind and often assaulting world, mothers were comforted by their children's special acts of assistance and caring" (Boxill & Beaty, 1990, p. 59). Younger children seemed in conflict over their need for attention and the need to be independent and often questioned the certainty of any aspect of their lives.

Frequently homeless families must deal with intrusion into family life by protective services staff, who often become involved with the family around issues of abuse or neglect. Bassuk and Rosenberg (1988) found that homeless women were more likely to be investigated for abuse or neglect than were housed poor mothers. Estimates of involvement with protective services agencies range from 7.6% (Weitzman et al., 1990) to 10.3% (Mills & Ota, 1989). When considering these findings, however, one must be cognizant of the fact that many protective service agencies consider the condition of homelessness itself to be a sign of neglect; thus it is not surprising that homeless families may be more involved with such agencies than housed poor families.

Thus homelessness disrupts normal family relationships that are usually carried out in the privacy of the home. Mothers may be especially sensitive to scrutiny and criticism from shelter staff, residents, or protective services staff. They may turn to older children for solace and assistance in performing parental duties. Children may sense their mother's fears and increase demands for attention or assert a false sense of independence.

## Services for Homeless Families

Private nonprofit and religious institutions that have traditionally served homeless individuals have begun opening their doors to families (Stoner, 1984). In 1983 the federal government began funding programs for the homeless through the Food and Shelter Program, which provided support to food kitchens and emergency shelters. By 1987 it was clear that the "emergency-response" approach was not sufficient to deal with the problem of increasing homelessness. The Stewart B. McKinney Homeless Assistance Act (P.L. 100-77) "was the first piece of legislation to recognize . . . that homelessness is far more than a housing problem" (Kondratas, 1991, p. 1228). The components of this act included housing and food assistance, substance abuse treatment, education, and job training.

Comprehensive services to homeless people include three tiers: (a) emergency shelter and services, (b) transitional shelter and services, and (c) stabilization or long-term services (Kauffman, 1984; Stoner, 1984). Although not all homeless people need all three types of services, female-headed families are likely to need all three tiers because they tend to have multiple, serious problems that are barriers to restabilization (Ziefert & Brown, 1991).

### Emergency Services

Emergency shelters provide time-limited shelter (often from 30 to 60 days) and some case management services to families (e.g., Hutchison, Searight, & Stretch, 1986; Kauffman, 1984; Ziefert & Brown, 1991). Prob-

ably the most well-known and infamous emergency shelter network exists
in New York City, where homeless families and individuals have been
warehoused in barracks, gymnasiums, and other very large congregate facilities, frequently in crowded and unsanitary conditions (Kozol, 1988;
Shinn, Knickman, Ward, Petrovic, & Muth, 1990). Recently, efforts have
been made to create new methods of providing emergency and other services in New York (Shinn et al., 1990; Travers, 1989).

*Transitional Services*

In addition to shelter, transitional services include more intensive case
management and advocacy to secure permanent housing, a stable income,
and any other services that may be necessary, such as treatment for substance abuse, mental illness, or health problems (Stoner, 1984). Residents
usually remain in these programs for 60-90 days. Some communities have
developed transitional services especially for families (e.g., Cornish &
Nelson, 1991; Heard & Boxill, 1988; Phillips, DeChillo, Kronenfeld, &
Middleton-Jeter, 1988). Again, probably the most horrific example of a
"transitional" living situation is in New York City, where homeless families
have been "temporarily" housed for years in unsanitary, crime-ridden welfare hotels that cost the city more than the price of renting an apartment
(Kozol, 1988; Shinn et al., 1990). Travers (1989) described how New York
is attempting to create new models of transitional housing that also include
appropriate services.

*Stabilization or Long-Term Assistance*

The tier of service varies depending on the capacity for the family to
live independently. While some poorly functioning people need a variety of ongoing services, most homeless mothers do not have such serious
problems that interfere with their ability to function on a day-to-day basis
(Stoner, 1984). However, formerly homeless mothers often continue to
need some type of assistance to pay for adequate housing as well as some
supportive services. Examples of such programs have been described by
Kauffman (1984), Phillips et al. (1988), and Bordeleau (1989).

While a comprehensive service system can be successful in helping homeless families become restabilized, the prevalence of homelessness will not
actually decrease while there is a scarcity of low-cost housing (Buckner,
1991). Some communities have taken a structural rather than a simply
individualistic approach to ending homelessness. For example, East Orange,

New Jersey, developed a program to "upgrade the community's stock of marginal housing . . . and to stimulate private sector activity in the development and maintenance of housing for low-income families" (Potter, 1989, p. 13).

## Theories and Explanations
## for Understanding Homelessness

Research on homelessness has focused primarily on individual-level explanations that study characteristics of homeless people. Societal problems that contribute to the growth of homelessness have often been ignored (Shinn & Weitzman, 1990).

### A Framework for Examining Theories of Homelessness

Shinn and Weitzman (1990) presented a comprehensive model for explaining homelessness that takes into account individual, social group, and socioeconomic factors. This model provides a framework for examining various theories regarding homelessness.

*Individual factors.* Studies focusing on individual factors associated with homelessness often assume a causal link between personal deficits and homelessness. According to Merves (1986), "the personal deficit theory or blame the victim model is proposed by those who point to alcoholism, drug abuse, mental illness, social disaffiliation, irresponsibility, laziness or free choice of this life style to explain why people are homeless" (p. 4). Other individual-level factors include youth, low income, ethnicity, physical disabilities (Shinn & Weitzman, 1990) and abuse, separation from one's family of origin, and exposure to domestic violence as adults (Bassuk et al., 1986; Goodman, 1991a). Also included in this category would be any individual factors that imply housing loss (such as eviction), factors that result in an increased demand for housing (such as pregnancy), or factors that result in a decrease in material resources (such as job loss or loss of welfare benefits).

*Social factors.* Social group factors focus primarily on social ties with friends and relatives and connections with community organizations or institutions such as churches, settlement houses, and social service agencies. Disaffiliation theory and attachment theory have been used to explain why certain people have such limited support networks that they become homeless. The disaffiliation perspective has long been used to explain homelessness, especially among single men. According to Crystal (1984), "disaffiliation was seen as extending to most aspects of social living, including family ties, conventional living arrangements, employment, and internalization of socially accepted norms and values" (p. 2). Using attachment theory, Passero, Zax, and Zozus (1991) explained how family history can lead to extreme disaffiliation and inability to use social networks. They suggested that "children who experience high degrees of abuse and family discord, low degrees of parental involvement, and poor family organization and social integration are likely to experience later difficulty in seeking out caregivers" (p. 70). Studies documenting high rates of early childhood disruptive experiences among homeless women indicate that they may be at particular risk for poor attachment and consequent social disaffiliation.

Theories based on the assumption that poor social networks are a causal factor in homelessness are not entirely supported by research. While several studies have found homeless families and individuals to have small social networks (Bassuk, 1990; Bassuk et al., 1986; Dail, 1990; Passero et al., 1991), others have documented no differences between poor housed and homeless families on measures of social support or network size (Goodman, 1991b; Molnar, Rath, Klein, Lowe, & Hartmann, 1991). Shinn et al. (1990) found homeless families actually to have stronger support networks and concluded that homeless mothers turned to friends and relatives until "their safety nets had worn too thin to support them any longer" (p. 1186). Although homeless families may have smaller support networks than the general population, "inadequate networks among homeless people may, in fact, be within the normal range for people living in poverty" (Shinn et al., 1990, p. 1186).

*Socioeconomic or structural factors.* Many researchers have asserted that homelessness is primarily a structural problem related to poverty and lack of low-cost housing (e.g., Buckner, 1991; Edelman & Mihaly, 1989; McChesney, 1990; Rossi & Wright, 1987). From 1977 to 1987, there was a "virtual decimation of the low-income housing supply in most large American cities" accompanied by a substantial increase in the urban poverty population, resulting in increased homelessness (Wright & Lam, 1987, p. 48). The low-income housing shortage was a result of inflation, which drove up the cost of housing; urban renewal; loss of single-room occupancy boarding houses; and abandonment of buildings by landlords unwilling to make repairs. In addition, the number of new housing starts decreased during the recessions of 1980-1982, and federal appropriations for subsidized housing declined 80% in constant dollars during the 1980s (Edelman & Mihaly, 1989; McChesney, 1990; Rossi & Wright, 1987).

At the core of the problem of homelessness is extreme poverty, which has increased during the past two decades. The poverty rate has risen from 12.6% in 1970 to 15.2% in 1983. In 1990 14.9% of families with children under 18 and 18.3% of families with children under 5 had incomes below the federal poverty level (U.S. Bureau of the Census, 1992). The increase in poverty has been attributed to reduction in the demand for low-skilled workers, the lowered real value of welfare payments, which have not kept pace with inflation, and the fact that the poor have had to pay increasingly large proportions of their income for housing (Edelman & Mihaly, 1989; Rossi & Wright, 1987).

The feminization of poverty has also contributed to the increase in the overall poverty rate. The number of female-headed families rose more than 84% from 1970 to 1984, primarily because of the increased divorce rate and an increase in never-married women having children (Sullivan & Damrosch, 1987). In 1990 42.3% of female-headed families with children under 18 and 57.4% of such families with children under 5 had incomes below the federal poverty level (U.S. Bureau of the Census, 1992). Female-headed families are more likely to be poor than two-parent families because there is no second wage earner and because of the lower average wages for women. No-fault divorce laws and low rates of child support payments have also contributed to the poverty rate among female-headed families (Sullivan & Damrosch, 1987).

McChesney (1990) asserted that homelessness is primarily a structural problem, because of an imbalance in the ratio between the number of low-cost housing units available and the number of poor families who need such housing. According to McChesney (1990):

> Homelessness is like a game of musical chairs. The more people playing the game, and the fewer the chairs, the more people left standing when the music stops . . . if homelessness is the net result of the aggregate low-income housing ratio, then . . . homelessness is *not* caused by individual characteristics or behaviors. . . . At most, personal characteristics operate as selection mechanisms. (p. 195)

Shinn and Weitzman's (1990) model posits dynamic relationships among individual, social group, and socioeconomic factors. While most effects are probably in the direction from the macro to micro level (as when economic downturns lead to job losses), "micro-level variables may also have intermediate-level consequences. For example, childhood abuse may lead to unreliable social relationships with the family in adulthood" (Shinn & Weitzman, 1990, p. 6). Buckner (1991) suggested that the individual level of analysis may be most useful in identifying which individuals or families will be least able to compete in a scarce housing market, based on certain risk factors or "markers of vulnerability." In terms of predicting the prevalence of homelessness, however, socioeconomic variables are the most important indicators (Buckner, 1991; Shinn & Weitzman, 1990).

*Stress Theory*

Milburn and D'Ercole (1991) used stress theory to explain homelessness among women, suggesting a transactional view of stress as "a relational process that occurs through the interaction of a threatening circumstance— or one that is perceived to be threatening—and the psychological and social resources that one calls on to address the threat" (p. 1162). Stress does not reside in the situation itself or in the person, but in the transaction between the two. Using this model, homelessness can be conceptualized in two ways. First, homelessness can be seen as "the potential outcome of various external pressures or stressors such as residential instability or poverty" (p. 1162). Second, homelessness can be seen as "a stressor, a condition that makes reacquiring stable housing . . . extremely difficult" (p. 1162).

People are at risk for becoming distressed when they are beset by major, acute life events, when they experience an accumulation of chronic annoyances and hassles, and when they experience interactions of acute events and chronic hassles. However, the extent to which one actually experiences stress is mediated by social and psychological factors. According to this model, the risk factors related to homelessness that women face include residential instability, poverty, employment problems, and victimization. Mediators of stress are considered to be social supports (a social resource) and coping abilities (a psychological resource). Acknowledging that homelessness is not primarily a psychological problem, Milburn and D'Ercole (1991) suggested that the "stress model brings a useful psychological perspective to this macro-level issue" (p. 1167).

Theories explaining homelessness vary in the extent to which causality is posited to reside in characteristics of homeless individuals, including their social networks, or in socioeconomic factors in the wider society. When attempting to explain the prevalence of homelessness, macro-level factors related to poverty and the low-income housing shortage must be considered. In the context of a low-income housing shortage, individual and social group levels of analysis and theories related to personal deficit, social disaffiliation, attachment, and stress are most useful in predicting which families and individuals will be most vulnerable to becoming homeless.

However, many factors that are seen as precursors of homelessness may, in fact, be potential consequences of homelessness, because the condition of homelessness itself can lead to disruptions in social ties, depression, substance abuse, job loss, and reduction in coping abilities.

## Future Directions

Most research on homeless families has focused on describing the characteristics of families and trying to explain how they became homeless. Questions that would be appropriate for future research include the following: (a) What are the characteristics, precipitating events, and coping strategies of nonurban homeless families? Are these similar to or different from those of their urban counterparts? (b) What is the process whereby homeless mothers are able to stably rehouse their families? What personal strengths and coping abilities of the mothers are associated with successful restabilization? (c) What types of services are the most effective in helping restabilize families? What services are valued by homeless mothers themselves? (d) How do homeless mothers and children perceive, and make sense of, their experience? (e) How do the social networks mediate poor families' risk of becoming homeless?

Most intervention programs are based on the assumption that individual or family characteristics are responsible for homelessness. However, when low-income housing is scarce, intervention programs designed to ameliorate individual-level factors will not be successful in reducing the overall homeless population. Thus programs aimed at reducing homelessness must address its root causes by making low-income housing available to people who need it at a price they can afford or by increasing the ability of families to pay higher rents. Programs aimed at ameliorating individual or family problems that interfere with families' abilities to secure and maintain adequate shelter can be helpful in assisting individual families to resolve their immediate housing difficulties, but ongoing financial and/or emotional support may be necessary for some families.

Homeless families headed by women differ according to various personal and familial characteristics as well as according to the various pathways that bring them to the condition of homelessness. Future research must take into account these differences, and programs designed to help homeless families must also acknowledge and respect their uniqueness as well as their similarities.

## References

Acker, P. J., Fierman, A. H., & Dreyer, B. P. (1987). An assessment of parameters of health care and nutrition in homeless children [Abstract]. *American Journal of Disease of Children, 141,* 388.

Alperstein, G., Rappaport, C., & Flanigan, J. M. (1988). Health problems of homeless children in New York City. *American Journal of Public Health, 78,* 1232-1233.

Anderson, S. C., Boe, T., & Smith, S. (1988). Homeless women. *Affilia, 3*(2), 62-70.

Bassuk, E. L. (1990). Who are the homeless families? Characteristics of sheltered mothers and children. *Community Mental Health Journal, 26*(5), 425-433.

Bassuk, E. L., & Rosenberg, L. (1988). Why does family homelessness occur? A case-control study. *American Journal of Public Health, 78*(7), 783-788.

Bassuk, E. L., & Rubin, L. (1987). Homeless children: A neglected population. *American Journal of Orthopsychiatry, 57*(2), 279-286.

Bassuk, E. L., Rubin, L., & Lauriat, A. S. (1986). Characteristics of sheltered homeless families. *American Journal of Public Health, 76*(9), 1097-1101.

Bernstein, A. B., Alperstein, G., & Fierman, A. H. (1988, November). *Health care of homeless children.* Paper presented at the meeting of the American Public Health Association, Chicago.

Bordeleau, N. V. (1989, Winter). From client to homeowner in Rhode Island: Project Independence promotes affordable housing. *Public Welfare,* pp. 16-18.

Boxill, N. A., & Beaty, A. L. (1990). Mother/child interaction among homeless women and their children in a public night shelter in Atlanta, Georgia. *Child and Youth Services, 14*(1), 49-64.

Buckner, J. C. (1991). Pathways into homelessness: An epidemiological analysis. In D. J. Rog (Ed.), *Evaluating programs for the homeless* [Special issue]. *New Directions for Program Evaluation, 52,* 17-30.

Burt, M. R., & Cohen, B. E. (1989). Differences among homeless single women, women with children, and single men. *Social Problems, 36*(5), 508-524.

Chavin, W., Kristal, A., Seabron, C., & Guigli, P. E. (1987). The reproductive experience of women living in hotels for the homeless in New York City. *New York State Journal of Medicine, 87,* 10-13.

Cornish, J., & Nelson, K. (1991). Families helping families. *Community Alternatives: International Journal of Family Care, 3*(2), 59-73.

Crystal, S. (1984). Homeless men and homeless women: The gender gap. *Urban and Social Change Review, 17*(2), 2-6.

Dail, P. W. (1990). The psychosocial context of homeless mothers with young children: Program and policy implications. *Child Welfare, 69*(4), 291-308.

Edelman, M. W., & Mihaly, L. (1989). Homeless families and the housing crisis in the United States. *Children and Youth Services Review, 11,* 91-108.

Goodman, L. (1991a). The prevalence of abuse among homeless and housed poor mothers: A comparison study. *American Journal of Orthopsychiatry, 61*(4), 489-500.

Goodman, L. (1991b). The relationship between social support and family homelessness: A comparison study of homeless and housed mothers. *Journal of Community Psychology, 19,* 321-332.

Hall, J. A., & Maza, P. L. (1990). No fixed address: The effects of homelessness on families and children. *Child and Youth Services, 14*(1), 35-47.

Hallahan, D. P., & Kauffman, J., M. (1988). *Exceptional children: Introduction to special education* (4th ed.). Englewood Cliffs, NJ: Prentice Hall.

Heard, D. R., & Boxill, N. A. (1988). Two steps back, one step forward: Homeless women and their children at a transition house. *SAGE, 5*(1), 50-51.

Hoombs, M. E., & Snyder, M. (1982). *Homelessness in America: A forced march to nowhere.* Washington, DC: Community on Creative Nonviolence.

Hutchison, W. J., Searight, P., & Stretch, J. J. (1986). Multidimensional networking: A response to the needs of homeless families. *Social Work, 31*(6), 427-430.

Johnson, A. K. (1989). Female-headed homeless families: A comparative profile. *Affilia, 4*(4), 23-39.

Johnson, A. K., & Kreuger, L. W. (1989). Toward a better understanding of homeless women. *Social Work, 34*(6), 537-540.

Kauffman, N. K. (1984). Homelessness: A comprehensive policy approach. *Urban and Social Change Review, 17,* 21-26.

Kondratas, A. (1991). Ending homelessness: Policy challenges. *American Psychologist, 46* (11), 1226-1231.

Kozol, J. (1988). *Rachel and her children.* New York: Fawcett Columbine.

Masten, A. S. (1990). *Homeless children: Risk, trauma, and adjustment.* Paper presented at the 98th Annual Convention of the American Psychological Association, Boston.

McChesney, K. Y. (1987). Women without: Homeless mothers and their children (Doctoral dissertation, University of Southern California). *Dissertation Abstracts International, 48,* 1032A.

McChesney, K. Y. (1990). Family homelessness: A systemic problem. *Journal of Social Issues, 46*(4), 191-205.

Merves, E. S. (1986). Conversations with homeless women: A sociological examination (Doctoral dissertation, Ohio State University). *Dissertation Abstracts International, 47,* 1898A.

Mihaly, L. (1991). Beyond the numbers: Homeless families with children. In J. H. Kryder-Coe, L. M. Salamon, & J. M. Molnar (Eds.), *Homeless children and youth: A new American dilemma* (pp. 11-32). New Brunswick, NJ: Transaction.

Milburn, N., & D'Ercole, A. (1991). Homeless women: Moving toward a comprehensive model. *American Psychologist, 46*(11), 1161-1169.

Miller, D. S., & Lin, E. H. B. (1988). Children in sheltered homeless families: Reported health status and use of health services. *Pediatrics, 81,* 668-673.

Mills, C., & Ota, H. (1989). Homeless women with minor children in the Detroit metropolitan area. *Social Work, 34*(6), 485-489.

Molnar, J. M. (1988). *Home is where the heart is: The crisis of homeless children and families in New York City.* New York: Bank Street College of Education. (ERIC Document Reproduction Service No. ED 304 228)

Molnar, J. M., Rath, W. R., & Klein, T. P. (1990). Constantly compromised: The impact of homelessness on children. *Journal of Social Issues, 46*(4), 109-124.

Molnar, J. M., Rath, W. R., Klein, T. P., Lowe, C., & Hartmann, A. (1991). *Ill fares the land: The consequences of homelessness and chronic poverty for children and families in New York City*. New York: Bank Street College of Education.

National Coalition for the Homeless. (1987). *Broken lives: Denial of education to homeless children*. Washington, DC: Author.

Passero, J. M., Zax, M., & Zozus, R. T., Jr. (1991). Social network utilization as related to family history among the homeless. *Journal of Community Psychology, 19*(1), 70-78.

Patton, L. T. (1988). The rural homeless. In Institute of Medicine (Ed.), *Homelessness, health and human needs*. Washington, DC: National Academy Press.

Phillips, M. H., DeChillo, N., Kronenfeld, D., & Middleton-Jeter, V. (1988). Homeless families: Services make a difference. *Social Casework, 69*(1), 48-53.

Potter, B. (1989, Winter). East Orange foregoes traditional models: An emergency program for the homeless has a broad impact. *Public Welfare*, pp. 13-15.

Rafferty, Y., & Rollins, N. (1989). *Learning in limbo: The educational deprivation of homeless children*. New York: Advocates for Children of New York.

Rafferty, Y., & Shinn, M. (1991). The impact of homelessness on children. *American Psychologist, 46*(11), 1170-1179.

Redlener, I. E. (1988). Caring for homeless children: Special challenges for the pediatrician [Entire issue]. *Today's Child, 2*(4).

Rescorla, L., Parker, R., & Stolley, P. (1991). Ability, achievement, and adjustment in homeless children. *American Journal of Orthopsychiatry, 61,* 210-220.

Reyes, L. M., & Waxman, L. D. (1986). *The continued growth of hunger, homelessness, and poverty in America's cities: 1986*. Washington, DC: U.S. Conference of Mayors.

Reyes, L. M., & Waxman, L. D. (1989a). *A status report on hunger and homelessness in America's cities: 1988*. Washington, DC: U.S. Conference of Mayors.

Reyes, L. M., & Waxman, L. D. (1989b). *A status report on hunger and homelessness in America's cities, 1989: A 27-city survey*. Washington, DC: U.S. Conference of Mayors.

Rossi, P. H. (1989). *Without shelter: Homelessness in the 1980s*. New York: Priority.

Rossi, P. H., & Wright, J. D. (1987). The determinants of homelessness. *Health Affairs, 6*(1), 19-32.

Ryan, P., Goldstein, I., & Bartelt, D. (1989). *Homelessness in Pennsylvania: How can this be?* Philadelphia: Coalition on the Homeless in Pennsylvania (CHIP) and the Institute for Public Policy Studies of Temple University.

Shaffer, D., & Caton, C. L. (1984). *Runaway and homeless youth in New York City: A report to the Ittleson Foundation*. New York: Division of Child Psychiatry, New York State Psychiatric Institute.

Shinn, M., Knickman, J. R., Ward, D., Petrovic, N. L., & Muth, B. J. (1990). Alternative models for sheltering homeless families. *Journal of Social Issues, 46*(4), 175-190.

Shinn, M., Knickman, J. R., & Weitzman, B. C. (1991). Social relationships and vulnerability to becoming homeless among poor families. *American Psychologist, 46*(11), 1180-1187.

Shinn, M., & Weitzman, B. C. (1990). Research on homelessness: An introduction. *Journal of Social Issues, 46*(4), 1-11.

Stoner, M. R. (1984). An analysis of public and private sector provisions for homeless people. *Urban and Social Change Review, 17*(1), 3-8.

Sullivan, P. A., & Damrosch, S. P. (1987). Homeless women and children. In R. D. Bingham, R. E. Green, & S. B. White (Eds.), *The homeless in contemporary society* (pp. 82-98). Newbury Park, CA: Sage.

Travers, N. M. (1989, Winter). New York launches two-pronged effort: The state meets emergency needs of the homeless while creating transitional housing models. *Public Welfare,* pp. 19-21.

U.S. Bureau of the Census. (1992). *Statistical abstract of the United States: 1992* (112th ed.). Washington, DC: Government Printing Office.

U.S. Department of Education. (1989, February 15). *Report to Congress on state interim reports on the education of homeless children.* Washington, DC: Government Printing Office.

U.S. Department of Housing and Urban Development. (1984). *A report to the secretary on the homeless and emergency shelters.* Washington, DC: Department of Housing and Urban Development, Office of Policy Development Research.

U.S. Department of Housing and Urban Development. (1989). *A report on the 1988 National Survey of Shelters for the Homeless.* Washington, DC: Department of Housing and Urban Development, Office of Policy Development Research.

van Ry, M. (1993). *Homeless families: Causes, effects, and recommendations.* New York: Garland.

Wagner, J., & Menke, E. (1990). *The mental health of homeless children.* Paper presented at the meeting of the American Public Health Association, New York City.

Weitzman, B. C., Knickman, J. R., & Shinn, M. (1990). Pathways to homelessness among New York City families. *Journal of Social Issues, 46*(4), 125-140.

Whitman, B. Y., Stretch, J., & Accardo, P. (1987, February 24). *The crisis in homelessness: Effects on children and families* (Testimony presented before the U.S. House of Representatives Select Committee on Children, Youth, and Families). Washington, DC: Government Printing Office.

Wood, D., Hayashi, T., Schlossman, S., & Valdez, R. B. (1989). *Over the brink: Homeless families in Los Angeles.* Sacramento, CA: State Assembly Office of Research.

Wood, D., Valdez, R. B., Hayashi, T., & Shen, A. (1990). Homeless and housed families in Los Angeles: A study comparing demographic, economic, and family function characteristics. *American Journal of Public Health, 80*(9), 1049-1052.

Wright, J. D. (1990). Homelessness is not healthy for children and other living things. *Child and Youth Services, 14*(1), 65-88.

Wright, J. D., & Lam, J. A. (1987). Homelessness and the low-income housing supply. *Social Policy, 17,* 48-53.

Ziefert, M., & Brown, K. S. (1991). Skill building for effective intervention with homeless families. *Families in Society, 72*(4), 212-219.

# 15

# Conclusion

## *Challenges for Family Intervention*

SHARON J. PRICE
PATRICK C. MCKENRY

The authors in this volume have addressed several major problems that confront families and that generally result in varying degrees of stress. These problems are both internal and external to families, predictable and unpredictable, and vary from family to family. Despite this variation, however, there are several general conclusions that can be drawn that have implications for researchers, educators, practitioners, and policymakers. These include an ever-increasing level of stress facing families, families coping as systems, gender and cultural variations in coping, the interrelationship of family problems to other social systems, the ambiguity of chronic stress, and variations in problems and stress across the family life cycle.

### Increasing Stress for Families

It is generally accepted that all families are coping with some problems in their daily lives that result in stress. However, the level of stress experienced by families, similar to that experienced by individuals, appears to be increasing because of the dramatic changes that have affected families in recent years. These changes include, among others, the decrease in the economic well-being of families including employment instability and downward mobility; the increase in the number of families in which both spouses plus adolescents are in the labor force; the increased mobility of families; the increase in drug use, alcohol abuse, suicide, and other self-destructive behaviors; and the increase in societal violence. Structural changes that have taken place in families have also contributed to increased stress, such as divorce and remarriage.

It is easy to see why many families are vulnerable to multiple problems and subsequent higher stress levels. Their stress levels also would be higher if the problems are unexpected or situational rather than normative or expected. Several authors have addressed the issue of multiple stressors in terms of "stress pileup" (Boss, 1987; McCubbin et al., 1980). Other researchers, including Holmes and Rahe (1967) and McCubbin, Patterson, and Wilson (1981), have discussed this phenomenon in terms of simultaneous multiple life events. However, many researchers, practitioners, educators, and policymakers still approach family problems as being the result of a single issue (unemployment, illness, alcohol abuse) that has the potential for stress without looking at other stressors (internal and external) that may be affecting families. In view of the number of problems that are confronting families and their higher levels of stress, more emphasis should be placed on the interaction of multiple problems as well as the impact of simultaneous problems. For example, if a family experiences the serious illness of one of its family members at the same time the major breadwinner loses her or his job, accompanied by the loss of income and health care benefits, it would be expected that the family's level of stress would be higher than if they were confronted with only one of these problems. It appears therefore that "the accumulation of stressor events may explain family crisis better than any one isolated event" (Boss, 1987, p. 700).

## Families Coping With Problems

Family scholars have historically exhibited an avid interest in family problems and how individuals respond to them. However, recently there has been an increased interest in how families as systems cope with their problems. In addition, several authors have applied individual coping frameworks to families (Boss, 1987). Other authors have developed models that have been used to measure and/or describe normal family functioning. Three of the most commonly used models in the assessment of family coping include Olson's Circumplex Model of Marital and Family Systems (Olson, Sprenkle, & Russell, 1979), the Beavers-Timberlawn (Lewis, Beavers, Gossett, & Phillips, 1976) model of how competent families relate, and the McMaster Model of Family Functioning (Epstein, Bishop, & Baldwin, 1982).

Olson's Circumplex Model classifies families on three dimensions of family life: cohesiveness, adaptability, and communication. Cohesion and adaptability are central dimensions in this model while communication is viewed as a facilitating factor. Olson reported that "balanced" families show moderate levels of cohesion and adaptability and were viewed as exhibiting the greatest marital and family strengths across the family life cycle.

The Beavers-Timberlawn approach focuses on negotiation, conflict, and closeness in "healthy" families. This approach is based on family systems theory and includes the assumption that power must be evenly divided between spouses for optimal family functioning.

The McMaster Model of Family Functioning (Epstein et al., 1982) is also based on systems theory and assumes that certain behaviors constitute healthy and "normal" families. It focuses on three "task" areas: basic (instrumental tasks), developmental (stages of the family life cycle), and hazardous (serious crises) and measures problem solving, communication, roles, affective responses, affective involvement, and behavior control.

Authors who have focused on individuals' response to problems include Lazarus (1977), Pearlin and Schooler (1978), and Moos and Schaefer (1986). Lazarus divided the coping process (cognitive appraisal of what is happening) from coping strategies (actual response to the problem), whereas Pearlin and Schooler described coping responses as falling into three categories: directly altering the problem, changing one's view of the problem, and managing emotional distress resulting from the problem. Moos and Schaefer developed a more elaborate model in their proposal that coping strategies are composed of both cognitive and behavioral responses and include (a) establishing the meaning of and understanding the personal significance of the situation; (b) confronting reality and responding to the requirements of the external situation; (c) sustaining relationships with family members, friends, and other individuals who may be helpful in resolving the problem and its aftermath; (d) maintaining a reasonable emotional balance by managing upset feelings; and (e) preserving a satisfactory self-image and maintaining a sense of competence and mastery.

These selected models have made a major contribution to our understanding of how families cope with problems and what constitutes healthy functioning families and individuals. In addition, frameworks provide a mechanism for addressing family-related problems and reinforce the need to deal with these issues from a family perspective. However, this focus on a general notion of family may have resulted in a neglect of the diversity that exists between and within families.

## The Role of Diversity

Ethnicity and racial identity provide a mechanism for identification, that is, belonging to a particular group, and are usually transmitted by families and reinforced by the larger community. Therefore most persons identify with a particular ethnic and/or racial group, and the variations between the various groups should be addressed when dealing with family problems. It is often accepted that family problems vary, as do their responses, but the racial/ethnic variations in coping are often ignored. For example, African American families have a long history of relying on the extended family and community for assistance, often because of racism and discrimination. In addition, many recent immigrant families rely heavily on their families for assistance.

Much of the focus on these families has been from a problem perspective (teenage pregnancy, single-parent families, female dominance) and has often assumed they are inferior because they deviated from the "model" of white middle-class families in their responses to these issues. Therefore it is the responsibility of researchers, educators, practitioners, and policymakers to respect the uniqueness and identify the strengths exhibited by these families while providing appropriate assistance.

Closely related to ethnic/racial differences is the issue of gender. It is imperative that race and gender be tied to the availability and use of resources in viewing how families cope with problems. Poverty is a problem for many families, and recently the "feminization of poverty" has been recognized. Although many poor families are identified as being part of a "minority" population, they also exist in the "majority" population. These families, however, experience an even greater lack of services and resources while at the same time being at greatest risk of experiencing more problems. This is particularly relevant in light of the proposed national health care reform. The lower wages of women and minorities, which result in inadequate economic resources to meet everyday expenses without considering possible emergencies, is but one example, and sometimes simple solutions result in even greater problems for these families. For example, the proposal to "force" welfare mothers into the labor market may, on the surface, may be a valid recommendation. However, we must also consider the issues of adequate job training; the availability and costs of child care, transportation, and work clothes; and the availability of jobs.

Feminist theory challenges us to "rethink both the separateness and the solidarity of families" (Ferree, 1991, p. 103). According to feminist theory, families should be viewed as integrated with wider systems of economic and political power, and at the same time the diverging and sometimes conflicting interests of each family member should be addressed. It is essential therefore that the availability of coping strategies within families be viewed as a reflection of and part of the larger political society, which historically has been male dominated. Although systems theory contributes much to our knowledge about how family members interact and cope with problems, it may also ignore the differential impact of family members to the degree that some family members (i.e., women and children) may be expected to sacrifice more than others for the sake of family equilibrium. The feminist argument that families must be viewed in the context of political and economic systems is applicable to other systems as well.

## Interrelationship of Families and Other Social Systems

There are several differences among researchers, educators, practitioners, and policymakers that should be confronted when focusing on family problems. This is a challenge to all groups because their perspectives and languages have historically differed. For example, until recently family scholars have shown little interest in the biological or health issues as related to families, while medicine and other health sciences have ignored families and the role they play in the health care system. A similar dichotomy has existed between the world of work and families. These dichotomies have resulted in a split between families and societal issues and a lack of recognition that families do not live in isolation from the larger society and the larger society does not function without families. Therefore there is an increasing need to address all issues as related to families, and it is extremely relevant in the 1990s and beyond as policymakers develop policies and interventionists develop programs and practices, which are pressured by the formation of an aging society. Several basic recommendations may apply to all involved groups (Moen & Shorr, 1987).

1. View families as active rather than passive (families can be defined as part of the solution rather than the problem). Such an approach would be conducive to policies supporting families in achieving their own goals rather than policies that replace families by substituting public services.

2. Enhance the awareness of the changing nature of families (alterations in family structure and composition, differential family needs at different stages of the life cycle, and the pluralistic and changing nature of families). This emphasis would remove the necessity, or the desirability, of framing a definition of the family before policy could be formulated.

3. Consider families rather than only individuals. For example, policies and programs directed toward teenage pregnancy should include the family context, and records of child abuse or spouse abuse should be kept in a way that would make it possible to trace the history of abuse to other siblings or spouses.

4. A "family impact" orientation could sensitize researchers and decision makers to look for inadvertent impacts on families. For example, programs that focus on children should be viewed as affecting parents.

### Ambiguity From Chronic Stress

Chronic stressors and acute stressors have been differentiated in this volume. A *chronic stressor* is "a situation that runs a long course, is difficult to amend, and has a debilitating effect on the family" (Boss, 1987, p. 699). A major effect of chronic stress is the production of ambiguity. Many researchers, interventionists, and practitioners, however, focus on family problems that are "concrete," observable, and measurable, resulting in a lack of emphasis on how families cope with the strain of uncertainty and continued ambiguity. For example, ambiguity generated by a family member's testing positive for HIV, discovering one carries the gene of Alzheimer's disease, or the uncertainty regarding whether a child support check will arrive, similar to the ambiguity generated by an absent family member, creates significant strain that could last for months or years.

Individuals also experience the strain of role ambiguity, often for an extended period of time. Appropriate role behavior is no longer clearly defined, and therefore it is not unusual that husbands and wives experience personal, and possibly interpersonal, conflict about this issue. In view of the many stressors and problems that may result in ambiguity, those persons focusing on family problems and stress may have to be increasingly process focused rather than issue or event focused. Such a perspective would contribute to greater awareness of the issues surrounding how families cope with chronic stress or strain.

## Family Life-Cycle Variations

The material contributed by the authors in this volume stresses the fact that family problems are often normative, corresponding to transitions in the family life cycle. For example, most families expect to make selected adjustments, such as persons entering and exiting the family at relative specific times, throughout the life cycle. Whereas these adjustments create some degree of stress, the fact that they are expected reduces the magnitude of this response. However, if family events occur "out of cycle" or "off time" (e.g., a child dies before parents), the adjustment demands are greater and accompanied by higher levels of stress. In addition, the life cycle supplies a frame of reference providing appropriate means and the timing of interventions (Mattessich & Hill, 1987) and mediates the impact of policies and interventions on families. Therefore knowledge about the stage in the family life cycle in which a particular event occurs would lend insight into the possible degree of normative stress a family may be experiencing—in addition to any unexpected stressor.

## Summary

Families are thought to be experiencing higher levels of stress today than ever before. Yet families vary in their responses to both expected and unexpected problems that confront them. Some families dissolve as a result of stress (which may be the best response), whereas other families are able to find ways to effectively deal with what seems like insurmountable odds. According to the ABC-X model, successfully meeting family problems depends partially on individual and family resources. Although most families will be confronted at some time with problems of such magnitude that additional resources are needed, resources are not distributed equitably. This is evident in the increased gap between the rich and poor in our society, and therefore some families need more assistance than other families.

310                                                          Families and Change

On the national level, the 1980s was a decade when little money was available to help families with their problems. In addition, there was an accompanying lack of expressed interest in family problems by many of our elected officials, while at the same time there was an increase in the impact of groups who claim to be "pro family" but advocate returning to a period of family life that probably never existed for the majority of Americans. Recently, however, with peacetime reductions in defense spending and an increased interest in families, there is a possibility that some of the issues presented in this volume will be addressed. There are still significant concerns, however, about fiscal restraint and cutbacks in many programs that are family focused, but there appears to be an increasing awareness of problems confronting families and at least verbal support of families who are living in an increasingly challenging environment. This awareness and support were evident in the passage of the Family Leave Bill.

Family life educators have the potential to play a key role in helping families cope with the issues discussed in this volume. Areas including sexuality, parent education, marriage, remarriage, and enrichment have recently entered the curriculum of family life education. In addition, families are increasingly turning to family life education programs to learn how to solve problems and to satisfy their desire to enrich and improve their quality of life. These programs, however, are often based on white middle-class and male-dominated models and the processes leading to marriage, emphasizing early marriage and early parenthood. Increasingly family life education programs should focus on problem-solving strategies applicable across the life cycle for a diverse group of families. For example, curricula should include how different racial/ethnic and SES families cope with problems as well as the strengths of a range of family responses across the life cycle. Instead of focusing on marriage and family life, as traditionally defined, an increase in the emphasis on relationship education—that is, concepts and theories that apply across the family life cycle, to friendships, or to the world of work—would make a major contribution.

## References

Boss, P. (1987). Family stress. In M. B. Sussman & S. K. Steinmetz (Eds.), *Handbook of marriage and the family* (pp. 695-723). New York: Plenum.
Epstein, N. B., Bishop, D. S., & Baldwin, L. M. (1982). McMaster model of family functioning. In F. Walsh (Ed.), *Normal family processes* (pp. 115-141). New York: Guilford.

Ferree, M. M. (1991). Feminism and family research. In A. Booth (Ed.), *Contemporary families: Looking forward, looking back* (pp. 103-121). Minneapolis, MN: National Council on Family Relations.

Holmes, T. H., & Rahe, R. H. (1967). The social readjustment rating scale. *Journal of Psychosomatic Research, 11,* 213-218.

Lazarus, R. C. (1977). Cognitive and coping processes in emotion. In A. Monat & R. S. Lazarus (Eds.), *Stress and coping* (pp. 145-158). New York: Columbia University Press.

Lewis, J. M., Beavers, W. R., Gossett, J. T., & Phillips, V. A. (1976). *No single thread: Psychological health in family systems.* New York: Brunner/Mazel.

Mattessich, P., & Hill, R. (1987). Life cycle and family development. In M. B. Sussman & S. K. Steinmetz (Eds.), *Handbook of marriage and the family* (pp. 437-469). New York: Plenum.

McCubbin, H., Joy, C., Cauble, B., Comeau, J., Patterson, J., & Neddle, R. (1980). Family stress and coping: A decade review. *Journal of Marriage and the Family, 42*(4), 855-871.

McCubbin, H., Patterson, J., & Wilson, L. (1981). *Family Inventory of Life Events and Changes (FILE): Research instrument.* St. Paul: University of Minnesota, Family Social Science.

Moen, P., & Shorr, A. L. (1987). Families and social policy. In M. B. Sussman & S. K. Steinmetz (Eds.), *Handbook of marriage and the family* (pp. 795-813). New York: Plenum.

Moos, R. H., & Schaefer, J. A. (1986). Life transitions and crisis: A conceptual overview. In R. H. Moos (Ed.), *Coping with life crises* (pp. 3-28). New York: Plenum.

Olson, D. H., Sprenkle, D. H., & Russell, C. S. (1979). Circumplex Model of Marital and Family Systems I: Cohesion and adaptability dimensions, family types, and clinical applications. *Family Process, 18,* 3-28.

Pearlin, L. I., & Schooler, C. (1978). The structure of coping. *Journal of Health and Social Behavior, 19,* 2-21.

# Name Index

Name Index 315

Chaudhary, B. S., 140
Chavin, W., 286
Cheal, D., 35
Chen, K. H., 132
Cherico, D. J., 178
Cherlin, A. J., 49, 198, 199, 205, 206, 207, 224, 227
Chi, S. K., 42
Chibucos, T. R., 247, 249, 250, 251
Chilamkurti, C., 269
Chilman, C. S., 71
Chiriboga, D. A., 201
Chodorow, N., 24
Christensen, D. H., 212
Christie-Seely, J., 144
Christopoulos, C., 267
Churchill, M. P., 178
Clark, A., 29
Clark, P. G., 184
Clarke, S. C., 219, 233
Clayson, D. E., 51
Clayton, P., 175, 184
Clayton, T. L., 157, 158, 163, 164
Cleek, M., 201
Clingempeel, W. G., 93, 225, 233
Cloward, R. A., 101
Coates, T. J., 131
Cobb, S., 9
Coe, R. D., 70
Coelho, G., 4
Cohen, B. E., 281, 283, 284, 286, 289
Cohen, F., 132
Cohen, S., 134
Cohen-Sandler, R., 99
Cohn, D. A., 267, 275
Cole, A. L., viii
Cole, C. L., viii
Cole, J. D., 163
Coleman, C., 49
Coleman, M., 49, 220, 227, 230, 233
Collier, A. M., 133
Collins, P. H., 24
Coltrane, S., 73, 74, 220
Comeau, J., 304
Condran, G. A., 45, 200
Conger, K. J., 48, 71, 98
Conger, R. D., 48, 71, 96
Consortium of Family Organizations, 145

Conte, J. R., 54
Cook, J. A., 182
Coombs, R. H., 249
Cooper, B., 157
Cooper, C. R., 97, 104, 250
Cooper, H., 49, 220
Cooper, K., 48,
Coppotelli, H. C., 132
Corcoran, M. E., 70
Corenblum, B., 54
Cornell, C. P., 266
Cornish, J., 293
Cosand, B. J., 99
Counts, D. A., 178
Counts, D. R., 178
Coverman, S., 72, 74
Cowan, C. P., 46
Cowan, P. A., 46, 49
Cowen, E. L., 208
Cox, M., 202, 206
Cox, R., 202, 206
Coyne, J. C., 44
Coysh, W. S., 204, 205
Craig, Y., 178
Creighton, J., 187
Crockett, L. J., 90
Cromwell, R. E., 95
Crosbie-Burnett, M., 219-241
Crouter, A. C., 47, 74, 78
Crutchfield, R. D., 98
Crutchley, E., 164
Crystal, S., 295
Csikszentmihalyi, M., 104
Curtis, L., 265

D'Amico, R. J., 78
Dahl, C. M., 212
Dail, P. W., 282, 283, 285, 289
Daly, K., 35
Daly, M., 221, 268, 272
Damrosch, S. P., 296
Danon-Boileau, H., 92
Darling-Fisher, C. S., 72
Daro, D., 265, 275
Datan, N. C., 91, 92,
Davenport, C., 99
Davidson, B., 42

Johnson, C. L., 44
Johnson, D., 200
Johnson, D. L., 166
Johnson, D. W., 43, 49
Johnson, J., 8
Johnson, L. B., 35
Johnson, M. A., 178
Johnson, S. B., 140
Johnston, J. R., 204, 205
Johnston, J. V., 134
Johnston, L. D., 100, 101, 244
Johnston, W. B., 69
Johnstone, E. E., 155, 156
Jones, S., 162
Jorgensen, S., 48
Jouriles, E. N., 46
Joy, C., 226, 304
Joyce, S., 267
Jurich, A. P., 96, 251
Jurich, J. A., 96, 251
Juster, F. T., 72

Kahn, D., 55
Kahn, M. D., 184
Kalish, R. A., 183
Kalmuss, D., 54, 221
Kalnins, I., 178
Kalter, N., 208
Kamerman, S. B., 78, 80
Kamo, Y., 74
Kandel, D. B., 101, 251
Kanouse, D., 42
Kantner, J. F., 97
Kantor, D., 177
Kaplan, H. B., 94, 98
Kaprio, J., 133
Karno, M., 153, 154
Karson, M., 90
Kasl, S. V., 134
Kasten, A. M., 166
Kastenbaum, R., 174, 178
Katz, M. H., 76
Kauffman, J. M., 179, 288
Kauffman, N. K., 292, 293
Kaufman, E., 54, 101, 251, 252
Kaufman, J., 269
Kazarian, S. S., 163

Kazdin, A. E., 46
Keith, P. M., 50, 76
Keller, J. F., 123
Keller, M. B., 164
Keller, S. E., 134, 174
Kelly, J. B., 102, 210, 225, 230
Kelly, J. R., 117, 118, 121, 122
Kelly, R. F., 76, 77
Kelman, S., 244, 245
Kendler, K. S., 157
Keppler, K., 161
Kercher, L., 161
Kessler, R. C., 77, 251
Khurana, R., 140
Kiecolt-Glaser, J. K., 134
Kiloh, L. G., 134
Kim, W. J., 99
Kimmel, M. S., 33
King, R. A., 99
Kingston, P., 47
Kirschling, J. M., 124
Kitagawa, E. N., 97
Kitsen, J., 140
Kitson, G. C., 201, 205
Klap, R., 276
Klass, D., 180, 183, 188
Kleban, M. H., 154
Klein, B. W., 70
Klein, J. I., 160
Klein, R., 133, 139
Klein, S., 179
Klein, T. P., 286, 295
Klerman, G. L., 157
Klerman, G. R., 164
Klesges, R. C., 131
Kline, M., 204, 205
Kling, M. A., 134
Knapp, J. R., 90
Knickman, J. R., 282, 283, 284, 287, 288, 289, 290, 292, 293, 294, 295
Knowles, G. A., 98
Kobak, R. R., 49
Koepke, L., 234
Kohen, J. A., 52
Kohlhepp, K. A., 43
Kolko, D. J., 46
Kolman, M. L., 140
Kondratas, A., 292

Polin, G., 140
Pollock, G. H., 188
Polonko, K., 35
Polson, C. J., 96, 251
Ponzetti, J. J., 178
Pope, C. R., 45
Potter, B., 294
Potts, M. K., 44
Potuchek, J. L., 22, 27
Powell, D., 226
Powers, S. I., 90, 91, 104
Prata, G., 164
Pratt, E. L., 42
Price, R. A., 132
Price, S., 1-20, 210, 211, 303-311
Procidano, M. E., 42

Quinian, D. M., 140
Quinsey, V. L., 270

Rabin, C., 55
Rabins, P. V., 154
Rabkin, J. G., 132
Radbill, S. A., 262
Rae, D. S., 153, 154
Rafferty, Y., 287, 288
Rahe, R. H., 3, 132, 137, 173, 304
Ramey, C. T., 133
Ramsden, P. G., 178
Ramsey, S., 212
Ranck, K. H., vii
Rando, T. A., 175, 177, 183, 184, 185
Rankin, J. H., 247
Ransom, D. C., 153
Raphael, B., 175, 183
Rappaport, C., 286
Rath, W. R., 286, 295
Redlener, I. E., 286
Rees, H., 7
Regier, D. A., 153, 154
Reid, J. R., 247, 250
Reid, W. J., 47, 55
Reinke, B. J., 43, 52
Reiss, D., 54, 138, 139, 163, 165, 179, 233, 246, 248
Renner, M., 224

Report of the Secretary's Task Force on Youth Suicide, 100
Rescorla, L., 286, 287, 288
Retherford, P. S., 71
Rettig, K. D., 212
Revenson, T. A., 44
Rexroat, C., 73, 74
Reyes, L. M., 282, 285
Reynolds, J., 187
Rhodes, J. E., 101
Rice, D. P., 244, 245
Richardson, D., 167
Richardson, L., 178
Ridley, C. A., 71
Riley, J. W., 114
Riley, M. W., 114
Risman, B. J., 25
Rita, H., 133
Rivers, C., 27, 31
Robbins, C., 98
Roberts, C. W., 48
Roberts, L. J., 50
Robins, L. N., 153, 154, 250
Robins, P. K., 212
Robinson, J. P., 28, 73
Rodgers, R. H., 211
Rodgers, W., 42
Roebuck, J., 97
Rofe, Y., 42
Rogers, J. A., 166
Rogers, T. R., 50
Roghmann, K. J., 136
Rogler, L. H., 42
Rojek, D. G., 250
Rolland, J. S., 185, 186, 187
Rollins, B. C., 45, 95, 97, 249, 250
Rollins, N., 288
Romig, C. A., 98
Rones, P. L., 70
Ronkko, T., 163
Rorabough, W. J., 242
Rosaldo, R., 179, 186
Rosen, E., 182, 185
Rosen, H., 188
Rosenbaum, A., 54
Rosenberg, L., 283, 284, 285, 286, 287, 289, 291
Rosenblatt, P., 176

Zammichielli, M., 47
Zankowski, G. L., 248
Zaslow, M., 79
Zax, M., 295
Zeiss, A., 48
Zelnik, M., 97
Ziefert, M., 291, 292
Zigler, E., 79, 269
Zill, N., 207, 225
Zipple, A., 166

Zisook, S., 174
Zola, I. K., 135
Zozus, R. T., Jr., 295
Zubin, J., 161
Zuckerman, A. E., 136
Zuckerman, D. M., 134
Zuckerman, S., 99
Zvonkovic, A. M., 71
Zweben, A., 53

# Subject Index

# About the Contributors

**Katherine R. Allen** is Associate Professor of Family Studies in the Department of Family and Child Development at Virginia Polytechnic Institute and State University in Blacksburg, Virginia. She also serves on the Virginia Tech Women's Studies Advisory Committee. She teaches classes on gender relations, family theories, research methods, and human sexuality. She received her Ph.D., M.A., and Certificate of Gerontology from Syracuse University and her B.S. degree from the University of Connecticut. She is the author of *Single Women/Family Ties: Life Histories of Older Women* (Sage, 1989) and the coauthor, with Kristine M. Baber, of *Women and Families: Feminist Reconstructions* (Guilford, 1992).

**Kristine M. Baber** is Associate Professor in the Department of Family Studies at the University of New Hampshire, where she also is a core faculty member of the Women's Studies Program. She teaches courses in family relations, human sexuality, research methods, ethics, and gender studies. She received her M.A. in Human Development and Family Relations and her Ph.D. in family studies from the University of Connecticut; her B.A. in Philosophy was from Southern Illinois University. She is coauthor, with Katherine R. Allen, of *Women and Families: Feminist Reconstructions* (Guilford, 1992).

**Patricia Bell-Scott,** Professor of Child and Family Development and Women's Studies and Adjunct Professor of Psychology at the University of Georgia, served as project codirector of the William T. Grant-funded Consortium for Research on Adolescent Development from 1986 to 1991. She is editor of *Life Notes: Personal Writings by Contemporary Black Women—*

the first collection of black women's journal- and diary-writing; principal coeditor of *Double Stitch: Black Women Write about Mothers and Daughters*; and co-founding editor of *SAGE: A Scholarly Journal of Black Women.* She has published broadly on African American family studies and women's psychosocial development.

**Rosemary Blieszner** is Associate Professor in the Department of Family and Child Development and Associate Director of the Center for Gerontology at Virginia Polytechnic Institute and State University. She received her Ph.D. from Pennsylvania State University in human development-family studies with a concentration in adult development and aging. Her research focuses on the contribution of family and friend relationships to psychological well-being in adulthood and old age. She is coauthor of *Adult Friendship* (with Rebecca G. Adams, Sage, 1992) and coeditor of *Handbook on Aging and the Family* (with Victoria H. Bedford, Greenwood, 1994). Her articles have appeared in journals such as *Journal of Marriage and the Family, Family Relations, Journal of Gerontology,* and *Journal of Social and Personal Relationships.*

**Thomas L. Campbell** received his undergraduate degree from Harvard College (1974) and his M.D. from Harvard Medical School (1979). He completed his family practice residency and fellowship in psychosomatic medicine at the University of Rochester School of Medicine and Dentistry. Currently he is Associate Professor of Family Medicine and Psychiatry at the University of Rochester, where he codirects the Family Systems Medicine Fellowship and psychosocial training for the Family Medicine Residency Program with Susan McDaniel. He has written extensively on the role of the family and medical practice and on the influence of the family on physical and mental health. His National Institute of Mental Health monograph, *Family's Impact on Health,* has been an influential review of the current research in this area. Other books he has coauthored include *Families and Health,* with William Doherty, and *Family-Oriented Primary Care: A Manual for Medical Providers,* with Susan H. McDaniel and David B. Seaburn. He is Board Certified in Family Practice and a Clinical Member of the American Association of Marriage and Family Therapy.

**Margaret Crosbie-Burnett,** Associate Professor, received her Ph.D. from Stanford University in 1983. She has been Professor of Counseling Psychology for 11 years, first at the University of Wisconsin–Madison and currently at the University of Miami. She was guest editor of a special issue of *Family Relations* on stepfamilies in 1989, and she has served for 7 years as cochair of the Focus Group on Remarriage and Stepfamilies within the National Council on Family Relations. Her research, teaching, and writing on stepfamilies has focused on the development of an instrument for the assessment of stepfamily adjustment and the development of theory and policy in this area.

**David H. Demo** is Associate Professor of Human Development and Family Studies at the University of Missouri. He received a B.S. in psychology and sociology from the University of Richmond, an M.S. in sociology from Virginia Commonwealth University, and a Ph.D. in sociology and human development and family studies from Cornell University. He serves on the editorial board of *Journal of Marriage and the Family.* His research focuses on the linkages between social structure and personality, and his current projects examine the influences of family structure and family relations on parents and children.

**Lawrence H. Ganong** is Professor of Nursing and Human Development and Family Studies at the University of Missouri. He received a B.A. in psychology from Washburn University, an M.S. in family studies from Kansas State University, an M.Ed. in counseling psychology from the University of Missouri, and a Ph.D. in family studies from the University of Missouri. He serves on the editorial boards of several professional journals, such as *Journal of Marriage and the Family, Family Relations,* and *Journal of Family Issues.* His primary research interests are remarriage and stepparenting, and family-related stereotypes.

**Stephen M. Gavazzi** is Assistant Professor, Marriage and Family Therapy Program, Department of Family Relations and Human Development, The Ohio State University. He received his Ph.D. from the University of Connecticut. He is a Clinical Member and Approved Supervisor of the American Association of Marriage and Family Therapy and has published articles on clinical issues in such journals as *Family Process, The American Journal of Family Therapy, Family Systems Medicine,* and *The Journal of Family Psychotherapy.* His research interests encompass a range of topics regarding adolescent development and well-being, including the interaction of family system and peer network characteristics, parenting styles and their connection to at-risk behaviors, and the use of rituals in prevention and intervention efforts with adolescents and their families.

**Richard J. Gelles** is Professor of Sociology and Psychology and the Director of the Family Violence Research Program at the University of Rhode Island. He received his A.B. from Bates College (1968), an M.A. in sociology from the University of Rochester (1971), and a Ph.D. in sociology from the University of New Hampshire (1973). He is the author or coauthor of 16 books and more than 100 articles and chapters on family violence. His most recent books are *Intimate Violence* (Touchstone, 1989), *Physical Violence in American Families: Risk Factors and Adaptations in 8,145 Families* (Transaction, 1990), *Intimate Violence in Families* (Sage, 1990), and *Sociology: An Introduction* (4th edition, McGraw-Hill, 1991). He received the American Sociological Association, Section on Undergraduate Education, "Outstanding Contributions to Teaching Award" in 1979.

**Kathleen E. Georgen,** who received her B.A. in psychology from the University of Colorado at Boulder, recently completed an M.A. in family life education and consultation at Kansas State University. Her areas of focus include family policy, work-family issues, and the effects of legislation on families. She served as a legislative intern at the Kansas state capital in Topeka and is currently a legislative aid.

**Irwanto,** a Fulbright Scholar from Jakarta, Indonesia, received his B.A. from Universitas Gadjah Mada in Yogyakarta, Indonesia. He received his M.S. and his Ph.D. in child development and family studies from Purdue University in 1990 and 1992, respectively. While at Purdue he was instrumental in the creation of two funded proposals: (a) AIDS Prevention in Indonesia: Workshops for Health and Social Work Professionals, and (b) A New Vision for CDFS 301: Families and Society. He has been a Lecturer of Educational and Developmental Psychology and Curriculum Development and Microteaching at the Faculty of Teacher Training, Atmajaya Catholic University and a researcher and A/V drug prevention specialist for a United Nations Development Program-sponsored prevention program. He is author or coauthor of several relevant publications including *Introduction to Psychology* (published in Jakarta, Indonesia).

**Robert A. Lewis** is the Norma Compton Distinguished Professor of Family Studies in the Department of Child and Family Studies, Purdue University. Since receiving his Ph.D. in sociology from the University of Minnesota in 1969, he has been engaged in research and teaching in family studies and sociology at the University of Minnesota, the University of Georgia, Pennsylvania State University, and Arizona State University before coming to Purdue University. He also has taught graduate courses and done cross-cultural research at the University of Uppsala, Sweden, in 1977 and in Budapest, Hungary, in 1987. He has published 58 articles and book chapters and written/edited eight books and special issues alone and with others, including *Assessing Marriage: New Behavioral Approaches, Family Assessment and Treatment of Drug Abusing Adolescents, Men in Difficult Times, Men in Families,* and *Men's Changing Roles in Families.* Many of these publications have been related to topics such as families and drug addictions.

**Elizabeth W. Lindsey** is Instructor in the School of Social Work at the University of Georgia and teaches courses related to marriage and family therapy. She received her M.S.W. in social work from the University of Georgia and her B.A. from the University of North Carolina at Chapel Hill. She has published articles related to public welfare, delinquency and prevention of delinquency, foster care review systems, and mental health programs in public schools. She is currently writing her dissertation for a Ph.D. in child and family development with an emphasis in marriage and family therapy at the University of Georgia. The dissertation explores the process by which homeless mothers are successful in stably rehousing their families.

**Jay A. Mancini** is Professor and Department Head of Family and Child Development at Virginia Polytechnic Institute and State University, Blacksburg and Falls Church, Virginia. He is the author/editor of *Aging Parents and Adult Children* (Lexington Books, 1989) and Senior Editor of the National Council on Family Relations book series on the contemporary family. His research has appeared in *Journal of Marriage and the Family, Journal of Gerontology: Psychological Sciences,* and *Family Relations: Journal of Applied Family and Child Studies.*

**Patrick C. McKenry** is Professor of Family Relations and Human Development, The Ohio State University. He received his Ph.D. in child and family studies from the University of Tennessee and served as a postdoctoral fellow in the Department of Child and Family Development at the University of Georgia. He is the author of more than 60 publications in the areas of family structure variations, stress and coping, and cultural diversity. He is coauthor, with Sharon Price, of *Divorce: A Major Life Transition.* He currently serves on the editorial boards of *Journal of Family Issues, Family Perspective,* and *Family Science Review.*

**Colleen I. Murray** is Associate Professor of Human Development and Family Studies at the University of Nevada, Reno, where she also is a faculty member of the Interdisciplinary Social Psychology Doctoral Program. She received her Ph.D. from the Ohio State University. Her research interests include bereaved parent-surviving sibling experiences, risk behaviors and environments of adolescent females, and feminist approaches to the study of families.

**Velma McBride Murry** is Assistant Professor of Child and Family Development in the College of Family and Consumer Sciences at the University of Georgia. She received her M.S. and Ph.D. from the University of Missouri–Columbia. She was a summer fellow to the National Institutes of Health Workshop on Families and AIDS and the International Society for the Study of Behavioral Development. Her research interests involve the sociocultural study of adolescent and young adult sexuality as well as family stress, coping, and adaptation. Her work has appeared in *Journal of Adolescent Research, Youth and Society, Family Sciences Review, The Black Family: Essays and Studies* (Staples, editor), and *Black Adolescence: Current Issues and Annotated Bibliography* (Bell-Scott and Taylor, editors).

**Briana S. Nelson** recently completed her masters degree in marriage and family therapy at Kansas State University. She received dual bachelor's degrees in psychology and life sciences from Kansas State. She was a Fellow in a National Institute of Mental Health Training Grant that focused on the rural elderly and severe mental illness. Part of this training included gaining clinical experience at the Veterans Administration Medical Center in Topeka. Her areas of research and clinical interest include working with trauma victims and their families, children of divorce, and later life couples' relationship changes. She practices marriage and family therapy in Colorado.

**Sharon Y. Nickols** is Professor of Family Economics in the Department of Housing and Consumer Economics and Dean of the College of Family and Consumer Sciences at the University of Georgia. She received her Ph.D. at the University of Missouri–Columbia in Family Economics and Management. Her research has focused on the division of labor in the home and women's employment. She has held faculty and administrative positions at the University of Illinois and Oklahoma State University.

**Sharon J. Price** is Professor and Head of the Department of Child and Family Development at the University of Georgia. She received her Ph.D. in sociology from Iowa State University. She is the author of publications in the areas of divorce, remarriage, fathers, marital adjustment, marital interaction, and parent-child relationships and is coauthor, with Patrick McKenry, of *Divorce: A Major Life Transition.* She is past president of the National Council on Family Relations, American Council on Education Fellow in the Administrative Leadership program, and recipient of the Osborne Award for outstanding teaching in the area of the family (presented by the National Council on Family Relations). She is a Clinical Member and Approved Supervisor in the American Association of Marriage and Family Therapy and editor of *Visions 2010: Families and . . . ,* published at the National Council on Family Relations.

**David W. Wright** is Associate Professor of Human Development and Family Studies at Kansas State University, where he has taught marriage and family therapy since 1985. He received his B.S. from California State Polytechnic University, his M.A. in marriage, family, and child counseling from Chapman College in California, and his Ph.D. in child and family development from the University of Georgia. He has published papers in the areas of adolescent sexuality and adolescent relationships, parent-adolescent interaction, the process of divorce, attachment between former spouses, postdivorce family life, and marital therapy. His current work focuses on how young adults develop the expectations that guide them in their relationships.